Future of Business and Finance

The Future of Business and Finance book series features professional works aimed at defining, describing and charting the future trends in these fields. The focus is mainly on strategic directions, technological advances, challenges and solutions which may affect the way we do business tomorrow, including the future of sustainability and governance practices. Mainly written by practitioners, consultants and academic thinkers, the books are intended to spark and inform further discussions and developments.

More information about this series at http://www.springer.com/series/16360

Peter Wollmann • Frank Kühn •
Michael Kempf • Reto Püringer
Editors

Organization and Leadership in Disruptive Times

Design and Implementation Using the 3-P-Model

Springer

Editors
Peter Wollmann
Bonn, Nordrhein-Westfalen, Germany

Frank Kühn
Dortmund, Nordrhein-Westfalen, Germany

Michael Kempf
Bad Honnef, Nordrhein-Westfalen, Germany

Reto Püringer
Ebertswil, Zürich, Switzerland

ISSN 2662-2467 ISSN 2662-2475 (electronic)
Future of Business and Finance
ISBN 978-3-030-63033-1 ISBN 978-3-030-63034-8 (eBook)
https://doi.org/10.1007/978-3-030-63034-8

This Springer imprint is published by the registered company Springer Nature Switzerland AG.
The registered company address is: Gewerbestrasse 11, 6330 Cham, Switzerland

Contents

Part V Helpful Design Concepts to Best Use the LEAN4.0 Model

About the Authors

Markus Beer has been supporting managers and their teams in complex change processes as an internal and external change manager for more than 20 years. In doing so, he draws on his experience in different sectors (retail, industry and consulting), different corporate functions (supply chain management, operations and human resources) and positions (project manager, manager and consultant). Markus is convinced that organizations and their members are successful when they continuously challenge their strategies, structures and processes while trying out and practising new forms of leadership and collaboration.

Philipp Bosselmann has been an experienced management consultant for over 15 years. Being trained as a physicist he started his professional career leading product development projects in the semi-conductor industry. Working as a management consultant since 2004, he first took a deep dive into process improvement, coaching projects and managing efficiency programmes in various industries. In the past 10 years, he has explored the emerging new innovation methodologies and ways of working and co-developed a unique innovation project management approach. Following the mission "help making good ideas change the world for the better", he co-founded SPROUT consulting in 2014, as an innovation platform for entrepreneurs from small and large technology companies. Philipp has been deeply involved in over a hundred innovation projects, providing focused acceleration and steering support, introducing new ways of working at project team and management team level and improving collaboration across organizations.

Nicole Hoenig de Locarnini is an executive consulting professional with one of the leading strategy firms focusing on organizations for the future and enabling lasting change. To date, she has devoted her professional life to developing deep technical insurance/reinsurance expertise at a major global insurance company (she originally trained as an actuary) and later leveraged this, matched with a diverse skill set in strategic transformation architecture and execution, operations, innovation, digital enablement and people and organizational design within the management consulting industry. Her work spans companies and business units within the financial services, life sciences and manufacturing producing industries. To satisfy her continuous passion for learning and growth, she has graduated in Consulting and Coaching for Change on the Specialized Executive Masters/MBA Program at the Oxford Saïd Business School and HEC Paris.

Giancarla Domini is an oenologist who has worked in famous wine companies in and outside the Piedmont region. She initially started working in industries unrelated to wine, e.g. in the arts and communication such as jewellery, radio and other related industries until she decided to follow her primary instincts and focus on the science of wine. Her broad experience and knowledge of the wine business covers several regions, beginning from the centre of Italy, through the Piedmont hills, to Virginia, USA. Through this intensive journey she has been able to gather different scientific experiences and insights worldwide. Now she works very closely with the well-known winery, La Mondianese, trying to create the perfect balance of wine and terroir. Her dream is to make a harvest in Australia before retirement.

Dieter Fellner is a qualified engineer for fundamental and theory in electrotechnics and biomedical engineering and has more than 30 years of professional experience in the area of the healthcare market. During his studies at the Vienna University of Technology, he worked at SIEMENS Medical Technology in the development of the latest magnetic resonance imaging. He started his professional career at PHILIPS Medical Systems in Hamburg and then led the development and introduction of the latest medical laser systems in Europe and Australia at KAPSCH Medical Technology.

He was able to further expand his leadership experience in the fields of intensive care, cardiac surgery and cardiology at the companies BAXTER and GUIDANT (now Boston Scientific). In his position as Country Director for Germany at EDWARDS LIFESCIENCES, he experienced the intensive journey from a listed spin-off MedTech company to a rapidly growing, patient-focused MedTech company in a top 30 global position. He strives to develop employees and drive innovation.

John Gray started leading technical accounting and business intelligence initiatives in Canada for Mozilla and Munich Reinsurance Company more than 7 years ago. In the past year, John has transitioned into IT application development and relocated from Toronto to Munich to become the latest Digital Finance team member. John competed in ice hockey at the level of Junior A throughout Canada and the USA, as well as holds a bachelor's degree in economics and a professional designation in risk management.

Dieter Haselbach is a sociologist by training, cultural advisor and researcher for more than 20 years. He taught sociology in universities in Canada, England, Austria and Germany. He is Managing Partner of ICG Culturplan, then Managing Partner of ICG Integrated Consulting Group Germany and now Business Partner in this company. He is Director of the Centre for Cultural Research in Berlin, develops business concepts, planning processes and strategies for institutions and local authorities and supports change management in public administration. He is Certified Systemic Interactive Coach. He created a furore as co-author of the book *The Cultural Heart Attack* (in German).

Paul Hombach is a musician, Improv actor and science communicator living near Bonn. He studied music, theology and geography at Bonn and Cologne Universities. As a certified teacher, he became a professional Improv player at the Springmaus Improv-theatre group in 1991 with broad experience in shows both for the public and for companies. He uses his knowledge and enthusiasm as an improvisational theatre trainer, editor of astronomical magazines and science speaker in English and in German. Paul is the founder of

"Meeting Music" - he attends congresses, conventions and workshops where he turns topics and key points of events into improvised songs.

Janina Kempf is a young professional who explores the intersection of international cooperation and digital development. Working with the GIZ (German development agency), she found the perfect spot to combine her drive for innovation and her passion for working with people from all around the globe, while being at the pulse of development politics. Within the organization she works in two positions, which complement each other: First, she is an advisor to the German Ministry for Economic Cooperation and Development and advises the unit which is concerned with the digital transformation of the global south. Second, she is a so-called IT Partner for the biggest department within the organization and supports the digital transformation of the department and beyond. She studied European Studies at Maastricht University and International Relations at the "Institut Barcelona d'Estudis Internacionals".

Michael U. Kempf has been an experienced management consultant (www.kempf-cp.com) for over 20 years. The driving force of his professional activities is his strong ambition to design processes and organizations in a sustainable manner. He relishes identifying key challenges, diagnosing complex relationships and assisting in shaping the future. Gaining experience and learning something new are indispensable parts of his life, which is why he likes to seize new opportunities. He began his career as a carpenter before studying social work, education and business administration. His career has spanned various jobs in social work, 10 years as a manager (HR and logistics) in industrial and retail companies and, since 1998, in advising people, leadership teams as well as working teams and organizations that are all very different. Michael has co-authored numerous publications in the field of leadership and organizational development.

Sebastian Kespohl has been working as a project manager and project portfolio manager in different verticals, mainly telco, FMCG and ecommerce in a highly tech-driven environment. Nowadays, he is a managing director of a regulated financial institute providing payment services to ecommerce merchants, for small and medium businesses up to the big global players. Sebastian has an educational background in bioinformatics and holds an executive MBA and a Certificate as an International Senior Project Manager, IPMA.

Frank Kühn has been supporting companies and institutions for many years in the areas of organization and leadership, change and project management. He brings his experience to developments such as the three-pillar model and systemic setting checks. Frank has a doctorate in work science. After leading positions in research and industry, he was a partner at HLP in Frankfurt and the ICG Integrated Consulting Group in Berlin and Graz. Today, he is an independent consultant, is a business partner of ICG, and is associated with other project partners and think tanks. He has published numerous articles in management journals and books.

Daniel Kunstleben has been the managing director of FABIDO since 2017. After studying political science, sociology and pedagogy in Münster and several years of professional experience in state politics, he held further positions as a personal assistant to a district manager and as head of department for central controlling in a district administration. Subsequently, he worked as a deputy mayor and department head for education, youth, social affairs, sport and culture of a medium-sized town in North Rhine-Westphalia before he finally came to Dortmund.

Christal Lalla is a certified sommelier, working in Italy, Germany, China, France and the USA since 2010, frequently as an international judge for tastings. She has established a fast-developing, innovative business around wine, wine services and wine education under the name VinAuthority and The Wandering Sommelier as well as providing out-of-the-box leadership training. Her approach, which is grounded on the premise that wine drinking is a holistic experience and event for all of the senses, including the winemaker's philosophy, motivation and techniques, the visual and haptic sensations of the vineyards and the cellars with their barrels and the taste of the wine combined with food pairings—and with well-fitting music or acting. Christal is also author of several manuscripts describing the connections between vinification, wine, spirits and food pairings.

Susanne Marell is CEO of Hill+Knowlton Strategies in Germany. Before joining H+K she was Managing Director at JP KOM and prior to that she served as CEO of Edelman for six years, overseeing the acquisition of and merger with ergo Kommunikation. After her studies, she started her career as a consultant with the agency Kohtes and Klewes (now Ketchum). In the following years, Susanne worked for companies such as Schering, Hoechst and Aventis CropScience. As Head of Communications and Market Services, her responsibilities included strategic communications support for merger and acquisition activities. In 2000, she moved to the chemical company Cognis and, as Vice President Corporate Communications, took over the management of worldwide corporate and sustainability communications. Following the acquisition of Cognis by BASF in 2010, Susanne was responsible for global brand management as Vice President Corporate Brand Management at BASF in Ludwigshafen. Susanne is a certified systemic consultant and change expert. She has many years of international experience in communications, marketing and sustainability, both on the corporate and agency side. In addition, she is co-founder of the German network of "Global Women in PR" and has built up the initiative "Next Gen Leadership" as a member of the extended board.

Lilian Matischok has a degree in mechanical engineering and is a systemic thinker and developer by vocation. Her favourite professional "brief job to be done" is connecting the dots of business strategy, product architecture and organizational development to holistic transformational programmes. She worked over 20 years as a manager, engineer and internal consultant at Robert Bosch GmbH in the automotive and in the industrial technology business area. Since 2020, she supports as a freelancing consultant for manufacturing companies in transforming from a brick-and-mortar business with tangible products towards digital and service business models and in collaborating successfully in platform-based ecosystems.

Mersida Ndrevataj is an architect and urban planner, currently working on a PhD in Urban Planning and Public Policy at IUAV University of Venice. Her professional objective is to help better shape the built environment through a multidisciplinary research-based and human-centred design process. To this end, she is involved in several academic research projects and works in the field of environmental psychology.

Reto Püringer has worked for more than 20 years in the banking and insurance industry. He has held various senior positions in global companies. His practical experience ranges from strategy development, business model design, product/proposition development/management, enterprise-wide portfolio management, program/project management, operations/IT management and large-scale change programme delivery to financial/actuarial management over different geographies and time zones, hierarchies and units, cultures and systems. Reto has managed multinational and multicultural change and transformation endeavours across the globe and managed teams of various sizes both on-site and remotely. Reto holds a degree in economical informatics and marketing and completed an Executive MBA at the University of Zurich.

Benjamin Rausch started leading global M&A, equity and corporate finance transactions more than ten years ago. For the past five years, Benjamin Rausch has been driving corporate performance management and developing software for financial organizations that enables faster and more effective strategic and financial decision-making. Benjamin graduated and received his doctorate in business administration on forward-looking corporate valuation techniques. Thereafter, he joined Rothschild's global advisory practice in Frankfurt and later Munich Reinsurance Company in Munich.

Ehssan Sakhaee is a passionate educator, engineer, philosopher and cartoonist, currently a lecturer and the Director of the UG Leadership Program at the Faculty of Engineering at the University of Sydney, Australia. His interests and passion lie in the area of personal and leadership development and helping people live more meaningful lives. He received his bachelor's and PhD in engineering from the University of Sydney in Australia. His career spans engineering, management and leadership consulting and research and higher education across Japan, USA and Australia. He has published works in engineering, leadership and management in project management as well as stories and poetry.

Jürgen Scherer holds an MBA and PhD from Cologne University in Germany. He has 30 years spanning broad industry experience in executive positions for global corporations in Germany and the USA, namely FMCG company Henkel, specialty chemicals company Cognis and industrial packaging company Mauser. He has been on the Cognis Executive Committee, was the Legal Representative of Cognis Germany and has led as Cognis Group Vice President the Corporate Sales/Key Account Management as well as the Supply Chain Services organization. He has published various papers in academic journals and readers and has presented business-to-business management topics at leading business schools and international conferences. Since 2019, he is a Business Consultant and Coach with www.bxb-exchange.com.

Marie Theres Schmidt studied Health Economics at the University of Rotterdam and SDA Bocconi School of Management where she graduated in 2012. She specialized in market access of pharmaceuticals and medical devices throughout her professional career and has led pricing and reimbursement processes for innovative medicines and medical devices for global companies. As Director Market Access and Government Affairs at EDWARDS LIFE SCIENCES, she is developing strategies to ensure patients' access to innovative, best-in-class medical technologies while pursuing political engagement for structural heart disease. Her projects are driven by strong cross-functional collaboration across organizational entities and healthcare authorities, always engaging multiple disciplines in decision-making processes. With her international working culture, she effectively manages diverse teams and projects in changing environments.

Lisa Schulze worked as an educational expert in a number of day-care facilities of FABIDO (family-complementary educational institutions for children in Dortmund) caring for children between 0 and 6 years, most recently as deputy head. During this time, she also completed her Master's degree in Elementary Education and Management in Social Economic and Diaconal Organizations. One of the major subjects was change management. This was followed by further training as a systemic consultant and then a transition to personnel development at FABIDO.

Jan Sølvberg spent the first 15 years of his work life in the ICT industry as a trainer, leader, project manager and consultant and the next 15 years as an organizational development consultant specializing on improvement and change processes, leadership development and coaching. Today, Jan is a senior consultant and partner with Innotiimi-ICG (Integrated Consulting Group) and President of the Norwegian chapter of International Coaching Federation (ICF). Inspired from emerging agile trends in software development that focus on closer customer involvement and shorter development cycles, he transfers those elements to organizational life and incorporates it into his professional work, feeling there a close connectivity with his clients.

Thomas Thirolf was born in Munich in 1963. He studied economics at the University of Augsburg. After obtaining his degree, Thomas completed a trainee programme at Hypobank, subsequently working in the credit and corporate banking department. He also worked in the central project office during the merger of Hypobank and Vereinsbank. Thomas joined Munich Re in 2001, becoming Head of Finance/Primary Insurance. In 2006, he became Head of Group Controlling. His main responsibilities are capital management (dividends, share buy-backs), performance and investment controlling of the business fields reinsurance and primary insurance as well as the development of economic steering methods. In this function he reports to the Group CFO and Member of the Board of Management, Dr. Christoph Jurecka. For the last 5 years, Thomas is further responsible for the Digital Finance Platform, which was set up and led by Benjamin Rausch.

Stefan Turnwald has been an experienced functional excellence and learning and development expert for more than 20 years in the pharmaceutical industry. He started his career as a commercial representative. After switching into the learning development function, he continuously grew his responsibilities and the geographic span of his activities. Stefan is driven by the continuous transformation and improvement of the interface of the pharmaceutical operation to external stakeholders. With his holistic approach, Stefan strives for the transformation of organizational structures, functions and business procedures for patient-centred and customer-focused way of working. He has managed and contributed to several change and business transformation projects at local, regional and global levels. His career has spanned roles and projects in established operations of various sizes as well as in start-up organizations. Stefan studied biology at the Friedrich-Alexander-University Erlangen-Nuremberg, Germany. Currently, he works and lives in Central Switzerland.

Jutta Wenzl is Head of Global HR at KraussMaffei Group, a manufacturer of machinery and systems for the production and processing of plastics and rubber. After her business studies, she started her career at Henkel and joined Cognis right from the start, when it was carved out from Henkel. During her time with Cognis, she held several operational and strategic HR roles. After the acquisition by BASF, she supported the Cognis integration being responsible for the Global HR integration before joining H.C. Starck, a leading supplier of technology metals, as Head of Global HR. Jutta is a certified systemic and hypno-systemic consultant and change expert. She has many years of international experience in HR, particularly in personnel and organizational development.

Georg Wiesinger develops and realizes innovative products for interior design. His focus is on integral, synergetic solutions for acoustics, lighting and cooling in rooms with special challenges, e.g., for open plan offices. He has extensive project experience as an engineer, architect and facility manager and is an all-rounder for the special challenges of holistic solutions along the property lifecycle. He obtained his doctorate in mechanical engineering and is a specialist for process-oriented planning and quality management. After performing leading roles in re-search and industry, he founded his own company BPE GmbH.

Peter Wollmann has been a responsible manager, initiator, mentor and facilitator in large, predominantly global transformations and strategic developments for almost 40 years. His specialties are the implementations of the three-pillar model in organizations and focused setting checks to identify strengths, weaknesses, opportunities and threats and facilitate optimization measures. Since 2017, Peter has been working independently on organizational projects and future initiatives. After graduating in mathematics and physics from the University of Bonn, he began his professional career at Deutscher Herold, then part of the insurance group of Deutsche Bank. Later he took on strategic leadership and most recently was programme director for global transformation in the Zurich Insurance Company (ZIC).

In his professional network, he has leveraged his experience and strategic thinking to the development of various leading companies. He is the author and publisher of a number of books and articles on strategy, leadership and project and project portfolio management. He is also the founder of wine business: VinAuthority.

Julia Zirn is an experienced consultant and coach with cidpartners, a renowned organizational consultancy for the facilitation and implementation of strategy and change processes located in Bonn and Berlin. Julia has been advising companies, teams and executives from a wide range of industries, whereby "Integrating Perspectives" is always at the heart of her client projects. With curiosity about people and an analytical eye for processes and structures, Julia facilitates and advises on the development of powerful solutions for complex challenges. Julia studied international business administration, sociology and cultural studies in Frankfurt, London and at Zeppelin University in Friedrichshafen and has been published in the *Journal for Organizational Development*, among others.

Part I

Introduction Chapters

In the two introduction chapters, the editors explain the purpose and trigger for the book as a further development of the approaches and experiences previously published in 'Three Pillars of Organization and Leadership in Disruptive Times—Navigating Your Company Successfully Through the 21st Century Business World' (Wollmann et al. 2020), i.e. on the one hand extending the scope e.g. to the public sector, and on the other hand stronger focusing on concretization and practical application in diverse industries.

Furthermore, the editors explain the structure of the book using various categories of use cases of the Three-Pillar Model (abbreviation: 3-P-Model). They give a brief overview of the essential contents and results of the various contributions, frame them and make the mutual links between the articles transparent. It becomes clear that the application of the model, as described in the previous book, has made further, important progress.

From a Retrospective to a Perspective View

Peter Wollmann, Frank Kühn, Michael Kempf, and Reto Püringer

Abstract

The editors explain the purpose and trigger for the book as a further development of the approaches and experiences previously published in the *Three Pillars of Organization and Leadership in Disruptive Times: Navigating Your Company Successfully Through the 21st Century Business World* (Wollmann et al., Three pillars of organization and leadership in disruptive times – Navigating Your company successfully through the 21st century business world. Berlin, Springer, 2020), i.e., on the one hand, extending the scope to the public sector, for example, and, on the other hand, focusing more strongly on concretization and practical application in various different industries.

The reason for the desire to continue work on the three-pillar model (abbreviated in the following as "3-P-Model") is the success in initial applications of the model in practice and the encouragement from numerous discussions with decision-makers and users experienced by the editors and authors of the previous book. Additionally, the "corona crisis" that happened while writing the book has underlined the relevance of the three pillars, the strength of the model, its universal applicability, and its value in finding solutions that work well even in

P. Wollmann (✉)
Bonn, Germany
e-mail: pw@peterwollmann.com

F. Kühn
Dortmund, Germany
e-mail: fk@kuehn-cp.com

M. Kempf
Bad Honnef am Rhein, Germany
e-mail: michael@kempf-cp.com

R. Püringer
Ebertswil, Switzerland
e-mail: rpueringer@hotmail.com

P. Wollmann et al. (eds.), *Organization and Leadership in Disruptive Times*, Future of Business and Finance, https://doi.org/10.1007/978-3-030-63034-8_1

extreme situations. This includes learning and developing for future challenges but also the growing awareness of people of the social purpose of organizations, the shared willingness to travel under unknown conditions and to experiment with how we can connect our resources even under unusual constraints.

In this chapter, a detailed recap of the 3-P-Model is documented, especially for all readers who have not read the previous book.

1 The Starting Point

Some days after the publication of our previous book with Springer (Wollmann et al. 2020) (Fig. 1), a representative number of the community—from this book and the previous one, all the editors and a large number of authors—met in mid-October 2019 for a workshop in Montalcino to discuss the lessons learned, to exchange first experiences in application and discussions of the 3-P-Model, and to decide the next steps (Fig. 2).

The development of the new 3-P-Model (for a quick recap, see below) and the writing of the book took more than 2 years and a lot of personal and virtual interactions, explorations, and applications to reach the necessary maturity. What now seems to be a quite simple and self-evident project was not at all like this in the beginning. The intensive engagement and the approach to develop the model step by

Fig. 1 The book published by Springer in 2020 and the editor and author community

Fig. 2 Impressions from the Montalcino workshop: retrospective on the former book process, approaching the new book (Photos by authors, used with permission. All rights reserved)

step led to constant new insights and understanding as well as to encouraging experiences concerning application of the model in various contexts.

Though this process was demanding, it created a high level of enthusiasm in the group which, on the one hand, led to a significant increase in the size of our community and, on the other, to the strong will to further tackle the topic, which meant covering a wider range of practical applications, widening the scope beyond enterprises to institutions, e.g., in the public sector, and further involving the societal relevance or "public value" (Moore 1995; Meynhardt 2009)—i.e., stressing the value-added for society as a whole by all sorts of organizations, e.g., enterprises, the public sector, global and local institutions, churches, and NGOs.

As a result of the review of the first book and the retrospective look at the process, all members of the community at the Montalcino workshop agreed that the success factors from the previous book should be maintained:

- Strong linkage of the chapters and articles of the new book to the daily work and experiences of people: Which new insights arise from the perspectives of sustainable purpose, travelling organization, and connected resources? What lessons learned and takeaways can be helpful for future situations and the overall transformation?
- Prevention of too strict, abstract, and dogmatic definition of ideas, concepts, and terms, but expectation of precise clarification, comprehensibility, and usability, e.g., through practical cases.
- Being mindful to involve cultural aspects that determine the success of any transformation process: How do they influence the way the three pillars are applied and how should the pillars create impact?
- Interconnecting authors and articles with certain interfaces to cooperate and align themselves—which means applying the three pillars to our own tasks.
- Keep diversity and freedom for the authors as a precondition for creativity—but referring to the 3-P-Model should be mandatory to develop joint knowledge from its application.
- Working on our model and its application needs vivid, regular, and frequent community discussion. This includes community events to jointly evaluate the maturity of the articles and align them, which we started to continue at the virtual level.

At this point, the overarching general purpose of the new book was to place the 3-P-Model in even more concrete terms, extend the number, range and areas of application, and summarize experiences to date.

This was before the "corona crisis" started, and our global society, not only the business world, was forced to embark on a challenging journey into the "known unknown." Now the purpose of the book has taken on an additional dimension as the meaning and importance of the three pillars has been underlined and even needs to be extended:

- Regardless of whether it is for commercial enterprises, public institutions, science, or NGOs, these days it seems impossible to reasonably define their purposes without connecting them to societal concerns or their "public value"(even more obvious in the Covid-19 pandemic starting in 2020). Nor is it possible to neglect or ignore intensive discussion about their real purposes in the future and how they relate to each other, in their ecosystems, and in the global contexts. Additionally, thinking in risk adjustment and business continuity management categories might impact on the calibration of purpose definitions. So, it is understood that the purpose in general must be rethought in and after the Covid-19 era to understand potentially necessary changes.

- It is impossible to regard the mindset and concept of a travelling organization only as a desirable option. A global journey has been started; we have to face it and the need to manage it in a responsible way, in our ecosystem and its global context. We are learning that starting journeys into the unknown or even "unknown unknown" are not preventable, for anybody. Such journeys can take dramatic turns that many of us could not have imagined so far. In the Covid-19 era, every individual, group, and organization is part of this journey and should be reviewed after the pandemic because our past normality will not be our future one. The global crisis will be—and this is evident—for most organizations, the major phase in their development and transition for years, even if they only struggle for survival. In any case, one thing is obvious: crisis becomes a significant part of the journeys—since other crises, such as climate change or migration, also must be coped with.
- It is impossible not to redefine connectivity demands and connection points in the society and in companies' and institutions' ecosystems with their world-wide partners. The new digital collaboration tools and practices or the reconfiguration of supply chains but also political influences and global crises as described not only are connected with each other but also highlight the need for joint action over decades. We have experienced that the connectivity of all our resources is crucial, going beyond national boundaries and closed-shop mentalities. Strong overarching global and local communities are more important than ever.

That means that the new book will be able to provide some valuable stimulation for a broad range of situations, even including coping with disastrous situations like the climate crisis, the Covid-19 pandemic, and "crises impacting on global and national economies" even though this was not the initial intention. But we added considerations to the book's purpose to increase the applicability, which means to also consider crises as a test case for the 3-P-Model.

Such crises are often, on the one hand, a catalyst for fundamental thoughts on recalibrating the 3-P-Model's application on an organization; on the other hand, they may act as "accelerators" for existing "hidden or well-known systemic developments" such as digitalization or social value shifts.

2 The Three-Pillar Model Recap and Further Development

The three-pillar model (3-P-Model), described in the previous book, was created to cover the urgent need of organizations in the current volatile, uncertain, complex, and ambiguous (VUCA) world to show adequate solutions to the question of how to be organized and managed in a dynamic way, how to commit to a clear direction and belief, and how to develop and connect the valuable resources they need to create impact and value. This includes embarking on the necessary journey even if all final clarifications have not been done, which means experimenting, prototyping, and piloting ideas and approaches to gradually find the right development path. Now the uncertainty of the VUCA world has been exponentially increased by the Covid-19 pandemic; experts estimate that its impacts might take a decade to finally get over (whatever this means) and that, potentially, the world will be different afterward in terms of the calibration of the relationship between governmental and societal system, enterprises and public sector, environmental and economic inter-relationships, etc. Clarifying and balancing this kind of connectivity will be a journey of its own, challenging new collective processes and practices.

The three main design principles for future organization and leadership can be described in detail as follows:

- *Sustainable purpose*
  The employees and teams in the organization but also its key stakeholders in the entire ecosystem and business environment must know what the organization stands for and what entrepreneurial value and societal contribution it creates. This includes the reciprocity of enterprises, public and social institutions, science, etc.
  The purpose must remain sustainable, reliable, and consistent, supported by leaders, employees, and stakeholders and lived by important representatives of the organization. The purpose aligns, convinces, and inspires the people involved in the joint endeavor, making them confident and proud to be a part of it and to contribute to it. Employees and team leaders can then take this overall purpose and translate it into what it means concretely for their teams and for them individually. Even—or especially—in crises, it proves its ability to provide orientation and energy and to keep the organization together on its way.
- *Travelling organization*
  Business consistency, strategic stability, and structural continuity with some episodic change projects from time to time. This has long been an illusion in disruptive and crisis-ridden times. Now, we must understand that organizations are continuously on a journey, experiencing twists and turns, following their purpose or even striving for survival, and always looking for the best way between poles, alternatives, and options. If the teams do not know what to expect around the next bend, they must take smaller steps and explore the terrain. Even if they don't know in advance what the best result will be, they will achieve it: they believe in their motivation and ability to manage the journey and to rely on their agile mindset, self-reflection, readiness to embrace change, and willingness to deliver. People in a travelling organization are curious, open, courageous, and keen to experiment, and they deal well with uncertainty, stress, and unforeseen incidents—and they are empowered to take decisions swiftly by themselves and to operate on their own.
  In the Covid-19 pandemic, the journey has become part of a global endeavor of the entire states, economies, financial systems, social systems, etc., all of them overwhelmed and stressed—there is no chance of being unable to cope with the dynamics.
- *Connecting resources*

The organization has to be aware that impact, value, and efficiency but also survival need multiple connectivity between humans, organizations, and ecosystems; between expertise and influence; between different political and social systems and cultures; between enterprises, scientific research, and public sector; between customer satisfaction and economic needs; between strategy, processes, and skills; and between risk management and business continuity. This means managing connectivity; preventing unconnected structural silos, boxed competencies, and echo chambers; and inspiring and supporting multilateral behaviors and initiatives in global and local professional communities, balancing the various, often contradictory, interests between the stakeholders.

All three pillars are key assets of systemic dynamics and high organizational effectiveness: They provide orientation and inspiration, giving fundamental impulses to start the journey and to connect the resources for joint success. Based on these findings, the 3-P-Model was created and its application tested, and mainly described, with reference to the business world. Now, a number of months later, after intense discussion and experiences, we have been struck by how well the model can also be applied to the current Covid-19 pandemic and to the public sector, including international institutions such as the UN, GIZ, etc.

3 Maturity Check for Your Organization: The 3-P-Model Questionnaire

In the previous book, a questionnaire was developed to check the 3-P-Model readiness of an organization in a simple way. For a focused application of the 3-P-Model to a specific organization, program or project, a tailor-made approach should be chosen, so the evaluation questions must be flexibly tailored to the concrete situation and setting. A more detailed version is documented in the appendix. You can explore the evaluation questions via three meta-questions:

- What are your needs, goals, and visions for each of the questions—and how do you share them with your team and in your organization?
- What have you achieved so far—and how do you get common evidence on this?
- What are the next steps on your journey—and how will you create commitment?

The result is a common understanding of the journey and its purpose, where you are on the journey and what the tasks are and next steps you will have to take. This will also lead to decisions concerning structural, processual, and practical questions. The purpose of this book is not to provide you with perfect recipes but to deliver helpful questions and inspirational examples. The key is to regularly check the organizational setting against the questions, underlining the relevance of sustainable purpose, travelling organization and connected resources.

How should this challenge be approached in practice? In our experience, it is best to use simple tools and formats. We have very good experience with, for example, backlogs, feedback practices, reviews, and forums. This means that you have a physical and digital board where you can collect, view, prioritize, organize, and track tasks. Continuous feedback loops and reviews help to create a common understanding of where you can strengthen, reduce, cancel, start, and keep the activities that are essential on your journey. Activities and tasks are key, as are their relevance and priority in the joint journey. Physical or digital forums are the communication hotspots that can take place at different physical or digital sites in the organization and its ecosystem, thus standing for the journey, its issues, and places: central marketplaces, IT working places, customer workshops, management discussions, meetings in the new factory, leadership and community conferences provide transparency, understanding, exchange, feedback, and new impulses.

After having given a first, quick feeling of how to proceed, the questionnaire is presented in which we have summarized the results of our previous book. This way you can get a good overview in a manageable format. This questionnaire will be further developed based on the following chapters and then presented in its new version in the final chapter.

The evaluation questions are listed along the phases of the journey:

- Awaken for the journey
  - How far did you explore the VUCA world with your team?
  - Were you able to create a shared understanding?
  - Is there a real commitment to a sustainable purpose?
  - Is the transition process toward becoming a travelling organization sufficiently prepared?
- Interlink for the journey
  - To what extent are teams and individuals involved and convinced?
  - Could an agile mindset be developed? To what extent?
  - Are differences in opinion and working styles used as learning opportunities?
  - How is exchange on the route and impact of the endeavor organized?
- Practice the future
  - Are all resources with each other effectively and efficiently connected?
  - To what extent is silo thinking overcome in favor of collaborative solution working?
  - Are the different working styles in your teams well connected?
  - What is the outcome of exploring various mindsets, experiences, and expectations?
- Lead on the journey
  - How is leadership as a servicing function realized and distributed?
  - To what degree is leadership practice connected to the purpose?
  - How is the communication about new policies and daily work organized?
  - Is there sufficient care for psychological safety from collective behavior?
- Establish new practices
  - To what extent are your portfolios, roadmaps, programs, and projects aligned to the purpose?
  - Has an agile communication platforms and practices been set up?

  - To what extent are liberating interventions applied?
  - How is success evaluated and how are new practices calibrated?
- Empower your people and organization
  - Is your recruiting focus on people with curiosity, openness, and agility?
  - Is there a climate of encouraging staff to take on roles and manage processes?
  - To what extent are feedback and learning procedures in place and working?
  - Is there a concept in place to evaluate success and calibrate development?

  Working on such questions leads to an intensive discussion, to a valid check of the maturity degree in terms of the 3-P-Model of an organization, and to some lessons learned along all phases of a travelling organization. It is a kind of concrete walk through the transformation (as in a movie). It ranges from the start phase to the continuation into a new quality of agile organization.

If the questions are asked regularly, we can see how the learning processes and the capabilities of the organization develop, which they need to do in an uncertain, disruptive, and crisis-ridden environment. Feel free to adapt the questionnaire to the situation in your organization and prototype it together with your employees. A company, its teams, and the people who conduct this kind of continuous evaluation are less prone to assuming obstacles, having perception biases, postponing conflict, and experiencing frustration due to the lack of connectedness in the journey.

First experiences and success stories show how the collective work on the three pillars, their questions, and impulses create a shift in the organization and leadership, from the illusion of stability and energy invested to stick to it toward the reality of travelling and the need to navigate the journey. The implementation strategies are different whether you want to discuss them regarding the entire organization or start with progressive units or test them in strategic programs or projects, then spread it into the organization. Thus, you have a dual, but closely connected, line of discussion: one on the content (see above) and one on the transition process, as described below.

4 Development of Your Organization: The 3-P-Model Concept Application Options

In addition to the questionnaire, the 3-P-Model community has created a rough development and consulting concept. The focus is on scalable flexible interventions based on the 3-P-Model. The process includes creation and learning loops, with regular progress and setting checks (Fig. 3). The concept is combined with an understanding of external, complementary support: In most cases, all necessary resources are in the organization, but externals can facilitate to connect them for new effectiveness—which results in the practical experience of a new quality of connectivity.

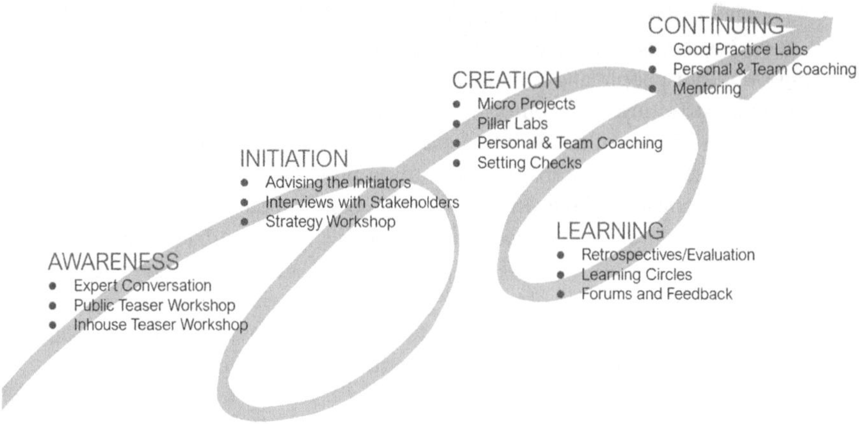

Fig. 3 The three pillars development concept (overview) (Illustrated by authors, used with permission. All rights reserved)

Regarding the questionnaire and the concept, we have now further developed the applicability of the model at a level that doesn't provide you with "cut and paste" recipes but approaches that practitioners can transfer to their work.

Our Own Journey and Self-Application

Our first book served to explore and develop the 3-P-Model. This second book aims to enrich the practical benefit for practitioners who want to prepare their enterprises, institutions, public services, administration, NGOs, etc. to cope with urgent challenges and future developments, disruptions, and crises.

Regarding this ambition, we are pleased with how well our community has developed, including the editors and authors as well as all other people involved who have contributed their experiences and shared their ideas with us. The authors collectively stand for both: a variety of topics, sectors, countries, personalities, and the common focus on our collaboration and further elaboration of the 3-P-Model. So, the editors and authors personally represent what the model stands for: sustainable purpose, travelling organization, and connected resources.

The common process also followed the model. After co-creating the purpose of the book in our meeting in Italy, we developed the iterative way of exploration, writing, evaluation, and connecting, being open on the way as well as involving the people, their experiences, the opportunities, the articles, and all the new information together, again and again. Then we had to face the global Covid-19 pandemic. So, we have co-created a book that we could not foresee in detail, but which should be fitting here and now and even for the "time after." And we will continue our journey.

5 Specific Insights from the 3-P-Model Application in the Case of the "Covid-19 Pandemic"

We started to work on this book in 2019, when many organizations considered themselves as "more or less" prepared to cope with the challenges of the VUCA world (already defined in the 1990s), after having coped with the financial crisis of 2009 (predicted a decade earlier) and now facing global crises such as climate change (already predicted by the Club of Rome in 1972) (Meadows et al. 1972), political turns, and transcontinental migration. It is a good question if these developments might be regarded as "unknown unknowns" (but they were predicted), "known unknowns," or even "known knowns"—and how humans, societies, and organizations could have coped with them better.

In 2020, while finalizing this book, we are all facing the Covid-19 pandemic (also predicted at least a decade before), and we have to state that the organizational journey is much more disruptive and turbulent than we presumed (but to be expected after former outbreaks of similar). Because of the dimension of this disruption, we also had to discuss the impact on our 3-P-Model and its application separately in a detailed article in the book (under the headline 'If not now—then when? Learning from the Pandemic for 3-P-Model Application') and in an article about leadership in crisis situations and in all other articles. Under the impression of the Covid-19 pandemic and its possible significance for the society and organizations, it has been crucial to "re-evaluate" the applicability of the 3-P-Model in the general and central statements made in the book or in the articles.

The key result of this re-evaluation—confirmed in the diversity of the analyzed cases—is that the three-pillar model also works very well to support organizations and leadership even in times of a significant crisis, of which the Covid-19 pandemic is just one example. This confirms its relevance at the organizational travel even in rough waters. This also means that it can be assumed that the 3-P-Model is relevant for managing the pluralism of "operating modes," i.e., routines, innovation, continuous improvement, and change or crisis mode—each mode for itself—or all in parallel and connected with each other. Whatever mode, they all need to have the same attitude and commitment to share and pursue the overall purpose, to actively contribute to the common journey, and to connect their developments and resources in a productive way and develop together.

References

Meadows, D. H., Meadows, D. L., Randers, J., & Behrens, W. W. (1972). *The limits to growth. A report for the club of Rome's project on the predicament of mankind.* New York: Universe Books.

Meynhardt, T. (2009). Public value. In *International encyclopedia of civil society* (pp. 1277–1282). New York: Springer.

Moore, M. (1995). Creating public value – Strategic management in government. Cambridge: Harvard University Press. ISBN: 978-0674175587, S. 64 ff.

Wollmann, P., Kühn, F., & Kempf, M. (Eds.). (2020). *Three Pillars of Organization and Leadership in Disruptive Times – Navigating Your Company Successfully through the 21st Century Business World.* Berlin: Springer.

Peter Wollmann has been a responsible manager, initiator, mentor, and facilitator in large, predominantly global transformations and strategic developments for almost 40 years. His specialties are the implementations of the three-pillar model in organizations and focused setting checks to identify strengths, weaknesses, opportunities, and threats and facilitate optimization measures. Since 2017, Peter has been working independently on organizational projects and future initiatives. After graduating in mathematics and physics from the University of Bonn, he began his professional career at Deutscher Herold, then part of the insurance group of Deutsche Bank. Later he took on strategic leadership and most recently was program director for global transformation in the Zurich Insurance Company (ZIC). In his professional network, he has leveraged his experience and strategic thinking to the development of various leading companies. He is the author and publisher of several books and articles on strategy, leadership, and project and project portfolio management. He is also the founder of a wine business: VinAuthority.

Frank Kühn has been supporting companies and institutions for many years in the areas of organization and leadership, change, and project management. He brings his experience to developments such as the three-pillar model and systemic setting checks. Frank has a doctorate in work science. After leading positions in research and industry, he was a partner at HLP in Frankfurt and in the ICG Integrated Consulting Group in Berlin and Graz. Today, he is an independent consultant and a business partner of ICG and is associated with other project partners and think tanks. He has published numerous articles in management journals and books.

Michael Kempf has been an experienced management consultant for over 20 years. The driving force of his professional activities is his strong ambition to design processes and organizations in a sustainable manner. He relishes identifying key challenges, diagnosing complex relationships, and assisting in shaping the future. Gaining experience and learning something new are indispensable parts of his life, which is why he likes to seize new opportunities. He began his career as a carpenter before studying social work, education, and business administration. His career has spanned various jobs in social work, 10 years as a manager (HR and logistics) in industrial and retail companies and, since 1998, in advising people, leadership teams, and working teams, and organizations that are all very different. Michael has co-authored numerous publications in the field of leadership and organizational development.

Reto Püringer has worked for more than 20 years in the banking and insurance industry. He has held various senior positions in global companies. His practical experience ranges from strategy development, business model design, product/proposition development/management, enterprise-wide portfolio management, program/project management, operations/IT management, and large-scale change program delivery to financial/actuarial management over different geographies and time zones, hierarchies and units, and cultures and systems. Reto has managed multinational and multicultural change and transformation endeavors across the globe and managed teams of various sizes both on site and remotely. Reto holds a degree in Economical Informatics and Marketing and completed an Executive MBA at the University of Zurich.

Contributions to the 3-P-Model Application: Overview and Connection of the Detailed Cases Presented in the Book

Peter Wollmann, Frank Kühn, Michael Kempf, and Reto Püringer

Abstract

The editors explain that the structure of the book is strongly based on the defined categories for detailed cases on the three-pillar model (abbreviated in the following as "3-P-Model") application as a further development of the approaches and experiences previously published in *Three Pillars for Organization and Leadership in Disruptive Times: Navigating Your Company Successfully Through the 21st Century Business World* (Wollmann et al. 2020), i.e., on the one hand, extending the scope to the public sector, for example, and, on the other hand, focusing more strongly on concretization and practical application in various industries.

The editors give a brief overview of the key content and outcome of the various contributions, frame them, and highlight links between articles. This chapter is important for the reader to decide which articles are most interesting for them and in which order they want to explore the broad spectrum of articles in the book.

P. Wollmann (✉)
Bonn, Germany
e-mail: pw@peterwollmann.com

F. Kühn
Dortmund, Germany
e-mail: fk@kuehn-cp.com

M. Kempf
Bad Honnef am Rhein, Germany
e-mail: michael@kempf-cp.com

R. Püringer
Ebertswil, Switzerland
e-mail: rpueringer@hotmail.com

P. Wollmann et al. (eds.), *Organization and Leadership in Disruptive Times*, Future of Business and Finance, https://doi.org/10.1007/978-3-030-63034-8_2

1 Introduction to the Case Categories

The benefit of the book is displayed in five sections of concrete 3-P-Model application to help readers to decide how to best apply the articles to suit their specific situation. The articles provide a wide variety of perspectives, insights, and benefits on different levels, from meta-level considerations of preconditions to concrete operational concepts, from enterprise-focused to global society-focused, from a private sector view to a public sector view, etc., and across all industries, functions, and professions.

1. *Fundamental thoughts with which to start the 3-P-Model journey*: The authors discuss cognitive, mental, and behavioral preconditions to best apply the 3-P-Model. The right understanding of the pillars and their dimension—also in the historical context—is crucial to tailor one's special approach to design in detail and to implement and apply the 3-P-Model.
2. *Leadership in the 3-P-Model—setting direction and motivation*: This section looks at the best preconditions for managing the application of the model and/or leading its implementation, i.e., how to prepare, facilitate, and track the application in the organization, programs, or projects, with practical examples of its impact on leadership, collaboration, and communication.
3. *3-P-Model application in the public sector*: The scope increases from the focus in the private sector in the previous book to a more holistic view, covering the public sector and global society, and connecting all across these spheres is a key target of the book. Practical experiences in applying the 3-P-Model in the public sector are analyzed, lessons learned documented, and a series of takeaways described.
4. *3-P-Model application in the private sector*: Here the authors focus on their various practical experiences in different industries and contexts in applying the 3-P-Model to their projects or in analyzing the outcomes using the three pillars. They have provided us with new lessons learned and many different takeaways. The journey in this section goes from examples from start-up and hybrid organizations to large transformations in established enterprises.
5. *Helpful design concepts to best use the 3-P-Model*: The authors show helpful concepts that are closely interlinked with applications of the 3-P-Model. Some concepts are new, while others are well-proven but develop new meaning in their interlinkage with the 3-P-Model.

We assume that readers will explore the book in a random but intelligent manner, moving between the general chapters of the introduction, which prepare the field, the application articles in the diverse categories, and the conclusion at the end of the book, i.e., finding the connections that are most suitable. The book is not intended to be read like a set text, from cover to cover. Even if it is read in this way, we have tried to ensure that articles containing fundamental thoughts are followed by concrete application cases, and input from them might be explored later, in greater depth, in the design articles.

Nevertheless, here are some helpful tips for navigating the book:

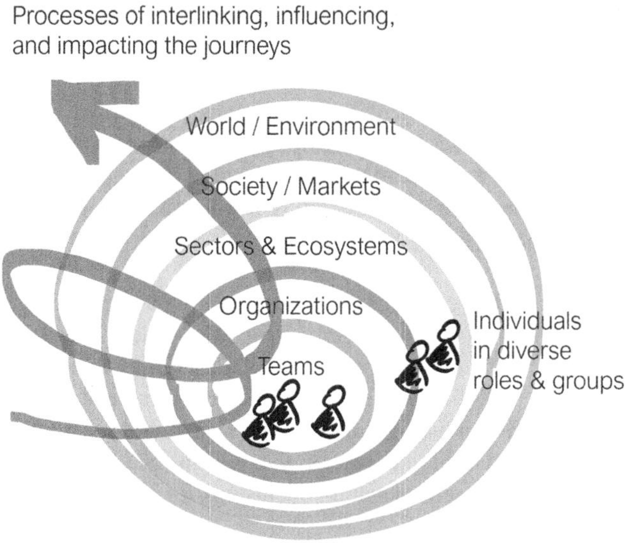

Fig. 1 Systemic and dynamic connectivity, in which all parts are connected with each other during their journeys and influence each other (Illustrated by Frank Kühn, used with permission. All rights reserved)

- In the table of contents, we have divided the articles into sections as described above.
- The following summaries of the articles provide an initial indication of how the articles relate to the three pillars and which elements of the broader system they touch on and connect with each other (Fig. 1).
- Cross-references in the articles interlink relevant questions.
- The biographical information about the authors provide further information about the professional background behind the articles.

Figure 1 emphasizes that sustainable purposes and traveling organizations are never "islands" but are connected to a broader system—as we have learned around the world not only from digitalization and big data but also from global crises and changes. Thus, it always was our intention for the wide range of articles in this book to cover this systemic and dynamic connectivity, where all elements are interlinked and influence the journey at all levels.

2 What the Articles Are About

The list of articles is developed—in a journey—in both a consistent and logical as well as a creative and unforeseeable manner and the interfaces and linkages of the articles developed in a similar fashion.

3 Fundamental Thoughts with Which to Start the 3-P-Model Journey

All three articles tackle fundamental preconditions in terms of mindset, attitude, intellectual understanding, resilience, flexibility, and curiosity on which leadership and management, well-fitting 3-P-designs, and successful applications might build. That is the reason to start with these articles as they facilitate the understanding of the more specific articles.

- The article "About Travelling in the Unknown in the 19th Century and Today. Pattern for Leadership and Management in 3-P-Model Context" explores the fundamental preconditions in terms of mindset, attitude, and resilience as well as the capabilities and skills needed and applied in the expeditions to Africa at the end of the nineteenth century (using, e.g., the expedition to find the mouth of the Zambezi) and the current journey of the Central Saint Martin's College in London—and derives useful general conclusions for the three pillars from these examples.
- In "Nature Eats Culture for Lunch: About Consonances and Dissonances Shifting or Limiting Harmony," the authors focus on the harmony between the natures, cultures, and structures of individuals, groups, and organizations. When these resources pull in opposite directions, it is difficult to create the collaboration needed to perform well and be satisfied with the situation we find ourselves in. The authors have placed the described dimensions in context and developed an effective model and practical methodology of how to apply it in social, business, and private contexts.
- The "Wicked Problems of Travelling Organizations" are undefinable and difficult to cope with—but they are all around. Currently, we face a pandemic as a new problem with its own wickedness, penetrating all systems. Nevertheless, wicked problems are not bad per se but are a natural part of our journey in the VUCA world. The article proposes discursive loops to cope with them and to finally manage them in a travelling organization.

4 Leadership in the 3-P-Model: Setting Direction and Motivation

All three articles illuminate important different perspectives of leadership in practice. The opener is an article stimulating analogy thinking and creating contexts to ludically (using play) learn or train good leadership and also management (improvisational theater); afterward an expert analyzes the importance and impact of intrinsic motivation as well as leadership in existential crisis before dysfunctional leadership is tackled. Without good leadership and connected management, 3-P-M cannot be successfully run.

- The principles of purpose, journey, and connectivity as unfolded in the 3-P-Model have a strong resemblance to the basics of improvisational theatre (improv). In other words, organizations can be regarded as a kind of improvisational theater. In "The Benefits of Improvisational Theatre," the author shows how helpful it is to learn to play in a proficient way or at least transfer key insights to shift the interaction and collaboration in the organization.
- The "Leading Organizations through Intrinsic Motivation" focuses on the overwhelming role of intrinsic motivation for individuals, organizations, and leaders and describes the historical development of the research into the subject. The author shows the fundamental role that intrinsic motivation takes in the most beneficial application of the 3-P-Model and in the interpretation of each of its pillar.
- In "The AAUL Framework of Leadership in Times of Crisis," the author explains his own leadership framework AAUL. It gives guidance, especially in crises. The understanding and application of a sophisticated leadership framework such as AAUL is significantly more focused, effective, and efficient if it is combined with the 3-P-Model, and crises become more easily manageable.

5 3-P-Model Application in the Public Sector

The five articles cover a broad field of topics, starting with an international organization and institution (UN), focusing then on globally important, but locally performed, tasks (urban planning) and afterward on the development of countries in a demanding context of different national, international, and local authorities. The last article covers the potential role of science on the journey of countries through unknown areas.

- The article on "Applying the Three-Pillar Model in UN Agencies" shows how global institutions—and especially the UN—are navigating troubled waters with the support of the 3-P-Model, coping with disruptive challenges and strong constraints using the example of a central UN agency. How should one navigate an organization that is connected in the entire system as displayed in Fig. 1?
- In "The Impact of Platform Economies on the Urban Structure," the impact of platform economies on cities and their urban planning is discussed with the help of the 3-P-Model using the example of the city of Venice and Airbnb. The topic is important as, in the digital age, cities are more and more organized around platform economies which are redefining urban life and transforming our relationship with space and people. The question especially of the purpose of a city or an urban area is raised and discussed and linked with journey thinking and the need for connectivity.
- The article "From the Inside and the Outside—A learning journey to mainstream the digital transformation in a federal enterprise" focuses on the continuous development of a federal agency, which acts on behalf of its commissioning parties and political agenda setting with employees all over the world. Following

sectoral structures, it is essential to connect resources such as talent, expertise, and motivation to create agents of change and enable a meaningful and effective internal digital transformation. This directly adds to the digital transformation of its service delivery, which was mainstreamed by the implementation of the "digital by default" concept.

- The "Scientific Guidance on Journeys in Unknown Areas—a Best Practice Example" describes the scientific guidance on the Covid-19 pandemic journey in Germany, where scientists were able to give significant guidance and support reasonable decisions in this unknown and threatening situation. The author shows how well the 3-P-Model can be applied on a journey in such a context—and what we can learn from scientific exploration journeys and their communication.
- In "Cooperation and Development in a Social Organization," the authors describe how a traveling organization is managed within an educational, socially, and politically determined ecosystem. It reports on a municipal enterprise in which daycare for children and family centers are coordinated. The teams working there pursue a clear purpose based on an advanced educational concept. Connecting resources here means harmonizing efficient processes and daily working practice, continuously networking the expectations and capabilities of the various stakeholders: children, parents, educators, cooperation partners, volunteers, administration, and politics.

6 3-P-Model Application in the Private Sector

The seven articles cover a broad field of situations in the different types of enterprises and industries, such as start-ups; organizations in hybrid situations; former start-ups which want to retain their original spirit despite being fast growing; enterprises in large, significant, and demanding transformations; and those from finance industry through retail, plant manufacturing, and medical technology to agriculture.

- The "Start-Up Development in Traditionally Operating Industries: Regional Subsidiaries of Pharmaceutical Companies" tackles a multitude of challenges arising with geographical expansion. The dynamic growth of the organization demands ongoing integration of new roles and assets but also of strategic elements and processes. Regarding the three-pillar model, "sustainable purpose" and "connecting resources" require continuous updating and adaptation to the current phase on the development journey to provide consistency and clarity for the "traveling organization."
- The article on "Applying the Principles of the 3-P-Model to Build an Agile High-Performance Team within Finance" describes and evaluates a Munich Re initiative. The new agile unit (built up like a start-up) within the classic finance and IT units, the management of the hybrid organization, and the arising tensions are described, using the three-pillar model effectively.

- The "Application of the 3-P-Model in a Start-up-like Environment of a Large Enterprise" concentrates on the leap from a small local team to a large global team: What capabilities had to be connected? What was the leap's impact on purpose; on mindset and spirit; and on roles, skills, and collective practices?
- The article "MedTech companies on their growth journey—Leadership responses to growth challenges in the light of the 3-P-Model" is a case study on how the 3-P-Model might influence this special industry on intensive growth journeys now and in the future, how it can help to integrate the change caused from outside and the change initiated from inside, and how it can combine change with existing structures by building hybrids.
- The article on "Building a Sustainable Brand in Specialty Chemicals. Carve Out from a Big Corporate" highlights and illustrates key components of this journey along the three organizational and leadership pillars of "sustainable purpose," "travelling organization," and "connecting resources." Each one represents a significant building block of the company's financial success, its reputation in the marketplace, and, most importantly, its strong bonding among its employees.
- The "Climate Change and Winemaking—a Significant Transformation in Agriculture" connects cultural and biological purpose with a journey in a critical environmental development which cannot be planned in a linear fashion. This requires a travelling mindset and connectivity in the wine-maker's ecosystem, i.e., with scientists, peers, etc., to master the journey. In the article, different geographies are mentioned. The article describes a context that is well known to everybody since wine is a "tangible good" of common interest whose growing number of consumers have increasing know-how and expertise—so it is an easy-to-understand case study.
- The "Trapped in the Bermuda Triangle among project, process and line organizations—accelerating complex tech development projects" describes an organizational development program deployed to stabilize and accelerate new product development projects in a high-tech industrial company. Initially, functional egotism, conflicts between project and line organizations, and inflexible processes frustrated the ambitions of all concerned. The program is evaluated retrospectively using the 3-P-Model.

7 Helpful Design Concepts to Best Use the 3-P-Model

These five articles cover different conceptual ways of applying the 3-P-Model. The broad range of topics covered goes from sophisticated ways of designing organization along the product life cycle to fast product development redesign, change management design in complex situations, creating and using a compass for entrepreneurial journeys and to crisis management with 3-P-using the example of the pandemic.

- The "Organizations Meandering in the Product Life-Cycle" describes the consistent connectivity between organization, ecosystem, and markets. Companies need to adapt their structures, processes, practices, and teamwork to the architecture and life cycles of their products so that their overall performance meets customer requirements and market developments. Since the different products are in different phases between genesis and commodity, a multiple organizational set-up is required to connect the resources in a challenging journey of the company as a whole.
- The "Transformation in the Field of Product Development: A Five-Day Micro Project" describes a 5-day microproject in the automotive industry that was set up to rebuild the product development process. The challenges of this process in terms of speed and effectiveness are triggered by a clear market-based purpose, which has also proven crucial for connecting, aligning, and energizing the project team and the main players. Both, the new process and the exciting experience of co-creation are key for the further corporate journey.
- The article "Emergent Change—Embracing Complexity as a Key Challenge in a Travelling Organization" provides a perspective on how to navigate an organization with a complexity mindset through emergent changes and even crises. The authors show how the management team can deal with complexity by exploring and connecting their diverse resources and aligning them to a joint management approach. They propose a map that can be used to collaboratively navigate the organization on its journey.
- The article "Building and Using a Compass for Travelling Organizations" underlines the need to connect the resources inside the company as well as with the ecosystem and the wider environment. A collaborative process of building and using a compass ensures a shared entrepreneurial mindset of a travelling organization and how to navigate it. Two cases are presented on how to create a compass from the top-down and the bottom-up.
- The authors of the article "If not now—then when? Learning from the Pandemic for the Application of the Three-Pillar Model" show that the 3-P-Model even works in the context of a global crisis, which is a pacemaker for fast learning, online communication, and self-organization but also questions the social purpose of organizations. Two practical approaches are presented to analyze the complex situation and to determine the specific need for action in the different phases of a crisis. Finally, the willingness to learn and develop is checked by looking back at the financial crisis of 2008/2009 and the discussion about resilience at that time.

8 How the Articles Are Linked

The course of the writing journey of writing was reminiscent of a long walk through an interesting landscape: scenic views produce new ways of looking at objects that were hitherto unknown, which always means new perspectives. The close interaction between all editors and authors produced so many linkages between key

Chapter	Chapters	3	4	5	6	7	8	9	10	11	12	13	14	15	16	17	18	19	20	21	22	23	24	25
3	About Travelling in the Unknown in the 19th Century and Today			●	●	●	●	●			●							●					●	
4	Nature Eats Culture for Lunch					●	●					●												
5	Wicked Problems of Travelling Orgs	●																●				●		●
6	The Benefits of Improvisational Theatre	●																						
7	Leading Organizations through Intrinsic Motivation	●	●				●	●				●												
8	The AAUL Framework of Leadership in Times of Crisis	●	●			●		●			●			●	●	●								●
9	Applying the Three-Pillar Model in UN Agencies	●				●	●			●														
10	The Impact of Platform Economies on the Urban Structure										●													
11	From Inside and the Outside – a learning journey to mainstream the digital transformation	●					●	● ●					●	●					●					●
12	Scientific Guidance on Journeys in Unknown Areas – a Best Practice Example	●					●		●									●						●
13	Cooperation and Development in a Social Organization		●																				●	
14	Start-Up Development in Traditionally Operating Industries					●				●				●			●						●	
15	Applying the 3-P-Model to Build an Agile High-Performance Team in Finance						●								●	●				●				
16	Application of the 3-P-Model in a Start-up-like Environment of a Large Enterprise						●							●		●				●				
17	MedTech companies on their growth journey - Leadership responses						●							●	●					●			●	
18	Building a Sustainable Brand in Specialty Chemicals. Carve Out from Big Corporate												●			●				●			●	
19	Climate Change and Winemaking – a Significant Transformation in Agriculture	●		●							●													
20	Trapped in the Bermuda Triangle among project, process and line organizations						●						●								● ●			
21	Organizations Meandering in the Product-Life-Cycle													●	●	●	●				●		●	
22	Transformation in the Field of Product Development: A Five-Day Micro-Project																		●	●				
23	Emergent Change – Embracing Complexity as a Key Challenge in a Travelling Org.			●																			●	●
24	Building and Using a Compass for Travelling Organizations	●											●			●				●		●		
25	If not now – then when? Learning from Pandemic for the Application of Three-Pillar-Model			●			●				●											●		

Fig. 2 Key chapter linkages and interfaces (created by Editors for the book)

content, insights, and takeaways: what was described in article A in its special context found an analogy in article B in the other special context. So, a glance at another article with linked content opens up a new perspective on the original one. In the table below, the key linkages between articles are shown—to be understood in the sense that if you are interested in the content and outcome of article A, reading articles B and C might be useful too (Fig. 2).

Please note that only the key connections from the editor's and author's perspectives are shown in the figure—you might discover many more connections and linkages during your own individual reading.

You will find more concrete hints on connections and linkages of the articles in the final concluding chapter, where the key conclusions of the articles and their takeaways are summarized and evaluated.

Peter Wollmann has been a responsible manager, initiator, mentor, and facilitator in large, predominantly global transformations and strategic developments for almost 40 years. His specialties are the implementations of the three-pillar model in organizations and focused setting checks to identify strengths, weaknesses, opportunities, and threats and facilitate optimization measures. Since 2017, Peter has been working independently on organizational projects and future initiatives. After graduating in mathematics and physics from the University of Bonn, he began his professional career at Deutscher Herold, then part of the insurance group of Deutsche Bank. Later he took on strategic leadership and most recently was program director for global transformation in the Zurich Insurance Company (ZIC). In his professional network, he has leveraged his experience and strategic thinking to the development of various leading companies. He is the author and publisher of a number of books and articles on strategy, leadership, and project and project portfolio management. He is also the founder of a wine business: VinAuthority.

Frank Kühn has been supporting companies and institutions for many years in the areas of organization and leadership and change and project management. He brings his experience to developments such as the three-pillar model and systemic setting checks. Frank has a doctorate in work science. After leading positions in research and industry, he was a partner at HLP in Frankfurt and in the ICG Integrated Consulting Group in Berlin and Graz. Today, he is an independent consultant and a business partner of ICG and is associated with other project partners and think tanks. He has published numerous articles in management journals and books.

Michael Kempf has been an experienced management consultant for over 20 years. The driving force of his professional activities is his strong ambition to design processes and organizations in a sustainable manner. He relishes identifying key challenges, diagnosing complex relationships, and assisting in shaping the future. Gaining experience and learning something new are indispensable parts of his life, which is why he likes to seize new opportunities. He began his career as a carpenter before studying social work, education, and business administration. His career has spanned various jobs in social work, 10 years as a manager (HR and logistics) in industrial and retail companies and, since 1998, in advising people, leadership teams, and working teams and organizations that are all very different. Michael has co-authored numerous publications in the field of leadership and organizational development.

Reto Püringer has worked for more than 20 years in the banking and insurance industry. He has held various senior positions in global companies. His practical experience ranges from strategy development, business model design, product/proposition development/management, enterprise-wide portfolio management, program/project management, operations/IT management, and large-scale change program delivery to financial/actuarial management over different geographies and time zones, hierarchies and units, and cultures and systems. Reto has managed multinational and multicultural change and transformation endeavors across the globe and managed teams of various sizes both on site and remotely. Reto holds a degree in Economical Informatics and Marketing and completed an Executive MBA at the University of Zurich.

Part II

Fundamental Thoughts with Which to Start the 3-P-Model Journey

The authors discuss in this part of the book cognitive, mental and behavioral preconditions to best apply the 3-P-Model. The right understanding of the pillars and their dimension—also in historical context—is crucial to tailor one's special approach to design in detail and to implement and apply the 3-P-Model.

All three articles tackle fundamental preconditions in terms of mindset, attitude, intellectual understanding, resilience, flexibility and curiosity on which leadership and management, well-fitting 3-P designs and successful applications might build. That is the reason to start with these articles as they facilitate understanding of the more specific articles.

About Travelling in the Unknown in the Nineteenth Century and Today: A Pattern for Leadership and Management in a 3-P-Model Context

Peter Wollmann and Reto Püringer

Abstract

Peter Wollmann and Reto Püringer explain some basic concepts for travelling organizations, meaning which different types of "travelling" exist, the specifics for journeys into unknown and dangerous areas (which is the most demanding category), which kind of leadership and management travelling organizations need, which mindset and capabilities are required in a team, how teams should be composed, which measurements in blurring situations are still helpful, and which are superfluous as well as how to cope with the lack of control in these situations.

It turns out that the expeditions to explore—the mostly unknown—Africa in the nineteenth century deliver perfect analogies and examples for journeys into unknown and dangerous areas, very different to safe movements in the simple, certain, and easily predictable world before VUCA and before the new realities with which we are confronted today.

To design an upcoming journey, it is therefore very helpful to understand which type of travelling a team does and which demands are connected with it. This allows one to prepare the journey based on learnings using analogies and examples which help to describe what the journey will mean in detail and enable the necessary decisions to be made in terms of travel approach, composition of the team, etc.

P. Wollmann (✉)
Bonn, Germany
e-mail: pw@peterwollmann.com

R. Püringer
Ebertswil, Switzerland
e-mail: rpueringer@hotmail.com

P. Wollmann et al. (eds.), *Organization and Leadership in Disruptive Times*, Future of Business and Finance, https://doi.org/10.1007/978-3-030-63034-8_3

1 Introduction

The travelling organization is the second pillar of the 3-Pillar Model,[1] described in the former book *Three Pillars of Organization and Leadership in Disruptive Times: Navigating Your Company Successfully Through the 21st Century Business World* (Wollmann et al. 2020) which aimed to provide direction and guidance in the current volatile, uncertain, complex, and ambiguous (VUCA) world. The term "travelling" defines the movement of an organization in the current volatile, uncertain, complex, and ambiguous (VUCA) world to follow its overarching purpose. Travelling in this context also means to be able to set off without all final clarifications, which means experimenting, prototyping, and piloting ideas and approaches to gradually find the right path. Travelling in organizations is, in itself, complex as various groups of people contribute to the overall purpose, each with a specific goal assigned. The coordination of scope and progress of those groups can be tedious, and an overarching purpose can unite these groups—especially if they connect with one another constantly.

A rough definition of "travelling organization" in the 3-P-Model can be found in the box below. In the current Covid-19 pandemic, which challenges a lot of putative certainties, it makes sense to understand travelling more broadly using also historical contexts in order to prepare a new perspective, especially regarding the potential loss of control during the journey—totally or at least to a certain and significant degree, which might be existential—and to develop the demanded resilience for this suitable mindset.

Travelling Organization

Business consistency, strategic stability, and structural continuity, coupled with change projects from time to time: this has long been an illusion in disruptive and crisis-ridden times. Now, we have to understand that organizations are continuously on a journey, following their purpose or even striving for survival, and always exploring the best path between poles, alternatives, and options. If the teams don't know what to face around the next bend, they have to make smaller steps and explore the terrain. Even if they don't know in advance what the best result will be, they will achieve it,

(continued)

[1]The other two pillars are:

Sustainable purpose: The people in the organization, but also its key stakeholders, need to know the mandate of the organization and the sustainable value it is creating. The mandate is giving clear and convincing orientation on the right level that aligns and inspires to go for a joint endeavor, which makes involved people confident, inspired, and proud to be part of and contribute to it.

Connectivity: The organization has to be aware that impact, value, and efficiency need connectivity between individuals; between people and organizations or institutions; between different systems and cultures; etc. Managing connectivity means preventing unconnected structural silos and boxed competencies and focusing on multilateral incentives and behaviors.

believing in their motivation and capabilities to manage the journey and relying on their agile mindset, self-reflection, readiness to embrace change, and willingness to deliver. People in a travelling organization are curious, open, courageous, and experimental, and they cope well with uncertainty, stress, unforeseen challenges, etc. Even a rudimental overview is difficult. And it is not possible to sidestep and prevent coping with the situation, and going on a journey is mandatory. Travelling in general can be more than running a transformation. In a transformation, the target situation is normally described to a certain scale on a detailed level. Even though it is clear that the desired target situation will only be reached to a certain extent, the target gives a lot of orientation. But there are also journeys to unknown areas where the target is to arrive wherever and to survive—just like in the crises today.

2 Categories of Travelling

It is helpful to start with a rough categorization of travel over the last centuries to understand the dimension of the topic.

Travelling in the twenty-first century often means going from A to B using reasonable infrastructure (highways, rail network, flight connections, etc.). Those trips can normally be planned in detail. Potential threats like severe traffic jams, delays, missing connections, crowded infrastructure, even accidents, or getting stranded because of an intervention like the current Covid-19 pandemic are annoying but manageable. Normally, the people involved stay connected with contact points needed to solve arising issues, and in the worst case, it takes time, so each loss of control is temporary and very rarely existential unless one has a severe accident, which is not so likely. The uncertainty potentially perceived in between is more trivial and focused on a temporary reduction of comfort. It is not a real adventure.

The descriptions and evaluations above are still valid when we consider the more unusual trips available today. Normally, things are well-organized in advance, there is a guide taking the lead, helpers are available, and continuous contact with friends and family via the Internet and mobile networks is possible. We would like to categorize these forms of travelling as "Routine Travel in the twenty-first century." The potential threats and unforeseen incidents are minimal and don't have significant impact. Neither a special mindset nor special capabilities are needed.

But there are also other types of travelling even in our days: the young man who recently walked without a passport from Germany to Iran to find his mother (Süddeutsche Zeitung Magazin 2020a), the young girl who sailed around the world all by herself (SZ.de 2017), the couple who visited 215 countries with their old car,[2] the man who went by bicycle from Germany to South Africa (Spiegel Online 2007), etc. All of these travellers allowed for all possibilities, including significant loss of control. Their purposes were both to follow a certain route (which might have to be modified in between) and to have experiences with themselves (what are we capable of achieving and how does this change us). The risk of these journeys was significantly higher, and the people embarked on them precisely because of this, to reach their limits, to get out of their comfort zones. Nevertheless, in all cases, support networks were in place. The young man on his way to Iran, for example, had mobilized friends of friends and friends of relatives as contact points along the route and to help him cross borders at spots where a passport was not necessary. His threat was to be captured by police or to get caught in cross fire. The girl sailing around the world had a professional sailing boat with advanced technology and connections to meteorological stations as well as with her parents and friends. Her threat was the weather—e.g., when rounding Cape Horn—and an accident with lost containers or with other boats and falling sick. The couple travelling round the world with their old car and the cyclist on his way to South Africa had flexible plans and a quite clear understanding of the challenges on the way, at least on a meta-level. And they also had access to modern communication devices. Their threats were falling sick, corrupt police and civil service, car or bicycle problems without being able to repair them easily, and also to get involved in gun battles or terror attacks. We would like to categorize these forms of travelling as "Advanced Individual Travel in the twenty-first century." The potential threats and unforeseen incidents are "medium severe," probably not really existential, but with some significant impact on health, physical integrity, personal freedom, etc. So, a special mindset involving a certain readiness to take higher risks, some resilience, and special capabilities to easily find solutions for issues is needed. The advantage for all travellers mentioned above is that there were quite detailed maps and a bundle of additional information available and that modern communication devices could be used and real-time solutions could, in theory, be found. That also means that, on a meta-level, the risks taken and potential incidents were quite transparent, but what could happen in detail was not.

Moving now to travelling in the nineteenth century, we find a significant different situation which we will describe in detail below (Livingston 2017). Very often, only the starting point was clarified in detail but not the destination which was only known at a high level without any details. Their exact course of the journey was mostly totally unclear as was the duration and any threats along the way. It was only understood that these threats might be existential with some significant impact on survival, health, physical integrity, personal freedom, etc. So, a special mindset based on a purpose and an absolute readiness to take highest conceivable risks, strongest resilience, and excellent capabilities to easily find solutions for issues are called for. Those travellers had neither detailed maps for orientation nor further

[2]https://www.mercedes-fans.de/magazin/sternstunde/g-modell-weltrekord-26-jahre-215-laender-900-000-kilometer-im-g-modell-35-jahre-mercedes-benz-g-klasse-jubilaeum-mit-weltrekord.7635

additional information nor any communication options in well-known locations. For those travellers, the purpose of the journey was worth the risk and uncertainty. We would like to categorize these forms of travelling as "Explorative Travel in the nineteenth century."

3 Explorative Travel in the Nineteenth Century as a Pattern for Travelling Organizations

In this paragraph, we would like to especially stress those famous expeditions in Africa, e.g., to explore and map defined parts of it or to discover the source of a river. The initial situation often was that the available maps reliably showed the right silhouette of Africa and a small strip of the interior of the country, charted in recent years with quite modern methods. The heartland was terra incognito, with only some information available from Arabian traders some hundred years previously and some maps that were more based on fantasy and anecdotal reports.

The African maps from the sixteenth century already show a certain level of detail which of course had not been created by modern cartographical methods. Nevertheless, one should not underestimate the level of documented facts and knowledge as well as the information that was communicated orally. The disadvantage compared to today was the lack of authenticated, absolutely reliable facts and knowledge; a certain level of healthy suspicion was crucial to prevent unpleasant surprises.

Even in the nineteenth century, the level of reliable geographic and cartographical knowledge of Africa was not sufficient for safe and focused travelling. This means that embarking on an expedition to find and explore the source of a river (like the Zambezi or the Nile) had significant challenges:

- It was clear that the source had to be somewhere as the river existed and parts of its course, and especially its mouth, were known.
- There was a rough idea where the source might be situated, but the detailed geography of the area was neither known nor had been carefully explored before.
- It was not improbable that the river was part of a drainage system so that there might be some tributary rivers—meaning it was not easy to decide which one was the main river and which one the tributary. This also means that even if the source was found, explorers would have to check whether it was the source of the main river or of the tributary.
- It was possible that the river courses were so nontransparent, e.g., in the context with large lakes, wetlands, and subterranean streams, that exploration would be almost impossible with the tools available at the time.
- There was no precise measurement to ascertain the exact position on the journey—in the unknown areas.
- It was very probable that there would be many unknown—potentially existential—threats on the journey, starting from exotic sicknesses to hostile locals, dangerous animals, lack of supplies of food and water, toxic food and water, insurmountable geographies, getting lost, etc. And it was nigh-on impossible to

Fig. 1 Africae tabula nova, 1570, Wikipedia, retrieved from Wikimedia Commons

prepare for these threats sufficiently or even prevent them from happening as a consequence of the lack of knowledge (Fig. 1).

Summarizing this, going on such an expedition meant:

- Knowing where to start from—normally from a place at the coast
- Knowing the destination, but only high level (it exists)—e.g., the source of a river
- Knowing a little about the overall direction for the journey, the first miles
- Knowing that there will be significant threats—but not which ones or where and when
- Not knowing where the destination will exactly be and how it can be reached
- Not knowing how to exactly get to the destination and how long it will take
- Not knowing how long the journey will take
- Not knowing at all what one would meet on the journey
- Not knowing whether one would be able to come back with or without success (Fig. 2)

It is clear that people and teams starting such an endeavor need very special preconditions, such as a very strong conviction and a yearning to follow the special

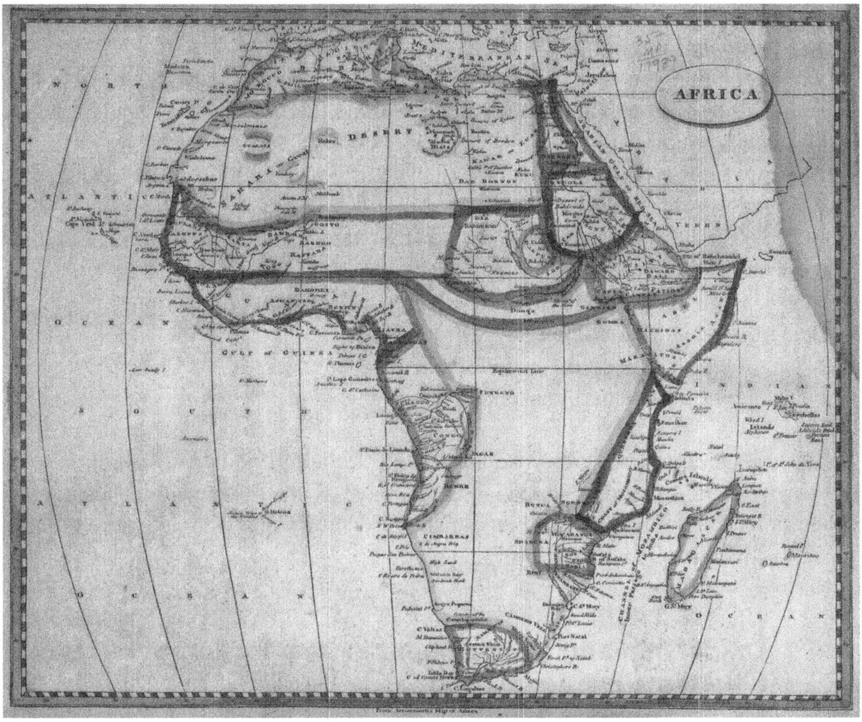

Fig. 2 Africa map 1812, Wikipedia, retrieved from Wikimedia Commons

purpose, an entrepreneurial, flexible, curious, resilient, and focused mindset together with the belief to achieve—together with the team—even very demanding tasks, and the capability to connect in an appropriate way with the encountered preconditions during the journey, especially within the expedition team and with the external world and here especially with the indigenous people encountered.

It has to be clear that learning every day is crucial for surviving, which means—following knowledge management theory—collecting data, extending the data to information by linking it with context, and developing it into knowledge by getting used to applying it in daily life. Finding a new herb is, in the beginning, a piece of data, describing it and exploring under which conditions and in which *terroir* it grows creates information, and using it for the daily preparation of meals or for healing sickness makes it a piece of knowledge.

Why is such a historic "hard-core" travelling concept nevertheless a pattern for modern travelling organizations? We are in a situation worldwide that is dramatic and does not have any real preference: the Covid-19 pandemic. It is absolutely clear that we need, in different perspectives, the spirit of those Africa expeditions:

- Accepting that there is no real preference, which means that we have to forget our well-known certainties and behavior patterns and start an exploration to unknown areas or even the unknown unknown. This also means accepting a loss of control and significant risks.

- Accepting that the destination and the target situation strived for cannot be defined, not even as a rough silhouette. So, the journey will be iterative, with a lot of changes on the way.
- Being aware that there will be unpleasant situations in between with threats, risks, fear, and negative emotions.
- Accepting that everybody will have to leave their comfort zone while travelling the journey.
- Being open to completely new experiences and focusing on learning.
- Being confident that the journey will lead to something of value.
- Trying the best to keep the team together and in good spirits.
- Focusing on trustful and transparent communication.

So, in the current crisis, too, we are starting from a difficult as-is situation to an unknown to-be situation. Maybe the analogy to the nineteenth-century risky expeditions is helpful—and the comparison also shows that we have more fallback scenarios than people had 200 years before.

4 Leadership and Management in Real Explorative Travel Situations

A key instrument for good leadership and management in travel situations is to create travel maps together with the team and communicate transparently.

Even if only the starting point is reliably known and the target not detailed, the daily progress on the journey can be described and documented—in both a qualitative and also partly in a quantitative sense. The questions how far are we still away from the destination, how long will the journey take toward it, etc. cannot be answered, but we know what we have achieved. We are also able to describe the assumptions about the journey and the destination—and their change from the daily experiences.

Taking the map of Africa—with a clear silhouette and only a small strip along the coasts described—and a large area where potentially the destination might be in the unknown heartland. We might enter the newly reached position daily, the results from the exploration of the environment of this position, additional learnings, and new perspectives on the assumed detailed position of the destination, even if there are different opinions, content of discussions, calculations of probabilities, etc. And we might also collect the update of the evaluation of assumed threats, risks, obstacles, etc.

This would all have to be based on clear briefing—re-briefing proceedings to create the transparency needed and to support honest exchange, which is crucial for mutual trust and for the level of confidence needed. The team leaders have to implement these mindsets and procedures in a way which enables the team to be able to steer itself autonomously in most situations—as self-initiative is crucial for travelling organizations, which means that the team is composed of different personalities with different strengths but all proactively taking responsibility.

The mentioned (daily) measurement of progress has to be regarded as "measurement in blurring contexts" as it only covers a small part of the reality: the key questions regarding the detailed position of the destination, the exact distance to it, the remaining time for the journey, etc. cannot be answered. So, it would be illusory to think that the measurement results guarantee full control of the situation. But it gives some control of the journey and allows one, at least retrospectively, to learn about journey optimization.

In that regard, it is important to have constant communication within the organization that is travelling, so everybody is clear where the group is in its journey and where they stand with their resources (e.g., water, food). To do so, standard data is required, so everybody has the same understanding when a situation is assessed. It is also crucial to have an idea every day of what the next action for every individual is, and to have transparency for the team, so it is clear who is contributing what based on a standard way of capturing and discussing the tasks.

The most important aspect when travelling in uncertainty is to provide transparency and feedback within the team. Constant feedback not only improves morale and trust within the team, but it allows one to identify threats and/or opportunities that an individual alone is not able to identify. The better the team members know each other, the better they understand who in the team has which competencies, and they can discuss together who is the best person to take on a task—especially when something unfamiliar needs to be done.

This is especially important when a team is on a journey that is full of risk. Imagine you set sail in the ocean and a mountain appears that splits the ocean in two. Do you sail left or do you sail right? There is no right or wrong decision as nobody knows the land and there is no GPS, Internet, etc. It is crucial that the team decides together as all of them will feel the consequences. Morale will increase as, in the event of failure, nobody can be blamed, and in case of success, everybody contributed. It's important to use a standard data set to ensure everybody has the same understanding about what has been decided, and afterward it can be reviewed.

To have such a team in place, people selection at the start of the journey is fundamental. Besides choosing the right mix of competences (people who can navigate a ship, people who can repair, etc.), you need to make sure the people have emotional intelligence and fit together as personalities. It would be very risky if people were meeting for the first time on the ship; team building before the journey starts is crucial to make sure everybody fits.

It's also important to understand why people want to go on this journey in case of travelling into unknown territory. The team needs to understand the drivers for each individual. Do people accept taking the risk because of curiosity, social responsibility, money, and fame? If the team hits a point of fundamental crisis, the resolution of the situation needs be on the back of clear purposes.

The last ingredient we should not forget is leadership. Even though the team can mostly organize itself, it needs individuals who see the big picture, who inspire and challenge the team and bring in positive energy to increase the mood, and who can speak up in case of conflicts. Imagine, as in the example above, the team needs to decide left or right, but after a long discussion, half of the group wants to go left and the other half right. You then need people who can take this conflict and nudge the teams toward deciding.

A Key Challenge of Travelling: The Exact Determination of the Current Position

One of the key challenges of travelling in unknown areas is the determination of one's current position in the best way possible, which depends, among other things, on available methods and tools. Today, GPS can determine geographic position quite reliably. Centuries ago, GPS was not available and methods and tools were limited. That was the reason why, 300 years ago, the English Admiral Sir Cloudesley Shovell, on his way back from Gibraltar to Portsmouth, wrecked his whole fleet off the coast of Isles of Scilly because he assumed he was in the middle of the entrance of the Channel. The reason for the accident was that, while the determination of the latitude could be exactly managed, the determination of the longitude was very imprecise in those days. This did not change before John Harrison finished the development of an astonishingly precise chronometer and won an award funded by the Board of Longitude. Prior to this, navigators only knew one of the coordinates of their position and had to speculate about the other by using rough auxiliary calculations (see Dava Sobel (1995): Longitude: The True Story of a Lone Genius Who Solved the Greatest Scientific Problem of His Time).

A situation like this looks familiar and arises the more complex and multidimensional a situation is: some factors are well-known, some a little bit and some absolutely not. To cope with this and to create an easily understandable analogue narrative, the above anecdote about navigation might be helpful.

Currently, the Covid-19 pandemic is creating such a multidimensional situation where only few coordinates can be solidly determined. Navigating in something like "Emerging Infectious Diseases" forces us to work with scenarios, not with prognoses which try to exactly draft a future development. It means "planning the non-plannable" which is realized using mathematical modeling. It is an iterative process where exact real-time measurement is used to continuously recalibrate the assumptions for the model calculation for the scenarios. The target is to gradually reach measures to make the most desired scenario the most probable one or even the one that actually occurs.

The takeaway for travellers is the following:

- It is crucial to understand which coordinates can be solidly determined, which only vaguely, and which not.

(continued)

- It is necessary to find an explorative and iterative way to increase one's ability to determine one's position step by step based on evaluated information or better knowledge.
- It is—especially for leaders—important to know exactly to what extent a situation is under control and to what it is not and to communicate this transparently.
- It is vital to stress the purpose and the necessity of connectivity (which is a driver for building up knowledge)—and to create confidence that navigation in an unknown area is achievable.

For this, the analogies described above may be helpful.

5 Another Journey Example from Central Saint Martins College in London in the Twenty-First Century

Another interesting example for travelling in the unknown or even the unknown unknown—beyond historical instances or the Covod-19 pandemic—is Central Saint Martins College in London. This old and extremely successful institution has had to reinvent itself as a consequence of large societal changes, climate change, consumption criticism, etc.

The dilemma can be summarized in some questions recently formulated in the *Süddeutsche Zeitung Magazin* (Süddeutsche Zeitung Magazin 2020b) where a long article, which was very worth reading, about the institution was published:

> But how does one nurture designers for a world that needs fewer, not more products? How does one prepare students for the cultural and ecological change that they should shape as Creative Directors, but which nobody yet knows what it will look like?

This dilemma is a good example for difficult journeys, during which the exact direction can only be developed step by step, based on interaction, experience, research, model calculations, etc.—in principle the same as journeys through the pandemic.

It is interesting to learn which special measures Central Saint Martins College took. In a nutshell, they can be summarized as follows:

- Enrichment of the role profile of designer: in the future, designers should understand their task not only as designing objects but as designing situations and systems.
- Involvement of the students in the journey to define their new role and the route how to get there.
- Cross-silo cooperation internally: the different ateliers were opened so as to be available for everybody.

- Cross-silo cooperation externally: student projects are directly realized together with companies and large brands in all industries.
- Increased cooperation with social, societal, and political projects.
- Encouragement of citizens from the neighborhood to get involved in the college's work.
- Involvement of scientists (e.g., biologists).
- In general, opening the college to all possible environmental influences.
- Special focus on civil responsibility, ecology, and climate change.

So, an important public institution sets off into an unknown future but is well prepared to design and shape the future on its way to this future.

6 Conclusions

In general, it is crucial to analyze the category of travelling and the intended journey that fits best and to envision which analogies and examples could be adduced to develop a comprehensive understanding of the necessary preparation and realization.

In a world which has tried for decades to reduce uncertainty to a minimum, the shock of realizing that one has lost detailed control—and perhaps never had it to the assumed degree—is quite significant and leads to the awareness that a lot of coping skills and mindsets in unknown and potentially dangerous areas and contexts have got lost and have to be re-established. Rather than developing detailed plans on how to do the journey, it is much more important to make sure the travelling team is resilient enough to manage the unknown by having the right people, communication, and tools in place—so they can execute their journey from day to day and adapt and/or adopt. An enterprise which starts a digital transformation often only roughly knows the overall target but not what it will look like in detail at the end, e.g., what a normal working week of each employee will look like afterward, so that a convincing film could be made upfront. On the contrary, people know that what they imagine will not become completely true, and potentially, the future will be totally different. But nevertheless, one has to move on—but with the right mindset.

That is the reason why studying the art of travelling and running excursions a hundred and more years ago is helpful—as the current demands are comparable in terms of mindset, skills, leadership, and management. The technical environment is, of course, different, but the principles regarding "how to" are still very similar.

7 Key Takeaways

- In general, a demanding and potentially risky journey into unknown areas can only be done successfully if there is a strong, convincing sustainable purpose in which the people believe and that serves as key motivation.
- Define the category of travelling the journey most likely will be and fix the preparation following analogies, examples, etc.

- Sufficient emphasis has to be placed on perfect connectivity: the composition of the team—to have a shared mindset, the same culture, and a balanced portfolio of capabilities and skills.
- During the journey, it is crucial to analyze regularly where the energy is flowing, if the energy is being used effectively and efficiently, and whether there are team members who are preventing high performance. This analysis of how the connectivity of the travelling team works should be regularly discussed in the team.
- Significant leadership efforts—by the official leader and by all team members—have to be made; especially proactive and independent entrepreneurial regulation of the journey's purpose and the objectives of each person's role are important.
- Absolute high transparency and honesty and consistency of the communication during the journey are required. This also means that autonomous action in a fully transparent environment is necessary, especially in complex contexts.
- Creative but data-driven maps—even if they are incomplete—can be used as an important instrument to move forward. If there are no official maps in place, own maps showing progress, position, etc. have to be developed and maintained (tailored to the journey or its purpose and the connectivity of its internal and external resources).
- Accept that the purposes of the journey might change during a journey (see examples from Africa expeditions and from fashion), and the team should not shy away from this debate.

References

Livingston, D. (2017). In H. Pleticha (Ed.), *Reisen und Entdeckungen im südlichen Afrika – Von den Kalahari zu den Victoria-Fällen* (3rd ed.). Wiesbaden: Edition Erdmann.

Spiegel Online, 04. Oktober 2007, 05:50: Mit dem Rad durch Afrika – 15.000 Kilometer auf Achse. Retrieved from https://www.spiegel.de/lebenundlernen/uni/mit-dem-rad-durch-afrika-15-000-kilometer-auf-achse-a-508575.html

Süddeutsche Zeitung Magazin, 06. Februar 2020a/Heft 6/2020: "Reise ins Ungewisse". Retrieved from https://sz-magazin.sueddeutsche.de/heft/2020/6

Süddeutsche Zeitung Magazin, 21. Februar 2020b/Heft 08/2020. Retrieved from https://sz-magazin.sueddeutsche.de/mode/central-saint-martins-college-wandel-nachhaltigkeit-88384

SZ.de, 17. April 2017, 19:45 Uhr: Laura Dekker: Die jüngste Weltumseglerin "wollte nie berühmt werden". Retrieved from https://www.sueddeutsche.de/panorama/laura-dekker-die-juengste-weltumseglerin-wollte-nie-beruehmt-werden-1.3467055

Wikipedia. Retrieved from https://de.wikipedia.org/wiki/Datei:Africae_tabula_nova.jpg

Wikipedia. Retrieved from https://commons.wikimedia.org/wiki/File:Africamap1812.jpg

Wollmann, P., Kühn, F., & Kempf, M. (Eds.). (2020). *Three pillars of organization and leadership in disruptive times – Navigating your company successfully through the 21st century business world.* Cham: Springer Nature.

Further Reading

Bäuerlein, T., & Tubali, S. (2018). *Quer denken, besser denken.* Hamburg: Hoffmann und Campe Verlag.

Covey, S. R. (2013). *The 7 habits of highly effective people – Powerful lessons in personal change*. London: Simon & Schuster.
Dignen, B., & Wollmann, P. (Eds.). (2016). *Leading international projects – Diverse strategies for project success*. London: Kogan Page.
Göpel, M. (2016). *The great mindshift: How a new economic paradigm and sustainability transformations go hand in hand*. Berlin: Springer International.
Heifetz, R. A., & Linsky, M. (2002). *Leadership on the line – Staying alive through the dangers of leading*. Boston: Harvard Business Review Press.
Kahneman, D. (2011). *Thinking, fast and slow*. New York: Farrar, Straus and Giroux.
Kühn, F., Kempf, M., & Chamberlain, J. (2020). The concept of purpose, travelling, and connectivity. In P. Wollmann, F. Kühn, & M. Kempf (Eds.), *Three pillars of organization and leadership in disruptive times – navigating your company successfully through the twenty-first century business world*. Berlin: Springer.
Laloux, F. (2014). *Reinventing organizations*. Nelson Parker: Brussels.
Willke, H., & Wollmann, P. (2012). Multi-level interaction resilience and cross cultural learning. In F. Kühn & P. Wollmann (Eds.), *Interaktion als Organisationsstrategie*. Berlin: Integrated Consulting Group.

Peter Wollmann has been a responsible manager, initiator, mentor, and facilitator in large, predominantly global transformations and strategic developments for almost 40 years. His specialties are the implementations of the Three-Pillar Model in organizations and focused setting checks to identify strength, weaknesses, opportunities, and threats and facilitate optimization measures. Since 2017, Peter has been working independently in organizational projects and future initiatives. After graduating in mathematics and physics from the University of Bonn, he began his professional career at the Deutsche Herold, then insurance group of Deutsche Bank, took on strategic leadership, and most recently was the program director for global transformations in the Zurich Insurance Company (ZIC). In his professional network, he brought his experience and strategic thinking to the development of various leading companies. He is the author and publisher of a number of books and articles on strategy, leadership, and project and project portfolio management. He also founded a wine business: VinAuthority.

Reto Püringer has worked for more than 20 years in the banking and insurance industry. He has held various senior positions in global companies. His practical experience ranges from Strategy Development, Business Model Design, Product/Proposition Development/Management, Enterprise-Wide Portfolio Management, Program/Project Management, Operations/IT Management, Large-Scale Change Program Delivery to Financial/Actuarial Management over different geographies and time zones, hierarchies and units, and cultures and systems. Reto has managed multinational and multicultural change and transformation efforts across the globe and managed teams of various sizes both on site and remotely. Reto holds a degree in Economical Informatics and Marketing and completed an Executive MBA at the University of Zurich.

Nature Eats Culture for Lunch: About Consonances and Dissonances Shifting or Limiting Harmony

Frank Kühn, Jan Sølvberg, and Mersida Ndrevataj

Abstract

There are numerous resources emerging from our nature, culture, and structures that affect our working lives and organizational journeys. By connecting these resources on a personal, group, and organizational level, we can share and pursue a sustainable purpose and achieve a joint successful future. When these resources pull in opposite directions, it is difficult to create the collaboration needed to perform well and be satisfied with the situation we find ourselves in. Following this consideration, the article demonstrates the value of harmony in disruptive times in the sense of a good balance between the resources. The author team carefully researched their working experiences and, based on their findings, developed an effective model and practical methodology on how to apply it in social, business, and private contexts.

F. Kühn (✉)
Dortmund, Germany
e-mail: fk@kuehn-cp.com

J. Sølvberg
Stabekk, Norway
e-mail: jan@solvberg.com

M. Ndrevataj
Venice, Italy
e-mail: mersida_n@hotmail.it

P. Wollmann et al. (eds.), *Organization and Leadership in Disruptive Times*, Future of Business and Finance, https://doi.org/10.1007/978-3-030-63034-8_4

1 Introduction

1.1 It's about Communication and Collaboration

In the VUCA (volatile, uncertain, complex, ambiguous) world, travelling organizations need more than a well-defined strategy to run their entrepreneurial activities successfully, with creativity and full engagement: They need an organizational model based on good collaboration and communication.

We notice that collaboration and communication is suffering in our everyday interaction with the social and working environment. We believe this is happening because there is a bad balance of resources originating from the individual's, group's, and organization's natures, cultures, and structures. Therefore, to figure out this challenging situation, recognize our resources, and identify their consonances and dissonances, we would like to propose in this article a theoretical model that considers "harmony" as a key for collaborative and communicative communities.

Research shows the consequences of bad collaboration and communication in terms of disengagement and even illness.

Around the world only 15% of full-time employees are "highly involved in and enthusiastic about their work and workplace." It means that "85% are not engaged or are actively disengaged in their job" (Gallup 2017).

Work-related mental illness can be significantly correlated with several findings about collaboration and communication.

"Inadequate health and safety policies; poor communication and management practices; limited participation in decision-making or low control over one's area of work; low levels of support for employees; inflexible working hours; and unclear tasks or organizational objectives" (WHO 2019).

Organizations (as well as societies and private life) function through communication and collaboration, for example, how urgent challenges are perceived and approached, how (and whether) agile working practices are co-implemented, how decisions are made and shared, how structures prevent or support fresh thinking for better living and working, how people are involved, etc. In other words and related to the studies quoted above, communicative and collaborative functionalities render human health and pursuits a joint success.

Whether all of these fail or succeed, these can be explored and explained via a look at the dissonances or consonances between individuals, groups, and organizations; between their natural, cultural, and structural resources; and how well these are balanced. Both the resources and their balancing affect our working lives and our organization's life cycle.

We are very aware that the definitions and distinctions between nature, culture, and structure can be the subject of passionate discussions in science or in ideologies. For this reason, we have formulated them as working hypotheses from a perspective of sufficient usefulness to understand the value of well-connected resources that lead

	Nature	Culture	Structure
Person	Needs & assets of people	Individual attitudes, norms & behaviors	Personal aims, priorities, ways of working
Group	Place of safety, empathy and hope	Communication & interaction patterns	Arbitrary distribution of roles & appreciation
Organi-zation	Purpose driven constellation of people	Common values, policies, attitudes, behaviors	Defined aims, functions, processes, etc.

Fig. 1 Overview of natural, cultural, and structural resources of individuals, groups, and organizations (Illustrated by authors, used with permission. All rights reserved)

to productive harmony or even creative stretching, rather than resource-wasting dissonance and dysfunctionality.

The first thing we need to do, when we encounter situations that we struggle with, is to draw a picture of it. How do we do that? We propose you create a matrix with three main resources (nature, culture, and structure) and their three different dimensional levels (individuals, groups, and organization) (Fig. 1).

Most of us know the individual resources. At work, as well as in our spare time, we all have needs such as safety and freedom, and we have assets such as talents and energy. We can call such resources a part of our personal nature.

Equally, we have attitudes (on social and political issues, on the need for collaboration, etc.), norms (about reliability, punctuality, work quality, etc.), and behaviors (how we deal with conflicts, support colleagues, address our own needs, etc.) which stem from our culture and are deeply imprinted by our personal impressions, experiences, and learnings.

Additional resources include individual goals and priorities (which can concern myself, family, workplace, society) and ways of working (alone or in groups), well-predetermined or artistic, sequential or cyclical, etc. They make up the structure or operating mode that we have individually developed for managing our private, social, and working lives.

Regarding groups and organization, we can also differentiate between nature, culture, and structure, as shown in Fig. 1. The natures of group and organization are indicated by their primary purposes, being a good place for people or a well-defined constellation of experts. Their cultures and structures are shaped, created, or even decided by the people who have lived or worked in them.

When we, as individuals, operate in a group and/or organization, the resources of our natural, cultural, and structural origin will be tested against the resources of the group or organization (themselves formed, represented, and even defended by other individuals).

Our belief is that when there is a large proportion of dissonance in the harmony of the resources, then the organization's effectiveness suffers. Dissonances—or a lack of harmony—between them prevent individuals, groups, and organizations from joint growth and true success. In other words, if the resources are in consonance or harmony, well connected, and in good balance, they can be a much more effective support to run the organization's purpose successfully.

As a result of what we have stated above, we assume harmony to be the key to new strategic and effective ways for good communication and collaboration, and we will propose some inquiry methodologies of the concept.

However, harmony must not be misunderstood as a comfort zone of the organization; it has a fragile state which requires continuous inquiry. We consider harmony to be a systemic resource of trust and open discussion on how to pursue our sustainable purpose, master our joint endeavor, and connect and bundle all our relevant resources for a travelling organization.

1.2 The Three-Pillar Model Application

The considerations in this article are closely interlinked with the concepts presented in the Three-Pillar Model (Wollmann et al. 2020), which are:

Sustainable purpose: The sustainability of an entrepreneurial strategy is closely linked to the well-being of its people; the economic model must have a sustainable social and environmental impact; the more we bring them in harmony with each other, the more we will realize inspirational collaboration, shared productivity, and joint success.

Travelling organization: In a VUCA world, our communication and collaboration models are also constantly changing and evolving. One of the main causes is certainly the acceleration of the digitalization process, the adoption of smart (co-) working practices and remote communication. Global crises even cause massive turns and leaps on this journey, which extremely challenge the cooperation and communication in the "travel group," its organizational framework, and the readiness of each individual.

Connected resources: All these need close connectivity far beyond classical command and control lines and silos which are not able to cope with the VUCA challenges quickly and efficiently. Communication and collaboration require the enhancement of individual, group, and organizational resources and their multidirectional interaction.

We consider that discussing collaboration and communication becomes important because if they are suffering this leads to a waste of both organizational and human resources. If we focus on the entrepreneurial ambitions and the individuals' needs, we should not be surprised if they are not all that different. Finding a model that holds them together can motivate people to a better engagement and motivation.

2 Painting a Picture

2.1 Putting Things into Perspective

We try to explain our reality with theoretical models, especially when faced with challenging or difficult situations. No theoretical model can completely capture the whole reality but will offer you aid in creating your own understanding of complex situations. Our model outlines three dimensions (nature, culture, and structure) we encounter when we find ourselves in situations that we struggle with. This picture might help you put things into perspective when dealing with such situations and provide a framework in which you might discuss with colleagues, business partners, and other counterparts and eventually find good solutions interlinking the ideas of sustainable purpose, travelling organization, and connecting resources (such as the ones described in this article). Thus, this model is not only useful for organizations but also useful for our personal work life and everyday challenges and interactions. It helps you to explore, explain, and express what it is about and how to deal with it.

2.2 Communication and Collaboration in Times of Pandemics

We started to write our article before the Covid-19 pandemic. Now our picture is being tested against the reality of this crisis. The working conditions created as a result of this pandemic have had an impact on the way we collaborate and communicate; how we deal with smart working and use technology; how collaborative structures emerge from a true problem; and how people are able to form virtual or distant groups, assume roles, and responsibilities, organize digital platforms—because it makes sense and meets the concerns of our global community.

"Normal" structures are lost for a period, mainly our way of working as people, groups, and organizations. Our individual reaction to the crisis develops our natural assets and fears as well as our culturally shaped behaviors. We seek safety in groups, but we probably do not find it in the usual constellations; instead, we connect emotionally by singing and applauding helpers from our balconies and open windows.

And the organizations emerge from the situation (implying the joint sustainable purpose) as helpful initiatives with dedicated people who contribute yoga videos, street fitness programs, or psychological advice. And what about the connectivity between human and organizational needs? We may be struggling with digital media and chaotic reactions, but we understand that we must solve them, get expert support, and develop new skills—because we see the need and meet concerns of our global community.

Now many of us have more time—what should we do with it? Reflect, write, post, observe our own feelings and reactions, and develop mindfulness? We must decide about our personal time structure and must take responsibility for ourselves and others, always questioning the harmony of our actions. New structures are emerging from the situation without any objectives or top-down commands because we see the need. At the same time, we see how others are overbusy to avoid any time for reflection, fearing panic and sticking to their "normalcy." This difference also applies to groups and organizations that use the situation for deep learning—because they are not willing or able to consider that something is happening. In this case we have an increasing stretch or even dissonance between them and the people who are experiencing a new quality of togetherness and sensitivity for good communication and now expect appropriate harmony in their future group and organization.

2.3 Harmony with Coping Mechanisms

When evaluating current experiences, we can identify different coping mechanisms on an individual level, which arise from our nature and are further strengthened in our cultural development. Such mechanisms are also relevant for groups and organizations. The difference between such mechanisms can be helpful or stressful, depending on how we manage them and how we look together at the sustainable purpose, organizational journey, and connectivity of our resources.

Perhaps you have experienced the "Five Levels of Focus" (Rock 2007) that we reinterpreted as five levels of coping with the pandemic?

- Visioning: Creating a positive post-pandemic big picture of future development
- Planning: Describing the challenge, prioritizing tasks, and starting projects
- Operating: Working away because someone must do it
- Problematizing: Searching for the causal problem which is difficult to solve per se
- Dramatizing: Making it more exciting than it is and, at best, triggering a clarification process

On the one hand, such coping modes can be valuable resources that complement each other—if we succeed in harmonizing them, following a shared purpose. On the other hand, they can trigger natural, cultural, and structural dissonances at all levels, in terms of individuals' loss of inner harmony, dysfunctional group dynamics, and losing connectivity and common energy.

But as we said above, we highlight the fact that no theoretical model can completely capture the whole of reality, but it will help you create your own understanding of complex situations.

2.4 Framing the Situation into the Matrix

So far, we have given an overview of the different impacts of the Covid-19 pandemic on the natural, cultural, and structural resources of individuals, groups, and organizations by using our harmony matrix.

In Fig. 2, we have applied our matrix to the pandemic. How are the resources developing in this situation—such as experiences, capabilities, and expectations—fit together? Now, in the transition phase, in the future? What opportunities and risks do

	Nature	Culture	Structure
Person	Personal resilience Empathy for people needing help Will to learn and grow even in crisis-ridden times	Experimenting with new coping behaviors Overcoming resistance to change, e.g., using digital tools Experiencing transparency & good communication	New working and time structures (working from home, online meetings) Balancing private and working structures Learning practices of others who take leadership in the crisis
Group	Stronger feeling of togetherness in the crisis Urgent challenge as binding force New understanding as part of global community	Taking an active part and responsibility in groups Supporting others to overcome barriers esp. in digital practices Sharing rituals and coping mechanisms	Creating online platforms Emerging structures based on people's energies, ideas etc. Evolving tasks and roles in coping with the common challenge
Organization	System trying to maintain itself, even relapsing into previous patterns Questioning own purpose and impact under challenging conditions Re-calibrating the understanding of "organization" and its purpose	Acceptance, avoidance or denial of seeing and dealing with crises Acceptance of purpose-driven, transparent leadership, also taken by experts Overcoming silo-thinking in urgent situations	New structures and ways of working Key players taking on their obvious roles in the crisis Rapidly developed temporary structures for delivering support material

Fig. 2 Matrix application to the pandemic situation

we see in relation to the three pillars, i.e., re-understanding, rebalancing, and recalibrating the purpose of individuals, groups, and organization? How can we strengthen the willingness and capabilities for joint travelling, and finally how can we connect all the resources that evolved in the situation? How can the transition to the "new normal" be co-created? How should we discuss in the organization and the ecosystems what the shared understanding of the "new normal" will be?

3 The Perfect Situation

3.1 A Personal Point of View

The situation is perfect for good communication and collaboration if I'm in harmony with myself, my natural needs and assets (using my talent and energy without fear, good space, valuable response, seeking happiness), my culture (what I have learned, what has imprinted itself on me), and my structure (how I approach things systematically)—and if this all fits together and is in good balance (Fig. 3). In addition, I'm in

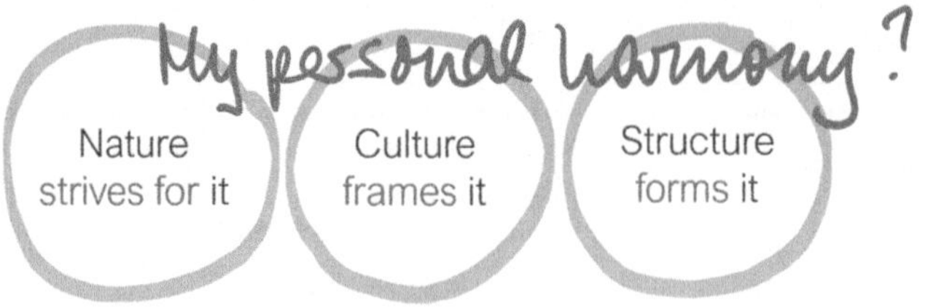

Fig. 3 Are my inner needs and assets in harmony with cultural and structural conditions and influences? (Illustrated by authors, used with permission. All rights reserved)

harmony with everything around me. Thus, I'm better equipped to cope with dissonances, i.e., I'm resilient and manage myself well and ready to contribute to a group's and organization's challenging journey through the VUCA world.

3.2 Understanding of Harmony

Harmony is here considered as a situation when natural, cultural, and structural resources are connected and in balance in their multiple interactions. These resources, originating from our nature, culture, and structure, affect our work lives as well as the organization's life cycle. When these three elements pull in opposite directions, it is difficult to create the collaboration needed to perform well and be satisfied with the situation in which we find ourselves. If they pull in the same direction, they create the perfect condition for successful performance; a fundamental part of this direction is created by a shared and sustainable purpose.

We can find the relevance and impact of harmony in our daily work, in projects, and processes but also in the interactions between these different levels. Meetings might be well prepared, projects well planned, and processes well organized in technical terms—but without harmony they will not deliver the best possible results because a lot of energy may be getting lost in emotional conflicts and tactical maneuvers. The more critical the situation, the more travelling organizations need to trust in their motivated travel group rather than in formal organigram with increasingly short half-life periods.

Thus, harmony operates in two dimensional directions, vertical and horizontal, between nature, culture, and structures as well as between individuals, teams, and organizations (Fig. 4). In most cases we need to look at both directions because the inner harmony of each dimensional level may be influenced by what is happening on the other dimensional level.

A good balance of our resources can be crucial in different aspects of our individual, group, and organization lives. How do individuals balance their natural gifts, cultural learnings, and structural settings? The same is valid for groups and organizations, which is described as the "harmony matrix" in Fig. 4. What is the nature of a group—expected by the humans joining it—and how does this agree with the group's real communication and interaction patterns, with the distribution of

	Nature	Culture	Structure
Person	Needs & assets of people	Individual attitudes, norms & behaviors	Personal aims, priorities, ways of working
Group	Place of safety, empathy and hope	Communication & interaction patterns	Arbitrary distribution of roles & appreciation
Organi-zation	Purpose driven constellation of people	Common values, policies, attitudes, behaviors	Defined aims, functions, processes, etc.

Fig. 4 Harmony matrix: harmony is based upon connectivity in two directions, vertical and horizontal, between nature, culture, and structures as well as between individuals, groups, and organization as a whole (Illustrated by authors, used with permission. All rights reserved)

roles and mutual appreciation in the group and with the culture and structure that has developed in the group?

Besides this horizontal balancing, the vertical balance is also crucial. How do the nature of the individual, group, and organization fit together? How do their cultures agree? How do their structures synchronize, e.g., how does my individual way of working fit with the organization's processes?

In the following case, we focus on "vertical" dissonance in culture. It's about teamwork and the leader of a hierarchical organization.

The development team was asked to deliver a project in a very short time. To date the team has created a culture of good communication and self-organization in order to manage their tasks and priorities—which was in perfect accordance with the attitudes and behaviors of the team members. In this case, they feel lost and unsafe as they don't understand their supervisor's request and fear the discussion (the supervisor is not open to communication), and they can't organize themselves (the supervisor asked them to follow a specific procedure). Thus, they cannot perform well, and they are dissatisfied with the situation. So, there is a harmony consonance between the team members and group and a harmony dissonance between the supervisor and group.

The next case focuses on "horizontal" dissonance: A person would like to get involved in a new project with a new team.

Alice is a young architect with a lot of creativity (nature) and has experienced open communication and participation in exciting tasks (culture). A year ago, she started working in a landscape architecture studio with a young team. Working in this studio is her dream job, but recently she has found it very exhausting because she got involved in a lot of projects without being able to calculate the workload and

	Nature	Culture	Structure
Person	Needs & assets of people	Individual attitudes, norms & behaviors	Personal aims, priorities, ways of working
Group	Place of safety, empathy and hope	Communication & interaction patterns	Arbitrary distribution of roles & appreciation
Organi-zation	Purpose driven constellation of people	Common values, policies, attitudes, behaviors	Defined aims, functions, processes, etc.

Fig. 5 In our daily life, the situation might be multidimensional. In this case we notice two diagonal dissonances: one between new standardized processes in the organization and the interaction culture of the group and the other between the personal way of working and the organization's purpose (Illustrated by authors, used with permission.)

coordinate it (structure). So, there is a typical dissonance between structure and nature (coordination vs. creativity) as well as between structure and culture (coordination vs. taking responsibility).

It can be more complex still; there might be multidimensional interactions of the different resources in different dimensional levels, as explained in the following case (Fig. 5).

The next case shows multidimensional dissonances about saving money, implementing new technologies, and decreasing performance.

This case is about a public company and its purpose to support other organizations and the public via highly relevant real-time information. So far, the process has been to receive specific requests by phone and give rapid replies while still on the call.

Their interaction has now been transferred to other media such as email and web solutions. The new operating mode affects two levels: the organization (standardized processes) and the group (culture of direct communication and interaction).

From the staff's view, the reasons for the change are not well founded. A practical challenge of their work is that most enquiries are very specific and have a limited time where they are valid; the incidents do not repeat themselves. This means that written info will be of interest to only a few and only at that particular time.

Many of them see personal communication as a crucial advantage of their work because they understand this direct way of communication to their clients as being closely connected to the company's purpose. Now they are no longer sure about the harmony between personal structure and organizational nature.

3.3 Degrees of Harmony

Harmony is not an end but helps humans, teams, and organizations to connect their resources and master the joint endeavor. This means questioning and discussing harmony in all directions, as shown above. It may also be reasonable to create a "stretch" for learning and development purposes (Fig. 6).

We know the procedure from creative workshops where we form three or four sub-teams that are asked to develop their various ideas in separate rooms and then compare the outcomes in the plenary session.

This kind of workshop is an example of harmony in content and process terms. In the first step, each group is on a creative journey of their own; this results in a variety of outcomes from the groups, but all of them are connectable around a minimum commitment of the workshop scope and process (middle part in Fig. 6, carefully balanced against the right part). A key in the harmony process is then to collect and blend the results—the harmony in this process enables and encourages the participants to discuss even dissonant outcomes in a productive way, based on the will to create a joint success (left part in Fig. 6).

Behind these experiences as explained in a qualitative way, there might be a desire for a quantification to measure the harmony status, identify the need for action, and follow up the development.

The questions are: (1) "How much" harmony is needed/useful in the situation? (2) How well are the resources connected, i.e., how much harmony is there between the items? (3) What reasons do you assume and what interventions seem adequate?

To define the levels of our personal, group, and organizational harmony, we can use a paired comparison as demonstrated in Fig. 7. This detailed focus on our

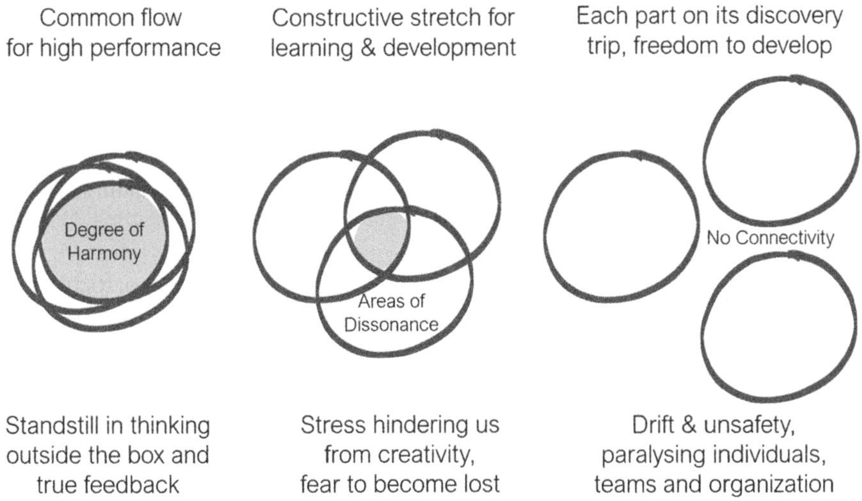

Fig. 6 What degree of harmony is helpful? Where do we have to stretch it for learning and development? (Illustrated by authors, used with permission. All rights reserved)

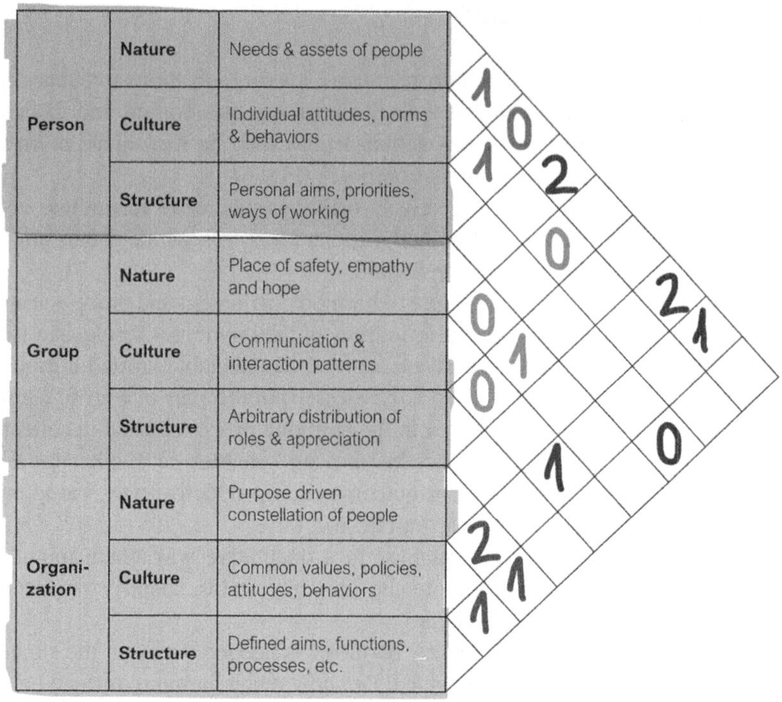

Fig. 7 Paired comparison to determine the degree of harmony (0: dissonance; 1: potential; 2: consonance) with some assessments as examples (Illustrated by authors, used with permission. All rights reserved)

multidimensional resources' interaction can facilitate a walk-through in a challenging context; it helps us to avoid mistakes and gives hints where further attention, actions, and interventions would be helpful. For further understanding, we have added an application case at the end of the article.

It is not just a math exercise. From our discussion, especially about quantification and paired comparison, we know the risk of a significant misunderstanding. Therefore, we want to share our thinking.

- Despite the appearance, we do not consider the harmony loop or in particular the "degree of harmony" as a measurable specialist knowledge. It is more of a creative tool that inspires dialogue but never provides an answer by simply summarizing points.
- If we take this seriously, the analysis requires a participatory approach in a workshop setting. We cannot discuss harmony without the people who are the key to development—it is about connectivity! If possible, the workshop should be conducted in a location and environment that encourages openness to discuss harmony or dissonance between resources.

- In efficiency-oriented, disruptive, or crisis-ridden times, people may think that discussing and building harmony has a lower priority—but this is not the case. It is the key to future fitness and investment in human resources, improving the capacity to adapt and respond to the VUCA world.
- This is not done in only one workshop. Knowing that this requires an investment of time and economic resources, a sustainable process should be agreed: how often do we think it is necessary to discuss harmony? Should we commit to a certain frequency or schedule? How can we give space and time to situational or urgent needs?

3.4 Harmony Loop

We already mentioned the need for harmony as a precondition of the travelling organization and connecting all our valuable resources. We would like to introduce here the "harmony loop" as a diagnosis and creativity tool for the Three-Pillar Model, which is able to challenge and discuss not only harmony at work but also harmony in the discussion of how harmony is experienced at work.

As Margaret Heffernan (2019) says: "We are brave enough to invent things we've never seen before; we can make any future we choose." But we must discuss it. The more we feel and think in our individual silos, rely on technological approaches, and understand the world mechanically (which may make life more comfortable), the fewer skills we have to face the unexpected, which includes the perceptions, opinions, and feelings of others.

So, we come to the harmony loop approach (Fig. 8). It starts at the bottom level, looking after our personal, inner harmony. If we are ourselves in optimal balance, this is a good precondition to approach the next level and care for harmony in our

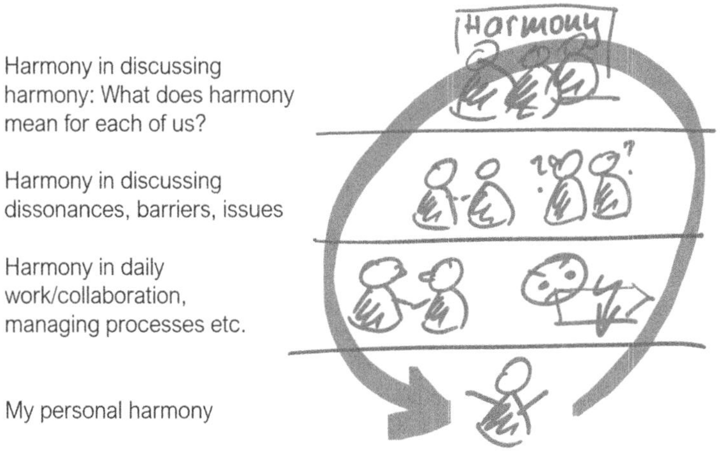

Fig. 8 Harmony loop (Illustrated by authors, used with permission. All rights reserved)

daily work, in our collaboration with our colleagues, and in our teams, in managing processes etc. When facing dissonances and conflicts, we take the next level (meta-harmony level) to discuss the issue. This will work if we are able to lead this discussion in harmony (which does not mean denying a conflict but discussing, handling, and solving it properly). If not, we can climb to the meta-meta-harmony level and discuss our understanding of harmony and its relevance for our travelling organization, for connecting our valuable resources, and for following our sustainable, shared purpose. This needs openness and passion for the discussion, exchanging our beliefs and views, accepting different beliefs and views, and being able to discuss them with respect.

How do we apply the harmony loop? This depends on the situation, its urgency, the people, teams, and organization involved. Which risks and barriers could endanger collective performance and success? What degree of harmony is needed at what level? Where should we approach the issue: with an exchange on personal feelings, with examining the harmonic dissonances and challenges that may pop up with the task, or with starting the work immediately?

The harmony loop gives precise hints where to pay attention, where to be mindful, where to redesign social processes, and where to clarify dissonances and conflicts. You can use it for your own reflection, but it is even more beneficial to apply it in your team. Thus, everyone formulates where they see a need for discussion and clarification on their joint journey; this will lead to a very intense exchange, learning, and development experience.

4 Application of the Harmony Model to a Case

In the following case, the methods presented in this article are applied step by step. Firstly, we use the harmony matrix to start identifying the natural-cultural-structural resources at stake. Secondly, we assess harmony recourses by paired comparison and identify the degrees of consonances or dissonances. Thirdly, we apply the harmony loop to reflect on the levels of discussion and indicate the level at which this should be further questioned and investigated.

4.1 Using the Harmony Matrix for Description

The case is about the change situation in a multinational engineering company that has built its understanding of itself on the people in its organizations. Their new strategy aims to better connect and integrate their knowledge, processes, and resources across countries and functions. In this way, they want to appreciate and retain employees who have proved to be competent and highly motivated. It has also been agreed that the future structure should neither be too complicated nor an obstacle to the desired culture of collaboration.

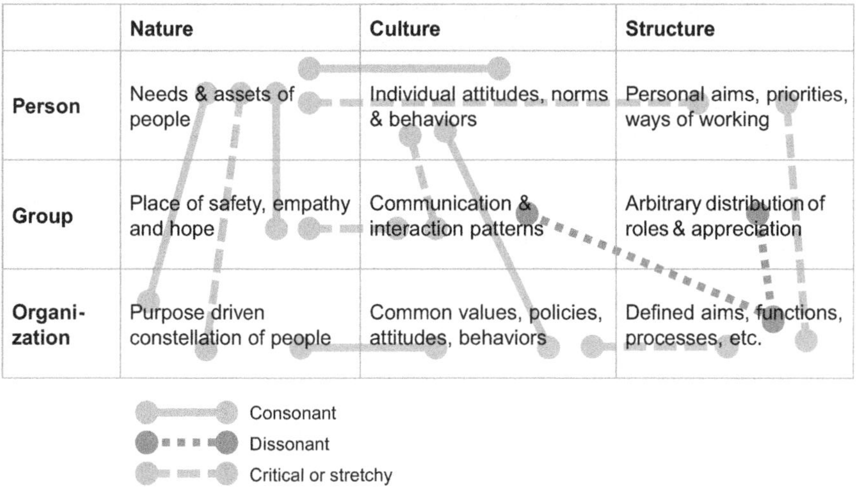

Fig. 9 Exploring perceptions and feelings of harmony and dissonances: the nature of the persons seems to be in harmony with the culture of the persons and the nature of the group and organization. But the culture of the group seems to be in dissonance with the organizational structure (Illustrated by authors, used with permission. All rights reserved)

But some uncertainty has arisen, especially in the subsidiaries. The people there liked the safety in their groups, but now they are wondering about the future of their local team within the overall organizational structure—what would this look like?

In this context, some differences between the local teams and the company have become apparent: the working methods and interaction patterns in the local teams are not only more informal and different to those in the current organization but also determined by some strong "influencers," which has led to some conflicts within the teams. It has therefore been assumed that many team members would be more likely to accept the policies and processes of the future organization if they helped to resolve such difficulties in their group dynamics.

After such initial impressions, the "harmony matrix" (Fig. 9) was used to identify the resources and the consonances (green lines) or dissonances between them (red lines) but also the critical connections (yellow lines), which are to be further analyzed as hindering or helpful stretches in the change situation. This initial view is later subjected to deeper analysis via the "pair comparison" and the "harmony loop."

Furthermore, we see dissonances between the culture and structure of the group and the organizational structure. The nature and culture of the individuals are perceived as being in good harmony. However, some further stretches around the organizational processes and their connections to the individual ways of working and to the organizational culture are needed. There also seems to be a critical situation between the culture of the people and the group culture, which needs to be analyzed in terms of stretch or stress and how to balance it.

4.2 The Degrees of Harmony to Assess the Situation

The deeper dive via the harmony assessment confirms the first impression. The dissonances within the groups have become even clearer (Figs. 10 and 11). On the one hand, the groups provide safety, which is highly appreciated. On the other hand, some individuals influence the collective culture negatively. Therefore, some colleagues seem to feel an emotionally higher affinity with the organization as a whole than with their own group.

The group culture gets the worst score (4 points) and, in comparison, the organization's culture the best one (13 points). This "numerical method" (at first sight) thus led to a comprehensive qualitative discussion—which was the most important effect and intention of the approach.

Following on from this, the challenge was to involve the people in the organization development; to appreciate their belief in the organizational culture as well as their individual ways of working, giving them safety and appropriate roles in the future organization; and to be a role model for good collaboration.

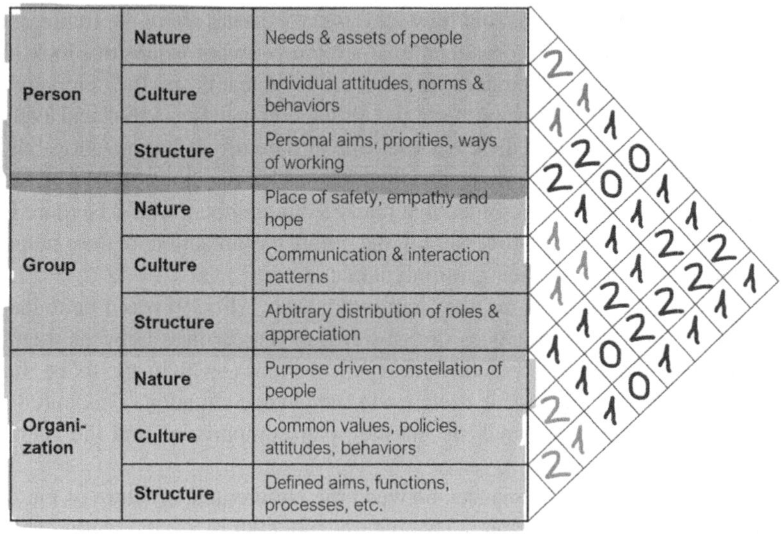

Fig. 10 Paired comparison to determine the degree of harmony between the nine resources (0: dissonance; 1: potential; 2: consonance). Each item can score 16 points max; total max is 72 points. In this case, the overall sum is 42 points, i.e., 42/72 = 58% harmony index (Illustrated by authors, used with permission. All rights reserved)

Person	**Nature**	Needs & assets of people	9	**30**
	Culture	Individual attitudes, norms & behaviors	11	
	Structure	Personal aims, priorities, ways of working	10	
Group	**Nature**	Place of safety, empathy and hope	12	**25**
	Culture	Communication & interaction patterns	4	
	Structure	Arbitrary distribution of roles & appreciation	9	
Organization	**Nature**	Purpose driven constellation of people	11	**32**
	Culture	Common values, policies, attitudes, behaviors	13	
	Structure	Defined aims, functions, processes, etc.	8	

Fig. 11 Summing up the points per dimension and resource (Illustrated by authors, used with permission. All rights reserved)

4.3 Discussion along the Harmony Loop

The individuals in the local groups did not seem to be in complete harmony with themselves, apparently because of a difficult group dynamic influenced by individual colleagues. This affected the harmony in the daily work; at the same time, there were expectations that the future organization of the company would offer better working conditions overall (although there was a certain degree of uncertainty about the structure). The harmony in the discussion of dissonances seemed to be suboptimal in the groups; otherwise disharmonies would have been addressed.

It is precisely this level of discussion that will now be the deciding factor for the further path of the change project to keep people on board and help shape the future culture and structure. The exchange about their expectations of harmony will be helpful to go this way together.

5 Conclusion and Take-aways

Harmony is the core of collaboration and communication, but its benefit must be reflected from time to time. Together with your teams and with your colleagues, you can build a professional understanding of harmony and how to understand it. It will lead to a more mindful thinking, communicating, and acting.

As authors of this article, we experienced the harmony approach on the writing process from the beginning
• Sharing our thoughts • Understanding our motivations • Doing something we like • Practicing nonjudgmental communication • Feeling our silent agreement • Collaborating from different places • Experiencing exciting moments
Mersida, Jan, Frank

In the following, you will find some takeaways on how to use the harmony approach in your organizational and team practice.

- A quick self-check in your teams may show the dissonances, harmony gaps, and consequences: Does your team situation or your organization influence your well-being, motivation, and performance? How do your personal beliefs and ways of working fit those of your team and the organization? What are the reasons and the effects?
- You may try a personal check: What in your own nature, culture, or structure prevents you from excellent performance?
- The harmony matrix exploration, the harmony degree investigation, and the harmony loop inspection can be applied to develop a new level of collaborative power. This needs an open discussion about harmony: What degree of harmony is optimum? How can you ensure this at all levels (personal, in your daily work, in reflecting on it at a meta-level, in discussing harmony as a core asset in your organization)?
- The practical application can be supported via a regular or situational feedback process including the harmony approach. This can easily be started as good practice in meetings or workshops, using the harmony or dissonance question in check-in/check-out situations.
- A wider application addresses the effectiveness of corporate activities, i.e., integrating the approach into setting checks of projects, processes, and units.
- You can also use the approach for creating a cultural shift, i.e., setting up a project to identify dissonances and to work on harmony as a cultural key.
- Finally, the leadership team should be involved actively because the Three-Pillar Model and the harmony approach will change your company's culture in a very productive way.

We see that there is a lot of mindful works needed to really connect natural, cultural, and structural resources and create joint success. The harmony approach application shows how difficult situations can be mastered and leads to the strengthening of internal communication and collaboration.

References

Gallup. (2017). *State of the global workplace*. Retrieved from https://www.gallup.com/workplace/257552/state-global-workplace-2017.aspx

Heffernan, M. (2019). *The human skills we need in an unpredictable world*. https://www.ted.com/talks/margaret_heffernan_the_human_skills_we_need_in_an_unpredictable_world?utm_campaign=social&utm_medium=referral&utm_source=linkedin.com&utm_content=talk&utm_term=business#t-935132

Rock, D. (2007). *Quiet leadership*. New York: HarperCollins.

Wollmann, P., Kühn, F., & Kempf, M. (Eds.). (2020). *Three pillars of organization and leadership in disruptive times – Navigating your company successfully through the 21st century business world*. Cham: Springer Nature.

World Health Organization (WHO). (2019). *Mental health in the workplace*. Information sheet; May 2019. Retrieved from https://www.who.int/mental_health/in_the_workplace/en/

Frank Kühn has been supporting companies and institutions for many years in the areas of organization and leadership and change and project management. He brings his experience to developments such as the Three-Pillar Model and systemic setting checks. Frank has a doctorate in work science. After leading positions in research and industry, he was a partner at HLP in Frankfurt and in the ICG Integrated Consulting Group in Berlin and Graz. Today, he is an independent consultant and business partner of ICG and associated with other project partners and think tanks. He has published numerous articles in management journals and books.

Jan Sølvberg spent the first 15 years of his work life in the ICT industry as a trainer, leader, project manager, and consultant and the next 15 years as an organizational development consultant specializing on improvement and change processes, leadership development, and coaching. Today, Jan is a senior consultant and partner with Innotiimi-ICG (Integrated Consulting Group) and the president of the Norwegian Chapter of the International Coaching Federation (ICF). Inspired from emerging agile trends in software development that focus on closer customer involvement and shorter development cycles, he transfers those elements to organizational life and incorporates it into his professional work, feeling a close connectivity with his clients.

Mersida Ndrevataj is an architect and urban planner, currently attending a PhD in Urban Planning and Public Policy at the IUAV University of Venice. Her professional objective is to help better shape the built environment through a multidisciplinary research-based and human-centered design process. To this end, she is involved in several academic research projects and works in the field of environmental psychology.

Wicked Problems of the Travelling Organizations

Dieter Haselbach and Frank Kühn

Abstract

Wicked problems are undefinable and difficult to cope with. Yet they are real. A typical example is climate change but also the fast-growing organizations in uncertain technical and social environments. Therefore, wicked problems are not bad per se, but they are different: They need an attitude and a mode of thinking that is fundamentally different to that used in solving linear problems. They do not fit into well-known categories of known or unknown, simple or complex and predictable or unpredictable problems or risks. The challenge of wicked problems is faced by organizations and teams that go on their journey through unknown territory in the VUCA world; they become part of the journey. If we accept wicked problems and the approaches they require, we will also better understand the nature of corporate journeys that no longer stick to experiences and prognoses, strategies, plans and structures, even the sophisticated ones. But we must be able to agree on how to deal with unclear challenges, how to connect our ways of thinking and acting, how to co-create the future step by step. Our attitude, readiness and creativity to deal, and make friends, with wicked problems are key to our joint endeavour. Following this approach, the article proposes discursive loops around wicked problems, and indeed wicked solutions, as a fundamental part of how to follow the sustainable purpose, manage a travelling organization and connect all relevant resources to master the joint endeavour.

D. Haselbach
Berlin, Germany
e-mail: haselbach@kulturforschung.de

F. Kühn (✉)
Dortmund, Germany
e-mail: fk@kuehn-cp.com

P. Wollmann et al. (eds.), *Organization and Leadership in Disruptive Times*, Future of Business and Finance, https://doi.org/10.1007/978-3-030-63034-8_5

If I knew the world would end tomorrow, I would plant an apple tree today. (probably not by Martin Luther)

We use the term 'wicked problem', but we do not follow the double negative connotation associated with it. Rather, we want to emphasize that a new way of thinking and course of action are needed to tackle the journey into the future of the society and organizations. The path will no longer be found using only our previous experiences, linear thinking and a two- or three-dimensional categorization of problems and risks. Travelling organizations will always have to deal with unpredictable developments, events that cannot be understood and influences that cannot be anticipated, and we still must make decisions. We want to try to illustrate what this means.

The topic of this article refers to all aspects of the three-pillar model (Wollmann et al. 2020):
- The 'sustainable purpose' as the real 'core' element of any organization is to give guidance and inspiration, which is even more fundamental when we have to cope with wicked problems and find the right way to address them and make effective decisions.
- The 'travelling organization' is a synonym for the dynamics, uncertainty and volatility of any company or institution, which includes well-planned development, market-driven transformation or even crisis-ridden disruptions even if we don't know the result of our interventions.
- 'Connecting resources' means not only to develop human experiences and creativity, as well as the corporate strategies and processes, but also to connect them to generate powerful solutions. Wicked problems need this capability because coping with them need real communication, collaboration and commitment

1 Term

A wicked problem is already wicked if one attempts to define it. That is, it is incomplete, complex, blurred, inconsistent and volatile, without a 'determinable stopping point' (Tonkinwise 2015). Therefore it (whatever it is) is difficult to solve. 'Solutions to wicked problems are not right or wrong' (Conklin 2006), but they do something. Sometimes something is solved for the moment, sometimes parts of the problem are solved, sometimes new problems arise while others are solved, sometimes the problem absorbs the solution and makes it a new part of itself, and sometimes it seems to disappear when you approach it or make itself appear smaller than it is (Fig. 1).

The only thing that is certain is that something must happen. The solution is just as unclear as the problem. For some people there seems to be a clear solution to a clear problem. But this solution raises new problems that cannot be solved easily. That is why we also argue about it. Some examples are climate change, election results and, in a company, the discussion about the change of markets and customer needs and the disagreement about the necessity of strategy and organizational change. Added to this is the experience that change is never completed anyway and only generates new questions—which is also an expression of wicked problems. And yet, action must be taken.

The financial crisis of 2008 led to very different decisions in companies. Sometimes there was a linear approach (Fig. 1), while elsewhere real entrepreneurship.

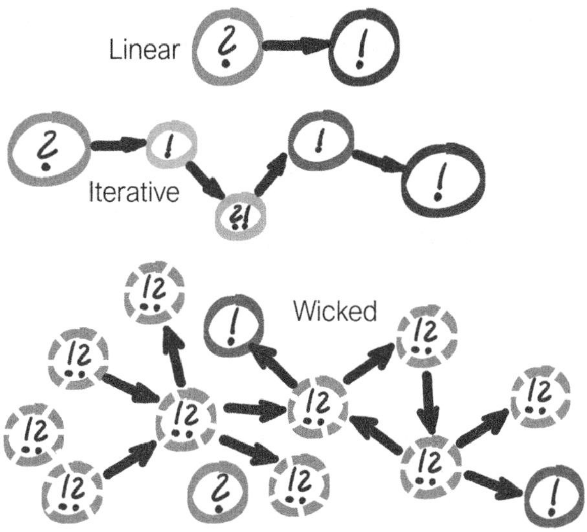

Fig. 1 For the clear problems, there are clear procedures for solving them; for some problems, solutions must be tried out step by step. For the wicked problems, there are, at most, apparent clarifications which, at the latest retrospectively, turn out to be ambiguities; apparent solutions contain new ambiguities and problems (Illustrated by Frank Kühn, used with permission. All rights reserved)

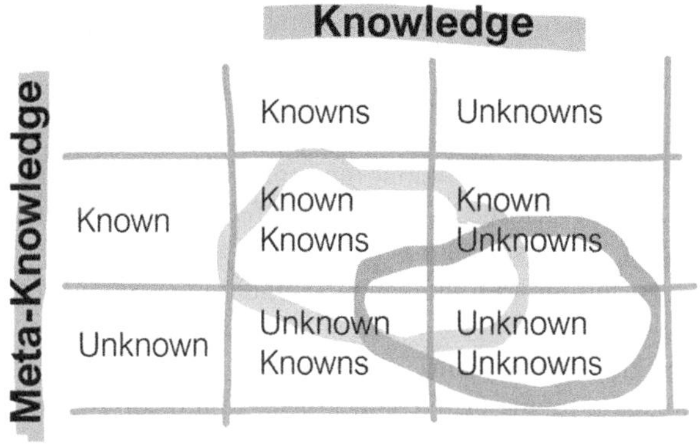

Fig. 2 An example of a categorization of problems and risks. Wicked problems elude such categories because they can change their classification unpredictably, when inspected closely, or when a solution is being tried (Illustrated by Frank Kühn, used with permission. All rights reserved)

Some investors immediately sold their companies to bolder ones; other companies reduced their workforce; those companies often managed by their owners, the bosses, still made a deal with their people: We will hang on, for the time being, with less work and less money. Some made something out of it with entrepreneurial confidence (in something that they could not really foresee), while others were no longer able to deliver after the reduction in staff when things suddenly started to improve again (which they could not have foreseen either) and had a new problem, especially since experienced staff had become scarce.

The simplification of a wicked problem to a linear solution thinking turned out to be a dead end. Every solution had its purpose and, at the same time, proved to be a new problem or, in other words, a real management task, leadership and decision-making task. Such challenges are part and parcel of any travelling organization.

Wicked problems make a difference to the so-called unknown unknowns (Fig. 2). Wicked problems do indeed occur, but they cannot be categorized; they may appear as if they can be (which we do not know), and this makes them particularly wicked. Known or unknown? Wicked problems are masters at fluctuating between categories—and thus equal companions of the travelling organization. The already not easy unknown unknowns (see below) have a property that distinguishes them from wicked problems: If we elevate them to known unknowns or knowns, they can be solved linearly—in the case where they were not hidden wicked problems. For insurance companies, for example, it was clear after the occurrence of asbestos claims that something similar could happen again, yet it was not clear when it would be. This is a typical case of known unknowns; when it occurs, it becomes a known known, which is solved linearly: problem, cause and then solution. In addition, the asbestos claims were used to learn how to deal with such problems.

When dealing with wicked problems is part of the travelling organization, the sustainable purpose takes on a whole new meaning and importance. By means of the purpose, the organization can decide what is at stake and in which direction action is taken. Is the purpose of state control to keep a government in power, to benefit its own people or to contribute to global well-being? Is the purpose of a company to generate profit for its shareholders, to contribute to society with its services or to give people work? Dealing with wicked problems, an unpredictable upheaval in society or ecosystems without any pattern of experience, will be different every time.

It is even better if people share the purpose of their organization's uncertain journey with real conviction. Only with the connectivity of all relevant resources can the journey into the unknown be tackled; problems must always be understood and reflected upon as solutions (and solutions as new problems). Now that resilience has long been identified as a necessary feature of the travelling organization (Kühn et al. 2013), a new standard is being set here.

According to Luhmann (1977), an organization consists of decisions. Decisions are making a choice between possibilities; otherwise they are not decisions. Not deciding when facing a problem is a decision too; this is also perceived very precisely by the people concerned. So how do we want to treat the problem? With 'merely' complex problems, we decide on a hypothesis for a solution and observe its effects; we can try. In the best case, we consider the side effects and long-term effects (Dörner 1997, 2015), which may, however, change quickly in disruptive times. Therefore, we already move on to experiments, rapid prototyping and minimum viable products in order to prepare ourselves in fast feedback and learning loops to test our hypotheses again and again.

Wicked problems are different; they are more challenging. 'Every solution to a wicked problem is a "one-shot operation", because there is no opportunity to learn by trial and error' (Rittel and Webber 1973). We cannot learn anything (or there is no use to try learning) yet still must do something. This means paying even more attention to effects and rebound effects.

Take the example of disposing of waste: If waste charges are high, garbage will be dumped in the forest. If the fees are reduced, more waste will be produced. Consumerism and waste are deeply rooted in us and in the social structures in which we move. They are both a concept and a problem for maintaining our prosperity. Markets and fiscal policy are designed to ensure that consumption is keen and that the economy grows; otherwise we will end up in a crisis. We should and must spend our money.

It is similar in organizations: When the controls fail, we tighten the reins, collect even more data, formulate even more sophisticated KPIs, keep our employees even more in check and alienate them even more from their valuable work. This is the only way that we have learned to go; this is our much-nurtured controlling illusion. We focus our energy on controlling rather than on supporting the staff on site, where the innovation in the market and the success with the customer is created. We pay more attention to balance sheets than to the performance motivation of the employees. The corporate journey connects with the financial market logic. Solutions become problems. How can this be overcome?

2 Wicked World

Globalization, digitalization, acceleration, information overload and fake news inevitably lead us into a wicked world: Everything is connected or not, true or false, reacts more or less sensitively to everything else, largely eludes our order of planning and control. How are we supposed to make good decisions (Fig. 3)? Many people follow their desire for simplification, which leads to inclusion and exclusion: nationalism of states, echo chambers of interest groups, division of organization into units and personal retreat into inner denunciation and depression. We can observe it in ourselves: Under stress, each of us becomes more binary, more violent; the shades of grey are lost.

Engaging in a common journey and the global community would require new trust in each other (Kühn and Wollmann 2018); at present, however, distrust is booming. How can we solve it? Somebody must start, somehow—a wicked problem.

If disruptions were predictable, they would be developments. We can manage developments, but disruptions happen and have repeatedly led to social upheaval: the steam engine on wheels, called the locomotive, just like the digital revolution and platform logic in modern business models. Technical innovations are always faster than the competent assessments of them. Innovations always have unexpected

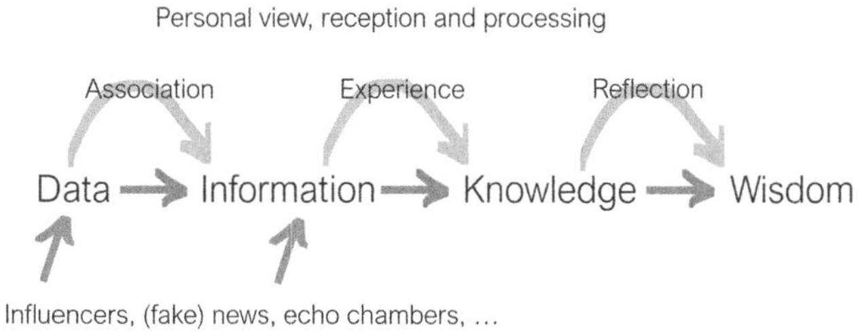

Fig. 3 How do we make wise decisions in societies and organizations? (Illustrated by Frank Kühn, used with permission. All rights reserved)

Fig. 4 Organization as a bundle of wicked problems (Illustrated by Frank Kühn, used with permission. All rights reserved)

consequences, and because they are also faster than cultural, organizational and political changes, we constantly produce dissonances and wicked problems.

Disruption results from an uncoupling of previously interdependent processes and a recomposition of business models. They are the most radical form of what Joseph Schumpeter (1926) called the 'new combinations'; here he had seen the source of all economic change. Habit, culture and morals no longer provide orientation; connectivity is lost for the moment and markets are uncoupled from ecosystems and one's own business. Leadership was called for when corporate structures could no longer provide a foothold. It is no coincidence that the call for meaning and purpose became louder and louder as the organization of companies reached its limits and orientation was sought. Agile organization is demanded when the speed of the old and familiar working methods does not suffice. At the same time, the definition of all these terms in companies is often unclear or arbitrary—this mirrors the overall situation.

With our travelling organization we must be able to master such disruptions. Or we can base the organization on development only, simply abandoning it in the event of disruptions and setting up a new one. Or we build hybrid organizations, as "ambidexterity" is booming. This terminology results from our biological evolution, which has provided us with exactly two hands, among other things. But the problem is much more diverse. How do you keep the balls in the air (Fig. 4)?

3 Desire to Act in the Midst of Desperation

Insecurity easily leads to despair. Where is the centre of despair? It is somewhere between what has been experienced so far and unclear perspectives, between problems and solutions or somewhere where the problem and the solution are unclear or where something is both at the same time. Since we do not know the problem and the solution, it remains unclear where the centre is. What remains is despair. We wander around in the wicked world between the problems and solutions, not even knowing what a solution and what a problem is.

While we can encounter simple problems with known procedure and solution models, complicated problems with shared expertise, such as complex problems with hypotheses and step-by-step verification, wicked problems remain chaotic (Fig. 5, cf. Snowdon and Boone 2007).

If chaos means not knowing, we are close to the essence of wicked problems. We would only have to admit to it; open ourselves to it, across the organization; and learn to communicate it. This would be a new management attitude and performance that stands for a traveling organization and real connectivity: openness to ask questions instead of feeling the pressure to provide answers; approaching the problems and do something about them, otherwise they will slip away.

Incidentally, asking questions is becoming increasingly important in view of the new dogmas and gurus, influencers and echo chambers. We need time to ask questions; we need to delve into topics. Anyone who asks is honest. Populists answer, not questions, but to discomfort. This makes for an ominous mixture: under-complex and destructive in the face of chaotic problems.

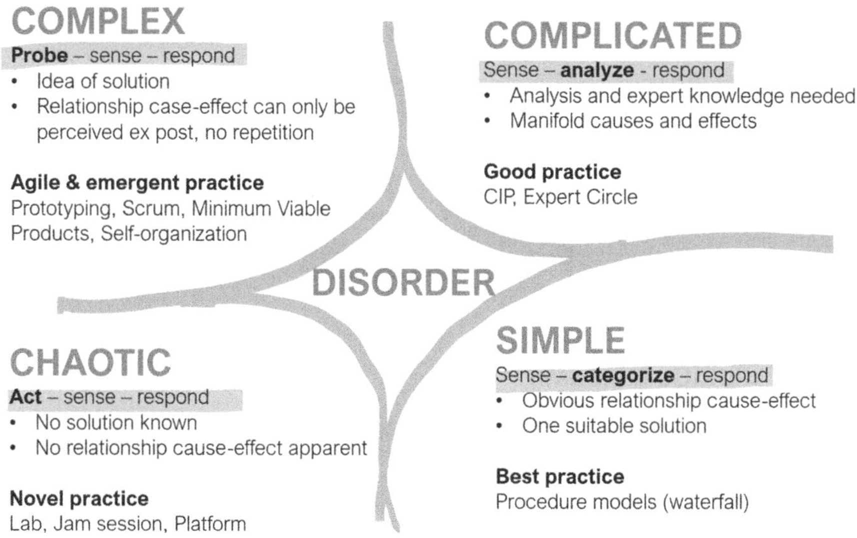

Fig. 5 Different situations and recommendations (Snowdon and Boone 2007) (Illustrated by Frank Kühn, used with permission. All rights reserved)

One possible path would be to first accept all of this, and to accept the confusion, even the despair. Accepting feelings and acknowledging them are important information: this is called mindfulness, and it is no coincidence that it is a current topic in the society and in organizations. In this context, mindfulness is also existentially important in business: only when we are aware of our confusion (when we admit that we do not know what we do not know, when we understand problems as solutions) can we avoid the mistake of hastily following our patterns of action and procedural models so often rehearsed for typical challenges.

Newer, agile ways of working must be critically assessed as well. Holacracy, iterative procedures, scrum, rapid prototyping, design thinking, etc. do inspire their communities. Often, however, the difference between dogma, method and organization becomes blurred. Many of the methodological ideas in these approaches are useful, but we must not follow them blindly.

Feeling and thinking for oneself are still the order of the day, even if it requires more attention and energy and our resources are getting scarcer and scarcer.

Thinking Games About the Organization (Haselbach and Kühn 2013)
Organization
1. We know that there are two sides of an organization, formal and informal.
2. Management invests in the formal: strategy, structure, control, etc.
3. What works: the informal.
4. What must an organization look like that takes this seriously?
Goals
1. We know that change projects can no longer be completed.
2. The management invests in goals and concepts to be achieved.
3. What works: going on the journey.
4. How must change be designed that takes this seriously?
Order
1. We know that only a minority of the employees are fully involved.
2. The management invests in their alignment.
3. What works: freedom.
4. What must leadership look like that takes this seriously?
Processes
1. We know that time and resources are limited.
2. Management invests in overhead structures.
3. What works: The company realizes itself in customer contact and on the shop floor.
4. How must processes be designed that take this seriously?

4 sPoRlOuBtLiEoMn

But back to the question of what is a problem and what is a solution? Or is it always both, a SpOrLoUbTlIeOmN?

Take, for example, the populist state leaders: They solve an imagined problem, which they put in words, with strategic ulterior motives, to appeal to the emotional state of many people (e.g. mistrust in the strategic ability and loyalty of governments, fear of foreign control by other states (communities), lack of orientation in the supposed chaos of the world, decreasing attention span in the internet age, lack of personal perspectives, social unrest) and create new problems (e.g. political division among the population, xenophobia, short-sighted and unpredictable leadership). More appropriate, albeit more sophisticated, solutions, e.g. social security, would also have been conceivable, but perhaps the cultural preconditions or the necessary space for imagination or information (beyond one's own echo chamber) or the patience or confidence in a sufficiently rapid realisation were lacking—all these are wicked problems. Nationalism, mistrust and dictatorship instead of cosmopolitanism and trust are the simple answers to emotional sensitivities, playing into the hands of those who are pressing for power and exclusion and for whom becoming a global community is the worst solution. Mistrust, however, is expensive and has already pushed some states into bankruptcy. The same applies to excessive centralized corporate governance, which leads to a lot of energy being directed inwards rather than outwards towards the market and customers.

Incidentally, we also have echo chambers in our organizations. Every vertical and horizontal silo is an echo chamber, fired by water cooler gossip and rumours that are only too happy to confirm our suspicions and prejudices.

How can problems and their solutions and their problems be reached?

Every wicked problem goes back to the fact that there was a wicked solution for a problem before. From the solutions we can learn about the extent of the problem and our strategies for dealing with problems—without finding any sustainable recipes. Otherwise the problem would not be a wicked one.

Wicked solutions are not meaningless. Today's world is as we have made it. From a systemic perspective, a problem has a meaning. It has not fallen out of the sky. It was a solution to something which, because it carries a problem within it, at best creates a countermovement and regulation, just like the digital or agile hype, which still produces overshoots and overreactions that gradually level off into feasible developments. Technically, many things will be possible, but what will they imply socially and organizationally? The discussion of social scenarios has long since begun (e.g. Frick and Höchli 2014). These scenarios lie between personal dedication to digitalization (full comfort of life with payment by personal data) and total refusal (exclusion from the mainstream of society with preservation of personal data). We do not know which way leads to which problem. But any action is nevertheless already part of a still unknown solution, thus a problem.

One must have touched the subject to see what happens, to be able to formulate questions and make it debatable. For this we need new ways of thinking, not to replace the old ones, but to expand our repertoire. Putting our perceptions into our thinking drawers or maps is no longer enough; we have to open up our thinking to other maps; and in the best case, we manage to reflect on our use of maps and thought structures (Kühn et al. 2020).

5 Make Friends with the Wicked Problems

The past is there to learn for the future; this is attributed to Stevie Wonder. Doing so requires a concept of thinking that understands the typical solutions retrospectively in order to find positive conclusions for future action. So that thinking again enriches our development (and not only makes us sad) and does not take energy from us, but rather gives it to us. Thus, problems become an important resource that is repeatedly linked to solutions.

Linear relations of the problem and solution are boring and can be passed on to algorithms. Also boring are questions that we can certainly work on iteratively; the appropriate agile instructions for action are available to us. The real potential lies in the wicked problems or in the way we deal with them, how long we ask and when we start something. This further defines the travelling organization: It includes the mutual awareness and care between the wicked problems and wicked solutions (Fig. 6).

We have no choice but to make friends with the fact that the wicked problems exist, just as we have to make friends with the time that simply exists. This means—as a new 'line of thought', or operative mode—to initiate and maintain a discursive loop, where the company develops its wicked problems, because only in this way can a truly sustainable organization throw itself into the adventure of the future. This requires a purpose: to help align and realign our thoughts and gain a new quality of trust and connectivity of our mindsets, ideas, assessments and feelings. How can we understand a problem as an exciting opportunity for development? The problem has been a solution to a problem—for which one, and what sense did the solution make, and why did other solutions seem more difficult? What solution is now conceivable? What new and inconceivable problems do we create with it? How do we accompany

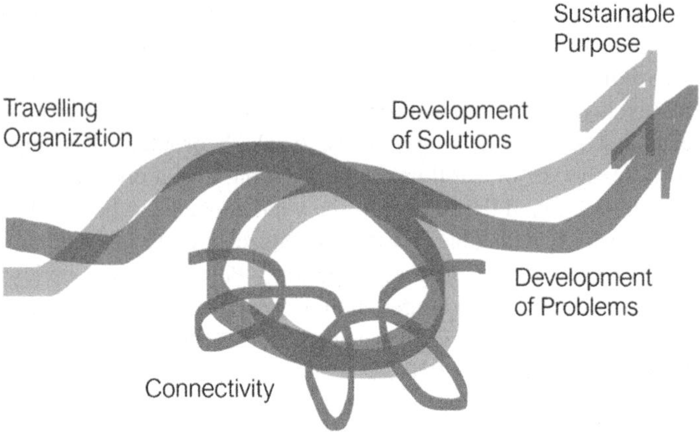

Fig. 6 Discursive loop in a travelling organization: the wicked problems and wicked solutions join in a joint journey (Illustrated by Frank Kühn, used with permission. All rights reserved)

the uncertain solution path, which we know is, at the same time, an unforeseeable problem path?

The travelling organization becomes a platform for a cooperation between the wicked problems and wicked solutions. When combined, both are resources which are effective. This makes an exciting task for management!

This discursive loop will therefore be a central skill.

6 New Travelling

We have argued that disruption is not predictable; otherwise it would be development. And that is why we do not have suitable answers immediately, because the world of our experience, our thinking, our language and our habits is based on the past.

This makes the journey doubly difficult for the organization. The travelling organization is not on a holiday trip; then we would not have to discuss it. Is it more of a caravan between endless sand, fertile oasis, fleeting mirage and predatory raid or a migration between two corporate cultures, where our data and experiences are of little help or simply meet with rejection?

One thing is clear. Everything that applies here and now will soon apply no longer, even if everything was better in the past (attention: personal echo chamber). The desertification and devastation of landscapes due to climate change will inevitably lead to a migration of people to the regions of the earth where the climate is more benign. We can build a wall as a wicked solution, and as a wicked problem, we may harvest a desperate rebellion of migrants. Or we can release scarce water to green deserted landscapes and reap a rebellion at home. Or we could do something about the glaciers melting; they do that because of global warming and air pollution. To do so, we could give up fast driving and New Year's Eve fireworks and reduce our meat consumption and online movies very easily. Then we would not have to build walls. But such a renunciation, practiced in masse, could destroy our growth-driven economy. No matter what we do, many citizens will rehearse the great uprising. Forbidding seems taboo. But calling for renunciation reaps a shitstorm. So, are we building walls after all? And can we even overlook the scenarios and developments?

Coming back to the organization, for which problems, for example, do models representing the developmental stages of human cooperation or organization (Glasl and Lievegoed 2011; Beck and Cowan 2005; Laloux 2014) offer a solution? For example, we may find that we are in a 'tribal' (based on the exercise of power and fear) or 'traditional' (based on formalized processes and roles) or 'modern' (focusing on competition and leadership) form of organization. What are such forms of organization solutions good for? For the unwillingness of employees to work (together) in a committed manner because they are X types according to McGregor (1960)? However, to date there has not been a study that proves the existence of X employees, but, instead, there are annual findings of 'inner resignation' due to poor leadership quality. Is this due to the lack of experience by the pioneers who want to build a new business and concentrate on the technical challenges or the lack of confidence in the middle management competencies (why modern organizations like to control them via the KPI recipe—in most cases without having read the side effects of the drug)? Or is it simply the overburdening of the middle management, which tries to keep the balls in the air (Fig. 4)? We also experience a lack of trust in the employees: they are often completely underrated—'that's not possible with them'. Yet employees have long known when a company is no longer functioning and wait in vain for constructive decisions from management. How difficult must it be to tackle wicked problems if we cannot think other than linearly?

So how do you create movement with all these people? It is by starting together with the employees—something that corresponds to the purpose and that seems plausible for tackling the wicked problems. And then, together, watch carefully how something thrives. That something will be relevant and good. Oddly enough, this is true for all levels of development of the organizations. Only in the so-called evolutionary developmental stage does it become almost part of the system; but this developmental stage is one that many leaders hardly trust their organizations, why the examples of application are scarce (e.g. Laloux 2014; Oestereich and Schröder 2017). This level requires mutual respect and more attention to people, including their own personal reflection on what they "really, really want" (Bergmann 2019; Breidenbach and Rollow 2019). What does this tell us? Are the development models a solution or a problem? Was it a problem that we have described here?

7 Lessons Learned: Provisional Thinking, Provisional Action

To deal with the wicked problems in a chaotic world, you need openness and composure. We need to understand that this world, its society and its organizations are made up of wicked problems. They belong to our travelling organization.

There are no clear solutions for wicked problems and no recipes for solutions. Approaches are made by questioning the problems: For what are the problem solutions and how did they come about? What can we learn from them? Any hostility towards the problems is taboo and would block our insight.

If we follow the definition that an organization consists of communication and decision-making, these two elements are the key to working on wicked problems and solutions. How do decisions about wicked problems work if solutions are not solutions, for example, when the concept of a solution is different depending on the nature of the problem? The solutions of linearly workable problems are as good as programmed. The solutions of wicked problems are a trigger of something difficult to grasp, requiring a high degree of attentiveness to see what it is and what happens.

A Test for Openness and Serenity

Can you agree to the following observations? Discuss them with your colleagues.

- We must pursue a sustainable purpose that makes a good contribution to the world and society. Only in this context can we ask ourselves the following questions. Otherwise, these questions would be grist for the mills of the populistic leaders of our time.

(continued)

• Everything is constantly moving and changing: Pausing is only possible through stopovers and snapshots. Organizational charts are also snapshots—tomorrow we will already have moved on in our thoughts. How long can and must we endure such dissonances?

• Mobile organizations 'resonate' which means interacting, sounding out and adjusting our timing and paces—always checking speed, rhythm and timing. What does time have to do with the wicked problems and our solutions?

• It is okay not to know everything: Do you want to continue to argue or accept and manage? Knowledge about the wicked problems only comes through doing. What goes, goes. Who remains is there. Now it is the right time. The wicked problems need stimulus so that we can recognize something from them. Every stimulus brings new impressions. Where can we try this out?

• Feeling and intuition are important for the wicked problems and wicked solutions—they are sometimes more valuable resources than rationality and cognition (otherwise the problems would not be 'wicked'). How do you build feelings—not just your own—into your business and organization?

• A culture of good leadership and cooperation creates an orientation on the journey in an unsafe territory: Trust, acceptance, reliability and fairness in the travel group provide support when traditional structures can no longer cope with volatile challenges and ongoing disruptions. Where do you start?

• Have confidence in the adaptability of the people. Since the financial crisis, we have learned that what used to be a crisis now comes under the heading of flexibility. Make the journey open and be honest with people. They are waiting for it. What is the first thing you want to tell them? Is this also a wicked problem or a wicked solution?

References

Beck, D. E., & Cowan, C. (2005). *Spiral dynamics: Mastering values, leadership and change*. Hoboken, NJ: Wiley-Blackwell.

Bergmann, F. (2019). *New work, new culture: Work we want and a culture that strengthens us*. Alresford: John Hunt Publishing.

Breidenbach, J., & Rollow, B. (2019). *New work needs inner work*. Munich: Vahlen.

Conklin, J. (2006). *Dialogue mapping: Building shared understanding of wicked problems*. Chichester: Wiley.

Dörner, D. (1997). *The logic of failure: Recognizing and avoiding error in complex situations* (4th ed.). Cambridge: Perseus.

Dörner, D. (2015). *Die Logik des Misslingens. Strategisches Denken in komplexen Situationen. 13. Auflage*. Hamburg: Rowohlt.

Glasl, F., & Lievegoed, B. (2011). *Dynamische Unternehmensentwicklung, Grundlagen für nachhaltiges Change Management* (4th ed.). Bern: Hauptverlag.

Frick, K., & Höchli, B. (2014). *Die Zukunft der vernetzten Gesellschaft*. Rüschlikon/Zürich: GDI Gottlieb Duttweiler Institute.

Haselbach, D., & Kühn, F. (2013). *Organisation der Zukunft: direkt, interaktiv, beweglich*. Trendforum, Berlin, 13.3.2013.

Kühn, F., Haselbach, D., & Gustafsson, T. (2013). *The art of travelling – Creating a shift towards a resilient organization*. Graz: ICG Change.

Kühn, F., Kempf, M., & Chamberlain, J. (2020). *The concept of purpose, travelling, and connectivity*. In P. Wollmann, F. Kühn, & M. Kempf (Eds.), Three pillars of organization and leadership in disruptive times – Navigating your company successfully through the twenty-first century business world. Cham: Springer Nature.

Kühn, F., & Wollmann, P. (2018). *10 wirksame Methoden, wie Chefs das Vertrauen ihrer Mitarbeiter zerstören*. Impulse online. Retrieved from https://www.impulse.de/management/personalfuehrung/vertrauen-mitarbeiter-chef/3560668.html

Laloux, F. (2014). *Reinventing organizations: A guide to creating organizations inspired by the next stage in human consciousness*. Brussels: Nelson Parker.

Luhmann, N. (1977). *Differentiation of society*. Canadian Journal of Sociology, Band 2, Nr. 1.

McGregor, D. (1960). *The human side of enterprise*. New York: McGraw-Hill.

Oestereich, B., & Schröder, C. (2017). *Das kollegial geführte Unternehmen*. München: Vahlen.

Rittel, H. W. J., & Webber, M. M. (1973). *Dilemmas in a general theory of planning*. Policy Sciences.

Schumpeter, J. (1926). *Theorie der wirtschaftlichen Entwicklung*. München: Duncker & Humblot.

Snowdon, D. J., & Boone, M. E. (2007). *A leader's framework for decision making*. Harvard Business Review.

Tonkinwise, C. (2015). *Design for transitions – From and to what?*. Taylor & Francis: Design Philosophy Papers 13/1.

Wollmann, P., Kühn, F., & Kempf, M. (Eds.). (2020). *Three pillars of organization and leadership in disruptive times – Navigating your company successfully through the twenty-first century business world*. Cham: Springer Nature.

Dieter Haselbach is a sociologist by training, cultural advisor and researcher for more than 20 years. He taught sociology in universities in Canada, England, Austria and Germany. He is the managing partner of ICG Culturplan, then managing partner of ICG Integrated Consulting Group in Germany, now business partner in this company, and director of the Center for Cultural Research in Berlin. He develops business concepts, planning processes, and strategies for institutions and local authorities and supports change management in public administration. He is a Certified Systemic Interactive Coach and created a furore as co-author of the book *The Cultural Heart Attack (in German)*.

Frank Kühn has been supporting companies and institutions for many years in the areas of organization and leadership and change and project management. He brings his experience to developments such as the Three-Pillar Model and systemic setting checks. Frank has a doctorate in work science. After leading positions in research and industry, he was a partner at HLP in Frankfurt and the ICG Integrated Consulting Group in Berlin and Graz. Today, he is an independent consultant and a business partner of ICG and associated with other project partners and think tanks. He has published numerous articles in management journals and books.

Part III

Leadership in the 3-P-Model: Setting Direction and Motivation

This part of the book is about best preconditions for best managing the 3-P-application and/or leading the 3-P-implementation, i.e. how to prepare, facilitate and track the application in the organization, in programs or projects, with practical examples of its impact on leadership, collaboration and communication.

All three articles illuminate important different perspectives of leadership in practice. The opener is an article stimulating analogy thinking and creating contexts to ludically (using play) learn or train good leadership and also management (improvisational theater), afterwards an expert analyzes the importance and impact of intrinsic motivation as well as leadership in existential crisis before dysfunctional leadership is tackled. Without good leadership and connected management, 3-P cannot be successfully run.

The Benefits of Improvisational Theatre

Paul Hombach

Abstract

The principles of purpose, journey and connectivity as unfolded in the three-pillar model (3-P-Model) have a strong resemblance to the basics of improvisational theatre (improv). That makes this form of art suitable to explore these principles in a literally playful manner. In this article the author discusses parallels between business transformation processes and the skills of that very agile, creative and highly connected art of acting.

The article shows that organisations can be regarded as a kind of improvisational theatre, which means that it is helpful to learn to act in a proficient way, or at least transfer key insights to shift the interaction and collaboration in the organisation. So, improv theatre can be seen as a highly effective coping mechanism for dealing with challenging organisational and leadership situations, which is also an emerging topic in neuroscientific research.

1 Principles of Improvisational Theatre

Improvisational theatre (improv) is a form of theatre played without a script. It is performed on different levels in lots of variations by numerous groups around the world. The common principle is the spontaneous development of scenes in close connection with the other players. This requires cooperation, spontaneity and an open mindset. When performed on stage, scenes mostly arise from the audience's suggestions, which make this particular form of theatre highly interactive. Some improv games follow certain rules and can be played from a beginner level, while others, the so-called long forms, are challenging even for the experts. Professional

P. Hombach (✉)
Sankt Augustin, Germany
e-mail: info@paulhombach.de

P. Wollmann et al. (eds.), *Organization and Leadership in Disruptive Times*, Future of Business and Finance, https://doi.org/10.1007/978-3-030-63034-8_6

improv actors often appear as comedians on stage or work as coaches. Improv methods can also be applied to training and education.

2 The Yes-And Principle

There is no such thing as right or wrong in improvised scenes. Look what's already there and deal with it. Don't deny or try to counteract it. Take it as a given reality and add something useful. It's a matter of acceptance and common development. The mindset behind it is that my idea is not better than yours. I realize what you bring on stage to start the scene. I and everyone else in the ensemble are committed to spinning the thread by trying to unfold the elements in a way that makes sense (which is, often enough, very funny!).

3 Acting Is Reacting

To act in today's VUCA world, organisations need to be adaptive, agile and flexible—just like in an improvised scene! In everyday life we are confronted with unplanned and unforeseeable incidents. The parallel to improvised acting is striking: one has to deal with the topics, figures and circumstances emerging on stage immediately and in an off-the-cuff manner (Fig. 1). It's not a one-way process, though. It's a creative give and take. As you are an involved and connected

Fig. 1 Improvisation of organisational issues (Illustrated by Frank Kühn, used with permission. All rights reserved)

participant in the play, your choices and decisions are relevant for the growth of the story. Others have to accept your contributions just as you have to accept theirs.

4 Failure Is an Option (and Opportunity)

We all remember the famous phrase 'failure is not an option' associated with the Apollo 13 mission. However, in improvisation failure *is* always an option. In the normal business life, the experiences of mistakes will have more or less negative consequences (which hinders evolution and learning—so, at least in a travelling organisation with all of its turmoil, we have 'to learn to fail'). Improv theatre provides a place where 'failure' is safe. Creativity may turn 'shit into gold'. As long as you stay connected, you're fine. Take the elements already in the stack and work with them. Furthermore, here we find a strong link to the 'fail faster, succeed sooner' idea (Sanabria 2020).

5 Link to the Three-Pillars Model (3-P-Model)

In their book *Three Pillars of Organisation and Leadership in Disruptive Times* (Wollmann et al. 2020), the authors outlined the importance of purpose, journey and connectivity in a rapid and unforeseeably changing world. These principles are generically embedded in the art of improvisation!

5.1 Sustainable Purpose

The purpose is to get the scene going, to enjoy performing and/or entertaining the audience (the 'customer'). Everyone is an equally accepted part in that play. The performance itself is processional at all times. Like the travelling organisation, the group of players embarks on a journey where the progression of the scene is a value in itself (note that here is an interesting parallel to the principles of Chinese philosophy and business habits as presented by François Jullien (2006, 2009, 2018)). Instead of thinking end-to-end and aiming towards a given close, the end of the scene (or, in a comedy context, a punchline) may emerge naturally 'out of the box'. Thirdly, connectivity is almost a prerequisite for improvisation, but a skill that can be explored and practised by performing scenes together. Other principles of modern management theory apply as well—it's that desired start-up feel with a lack of hierarchy, a cooperative and sharing approach of the workflow.

5.2 Travelling by Nature

Improv theatre offers a vivid platform for interaction. It is the only kind of acting that enables participants to experience the magic of the ongoing development of a common story. In order to create meaningful, plausible or even entertaining content, one has to work together over time and have faith in the group's creative potential. In-depth analysis of storytelling techniques reveals that a good story follows a road map. Screenplay authors often populate their world with archetypal figures and have them face more or less dramatic hurdles. Humans have been familiar with such concepts since the dawn of time. The path of a collectively told story has yet to be explored. Elements added to the narrative may arise from the participants' own experiences with stories and their cultural diversity. Likewise, similar to the parallels between a road movie and a travelling organisation (Wollmann 2020), the road along a collectively told story provides insights into the process of recalibration and adaptation. The process of transformation becomes tangible.

5.3 Genuine Connectivity

Connectivity is in the DNA of improvisation. It is essential to stay connected with all other players. There is a play happening on stage with a strong commitment to a shared world, place and set of figures. This needs to be focused on by everyone all the time. When you start to 'script' *off stage*, you lose connection to the process happening *on stage*. So, one of the oft-quoted wisdoms of improv is 'kill your darling'. Don't try to find a clever line in the wings while you're not involved in the events happening on stage. Otherwise you might just enter the scene unable to cope with the elements evolved.

A sustainable purpose, a mindset as a travelling organisation and the ability of connectivity foster a special and valuable quality both for individuals and for organisations alike: resilience. The strong linkage between improv and resilience is explained and detailed in the interview with Dr. Benjamin Hartwig, an expert on both improv and resilience.

Improvisational Theatre and Neuroscience: An Interview Between Paul and Dr. Benjamin Hartwig
Question: How can improv enhance resilience? *Answer*: To answer this question, we have to define improv. In terms of improv, in this context, we're talking about methods based on improvisational theatre. There are a few studies coming out now about how improvisational theatre techniques can help with anxiety, depression or PTSD (*post-traumatic stress disorder*). A recent study was conducted by Peter Felsman at the Alan Alda Center for Communicating Science at Stony Brook University in New York. Dr. Felsman has studied improvisational theatre comparing sentiments and abilities of people after 20 min of improv exercises to 20 min of exercises not involving improvisation. He found that, with proper selection of the exercises to make them comparable, he could see effects on divergent thinking, anxiety and happiness. The participants who did improv for 20 min felt less uncertainty, less anxiety, were better at divergent thinking and felt happier. In my opinion these points are really important for resilience work. We can grow our resilience on three levels: Instrumental changes, cognitive changes and regenerative changes so we can do something about our environment; we can think differently about the situation; we can learn to relax and engage our nervous system differently. Improv and resilience seem to interlink on all

(continued)

three levels. The most potent way to be become more resilient is called cognitive reappraisal. It's the ability to change your story and it helps out when you go into negative rumination. So that's where improvised theatre is extremely potent and where I see effects in my courses and seminars.
Question: Is there scientific evidence that improv shows neurophysiological effects?
Answer: I haven't found any convincing scientific study that shows neurophysiological effects of improvised theatre yet. When it comes to improvisation per se, there are some studies that were conducted by Charles Limb at the University of California in San Francisco. He used functional MRI (*magnetic resonance imaging*) to study the brain activity of jazz musicians when they were improvising compared to when they were playing a previously rehearsed piece. *Dr Limb could see different regions of the brain light up. For instance, when music was improvised back and forth between two musicians, the language centre of the brain was very active.*
That is the only evidence I can think of where we have something biological as evidence that improv has an effect. It's hard to study improvised theatre because it is a multilayered skill; it's verbal, physical, emotional all at once so you would have to ask a more specific research question and come up with a way to improvise in an MRI scanner. That is a challenge and will likely need a lot of money and time.
(https://www.researchgate.net/publication/314223256_The_Neuroscience_of_Improvisation)
Question: Just now the world is experiencing the unexpected Covid-19 pandemic. Can improv teach us how to cope with unforeseen and disruptive situations?
Answer: I think the mindset of an improviser is very helpful. In terms of science, it's been shown many times that improvised theatre enhances your ability of divergent thinking, i.e. finding multiple solutions to a given problem. You're not trapped and you're not stuck with just one or two solutions; you can think out of the box. Improv increases your chance of adaptation and dealing with the crisis in a better way.

Dr. Ben Hartwig is a professional actor in improvised theatre, philanthropist and science trainer living in Brussels and Cologne. He has a Ph.D. in genetics and has worked at the Max Planck Institute for plant breeding research in Cologne. He became a member of the Springmaus Improv theatre group in 2012. In 2017, he founded the start-up company Neuroblitz®. He was the first trainer in Germany to professionally combine science and applied improvisation. Today he focuses on improv theatre, science and personal development in training, coaching and seminars. He works with companies, institutes and universities in English and in German.
www.neuroblitz.de
Both interview partners, Paul and Ben, are starring in an improvised musical show in Cologne.

6 The Role of Improv Theatre in the Context of Business and Companies

Being almost 30 years in the improv business, I have performed improv theatre for many companies, big players as well as smaller ones. The function of professional comedians in such a context is often to accompany change processes or new product roll-outs, address crucial topics or simply act as an incentive on the company premises. Rather like the tradition of a court jester, the free speech of a comedian can address and express uncomfortable topics. I remember a typical case in a merger situation. A major financial company had bought another. There were different cultures at different locations, prejudices about 'the new ones', silo thinking. Improvised scenes helped to expose those habits in a very entertaining way. Taboos were resolved by laughing *with* each other (not *about* each other). Turn rumours into comedy rather than allowing them to spread amongst the staff! Furthermore, the event was remembered positively by the participants years later. You certainly can give people something to talk about!

7 Lessons Learned/Practical Takeaways

Improv is an established technique in business coaching. Some games frequently used as 'warm-ups' in theatre rehearsals as well as basic exercises can be played by anyone with the assistance of a coaching improv actor. The method is perfect for team building. Participants explore their ability to react spontaneously, foster communication and learn to act collectively in situations happening here and now. Sessions with an improv coach can take place on the company's premises in suitable rooms. In a multipurpose modern architecture (Wollmann and Ndrevataj 2020), a meeting room with enough space in the middle will do. I would recommend a group size of ± 10 people at a time and a least 1 day of training. At best, the lessons will empower the group with various soft skills. HR persons may even spot some really gifted individuals. In a 'worst case', the improv session is just fun for everyone with some gratifying hours of laughing and acting together. And that's a value in itself!

So, let your colleagues embark on a vivid and inspirational journey into the unknown!

References

Jullien, F. (2006). *Vortrag vor Managern über Wirksamkeit und Effizienz in China und im Westen.* Berlin: Merve Verlag.

Jullien, F. (2009). *Les transformations silencieuses.* Paris: Éditions Grasset & Fasquelle.

Jullien, F. (2018). *Vom Sein zum Leben.* Berlin: Matthes & Seitz.

Sanabria, F. (2020). Purpose, journey thinking, and connectivity people to people in global companies. In P. Wollmann, F. Kühn, & M. Kempf (Eds.), *Three pillars of organization and leadership in disruptive times – Navigating your company successful through the 21st century business world.* Springer Nature: Cham.

Wollmann, P. (2020). The art of travelling in films. In P. Wollmann, F. Kühn, & M. Kempf (Eds.), *Three pillars of organization and leadership in disruptive times – Navigating your company successfully through the twenty-first century business world.* Springer Nature: Cham.

Wollmann, P., & Ndrevataj, M. (2020). Modern architecture supporting organization design. In P. Wollmann, F. Kühn, & M. Kempf (Eds.), *Three pillars of organization and leadership in disruptive times – Navigating your company successful through the 21st century business world.* Springer Nature: Cham.

Wollmann, P., Kühn, F., & Kempf, M. (Eds.). (2020). *Three pillars of organization and leadership in disruptive times – Navigating your company successfully through the 21st century business world.* Cham: Springer Nature.

Paul Hombach is a musician, improv actor and science communicator living near Bonn. He studied music, theology and geography at Bonn and Cologne Universities. The certified teacher became a professional improv player at the Springmaus Improv theatre group in 1991, with a broad experience in shows both for the public and for companies. He uses his knowledge and enthusiasm as an improvisational theatre trainer, editor of astronomical magazines and science speaker in English and in German. Paul is the founder of 'Meeting Music'—he attends congresses, conventions and workshops where he turns topics and key points of events into improvised songs.

Leading Organizations Through Intrinsic Motivation

Ehssan Sakhaee

Abstract

Ehssan Sakhaee explains in his article the overwhelming role of intrinsic motivation for individuals, organizations, and leaders that promotes autonomy and describes the historical development of research on it. He shows which fundamental role intrinsic motivation takes within the 3-P-Model: convincing purposes animate and support intrinsic motivation, a mindset as travelling organization calls for autonomously thinking and acting people with high-quality motivation, and connectivity in the large networks needed is a lot more easily achieved between intrinsically motivated people who share the enthusiasm of a large endeavor. This is brilliantly stressed and made transparent in the following: in his book *Influencing Human Behavior*, Harry A. Overstreet states, "Action springs out of what we fundamentally desire ... and the best piece of advice which can be given to would-be persuaders, whether in business, in the home, in the school, in politics, is: First, *arouse in the other person an eager want.* (One) who can do this has the whole world with (them). (One) who cannot walk a lonely way."

1 Brief Introduction

The article will connect motivation in the theory, research, and practice with the three-pillar model (3-P-Model), which was developed in the former book *Three Pillars of Organization and Leadership in Disruptive Times: Navigating Your Company Successfully Through the 21st Century Business World* (Wollmann, P.;

E. Sakhaee (✉)
The University of Sydney, Sydney, NSW, Australia
e-mail: ssan.sakhaee@sydney.edu.au

P. Wollmann et al. (eds.), *Organization and Leadership in Disruptive Times*, Future of Business and Finance, https://doi.org/10.1007/978-3-030-63034-8_7

Kühn, F.: Kempf, M. (Ed.) (2020); Cham/CH: Springer Nature) to give orientation in the current volatile, uncertain, complex, and ambiguous (VUCA) world.

Sustainable purpose: The people in the organization but also its key stakeholders need to know the mandate of the organization and the sustainable value it is creating. The mandate gives clear and convincing orientation on the right level that aligns and inspires to go for a joint endeavor, which makes the people involved confident, inspired, and proud to be part of and contribute to it.

Travelling organization: The organization needs to understand that it is continuously on a journey toward the best possible result and joint success, in the context of the agreed sustainable purpose, coping with all—partly unforeseeable—influences, away from the illusion of consistency, stability, and structural continuity in disruptive times. Travelling organizations need holistic agility in their mindset and DNA, covering an agile mentality, self-reflection, readiness to embrace change, and willingness to deliver.

Connectivity: The organization has to be aware that impact, value, and efficiency needs connectivity between individuals; between people and organizations or institutions; between different systems and cultures; etc. Managing connectivity means preventing unconnected structural silos, boxed competencies, focusing on multilateral incentives and behaviors.

2 Explanations on Motivation

2.1 What Is Motivation?

> Motivation is an intrinsic phenomenon. Extrinsic satisfaction only leads to movements, not motivation.—Frederick Herzberg

Motivation is an *internal* drive to want to do something. It almost acts as an invisible force that pushes you to take action. In motivational psychology, motivation is classified into two categories, intrinsic and extrinsic motivation, which we will cover in this article. In this chapter we will look at how these can be achieved.

2.2 The Importance of Motivation

Problems arising from the lack of motivation are multidimensional—on the individual level, someone with low motivation can suffer psychologically and emotionally from a lack of engagement (that naturally induces satisfaction and mental stimulus). From the organizational perspective, the individual would be lacking in performance. It has been shown that we can, in fact, represent performance as a function of several parameters, namely, abilities, motivation, and opportunity or situational factors (Ramadhar 1988). Some management writers replace opportunity with personality (Lynch 1984), so it may seem valid to introduce here a more refined equation for performance that integrates the complete set of factors. This new equation is:

$$\text{Performance} = \text{Motivation} \times \text{Abilities} \times \text{Opportunity} \times \text{Personality}$$

In the equation, *motivation* reflects the person's desire to want to utilize their abilities (e.g., the drive to learn and engage in an activity). Abilities are the current skills of the individual and their ability to learn new requisite skills for the task at hand. Opportunity reflects the resources and support available to do the task, while personality is an individual's psychosocial traits that allow them to maintain motivation and not be influenced by obstacles and setbacks. We note that an individual's personality *may* change. There may also be some overlap of abilities and personality, for instance, an individual's *resilience* (ability to bounce back from crisis) is a skill/ability but can also be a personality trait (someone may naturally be resilient but also an individual can develop skills in resilience). The ability to self-manage also falls into this category. The best performance is reached if the parts of the equation combine or fit best to each other. This perfectly fits to the pillar of "connectivity" of the 3-P-Model; the best results are achieved if the right connectivity is reached.

2.3 The History of Motivation

In 1949, Harry Harlow and colleagues performed a two-chapter experiment on a group of monkeys—they placed the monkeys in cages with puzzles that consisted of a complex contraption. Without any form of force or encouragement, the monkeys began trying out the puzzles, in fact, really engaging in the activity of solving them. Soon, they were able to solve these puzzles. What was strange, however, to Harlow and his colleagues was that the monkeys were not given any incentives to solve these puzzles. At the time psychologists knew of two motivational drives, namely:

1. Internal or biological urges (food, water, sex)
2. External (rewards and punishments)

However, since neither of these two was present to explain the monkeys' intense drive to solve the puzzles, this perplexed the group of psychologists, as stated by Harlow:

> Solution did not lead to food, water, or sex gratification.

So, what is the third driver that the psychologists had not considered until this time? The drive seemed so *intrinsic* in nature, showing the monkeys' inherent desire in the task, finding the task satisfying without needing any other rewards. Harlow was the first to coin this type of motivation, *intrinsic motivation*.

Harlow then thought perhaps adding a *reward* may further increase the monkeys' motivation, so he rewarded the monkeys with raisins. To his surprise, when rewards were introduced, the monkeys made more errors and even solved the puzzles less frequently. Harlow writes:

> Introduction to food in the present experiment served to disrupt performance, a phenomenon not reported in the literature.

It seemed that introducing the reward when *intrinsic motivation* was present actually had a detrimental effect on performance! This was very surprising for Harlow, and although Harlow urged psychologists to be aware of this third drive, he himself did not want to spend his time fighting the establishment and dropped this research altogether.

2.4 Intrinsic Motivation and Impact of Rewards

What Harlow dropped in the 1950s was picked up again 20 years later by another psychologist, Deci, who, at the time, was with the business school at the University of Rochester and who had also recently received his MBA from Wharton and was very interested in and intrigued by *motivation*. He began with an experiment. This time on humans, a special sort—university students in their prime. He placed the students in two groups. Both groups were given soma cube puzzles over 3-hour periods and over 3 consecutive days. A few other goodies were placed at the students' disposal, *Time* magazine, the *New Yorker*, and *Playboy* (to ensure everyone's interest was covered).

On the first day, both groups of students were asked to solve the soma puzzles.

On the second day, *one* of the groups was told that, for every set of puzzles they could solve, they would be rewarded with $1 (that was two pints of beer in 1969!), while the other group got nothing. On the third day, both groups continued without any rewards.

Halfway through each experimental day, Deci would leave the room and observe the behavior of students from the outside via a one-way mirror for about 8 min to see what the students in each group did.

The first day offered nothing surprising; both groups began solving the puzzles for about half of the time Deci was not present with them. On the second day, the group that was to be rewarded for solving puzzles had become very interested in solving the puzzles and tried to solve as many as they could. This was again not surprising as it matched the motivation philosophy of "reward me and I'll work harder."

The surprise however came on the third day. While the group that was never rewarded continued to solve the puzzles with almost a little more enthusiasm than the first 2 days, the group that was rewarded on the second day were even less enthusiastic than not just the second day when they were paid but also the first day when they weren't! Paying them actually had a detrimental effect on their natural desire to want to solve the puzzles for the sake and enjoyment of doing so, i.e., *a negative* impact on their intrinsic motivation (Pink 2009)!

2.5 Motivation Is a Spectrum

Although we explicitly talk about intrinsic and extrinsic motivation, in reality and according to SDT, motivation is a spectrum as shown in Fig. 1. On the far left, we have no motivation at all (amotivation), whereas on the far right, we have pure intrinsic motivation (intrinsic regulation). What is important to note is that people flourish when they operate in what is called autonomous motivation. This is where what individuals do is either personally meaningful and important and or enjoyable and interesting to do.

Autonomous motivation causes individuals to feel volition. Here, motivation requires no effort and the quality of motivation is high, and, with it, individuals have higher levels of well-being as well. Autonomous motivation is aligned with commitment as it is interest and value-based functioning; we could call this thrive-mode operation. Controlled motivation primarily makes people comply but not necessarily commit, in order to seek some external reward (such as a bonus and/or promotion) or avoid a punishment (being fired, reprimanded).

2.6 The Power of Purpose, Autonomous Motivation, and the 3-P-Model

Autonomous motivation combined with purpose and vision that inspires employees helps individuals and teams to not only gain a greater sense of motivation but also what is termed in positive psychology as "meaningful life"—that is highly correlated with life satisfaction and well-being. Purpose and meaning are essential components of the 3-P-Model. The combination of these provides a high-quality and sustainable motivation aligned with well-being, happiness, and life satisfaction. When individuals and teams identify with the purpose of the organization, and it becomes personally important for them (identified regulation) as in Fig. 1, it can become part of their identity to meet organizational objectives (integrated regulation), and so this high-quality autonomous motivation is far more powerful and aligned with well-being than extrinsic motivators (bonuses, promotion).

In the words of the 3-P-Model, the autonomous motivation is supported by the meaning of my work and how it fits with the *sustainable purpose* of the organization I am working for. And vice versa, the purpose offers orientation to my autonomy. The interest and enjoyment depend on the *organizational journey*, when exciting and even astonishing perspectives and challenges evolve. This is all supported by the third pillar, i.e., if it is connected with other resources that create a context of relevance, safety, etc. (*connectivity*).

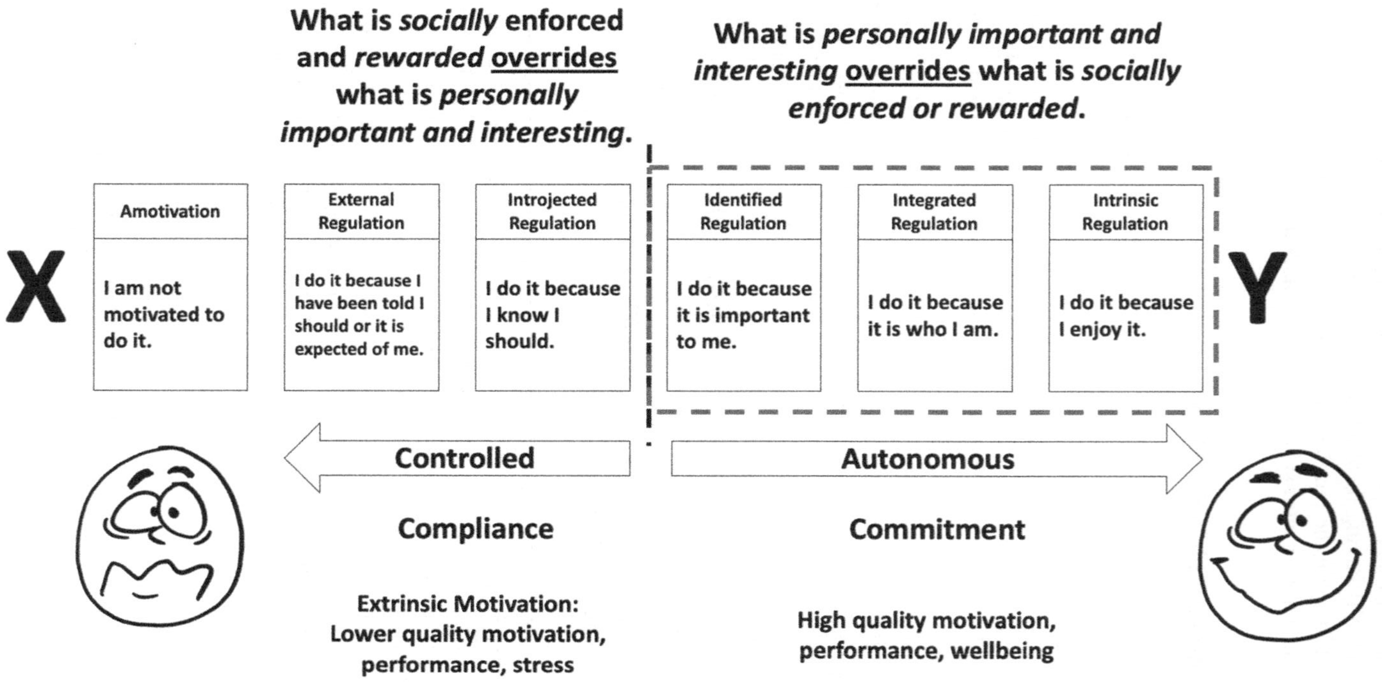

Fig. 1 Motivation is a spectrum (Illustrated by the author, used with permission. All rights reserved)

2.7 Self-Determination Theory

Self-determination theory states that there are three basic psychological needs that all people have, regardless of where they are from: race, culture, gender, age, experience, status, etc. all have three basic psychological needs. When these psychological needs are satisfied, then people feel volition and well-being. Individuals can then move toward autonomous and intrinsic motivation and be self-determined. According to the theory, the three basic psychological needs are:

1. Autonomy
2. Competency
3. Relatedness

Autonomy refers to having the feeling that one is in control of one's own life—feeling that one has the ability to choose how they want to do something. It does not mean freedom; it is power to choose a course of action without feeling that one is being controlled. In 1930, the psychologist Alfred Adler describes having control over one's own environment as "an intrinsic necessity of life itself." In the 3-P-Model, this applies well to the traveling organization.

Competency is the feeling that one's work is significant, that one is capable of accomplishing tasks, and that these tasks matter to the individual. When people feel competent, they feel they are able to get things done. In this 3-P-Model, this notion of competency fuels individuals and groups toward the *sustainable purpose* and the efficacy required to engaged with the wide variety of stakeholders through *connectivity*.

Relatedness refers to the feeling that you belong to a community, society, and to other people. It includes feeling cared for and being able to care for others. This is a feeling of connectedness, another basic psychological need supporting autonomous motivation and well-being. In the 3-P-Model, this further creates a strong connectivity as trust and bonding can flourish between the various stakeholders in the system.

Research into the self-determination theory performed over the past 40 years by Edward L. Deci and Richard Ryan (Ryan and Deci 2000, 2015) and thousands of researchers around the world have shown that these factors play an important role in motivation, engagement, productivity, and well-being. When basic psychological needs are satisfied, it supports the high-quality motivation (autonomous and intrinsic motivation) and well-being.

Leaders can facilitate a climate where basic psychological needs are satisfied. This in turn will result in high levels of motivation, engagement, and productivity—improving outcomes for individuals, teams, organizations, *and the wider society.*

3 Motivation and Leadership in Organizations

We will now look at how the theories above apply to leadership in organizations as well as the 3-P-Model. When we refer to leadership in this article, we basically mean anyone who can exercise influence on others, teams, and the whole organization.

3.1 Leader's Mindset and Heartset

The leader's mindset is an important element. If a leader is functioning in "thrive mode," they are more likely to have their psychological needs satisfied and then, in turn, be more able to behave in ways that support autonomy among their employees. So, the leadership here starts with self-leadership, and one of the primary ways to do this is through the practice of mindfulness, which is described in the article *Leadership in Times of Crisis* in this book.

When leaders feel safe and operate in "thrive mode," they intrinsically focus on both values, purpose, and relationships, driving the strength of the 3-P-Model. Their desire for organizational success stems from integrated internalized regulation (values) rather than introjections (fears). Additionally, seeing others as individuals who the leader wishes to develop and empower, with a deep sense of care for their well-being and development, is essential in everything else that follows.

3.2 Leadership that Supports Autonomy

Leaders can facilitate autonomous motivation by focusing on employees' own interests, values, and approaches to getting things done. This can be facilitated by engaging employees in executive decision-making and their involvement in setting deadlines, goals, expectations, and processes. This, of course, requires the leader to trust the competency and capability of the employees. When you have the right people in the team and in the organization, it is easier to impart such trust and responsibility. As famously spoken by 3M President and CEO, William L. McKnight, in 1948, "those men and women, to whom we delegate authority and responsibility, if they are good people, are going to want to do their jobs in their own way."

3.3 Communication that Supports Autonomy

Communication that supports autonomy is communication that fosters behavior supporting autonomy. For example, instead of using directive language (control-oriented language) such as "you should, you must, . . ." or using any approaches that make employees feel they are being controlled rather than supported, leaders use language that supports autonomy. This gives autonomy to employees to seek help when they need it. It does require higher levels of pro-activity on the part of employees, which ultimately results in commitment rather than compliance.

3.4 Competency and Trusting in Your People

Being optimistic and believing in your people makes a great difference to their level of competency. The Pygmalion effect shown in an experiment by Rosenthal and Fode in 1963 (Rosenthal and Fode 1963) is just one powerful experiment which shows how the "leader's" (in the case below, the scientist) expectation had an effect on the competency of the mice. Identical rats were labeled "smart" and "dumb." The expectation and corresponding treatment affected their performance where the mice that were *expected* to be smart eventually were able to learn the maze faster than those who were *expected* to be dumb. What the scientists were not told is that both groups had the same level of intelligence! This confirmed that the expectation of the scientists alone had a significant effect on the performance of the mice. I have tried to depict this in the cartoon in Fig. 2.

Similar studies have been done with teachers and students. Rosenthal and Jacobson performed an experiment in 1966 (Rosenthal and Jacobson 1966) that demonstrates that a teacher's expectation and belief in their students' capabilities actually affected the students' IQ! In the experiment, a randomly selected number of students were labeled and reported as having "unusual potential for intellectual gains" to their classroom teachers. As they outline in their paper:

> Within each of 18 classrooms, an average of 20% of the children were reported to classroom teachers as showing unusual potential for intellectual gains. Eight months later these "unusual" children (who had actually been selected at random) showed significantly greater gains in IQ than did the remaining children in the control group.

These results show that trusting in others' competency and capability could have a positive impact on their performance. The expectation and belief of the leader has a

Fig. 2 The Pygmalion effect on mice (Illustrated by the author, used with permission. All rights reserved)

crucial impact on the subordinate's self-efficacy and belief in themselves and their competency (perceived competency).

3.5 Competency and Flow

Mihaly Csikszentmihalyi (1990) talks about the concept of *flow* where the challenge level is just right—this concept is shown in Fig. 3. If the challenge is too high, this could result in anxiety or worry; if the challenge is too low, this could result in boredom and apathy. If the challenge is just right, one feels in control and can enter flow—also known as "being in the zone"—so engrossed (Slocum et al. 1989) in the task that one can lose oneself in it, losing track of time and space. Leaders can provide tasks that match the skill level of employees so that they are more likely to experience flow. There are two other ingredients for flow: clear goals and immediate feedback. The combination of these three provides the best opportunity for individuals to engage at a high level and have an optimum experience in their work.

4 Relatedness and Positive Relationships

Developing genuine care for others is the source of satisfying this component of basic psychological needs. When employees are seen as human beings with ambitions, goals, and the desire to develop, grow, and contribute, they are no longer seen as just resources, or cogs in the machine. When a leader shifts their mindset from seeing their people as resources to seeing them as aspiring, intrinsically motivated individuals that the leader will have the opportunity to develop, positive relationships will begin to develop.

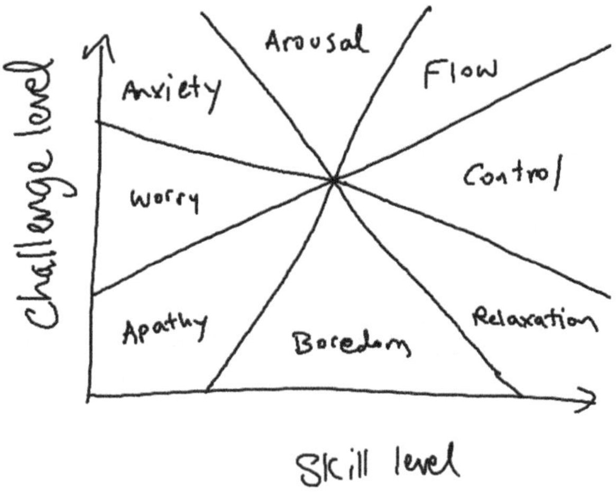

Fig. 3 The concept of flow in positive psychology (Illustrated by the author, used with permission. All rights reserved)

4.1 An Important Note on Leader Mindset

This article provides a framework that allows a leader who genuinely cares for his/her people or is willing to develop a genuine sense of care for them people to better facilitate their motivation and well-being. If the approach is applied in a way that merely gets results (e.g., higher motivation, higher productivity, etc.) and there is no genuine authentic care behind the actions and behaviors, then it is very unlikely that the approach will work effectively or be sustainable. Hence a genuine sense of care is a prerequisite for the behavioral suggestions in this article.

5 Connection with the 3-P-Model

5.1 Sustainable Purpose

When the sustained purpose of the organization is inspiring to the employees and aligned with their own personal values, employees' motivation begins to shift toward autonomous motivation (i.e., identified regulation and integrated regulation).

Doing what is difficult and tedious but highly valuable and important, in a situation where one exercises volition to do the task, is very much in the autonomous motivation region. The individual does not have introjections that they feel they are controlled by. Instead their motivation is replaced by a high-quality drive that is ignited by values and interests. They engage at a high level, driven by an inspirational sustained purpose. Sustained purpose allows individuals and teams to maintain their engagement despite challenges as the level of commitment is higher than when there is no clear and sustainable purpose.

5.2 Traveling Organization

Leadership that supports autonomy allows for seamless exploration. There is no top-down directive of how to do things in a VUCA world; there needs to be autonomy for employees to think independently and collaboratively—to seek out each other's strengths and knowledge and collectively explore the unknown landscapes they are exploring on the journey to discovering the solutions. No leader can know what the future holds and relinquishing control and trusting their people is the only way for the traveling organization to survive and thrive in a VUCA world. Intrinsic motivation that supports autonomy is particularly important in disruptive times as it is sustained through crisis and change. This is because the level of commitment is far higher than that of traditional motivational approaches (extrinsic motivators).

5.3 Connected Resources

Since now there is a focus on relationship building and genuine care and connection, a deep sense of relatedness arises that builds stronger bonds, trust, and collaboration. The power of autonomy and relatedness will be the driving forces to bring full awareness of the complex web of resources available to the organization and its sustainable purpose. Since resources are not managed from the top-down, and full trust is given to those who lead the resources from the bottom-up, the efficiency and effectiveness of resource use will be fully realized and sustainably managed. There is also a higher sense of responsibility for the utilization of these connected resources and the dissemination of important knowledge regarding how to best utilize the resources to avoid failure. This is due to the recognition by all parties that there is no central authority to manage the resources but, instead, a collective who are custodians of the complex web of connected resources, and who harmoniously coordinate and replenish the resource pool.

6 Key Conclusions and Takeaways

Derived from recent state-of-the-art theory and research about motivation, four ingredients to enhance intrinsic and autonomous motivation in organizations should be always focused on:

1. Leader's mindset and heartset
2. Trust in others' capability and effectiveness
3. Providing a clear vision and purpose that inspires and motivates employees
4. Providing clear goals, tasks that match skill level, and supplementing these with regular feedback

These four ingredients allow for a high-quality motivation and engagement as well as employee well-being. This is sustainable motivation at its very best that is essential in a VUCA world that functions using the 3-P-Model.

References

Csikszentmihályi, M. (1990). *Flow: The psychology of optimal experience*. Harper & Row. ISBN: 978-0-06-016253-5.

Lynch, D. (1984). *Your high performance business brain*. Englewood Cliffs, NJ: Prentice Hall.

Pink, D. H. (2009). *Drive : The surprising truth about what motivates us*. New York: Riverhead Books.

Ramadhar, S. (1988). Life performance = motivation x ability x opportunity: Individual differences in predictive models. *Genetic Social and General Psychology Monographs, 114*, 191–210.

Rosenthal, R., & Fode, K. (1963). The effect of experimenter bias on performance of the albino rat. *Behavioral Science, 8*, 183–189.

Rosenthal, R., & SL Jacobson, L. (1966). Teachers' expectancies: Determinates of pupils' IQ gains. *Psychological Reports, 19*, 115–118.
Ryan, R. M., & Deci, E. L. (2000). Intrinsic and extrinsic motivations: Classic definitions and new directions. *Contemporary Educational Psychology, 25*(1), 54–67. https://doi.org/10.1006/ceps.1999.1020.
Ryan, R., & Deci, E. (2015). *Self-determination theory* (pp. 486–491).
Slocum, J. W., et al. (1989). *Organizational behavior*. St. Paul: West Publishing.

Ehssan Sakhaee is a passionate educator, engineer, philosopher and cartoonist, currently a lecturer and the Director of the UG Leadership Program at the Faculty of Engineering at the University of Sydney, Australia. His interests and passion lie in the area of personal and leadership development and helping people live more meaningful lives. He received his Bachelors and PhD in Engineering from the University of Sydney in Australia. His career spans Engineering, management and leadership consulting, and research and higher education across Japan, the United States, and Australia. He has published works in Engineering, leadership, and management in project management as well as stories and poetry.

The AAUL Framework of Leadership in Times of Crisis

Awareness, Acceptance, Understanding Leadership (AAUL) Framework in the Context of Self, Others, and the Wider VUCA Organization, Society, and the World

Ehssan Sakhaee

Abstract

Ehssan Sakhaee explains the AAUL framework which gives guidance for leadership, especially in crisis situations. He shows the strong linkage of AAUL to the three-pillar model (3-P-Model) and that the understanding and application of a sophisticated concept such as AAUL is significantly more focused, effective, and efficient if it is combined with the 3-P-Model. The steps from awareness through acceptance and understanding to applying good leadership are transparently and plausibly demonstrated.

1 Brief Introduction

The article will connect a transparent leadership framework, especially appropriate in crisis situations, with the three-pillar model (3-P-Model) which was developed in the former book *Three Pillars of Organization and Leadership in Disruptive Times: Navigating Your Company Successfully Through the 21st Century Business World* (Wollmann et al. 2020) to give orientation in the current volatile, uncertain, complex, and ambiguous (VUCA) world.

Sustainable purpose: The people in the organization but also its key stakeholders need to know the mandate of the organization and the sustainable value it is creating. The mandate gives clear and convincing orientation on the right level that aligns and inspires to go for a joint endeavor, which makes

(continued)

E. Sakhaee (✉)
The University of Sydney, Sydney, NSW, Australia
e-mail: ssan.sakhaee@sydney.edu.au

P. Wollmann et al. (eds.), *Organization and Leadership in Disruptive Times*, Future of Business and Finance, https://doi.org/10.1007/978-3-030-63034-8_8

involved people confident, inspired, and proud to be part of and contribute to it. The article shows how this applies to the question of an individual's depth of awareness and how this leads to social and VUCA understanding, and why this consideration is crucial for effective leadership.

Travelling organization: The organization needs to understand that it is continuously on a journey toward the best possible result and joint success, in the context of the agreed sustainable purpose, coping with all—partly unforeseeable—influences, away from the illusion of consistency, stability, and structural continuity in disruptive times. Travelling organizations need holistic agility in their mindset and DNA, covering an agile mentality, self-reflection, readiness to embrace change, and willingness to deliver. In terms of leadership, this means being aware of and understanding the dynamics in ourselves as individuals, our social systems, and the VUCA world and how to synchronize their journeys.

Connecting resources: The organization has to be aware that impact, value, and efficiency need connectivity between individuals; between people and organizations or institutions; between different systems and cultures; etc. Managing connectivity means preventing unconnected structural silos, boxed competencies, and strategic and processual gaps, focusing on multilateral incentives and behaviors. This article focuses on how good leadership evolves out of the connectivity and comprehensive understanding of self-leadership, leading of others, and leadership in the VUCA context.

2 The AAUL Framework at a Glance

The awareness, acceptance, understanding leadership (AAUL) framework (pronounced Owl) (Sakhaee 2020) shown in Fig. 1 is a framework for leadership in a VUCA environment that aligns and cultivates the mindsets and skillset that enable the realization and implementation of the three-pillar model. In particular, the AAUL framework is ideal in a crisis situation as the self-awareness aspect enables rapid self-leadership to return from panic mode to a calm state for making more informed decisions. The AAUL framework aims to develop a holistic mindset that begins from self and extends to a VUCA world environment. The attitudes, mindsets, and skills developed at the individual level are naturally extended to one's immediate environment and relationships and then further expanded at a global level spanning in our VUCA world. Essentially AAUL brings a sense of holistic awareness and understanding that recognizes the interconnectedness of all things, from self to others, and the natural environment, locally and globally. This mindset is nonjudgmental, open, and curious with a deep sense of caring for the well-being and sustainability of the collective that incorporates self, others, the collective system one contributes to (the organization), and the wider society and the environment.

The AAUL Framework at a Glance

Fig. 1 AAUL framework: leadership in a VUCA world © Ehssan Sakhaee

3 Awareness

Awareness is about being conscious of what is, from ourselves to our environment, across time and space; how everything is influenced and affected by everything else; and how we influence and are influenced by our environment, experiences, culture, values, personality, and our strengths and limitations as well as by which purpose we are pursuing. Awareness is simply having the power to observe reality as it is and dig deep into understanding the nature of reality for what it is. This awareness also recognizes that knowledge is always evolving, and, although it realizes on the intellect and perspective, it always subjects this to scrutiny and opens to constant evolution of beliefs and thinking processes about the nature of the self, others, and the world. This awareness is akin to being an outside observer of oneself and others, the environment from an external, curious, and nonjudgmental perspective. Heightened awareness allows us to witness our common purpose, the interconnectedness of our world—leading to a better understanding through curiosity and effective leadership that entails positive action toward positive change. This is the stepping stone that sheds light on seamless implementation of the three-pillar model.

3.1 Self-Awareness

Self-awareness is an awareness of ourselves, our own thought processes, constructed identities, our emotions, hot buttons, our psychological, and psychophysical and physiological reactions to our environment. These become especially apparent in times of crisis when unexpected events take place and we experience turbulent emotions and worries about the future.

Through self-awareness, leaders are able to rapidly become aware of how they function in crisis and VUCA environments and then manage them effectively, before becoming a victim of uncertainties and circumstances. This also relates very closely to the self-reflection component of the *traveling organization*, the second pillar of the 3-P-Model. The innate return to a calm and collected state in a crisis or VUCA environment is an essential stepping stone in the leadership of others and of the organization as a whole.

When a leader develops a heightened sense of self-awareness, they may still experience negative emotions such as anger, frustration, sadness, and worry. However, the frequency and intensity of these may be diminished as they are able to rapidly become aware of these emotions, manage them effectively, and choose not to have the emotions control their behavior. Emotions are treated as information that can be used to make proactive, conscious decisions rather than abrupt reactions to situations. As a result, leaders are able to make better decisions from a calm and collected state or delay making abrupt unhelpful decisions until they can use clear discernment and are thus able to make better decisions.

3.2 Social Awareness

According to Daniel Goleman, author of *Emotional Intelligence* (Goleman 1996), self-awareness leads to social awareness. Social awareness is the ability to tune into other people's emotions and feelings. This of course leads to the ability to empathize and listen empathetically, gaining a deeper understanding of others, their feelings, and their perspectives. Effective communication only takes place when individuals are willing to empathetically listen to others. As Stephen Covey, author of *The 7 Habits of Highly Effective People* (Covey 2013), notes, often most people listen autobiographically to give advice (e.g., offer a solution) or evaluate (judge), rather than deeply understand the other person. Social awareness allows an individual to dig deeper to understand others more effectively. The development of the social awareness component leads to a deeper understanding of *connectivity*, the third pillar in the 3-P-Model. The leader has essentially broadened their awareness to deeply understand the interconnectedness of their social environment, and a deeper understanding of all stakeholders will emerge.

3.3 VUCA World Awareness

VUCA world awareness is an important skill for a leader as it tries to observe things from a "birds-eye" perspective and identify the cause and effect. How are the current systems in place impacting on people, teams, and the organization? How are current practices and products impacting the society and the environment in the short and long term? Through this VUCA world awareness, *sustainable purpose* (the first pillar in the 3-P-Model) is seen more vividly at both the organizational level and the societal level. Sustainable purpose can be lived and breathed through this mode of awareness as its holistic implications become readily apparent in the present moment.

These are important questions for a leader. You may have come across the saying "leadership is about doing the right things, management is about doing things right"—quotes from Peter Drucker and Warren Bennis (Drucker 2006; Bennis and Nanus 1997). The fact is that to know what the right things are, a leader should have a good understanding of all the various interdependencies, how everything impacts and affects other things over time and space. What is the root cause of whatever is observed on the surface? These are important "systems' thinking" questions and mindsets. Leaders who develop this high-level awareness can understand how their actions affect themselves, others, their organizations, and their external environment through time and space. Such a VUCA world awareness brings the collective three pillars of the 3-P-Model together, the *sustainable purpose* for the self, organization, and the world; the interconnectedness, complexity, and rapid change of the *traveling organization*; and the *connectivity* between all resources.

4 Acceptance

Acceptance is a prerequisite to *understanding* as, without acceptance, there will be denial, and denial acts as an obstacle to a deep understanding. The acceptance attitude is to embrace what is for what it is, without resisting it, without fighting it, and without the need to immediately change things before understanding them more deeply. Acceptance does not result in complacency. On the contrary, it empowers one to perform value-based actions, rather than actions that come from resistance. Acceptance allows leaders to accept themselves, as they are—becoming comfortable with their weaknesses and shortcomings. This leads to admitting mistakes and rapidly rectifying problems, being open to feedback. This attitude extends to accepting others, empathy, and nonresistance to how reality unfolds. Instead of resisting and denying crisis, they fully accept and then manage it effectively. The realization of the complexity and the need to rapidly change through the reality of a *traveling organization* and complex web of *connectivity* becomes a part of life—a part of one's functioning through a deep sense of acceptance of this reality in a VUCA world and to keep orientation on this journey through the inspirational *sustainable purpose*.

4.1 Self-Acceptance

William Ury (2015) says it best in his book *Getting to Yes with Yourself*: "If self-judgment is no to self, self-acceptance is a yes to self, perhaps the greatest gift we can give ourselves."

Carl Rogers (1967), one of the founders of humanistic psychology, stated, “The curious paradox is that when I accept myself as I am, then I change.” Self-acceptance does not equate to complacency if it is coupled with the desire to evolve and contribute, as well as focus on values, strengths, and being of service. When you accept yourself, you become your own ally, rather than your own opponent. This is contrary to the popular belief that to change we have to be self-critical and self-judgmental. Self-judgment and self-criticism often close us down and stop us from seeing the possibilities toward growth, development, and change. Self-acceptance allows one to be human, to be imperfect, and to seek help when required. It allows one to become non-defensive when one realizes a mistake and to take responsibility for positive action instead of resorting to either denial or guilt which both act as obstacles to positive change.

Self-acceptance leads to non-reactance and nonresistance to what is. Coupled with curiosity and compassion (see next section), it leads to self-understanding and self-growth.

4.2 Other-Acceptance

When we fully accept ourselves, we can then begin to accept others as they are, not as we want them to be, while being able to empower them toward positive change of their own accord, rather than to please others or in order to stay in a job. Accepting others allows us to be able to fully tune into others, as we have now removed the veils of judgment. Empathy becomes natural, a direct by-product of this acceptance. We are then able to fully understand others’ perspectives, realities, and values, which leads to higher quality of communication and engagement. Other-acceptance does not always equate to agreement with others without question. It simply means that you accept them and their perspectives and values as their current truth without denial, and work with the mental models and beliefs of others to integrate with one’s own and those of the organization. The flow and integration of meaning and understanding takes place when one accepts the others’ worldview that is affected by experience, cultural values, and personality.

4.3 VUCA World Acceptance

When we begin to accept the nature of our VUCA world as a natural phenomenon that results from the ever-increasing complexity of the world we live in, we become comfortable with the nature of our VUCA world. We no longer have to become critical and angry when events don’t unfold as we expect and want them to, and instead embrace volatility, uncertainty, complexity, and ambiguity as the reality of our current world. As with other forms of acceptance, the leader’s acceptance of what unfolds does not lead to complacency, but value-driven action toward positive influence and change.

5 Understanding

Through awareness and acceptance comes the ability to fully understand ourselves, others, and the world we live in. We can gain a deeper insight into why we operate in the way we do, why others are the way they are, how we function at our best, and then how to get the best out of ourselves and others. We also gain a deeper insight into interdependencies and influence. We are able to solve problems from their root cause rather than patching issues with symptomatic and quick-fix solutions. The attitude that can be cultivated toward understanding is curiosity. To be curious naturally creates the emotional energy required to be able to understand. Here, curiosity replaces criticism. Where criticism closes one down, curiosity opens one up toward understanding.

Understanding how we, others, and the world work is a crucial step to knowing what to do next in order to not only survive but thrive in a VUCA world. The lack of a deep understanding of how we influence others, how others influence us, and how collectively we impact our organizations and our world allows us to make more conscious and wiser decisions for the benefit of the collective. This understanding feeds back into the *sustainable purpose* and a deeper understanding of *connectivity* within ourselves and with the system around us and change as a *traveling organization* in a VUCA world.

5.1 Self-Understanding

Self-understanding is an attitude that is coupled with acceptance to dig deeper into the nature of ourselves, how we function, why we function that way, and how we can be better versions of ourselves. Understanding leads to knowing how one can further develop, how one can function at one's best in difficult circumstances, and how to lead ourselves. This arises from the self-reflection and the understanding of our interconnected impact and influence on our environment. Understanding how we function and how we influence and are influenced places us in a better position to make well-informed decisions.

5.2 Other-Understanding

Developing the mindset and attitude of understanding oneself leads to an attitude of understanding toward others, empathetically. It becomes natural to develop a desire to really understand others' perspective, views, and values and integrate them with our own. We can now see others as an extension of ourselves with the same *sustainable purpose*, navigating through complexity but with the same essential goal. A deeper sense of cooperation and collaboration arises through understanding others deeply and bringing the best out of others to achieve the collective sustainable purpose.

5.3 VUCA World Understanding

Understanding the VUCA world requires a leader to develop a systems' thinking approach to problem-solving. This allows the leader to understand the interdependency between people, organizations, and the wider environment. The impact and influence of social, organizational, economic, and political factors and their interplay across time and space can be understood from a *systems' thinking* view of these interactions and interdependencies. This is where the sustainable purpose of a traveling organization in a complex connected world is fully realized and understood. Although there is still uncertainty and unpredictability in a VUCA world, there is also a deeper understanding of how to navigate this individually and collectively so as to increase the probability of the best outcomes.

However, a VUCA world understanding is not just about the leader having a holistic perspective. It is also about combining the perspective of others through the two other pillars of the 3-P-Model: *travelling organization* and *connectivity*. To exemplify this, I would like to share the story of the *elephant in the dark room* found in some ancient eastern texts. Several people are exploring a creature in a dark room, experiencing the creature from their own individual perspectives. One calls out "it's a throne"; another, "a trunk"; another "a hose"' depending on which part of the creature (elephant) they are experiencing. It is only when they combine their perspectives that a more accurate representation of the elephant is achieved. This story illustrates the limitations of an individual perspective and the need to integrate various perspectives and views to obtain the most accurate picture of reality. Hence for leaders to get a deeper understanding of the VUCA world, they need a system's perspective of reality and combine their perspectives with the knowledge and perspectives of others.

6 Leadership of the Self

This is where we can apply the 3-P-Model in the context of self. Self-awareness has led to an individual identifying their own purpose, their personal "calling," and their reason for *being*. This becomes their *personal sustainable purpose*. However, this personal sustainable purpose is not in isolation of the extended organization, society, and the world, which essentially is an extension of the self. The *traveling organization*, in the context of self, is the *traveling organism* interconnected with this natural environment, capable of influencing and being influenced by others and the context and culture in which it resides. Leadership of the self means to be the master and agent of one's own functioning in the VUCA world, to be completely responsible for leading oneself through complexity and change, and being fully responsible for the impact one has on one's own environment, on others, on the organization, and on the wider society though time and space.

6.1 Leadership of Others

Through leading and sustaining oneself, one is now effectively able to lead others. As a culmination of the preceding qualities of awareness, acceptance, and understanding, one extends the leadership of others through empathy and collective effort. Leadership of others encompasses a deep sense of care for others' well-being and their effective functioning. Effective leadership can now be achieved here where others can now function optimally in the complex VUCA world in which they find themselves. Influence is based on a deep sense of awareness, acceptance, and understanding and is thus natural, harmonious, and without force.

6.2 Leadership of VUCA

Through leading oneself and others effectively, and through the deeper awareness and understanding of VUCA, the organization, and wider VUCA world, individual and collective action and leadership have the best chance of positive influence at a local and collective level. The organization is now an organism in a wider VUCA world, operating in synchrony and harmony with its natural environment. What the individuals, teams, and organizations do is now completely aligned with collective well-being of the world, not just of the human race but of the natural environment that the human race finds itself in. Leadership of VUCA does not mean *controlling* VUCA, but it means positively influencing it and also accepting outcomes as they arise, for the VUCA world will remain an unpredictable and uncertain place to operate. However, leadership becomes seamless and adaptable in the reality of VUCA and does not result in confusion or panic. Instead, it results in a deep sense of acceptance of what unfolds an effective leadership to thrive in a VUCA world. This completes the 3-P-Model at the highest level possible, seamlessly, and effectively.

7 The Interplay Between AAUL

In the previous sections, we have shown the various aspects of the AAUL framework and how one leads to the other, with the starting point being a deeper and holistic sense of awareness, starting with self-awareness and leading to awareness of others, the organization, and the wider VUCA world and the interconnectedness of everything. It is important to highlight that the interplay and collective development of all the faculties mentioned is essential for the framework to work, and one cannot apply any of them sustainably and effectively in isolation. AAUL is a holistic framework, and as one advances through the various faculties vertically from awareness to leadership and horizontally from self to others and the VUCA world, one is able to apply the framework at a complete and holistic level simultaneously. A leader applying AAUL will continue to develop and cultivate all 16 dimensions of AAUL simultaneously. This can be achieved from a continuous development of deep awareness and acceptance of the current condition without resistance as the starting point, and as an anchor for all the others. One technique that can be effectively used is the practice of *mindfulness*.

7.1 Mindfulness

Mindfulness (Sakhaee, n.d.-a) is a practice that an individual can do on a daily basis which leads to a deeper sense of awareness in its purest form. This could simply be spending a few minutes paying attention to one's breathing. This is simply observing breathing for several minutes. It may be that while observing breathing, an individual is distracted by their environment, by their thoughts, and by their emotions. This is fine. The idea of this practice is to notice disturbances with openness and curiosity rather than resistance. There is no need to feel a certain way. The practice is paying simple and gentle attention, observing the present moment and current condition, and completely accepting whatever is present here and now in the mind and body. Mindfulness is training the mind to become still and nonreactive (though proactive and responsive) to the current environment. Regular practice of mindfulness brings about a sense of calm and serenity that allows one to make clear decisions in difficult and chaotic situations, rather than reacting to situations based on abrupt emotions that may arise. Guided mindfulness meditations are available on various apps and platforms (Sakhaee, n.d.-b) that assist in the regular practice of mindfulness to cultivate awareness, acceptance, and compassion.

8 Summary

This paper covered the awareness, acceptance, understanding leadership (AAUL) framework that aligns leaders and organizations in the path of enabling and implementing the 3-P-Model at the individual, organization, and universal level and is highly suitable in times of crisis as well as in our VUCA world. It aims to provide the foundation of personal mindsets, skills, and attitudes to lead in a VUCA world aligned with, and significantly supported by, the 3-P-Model, which provides focus and deeper understanding. It also reflects how this leadership starts with self-awareness, self-acceptance, and self-understanding and how it can be extended to others and the VUCA world to effectively lead the interwoven complexity of this large-scale system that includes the individuals, teams, organizations, and the wider natural world. It is crucial that the elements of the AAUL framework are very well connected and balanced, especially in crises, e.g., self-acceptance without self-awareness would be a toxic combination in a crisis for anybody in a leadership role (Fig. 2).

Fig. 2 AAUL developing around the three pillars that help to focus the application in a practical way

9 Takeaways

An effective leader can take advantage of the awareness, acceptance, understanding leadership (AAUL) framework to develop a holistic approach, effectively supported by the three-pillar model of organization and leadership. The leader becomes a calm, collected conscious observer of themselves, others, their organization, and their environment, locally and globally—from a deep inner knowledge of themselves and others and a holistic view of their VUCA world. To implement AAUL:

1. Develop a deeper sense of one's self-understanding, own functioning, strengths, and weaknesses. Lead oneself on the basis of this deeper understanding which is an ongoing process.
2. Apply this to others, whether they are subordinates, colleagues, or other leaders and stakeholders, acknowledging, accepting, and integrating their perspectives and values to your own to foster the development of a shared *sustainable purpose*.
3. Be aware of the *connectivity* of the self, others, the organization, and the wider VUCA world through a systems' thinking perspective.
4. Develop a deeper understanding of the interconnectedness, dynamics, and the functioning of the organization in relation to the individual and teams in the organization but also to the external context by which the organization functions as a *traveling organization*.
5. Accept the nature of VUCA and become comfortable with this nature of reality without resistance, accepting the unforeseeable journey, even facing disruptions and coping with crises as integral parts of the future operating mode.
6. Lead through collective values and a common *sustainable purpose* in order to function harmoniously and effectively in a VUCA world.

References

Bennis, W. G., & Nanus, B. (1997). *Leaders: Strategies for taking charge* (2nd ed.). New York, Harper Business.

Covey, S. (2013). *The 7 habits of highly effective people: Powerful lessons in personal change* (25th anniversary ed.). New York: Simon & Schuster.

Drucker, P. (2006). *The essential Drucker: The best of sixty years of Peter Drucker's essential writings on management* (1st paperback ed.). New York: Collins Business.

Goleman, D. (1996). *Emotional intelligence: Why it can matter more than IQ*. London: Bloomsbury.

Rogers, C. (1967). *On becoming a person: A therapist's view of psychotherapy*. London: Constable.

Sakhaee, E. (2020). *Awareness, acceptance, understanding leadership framework*. Retrieved from www.ehssansakhaee.com/aaul-framework

Sakhaee, E. (n.d.-a). *Mindfulness crash course – A way to exercise self-awareness and self-regulation*. Retrieved from www.ehssansakhaee.com/mindfulness

Sakhaee, E. (n.d.-b). *10 minutes of mindfulness*. Retrieved from https://insighttimer.com/esakhaee/guided-meditations/10-minutes-mindfulness

Ury, W. (2015). *Getting to yes with yourself: (and other worthy opponents)* (1st ed.). New York: HarperOne.

Wollmann, P., Kühn, F., & Kempf, M. (Eds.). (2020). *Three pillars of organization and leadership in disruptive times – Navigation your company successfully through the 21st century business world*. Cham: Springer Nature.

Ehssan Sakhaee is a passionate educator, engineer, philosopher, and cartoonist, currently a lecturer and the Director of the UG Leadership Program at the Faculty of Engineering at the University of Sydney, Australia. His interests and passion lie in the area of personal and leadership development and helping people live more meaningful lives. He received his Bachelors and PhD in Engineering from the University of Sydney in Australia. His career spans Engineering, management and leadership consulting, and research and higher education across Japan, the United States, and Australia. He has published works in Engineering, leadership, and management in project management as well as stories and poetry.

Part IV

3-P-Model Application in the Public Sector

The scope of this book increases from the private sector focus in the previous book to a more holistic view, covering the public sector and global society and connecting all across the spheres is a key target of the book. Practical experiences in applying the 3-P-Model in the public sector are analyzed, lessons learned documented and a lot of diverse take-aways described.

The five articles cover a broad field of topics, starting with an international organization and institution (UN), focusing then on globally important, but locally performed tasks (urban planning) and afterwards on the development of countries in a demanding context of different national, international and local authorities. The last article covers the potential role of science on the journey of countries through unknown areas.

Applying the Three-Pillar Model in the UN Agencies

Peter Wollmann

Abstract

Lately, global institutions—and especially the UN—have been in troubled waters. The UN's "sustainable purpose" is being challenged: the diverse global conflicts and the underlying warring interests are having a severe impact on the UN's decision-making, and its financial stability is also being closely scrutinized. How the various UN agencies cope with such disruptive challenges and strong constraints is described in the interview below.

1 Introduction

The world is faced with a paradox of needing international/global institutions, such as the United Nations (UN), to address global issues, but also questioning their significance. Never in the last 75 years has the UN been under as much pressure with having to convince the Member States of its mandate, to balance the various interests of the Member States, and to create sustainable solutions under the existing constraints. In a world where today's society is globally interconnected, the UN is patiently finding the right journey through troubled waters and maintaining the networks needed to fulfill its mandate, all the while having to deal with powerful players resisting and wanting full autonomy. The interview below delves into how the UN copes with the aforementioned pressures within the concrete context of a specific UN agency, the United Nations Volunteers (UNV) program. The exploration is made by interviewing the UNV's Executive Coordinator, Mr. Olivier Adam, and applying the three-pillar model (abbreviated 3-P-Model), developed in 2019 by an international team of editors and authors (see *Three Pillars of Organization and*

P. Wollmann (✉)
Bonn, Germany
e-mail: pw@peterwollmann.com

P. Wollmann et al. (eds.), *Organization and Leadership in Disruptive Times*, Future of Business and Finance, https://doi.org/10.1007/978-3-030-63034-8_9

Leadership in Disruptive Times by Peter Wollmann, Frank Kühn, and Michael Kempf [editors], SpringerNature, 2020).

2 Recap of the Three-Pillar Model

The 3-P-Model[1] was created to address the urgent need of global institutions in the current volatile, uncertain, complex, and ambiguous (VUCA) world, in order to provide adequate solutions to the questions of how such institutions should be organized and managed in a dynamic way, how to get commitment to a clear direction and belief, and how to develop and connect the valuable resources such institutions need to create impact and value. This includes going on the necessary journey even without all final clarifications by experimenting, prototyping, and piloting ideas and approaches to find the right step-by-step development path.

The three main design principles for this type of modern organization leadership can be described as follows:

- *Sustainable purpose*: The people in the organization but also its key stakeholders need to know the mandate of the organization and the sustainable value it is creating.
  The mandate has to remain very stable; be supported by leaders, staff, and stakeholders; and be inspirational. Key representatives of the organization have to live the mandate.
  Or in other words, the mandate gives clear and convincing orientation on the right level that aligns and inspires people to go for a joint endeavor, which makes the people involved confident, inspired, and proud to be part of and contribute to it.
- *Travelling organization*: The organization needs to understand that it is continuously on a journey toward the best possible result and joint success, in the context of the agreed sustainable purpose, coping with all—partly unforeseeable—influences. On the map, it will potentially have to zigzag, always exploring the best path between poles, alternatives, and options. Sometimes the people in the organization don't know the whole environment and thus have to take smaller steps and explore the terrain.
  Even if they don't know what they will have to face around the next bend and what the best result will then be, they believe in their motivation and capabilities to manage it. This makes a fundamental difference to the illusion of consistency, strategic stability, and structural continuity in disruptive times. Travelling organizations need holistic agility in their mindset and DNA, covering an agile mentality, self-reflection, readiness to embrace change, and willingness to deliver.
  People in a travelling organization are curious, open, and impartial; have the

[1] *Three Pillars of Organization and Leadership in Disruptive Times: Navigating Your Company Successfully Through the 21st Century Business World* (Wollmann, P.; Kühn, F.: Kempf, M. (Ed.) (2020); Cham/CH: Springer Nature).

capacity for self-reflection; are experimental; and cope well with uncertainty, stress, special challenges, and unforeseen obstacles.

- *Connecting resources*: The organization has to be aware that impact, value, and efficiency need connectivity between individuals; between people and organizations or institutions; between diverse global experts and influences; between different political and social systems and cultures, etc.; between ways of working and customer needs; and between strategy and skills. This means managing connectivity, preventing unconnected structural silos and boxed competencies, and focusing on multilateral incentives and behaviors. And there is one additional huge advantage: only with an intelligent and flexible connectivity is it possible to balance the (increasingly) different interests between its multiple key stakeholders. This is a systemic asset that is not to be underestimated.

Based on the aforementioned three principles, the three-pillar model (3-P-Model) was built and its application tested and described mostly in, or with reference to, the private sector. But it is striking how well the model can also be applied in the public sector, including international institutions such as the UN, as we will see shortly.

3 Interview with Olivier Adam, Executive Coordinator of the United Nations Volunteers Program

3.1 Introduction of Olivier Adam

Olivier Adam is the current Executive Coordinator of the United Nations Volunteers (UNV) program since 2 January 2017. He joined the UNV after having served as the United Nations Development Program (UNDP) Deputy Regional Director and Deputy Assistant Administrator of the Regional Bureau for Europe, Commonwealth of Independent States (2014–2016). Prior to this, Olivier was the Manager of the UNDP Bratislava Regional Center (2012–2014) and before that UN Resident

Coordinator/UNDP Resident Representative in Ukraine (2009–2012). He served in different capacities at UNDP headquarters in New York, Argentina, and Haiti and has a wide UN experience for more than 30 years. Olivier holds a Master's degree in Public Administration from the Kennedy School of Government at Harvard University and a Master in Economics from the London School of Economics and Political Science and is a graduate of the Paris Institute of Political Studies (Sciences-Po).

3.1.1 The Interview

Question

Olivier, we had a lot of conversations about the 3-P-Model, based on the recent book *Three Pillars of Organization and Leadership in Disruptive Times* in the last couple of months. And we also spoke about the big challenges for the UN in general and for your UN agency specifically. In this context, we touched on the question of whether, or to what extent, the 3-P-Model is applicable to the UN and thinking accordingly creates some value.

Answer

Oh, I am very convinced that the 3-P-Model and all the examples and conclusions based on it are of significant value and applicable also for the UN and its entities. Applied concretely, it helps to make things really transparent from a different perspective.

Question

So, might we perhaps start with the first pillar, the sustainable purpose?

Answer

Sure, that's an easy one. The sustainable purpose of the UN—its value proposition—is perfectly documented in the UN Charter, which describes, on the one hand, the UN's mandate and, on the other, the value that the UN adds to the world. The UN Charter is, in general, very inspirational. It was created after the Second World War, in order to prevent similar conflicts or catastrophes and to rebuild parts of the world post-war. So, coming from this, it has been engaging and is still engaging people all over the world to support it.

If we go more into detail—such as, for example, defending children's rights or the support for refugees—the purpose of the UN in such thematic areas is intuitively transparent and finds immediate commitment. The same is valid for the special mandate of the UN to fight climate change and its impacts. Or think of the World Health Organization (WHO) and its crucial role in the current Covid-19 pandemic. There is a nearly infinite number of similar or comparable examples which are based on well-recognized and accepted principles.

There is significant demand for global order in the world—such as for reasons of stronger economic stability—perhaps today more than 50 or 60 years ago. The UN, with its diverse bodies, has the purpose to build, detail and further develop this global order. The limited success of attempts to bypass the UN in some cases confirms the necessity of official UN mandates for acting—but for this, the UN needs its strong global mandate, built on a clear and transparent purpose in general and also in defined situations.

It is important to add that the UN is a global institution which has to spend money on its approved projects and activity, not to make money. That means that the money spent has to be raised beforehand by the UN through not only the Member States' annual financial contributions but also through volunteer contributions for special initiatives or projects supported by Member States.

Question

That means that the overall purpose is accepted and only challenged in certain contexts, for example, on how to concretely proceed in a defined initiative?

Answer

Absolutely. You must consider that, often, an overall direction finds complete support, but the detailed elaboration for implementation affects different interests and, thus, must be carefully negotiated and balanced.

Question

What about the idea of the "travelling organization," does it reflect the continuous change and the needed agility of the UN?

Answer

I would like to answer this question together with a link to your third pillar "Connectivity."

In general, we have some significant environmental constraints for our "journeys" such as in our respective UN agencies, in our UN projects and initiatives, etc.

The constraints may relate, for example, to the mobilization of funds, the fundraising might be connected with some preconditions—or to the available resources—we might not have the full autonomy to assemble the teams for a defined journey. This has different reasons. On the one hand, the UN and the UN agencies are governed by different bodies. Our stakeholders, such as the Member States, have different interests and objectives and carefully insist on being sufficiently represented in all contexts in our agencies and our projects.

Referring to the UN agency I represent—the United Nations Volunteers program—we mobilize volunteers for UN projects and initiatives in areas such as peacekeeping, security, human rights development, humanitarian issues, medical emergencies like Ebola, etc. UNV as an organization has a dual mandate: on the one hand, to support Member States to deliver on the 2030 Agenda through volunteerism as an effective means of implementation and people engagement, and on the other, to support the UN system to deliver on the 2030 Agenda through the engagement of UN Volunteers. UNV manages a global talent pool of approximately 36,000 candidates who have particular capabilities, skills and expertise in approximately 170 categories of work, or what we call "profiles."

When a particular request comes in from a UN entity, the criteria for the placement of UN Volunteers has to reflect beyond their availability and their "technical" profiles but also in diversity and inclusion, such as balance in representation of gender and nationality. However, when responding to urgent crises, UN Volunteers are often deployed in teams with limited onboarding, which is not the best precondition for having a mindset as a travelling organization. On the other hand, our UN Volunteers go into their assignments with a strong volunteerism mindset and are very committed, flexible and willing to make a valuable contribution to their host entities' mandates. As it is our organization's responsibility and duty of care to the UN Volunteers, UNV ensures that the volunteers are properly insured with a fair monthly volunteer living allowance provided.

Question
I could imagine that this puts a strong focus on connectivity.

Answer
That's absolutely right. For example, UNV has representation in about 60 countries to cultivate close relationships built on mutual trust with Member States and other UN entities. These representations, or what we call UNV Field Units, are necessary to be able to act efficiently and with flexibility in case of an urgent demand. In 2019, we had 8282 UN Volunteers serving with 54 UN entities in 153 different countries.

This is only possible if one has—beyond a professional and continuously updated database—a network of close and trustful contacts to the Representatives of the diverse UN entities, Member States, other international institutions, etc. Using these connections, it is possible to often get great teams in place at short notice and smoothly commence and deliver on the relevant work.

To create the preconditions, my Deputy and I travel all over the world to cultivate the needed relationships with the key contacts and to solve urgent issues related to our Volunteers. Only in personal conversations do we get the valuable background information we need, which is all part of strategically communicating and coordinating with our UN partners.

Let me explain this further with an example. If we have an Ebola outbreak in a country and need a certain number of medical specialists and service people there within 72 hours, UNV first checks the UNV global talent pool database and identifies candidates with the right profile and experience and checks the potential candidate's availability. UNV then proceeds to contact key reference persons in the various UN entities linked to responding to medical emergencies to get more potential candidates to be contacted, checked and—once identified as selected candidates—briefed and activated. This might also be a step-by-step process where UNV deploys a core team immediately and gradually scales up according to the needs of profiles to further expand the team.

The reasons why the UNV program works well, despite all constraints, are mainly due to the high commitment of both the UNV staff and the UN Volunteers dedicated to supporting the UN system to deliver on the 2030 Agenda, as well as the diversity of candidates in UNV's global talent pool database and the professional network of partnerships the organization has developed. It is truly a connection between the so-called "travelling mindset" and "connecting resources" of the diversity and expertise of our Volunteers. And to add one more aspect: the quality of the UN Volunteers is a success factor to make donors and UN entities satisfied.

Overall, the more competent and successful an organization is in their "journey," the more support and resources the organization will mobilize from donors. Being really good as a "travelling organization" means that the organization is agile.

I think the UNV program is a really good and concrete example of a "travelling organization" within the context of the UN.

Question
I could imagine that this puts some significant pressure on the UN's human resources.

Answer
That is right. When hiring somebody as a UN staff with a permanent contract, you have to be sure that the person fits very well. Compared to the private sector, it is very difficult to let go of a UN staff member who is on a permanent contract. That's the reason why the category of UN consultants with contracts for a limited time period was introduced: to ensure people adapt and fit well within a certain team.

We have a real "civil service situation" to cope with. I already mentioned the other constraints for hiring in terms of the needed political balance of gender and diversity. So, you need to have special management skills to successfully lead in this framework.

The profile for UN staff, beyond technical skills, is quite clear. Successful candidates who work for the UN have to be very flexible and agile. They have to know that they will often be in unfamiliar and extreme situations. They have to also be able to connect and build trust with relevant stakeholders to successfully deliver on a UN entities' mission.

Overall, I think that your 3-P-Model is applicable generally to institutions like the UN, and specifically to UN entities like the UNV program. The concept helps to understand situations and demands from a different perspective, so it is really valuable.

4 Conclusion

On a meta-level, the 3-P-Model can be easily and successfully applied even in the context of global institutions like the UN. The three pillars help to concretely understand the demand of action in terms of purpose, and especially connectivity, and the necessity of developing coping mechanisms for keeping the mindset of a travelling organization also in frameworks with some constraints. Enterprises can learn from this situation even though they act in a significantly smaller context.

5 Lessons Learned and Practical Takeaways

One of the key insights from an intensive look at the UNV is that a strong and convincing purpose, together with a feeling of urgency and importance, has the strength to quickly form high-performing teams of people who have not necessarily met before. The crucial precondition is "only" that the potential candidates have been carefully selected and registered in a community or via recommendations of trusted professionals in the network of the responsible manager. This means that the necessary human resources work has to be accomplished upfront, even before the project to be started was known. People fitting these contexts have a special personality; they are professional experts in something; they are idealistic and ready to support global society; they are curious, flexible, and ready for journeys into unknown areas; they are pragmatic and solution-oriented; and they know how to connect.

What does this mean for enterprises, how can this be translated? The more the sustainable purpose of an enterprise and/or of one of its projects links with people's beliefs, values, and desires to contribute to something significant, the easier teams with the mindset of a "travelling organization" can be built up. The enterprise's HR has to regard the linked general personality attributes during the selection process and afterward to facilitate testing the further development in concrete projects of the enterprise. So, a documented overview of appropriate candidates for demanding projects and journeys is built up and updated on a regular basis.

In communication, it makes sense that the enterprise—or any kind of organization—gets straight in its own mind, what its own project, comparable to an endeavor such as a UN assignment in an Ebola area, would look like and how this could be described to candidates. The chosen narrative should create a comparable desire and motivation.

Peter Wollmann has been a responsible manager, initiator, mentor, and facilitator in large, predominantly global transformations and strategic developments for almost 40 years. His specialties are the implementations of the three-pillar model in organizations and focused setting checks to identify strength, weaknesses, opportunities, and threats and facilitate optimization measures. Since 2017, Peter has been working independently in organizational projects and future initiatives. After graduating in mathematics and physics from the University of Bonn, he began his professional career at the Deutsche Herold, the then insurance group of Deutsche Bank, took on strategic leadership, and most recently was program director for global transformations in the Zurich Insurance Company (ZIC). In his professional network, he brought his experience and strategic thinking to the development of various leading companies. He is the author and publisher of a number of books and articles on strategy, leadership, and project and project portfolio management. He also founded a wine business: VinAuthority.

The Impact of Platform Economies on the Urban Structure

Mersida Ndrevataj and Peter Wollmann

Abstract

In the digital age, cities are more and more organized around platform economies. These digitally based platforms are redefining urban life and transforming our relationship with space and people, with the consequences becoming more and more evident, currently even exacerbated by the Covid-19 crisis.

The aim of this article is therefore to analyze the ongoing transformation, using the 3-P-Model, developed in the book *Three Pillars of Organization and Leadership in Disruptive Times: Navigating Your Company Successfully Through the 21st Century Business World* (Wollmann, P.; Kühn, F.: Kempf, M. (Ed.) (2020); Cham/CH: Springer Nature), and identify the urban dimension of platform economy leaders, such as Airbnb, to measure its economic and social impact.

The first part of the article focuses on some generic characters of the business model of platform economy leaders such as the model's creative aspects, its geographical dimensions, and its global nature.

The second part focuses on the costs and benefits of an urban economy based on digital platforms and, in particular, the case of Airbnb. Through a theoretical analysis of the case of Venice city, we investigate different issues like the production of a monoculture industry linked to tourism; the "digital gentrification" of the urban centers linked to the increase in costs of living and housing prices, changing employment dynamics; and the "devitalization" of public space.

On the basis of the preceding considerations, the final section attempts to give some different governmental and entrepreneurial responses to the consequences of the platform economy business model.

M. Ndrevataj (✉)
Venice, Italy
e-mail: mersida_n@hotmail.it

P. Wollmann
Bonn, Germany
e-mail: pw@peterwollmann.com

P. Wollmann et al. (eds.), *Organization and Leadership in Disruptive Times*, Future of Business and Finance, https://doi.org/10.1007/978-3-030-63034-8_10

It is becoming evident how important broad discussions on the real sustainable purpose of cities to be strived for by the city authorities are, how difficult the journey is that cities are going through at present with the platform economies as a driver, how critically some influences of platform economy business have to be highlighted, and what this demands of all stakeholders: authorities, citizens, and the public and private sectors.

1 Structure Details

The concrete analysis, descriptions, and insights in the case study of Venice are framed by meta-level general considerations valid for all cities.

2 Introduction

In the last decade, one of the main drivers of urban transformation has been the rise of the platform economy which has led to the digitalization of everyday practices of work, study, commerce, travelling, and socialization and has had a strong impact on the traditional urban economy and its local development model.

In the platform economy, also known as the web economy or digital economy, we can recognize a wide range of sectors, from e-commerce to social networks or to the sharing economy, and well-known players such as Facebook, Airbnb, Amazon, Uber, WeWork, Scribd, Ouishare, Couchsurfing, Etsy, Prontopia, Kickstarter, etc. (Srnicek 2017).

In urban planning, the platform economy can be related to the term digital infrastructure as it has contributed to the invention or redefinition of a new socio-spatial structure based on information technology (Zimmerman and Horan 2004). This invisible structure has modified our consumption attitudes and community interactions and altered our relationship with public space and has led us to a lifestyle that is more geared to comfort and convenience.

In this article we have chosen to discuss one of the most influent sectors of this platform industry, the so-called sharing economy (SE), and explain how it has caused the structure, functions, and life of the contemporary city to mutate. On the one hand, this article discusses how this economic model has contributed to the generation of sharable goods and services and to new opportunities for profit—and on the other hand, its more negative impacts, the impoverishment of urban spaces, and the emergence of a monoculture urban economy, closely related to tourism.

The main characteristics of the digital platform economy (and sharing economy) are the rapid spread and coverage of client demands; high flexibility, scalability and easy accessibility of goods and services; creativity; and authenticity.

But besides these positive aspects, there is a hidden dimension of this economic model related to security, control, and monitoring issues; the conflict between the traditional industries and ways of working and the new and innovative ones; and the general impact on the social and physical structure of the living ecosystem.

We will consider here one of the main players which has changed urban planning tremendously: Amazon (with its impact on the city's retail landscape) and Airbnb (with its impact on real estate and especially on the rental market). The impact is fundamental and leads to serious considerations of systemic and concrete operative levels which can be perfectly expressed using the 3-P-Model, (Wollmann et al. 2020) which was created to address the urgent need of global institutions to find adequate solutions in the current volatile, uncertain, complex, and ambiguous (VUCA) world:

2.1 Purpose Driven

The first pillar of the 3-P-Model stresses the preeminence of a sustainable and convincing purpose for all kinds of organizations including urban societies such as cities, etc. All stakeholders need to know the mandate and philosophy of the organization and the sustainable value it is creating. In the best case, this mandate has to remain very stable, to be supported by all stakeholders, and to be inspirational. Key representatives of the organization have to live the mandate.

In the concrete context of this article, the principle of a sustainable purpose is often contradicted, as the platform economy becomes unsustainable when it contributes to individual or entrepreneurial capital accumulation with nothing in return for the city and its citizens; when it generates a growing economic, social, and spatial inequality. Therefore, the purpose of urban planning in relation to its economic model is to have a sustainable urban economy that generates equally shared profit and is accessible by a wide group of people. In the case of historical cities like Venice, the main purpose of the urban economy might be to "diversify" the offer in order to satisfy the permanent residents' needs and not only those of the tourists. And, furthermore, it should consider a new model of "neighborhood trade" to respond to the needs of a growing elderly population and to the promotion of sustainable mobility.

2.2 Journey Driven

The second pillar of the 3-P-Model stresses the preeminence of a mindset as a "travelling organization": The organization needs to understand that it is continuously on a journey toward the best possible purpose-linked result in the current challenges of, e.g., climate change, environmental issues, economic impacts from crises like the Covid-19 pandemic, etc., coping with all—partly unforeseeable—influences. On the map, it will potentially have to zigzag, always exploring the best path between poles, alternatives, and options with the confidence to manage the journey at all times. People in a travelling organization are curious, open, and impartial; have the capacity for self-reflection; and are experimental and cope well with uncertainty, stress, special challenges, and unforeseen obstacles.

In the concrete context of this article, the perception of being on a journey in an urban planning context is very common. Platform economies have been strongly criticized by urban planners for their negative environmental impact which does not necessarily mean that they should cease to exist, rather they should increase their regeneration capacity and become part of the circular economic model that urban planning is aiming for in the future. Let us remind ourselves that a joint successful journey to the future also means a joint responsibility for the environment!

A joint journey requires us to further consider the importance of collaboration between the global economy and the national and local ones. This need has been made even clearer by the Covid-19 pandemic and the fragility of local services that it has exposed.

2.3 Connectivity Driven

The third pillar of the 3-P-Model stresses the preeminence of the mindset and ability to connect all needed resources: The organization—and so urban society—has to be aware that impact, value, and efficiency need connectivity between individuals; between geographies to learn from each other; between people and organizations or institutions such as associations, universities, and scientific boards; between diverse global experts and influences; between the different political and social systems and cultures; etc.

In the concrete context of this article, the realization of connectivity is very demanding as so many different interests have to be aligned. City authorities are facing an increasing lack of trust from their citizens due to their inability to properly understand their citizens' needs and rights. Therefore, in order to make the platform economy a reliable urban economic sector, the connectivity of human and environmental resources becomes a crucial driver. On the one hand, a better connection of the local economic model with the context where it is applied is needed. The economy has to adapt, it has to be city-based, and it has to define its purposes in collaboration with the cities' and citizens' needs. In this way, the connectivity of territorial resources with the enterprising capabilities of this economic model could offer a multitude of innovative good practices. At the same time, this can only happen by means of good collaboration and communication between the various forms of interaction—between the large number of stakeholders, authorities with the experts, old businesses with new platform economy businesses, businesses in general with citizens, providers with their urban clients, private with public sector, etc.

The above considerations show the relevance and applicability of the 3-P-Model—with its "pillars" of "sustainable Purpose," "travelling organization," and "connecting resources"—to urban planning aspects in the context of platform economy business. These considerations will be explored later in the article using the example of Airbnb.

3 Some Considerations on the Rise of the Sharing Economy Business Model: The Origin and Developments of the Home-Sharing and Short-Term Rentals

3.1 The Rise of the Sharing Economy

The sharing economy emerged following the global financial crisis of 2008, in an environmental context characterized by economic, social, and political transition. It developed, following Jeremy Rifkin's reflections on *The Third Industrial Revolution* and the possibility of transforming that crisis into an opportunity for sustainable growth, in three main directions (Rifkin 2011):

1. Due to the environmental crisis, awareness of climate change and the scarcity of natural resources was rising, so there was an opportunity to embrace an alternative journey where our relationship with earth could be recovered.
2. Due to the growing urban population and increasing economic inequality and unemployment, there was an opportunity to make the economy more accessible, increase the redistribution of wealth, and decrease inequality.
3. Due to the technological spread and connection, it was possible to manage economic activity differently. Therefore, there was an opportunity to make traditional entrepreneurship and ways of working and collaborating more innovative; it was possible to increase the efficiency of economic activity through new means of communication, through the empowerment of resources and the new modes of mobility (transportation logistics).

Sharing economy, peer-to peer-economy, new economy, collaborative economy, or experience economy, with slightly different meanings, all these terms refer to the same new business model which promotes a form of collaborative consumption and is based on the practices of exchange and sharing of resources and services (Botsman and Rogers 2010). The sharing practice is based on digital platforms that serve as an intermediation hub between producers of resources or services (individuals, micro-entrepreneurs, freelancers, etc.) and users who want to use those resources or services (goods, time, skills, money, experience). The basic principle of the sharing economy model is based on the reuse of underutilized resources in order to reduce the use of limited natural resources and on the valorization of new skills and agile ways of working. Moreover, collaboration facilitated by digital hyper-connection can generate profit or economic savings on the one hand and, on the other, promote social experience and new forms of digital communities.

3.1.1 What Was the Impact of these Digital, Environmental, and Social Trends on the Evolution and Organization of Cities?

This digital shift was challenging for urban social and physical assets, too. But, what was the nexus between the new economy and the urban planning debate? How does this invisible platform affect the visible and physical structure of the city?

The emerging climate change as well as the information and technology shift brought new concepts to urban planning such as smart cities and sustainable urban development (European Union 2020 strategy), global cities (Sassen 2001), and creative cities (Carta 2007).

Urban government started addressing questions such as how could the city ensure a better quality of life to more people living in urban conurbations? How could the city provide new job opportunities to the traditional enterprises that were challenging the digital shift? How could the city increase its productivity without externalities and through a green or ecological footprint? How could all this be achieved through the new sharing economy model?

3.2 Home-Sharing Practice

According to Rachel Botsman, the "sharing economy is an economic system that unlocks the value of underused assets through platforms that match 'needs' with 'haves in ways that create greater efficiency and access" (Botsman and Rogers 2010). This system provides resources and services through different forms of value exchange: rent, swap, borrow, lend, etc.

Luis is a young mechanical engineer who has moved to Venice for work. He loves to walk around the city in his free time and discover every secret corner of it. Lately he joined the website Couchsurfing to meet new travelers and share his knowledge of the city with them.

Mary is an architect who lives and works in Milan. She lives alone in a very large house located in the city center. She enjoys her work, but sometimes finds it very demanding and her job is not sufficiently well paid to enable her to pay her monthly expenses. She has recently decided to rent a room in her house on Airbnb so she can make extra income and, at the same time, take the opportunity to meet and socialize with people from all around the world.

Alicia is a retired teacher who lives alone in a beautiful house in Turin. She loves to travel with her friend Laura and experience new countries and cultures. Both have recently registered on HomeExchange and plan to exchange Alicia's house with that of an elderly couple living in Lisbon during the first 2 weeks of August.

The three protagonists in the above stories have something in common: all of them are sharing their property with other people through a digital platform, in different forms of value exchange.

3.3 Home-Sharing Economy and Tourism

The widespread use of information and communication technology also changed the travelling experience. The traditional tourism industry became one of the primary targets for the sharing economy business model and a new form of short-term rental accommodation emerged in the real-estate market.

Airbnb is certainly one of the main players in the home-sharing market based on a short-term rental and closely related to tourism. The platform connects travelers or people who need accommodation with people who want to offer their home; it gives travelers the opportunity to stay with a local in town and enables homeowners to make extra income by renting out (part of) their property.

Home sharing was conceived as a business model that allows people to generate extra income from renting an underutilized space/room. In order to prevent it from becoming a hotel-like for-profit business, a limit of 30 days per year was introduced. This new limited rental of residential properties has been licensed differently in different contexts.

The success of home sharing has generated new sharing forms that are connected to the tourism industry. One example is Prontopia, an app that travelers can use to contact a local guide who can help them reach their rented accommodation, prevent them from getting lost in the city, and give them local tips.

A first provisional analysis shows that the rise of the platform economy or sharing economy has had a significant impact on the sustainable purpose of the city and its urban planning demands, its development journey (and the necessary mindset as a travelling organization), and its connectivity (its ability to best connect resources, etc.).

This new type of economy has been on the rise for a decade now. What do we know about the impact of the sharing economy on the urban fabric? What are the challenges and opportunities of this business model for the future?

A short but comprehensive insight into the relation between urban planning and the sharing economy will be further developed using the example of the city of Venice.

What we assume at this point is that the sustainability of the platform economy and its journey into the future depends on its ability to develop its strategies in collaboration with the city in order to co-design an attractive local development model and discuss and communicate this in a transparent way.

4 The Death and Life (Jacobs 1993) of the Home-Sharing Economy

4.1 Enhancing the Cultural Tourism Industry

As the interconnected world and the so-called platformization industry evolves, the urban factory transforms itself into an "intelligent machine" for the production and exchange of goods and services in an economic network of global scale. In the new urban context, tourism takes on an important role: it becomes an agent of change in the urban economy and is used by city governments as a tool for the creative economic revival of the city, especially in cities with significant cultural and historical values.

In the course of a few years, the innovative tourism industry, together with the home-sharing business and all the other intrinsic sectors, has managed to trigger an invasive and frenetic expansion, changing the morphological profile and the very function of the city.

The promotion and growth of tourism has led to a break in the balance between city users and residents of urban centers. The urban landscape, its image and soul, is undergoing a constant transformation to respond more and more to the needs of temporary residents and less and less to the permanent ones. The main streets are full of souvenir shops, clubs, restaurants, and of course signs advertising rooms for rent; they have become the symbol of a monocultural and superficial tourist industry. In other words, it is a process of impoverishment of the soul of the public space, the conversion from a meeting space to a consumer space to an impoverishment of the tourist experience itself.

This has led to an increased cost of living and a reduction in the quality of life for the residents of urban centers and consequently to a process of depopulation, or rather a process of tourism gentrification.

4.2 The Case of Airbnb in Venice

In the historical city of Venice, the new home-sharing economy matched with the tourism industry managed to progress rapidly in a disruptive business model for the traditional short-term rental sector as well as the long-term one.

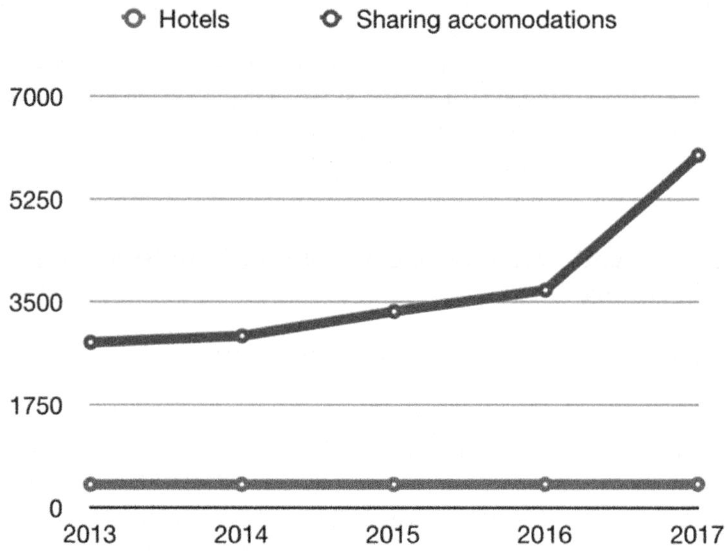

Fig. 1 The supply of tourist accommodation in Venice 2013–2017 (Source: Comune di Venezia, 2018)

The graph in Fig. 1 shows the comparison between the growth of the hotel availability and that of extra-hotel accommodation (comparable to sharing accommodation) in the city of Venice between 2013 and 2017 (Table 1: Comune di Venezia, 2018). This comparison clearly shows how the rising demand for accommodation from tourists is covered by the extra-hotel sector.

One of the most successful home-sharing economy platforms in Venice (and worldwide) is Airbnb. And it's generally said that the evident success of the platform in the tourist accommodation market comes from its promising slogan for an authentic local experience for the new millennium tourist: "live like a local."

Airbnb was initially introduced as a home-sharing economy platform that allowed householders (hosts) to rent to travelers (guests) a room in their home or a second property for a limited time (up to 30 days) in return for extra income. But in the meantime, Airbnb has turned into a proper commercial business, often abusive.

Box: Airbnb Statistics

According to Inside Airbnb estimates, on August 12, 2019, the total number of Airbnb official listings in the Municipality of Venice was 8907 with the following characteristics:

75% of the official listings rent the entire houses.
77% of the hosts could be identified as active hosts—this category includes ads with at least one review received in the 180 days prior to the reference date.
59% of the listings could be defined as commercial activities.
63% of the listings are rented by multi-hosts.
61% of the total reservations have been rented for 60+ nights during the last year.
75% of the total listings are located in the historical center where *82%* rent the entire houses.
27% of the listing are from noncommercial hosts.

In Venice, according to the Inside Airbnb (http://insideairbnb.com/venice/report.html) database, it is evident that the Airbnb accommodation platform is primarily used for commercial purposes (which means that during the year hosts rent their properties for more than 58 days and their empty rooms for more than 88 days) and that the sector is controlled by landlords identified as multi-hosts (hosts who rent more houses or rooms spread throughout the city) (Box above).

The database also shows very unequal financial revenue between multi-hosts and noncommercial hosts: 27% of hosts manage 20% of ads and earn 4% revenue and 5% of hosts own 30% of ads and 5% of hosts earn 35% of the total generated by ads.

Airbnb has additional significant impact on the housing sector and on the social structure of the cities. Due to the phenomenon of "platformization" and the city's tourist specialization, Venice's historical center has experienced a growth in short-term rental offers and therefore a lack of availability in the long-term rental market. This shrinking offer and the increasing market price for long-term residential

Fig. 2 Signs protesting about the abusive short-term rental accommodation hanging outside the window of a building located near the Rialto Bridge: "Stop abusive B&B! Violated House." (Photos by Mersida Ndrevataj, used with permission. All rights reserved)

housing has become one of the main reasons for the rapid decline in the numbers of people living in the city and their displacement to peripheral areas.

> In relation to the inhabitants, there are 12 Airbnb ads for every 100 residents. In relation to the total housing stock, about 12% of the housing is on Airbnb.

The physical and morphological structure of the city has been profoundly changed by the pervasive presence of short-term rented houses. The city has been invaded vertically by Airbnb apartments (entire buildings) (Fig. 2) and horizontally (entire neighborhoods).

Lastly, along with Airbnb's horizontal expansion, we encounter the proliferation of complementary facilities for tourist purposes and the alteration of the social and economic structure of the city and its quality of life. According to the research carried out by Visentin and Bertocchi (2019), the decrease in the number of local residents in the historical center of Venice is linked to increased tourism in the residential areas and to the decline in services for residents, leading the city into a monoculture for the tourism industry. The research examines the geographical location and dynamics of Airbnb accommodation, its link with the traditional accommodation sector, and the complementary tourist services (food shops or nonfood shops).

The results show how Airbnb accommodation and food shops are located close to the main tourist sights and how they spread intensively through the residential areas of the city. Meanwhile, traditional accommodation and nonfood shops are mainly located inside the area popular with tourists. Therefore, the presence of food shops and Airbnb accommodation in residential areas means that we find a mixed use of space for tourists and residents. This changes the life of the residents significantly and requires balancing measures.

5 The Impact of Covid-19 on the Platform Economy

The situation created by the pandemic has highlighted the two extreme sides of the platform economy.

On the one hand, it has proved itself to be indispensable in times like these when mobility is limited. The possibility of being able to order shopping online and have it delivered to your home, thus limiting your number of social contacts, and consequently the risk of infection, and saving time with one simple online order, rather than standing in long queues in front of the supermarket, is extremely valuable. Furthermore, it has value as a source of entertainment, learning, working, and of course communication. This is countered by the fact that it can be an unsustainable economic model if we think, for example, of the Airbnb platform.

Venice has had two emergencies within a few months which demonstrated that the economy on which the income of most of its residents is based (around 67% of them are related to the tourism industry) is unsustainable if it is the only source of income. Because of the floods and then the pandemic, the city turned into a large deserted ship. If that weren't enough, both emergencies happened at two crucial times for an urban economy based mainly on tourism: in November, near the New Year festivities, and in February, in the last week of the Venetian carnival.

As early as January 2020, Airbnb renters were already noticing a decrease of 80% of their bookings compared to the same month of the previous year, due exclusively to the pandemic and its initial worldwide spread. However, if everything were to end soon and everything were to go back to the way it was before, the "high season" from May to October would suffer a decrease due to another indirect but very important factor: the postponement of the opening of the Venice Biennale in 2021 and consequently the cancellation of all the bookings by the considerable number of missed *guests*.

Yet there are more bad news for the home-sharing economy! The long-term unsustainability of this economic model has induced some tenants to abandon the platform and the short-term rental model for the long-term one. Based on these facts, the IUAV University of Venice has taken the opportunity to propose to these landlords that they rent their homes at affordable prices to students for an initial 6-month period beginning from September 2020. It is certainly a good opportunity to restart the city and build a more liveable urban environment than the previous one, which was dedicated almost exclusively to a transitory population.

6 Challenges and Opportunities of the Tourism-Sharing Economy

Considering the Airbnb experience in the local community of the historical city of Venice, a remediation and an intervention are necessary in order to find a co-solution and promote a more sustainable and responsible form of urban economy.

The challenges and opportunities facing cities dominated by short-term rentals and the future development of the local economy, highlighted also by the Covid-19 pandemic, need to be addressed starting from the following points:

- How can we rethink policies on the urban-sharing economy following the pandemic?
- How can we recover the tourism-sharing economy while restoring the negative effects of the previous conditions?
- How can we make living in urban touristic centers more affordable so that cities are not emptied of inhabitants and filled up with temporary visitors? This is also a precondition to keep tradespeople and other services in city centers.
- How can we promote the welfare of local communities and the idea that the city is a common good (Timo Meynhardt 2019) to which everyone is entitled (residents, city users, tourists)?
- How can we stimulate a responsible market choice based on socio-environmental quality and not only on price or profit?
- How can we activate processes of reusing empty urban spaces capable of generating value in the local communities?

The sustainability of the home-sharing economy and its future journey may depend on its ability to develop a strategy in collaboration with local government.

7 Setting the Right Stage for the Platform Economy

As mentioned above, the platform economy is closely linked to the tourism and housing sectors. Through the use of the platforms, both these activities have led to an overwhelming process of alteration of the socio-spatial structure of the city and its economy.

7.1 Taxation

One of the most acknowledged benefits of the platform economy is certainly the possibility of an economic return from the use of underutilized resources and the easy accessibility by a wide range of the population. But, as we have seen in the case of Airbnb in Venice, facilitated and uncontrolled access to the short-term rental market has led to the saturation of supply and, moreover, to unequal competition with the traditional accommodation sector. As a result, the taxation of rental activity was introduced and adopted as a form of regulation of the operating framework and market competitiveness. "In Italy there are two tax regimes for short-term rental activity: the ordinary tax regime IRPEF (taxation is calculated on the basis of total annual income, ranges from 23% to 43% and allows for various deductions of costs and expenses); the flat-rate tax regime (introduced in 2017, it forces platforms and other intermediaries to levy taxes and establishes a flat-rate of 21% to be applied to the income generated by the rental but does not provide for deductions)." (https://www.airbnb.it/help/article/1394/ospitare-responsabilmente-in-italia) In addition to the taxation of hosts on their rental income, there is also a visitor's tax levied by some local or regional governments and which varies from one city to another.

7.2 Platform Innovation for Sustainable and Unique Travel Experiences

However, the national and local taxations have proved to be inappropriate and inefficient political restrictions if assumed only as a quantitative measure, so they must be integrated with other qualitative ones. As the supply of short-term rental accommodation grows, the income opportunities for the hosts decrease, and the quality of a multiplicated and standardized service is threatened. It is therefore important that platforms regenerate their original attractiveness and generate socio-environmental value. In the following we mention three different experiences of home-sharing platform regulations and innovation:

(a) Airbnb self-regulation
Grottole (https://news.airbnb.com/it/a-grottole-matera-per-cambiare-vita-e-salvare-il-borgo/) (Matera, Italy) is a depopulated historic city of 300 inhabitants with more than 600 empty houses and is an example of self-regulation and corporate social responsibility by Airbnb that consists in the revitalization of the area through so-called active or temporary citizens. Together with a local nonprofit organization called the Wonder Grottole Airbnb, it offers four citizens the possibility to move to the village in order to contribute to its rebirth and cultural enhancement of its historical heritage by engaging in voluntary activities.
(b) Eco-friendly home-sharing economy (eco from ecological, environmentally friendly)
Casa Anconeta (https://casanconeta.it) in Venice is an example of an ecobnb experience that promotes a new form of sustainable traveling. In addition to the opportunity to share a home and a local experience, the initiative aims to promote slow mobility, and to do this the price of the stay is based on the means of transport used to reach the city and the number of days of your stay.
(c) Equo-friendly home-sharing economy (equo from equity, fair-share of profit)
Fairbnb.coop (https://fairbnb.coop/it/) is an accommodation platform that promotes an equo-sustainable form of tourism and supports local initiatives and projects. The platform regulates competitiveness and quality of service by

giving only one possibility of home renting to the host. Besides, guests may choose to invest 50% of their booking commission in a project of their choice in the local community they are visiting.

7.3 ID Code Against Abuse

In terms of the quality and quantity control of the provided service, another difficulty often encountered in the short-term rental market is the abuse, i.e., the presence in the territory of houses or apartments that are not registered for tourist use.

With the aim of managing and stopping this phenomenon of illegality and tax evasion, the Italian government has introduced a *regional identification code* (comma 4 art. 13 quater del decreto-legge, 2019) which allows greater market transparency. The identification code is issued following a verification of the security and safety of the property, an attempt to protect the consumer and guarantee quality of the service.

Paris has adopted the same political restriction in order to have a transparent market and to be able to monitor compliance with the total number of nightly bookings granted (120 nights a year).

7.4 Zoning Restrictions with the Aim to Fight Progressive Spatial Spread of Shareable Housing and Digital Gentrification of Urban Residential Areas

The definition of strategic economic areas has been introduced as a form of limiting the spread of tourist accommodation in urban residential areas and consequently their impoverishment as a result of the pressure of tourist numbers. Barcelona was one of the European cities that adopted this zoning policy to counter the congestion of the city's tourist rentals through the implementation of a special urban plan (Peuat (https://ajuntament.barcelona.cat/ecologiaurbana/en/bodies-involved/citizen-participation/tourist-accommodation)) that divided the city into four different areas. In the first area, the historic center, the plan forbids new licenses for tourist rentals; in the second area, new licenses are granted provided that the occupancy of tourist apartments remains below a fixed density; in the third area, the one furthest from the historic center, new licenses can be obtained more easily but always with a maximum density quota set by the local government; the fourth area contains new urban areas under construction: these are subject to the same quotas of maximum density as the third area.

8 Conclusion and Takeaways

In this article we have tried to explain the central role of platforms in the creation of the home-sharing economy and the transformation of cities.

The platforms and all the dynamics linked to them such as mass tourism, the housing crisis, or the impoverishment of the quality of space and social interaction show us the gap between the digital logic and the analogical logic of the urban economy development; how individual welfare policy support comes at the expense of collective welfare; how the debate on the issue involves different urban stakeholders (public, private, third sector, civil society); and how the process of understanding and managing the phenomenon needs an inter-sectoral policy.

Moreover, the Covid-19 pandemic has further highlighted the debate and the critical issues related to the platform system. On the one hand, there is hope for the regulation and improvement of the market following the cessation of activity, but on the other hand, the economic crisis has further legitimized the need and right of homeowners to derive income. Following this pandemic, the question of the future of the collaborative economy implies reconfiguring a model of urban economic development.

In the following, considering the multifaceted impacts of the platform economy, we consider the role of the platform economy in the sustainable purpose of urban governments, and we build on our lessons learned about the topic. We focus on the critical issues and weaknesses of the system in order to regenerate its opportunities and benefits, and we consider the role of the platform economy in the sustainable purpose of the urban governments.

1. First of all, it has become evident that the 3-P-Model can be very well applied to the public sector in an urban planning context—it helps to analyze deficits especially in a situation of a significant transformation (like the rise of platform economies).

   In general, it makes a lot of sense to discuss fundamental topics at the meta-level of the 3-P-Model instead of getting bogged down in the "technical debate" of single issues. The 3-P-Model gives the right orientation to solve single questions—and this is valid for all of the three pillars.
2. The identified significant deficits with also significant (negative) impacts are:
   - The lack of a widely shared sustainable purpose of urban development between the local government and civic society—what sort of life should a city offer and guarantee to its citizens and stakeholders? What should it stand for? What is the intuitive narrative and video in the heads which is animating and promising?
   - The lack of a well-guided journey into the unknown area of the future, giving the involved people the feeling that they are respected, supported, and appreciated in contexts where openness to change and exploration of the new is called for.
   - The lack of sufficient connectivity: the various parties in the urban planning context often don't cooperate sufficiently.

3. On a more detailed level, we can state that the platform economy has been widely criticized for its negative impacts on the urban structure and on the quality of life of the local communities. Therefore, for a long-term sustainability, these platforms must embrace a community-based business model which reflects the sustainable purpose of urban areas. But on the other hand, besides the criticism and policies of regulation, the local government needs to consider and sustain the innovative side of these important urban players.
4. We perceive a lack of dialogue between entrepreneurs and urban planners. Using the 3-P-Model, we can analyze this lack of communication and enhance powerful collaboration for future developments. Cities and platforms have to focus more on an interactive and communicative process. It should be carefully considered which people and parties of the urban area and from the outside should be involved in which form on a regular basis. The convening of suitable committees, panels, or bodies for involvement and empowerment, carefully tailored to the individual situation of an urban area and inspired by comparable experiences elsewhere, is crucial.

References

Botsman, R., & Rogers, R. (2010). *What's mine is yours: The rise of collaborative consumption*. New York: Harper Collins.

Carta, M. (2007). *Creative city. Dynamics, innovations, actions*. Trento: List.

comma 4 art. 13 quater del decreto-legge 30 aprile 2019, n. 34 in https://www.gazzettaufficiale.it/eli/id/2019/06/29/19A04303/sg

http://insideairbnb.com/venice/report.html

https://ajuntament.barcelona.cat/ecologiaurbana/en/bodies-involved/citizen-participation/tourist-accommodation

https://casanconeta.it

https://fairbnb.coop/it/

https://news.airbnb.com/it/a-grottole-matera-per-cambiare-vita-e-salvare-il-borgo/

https://www.airbnb.it/help/article/1394/ospitare-responsabilmente-in-italia

Jacobs, J. (1993 [1961]). *The death and life of great American cities*. New York: Random House.

Rifkin, J. (2011). *The third industrial revolution: How lateral power is transforming energy, the economy, and the world*. London: Macmillan.

Sassen, S. (2001). *The global city*. Princeton University Press.

Srnicek, N. (2017). *Platform capitalism*. Oxford: Polity Press.

Timo Meynhardt, T. (2019). Public value. In *International encyclopedia of civil society* (pp. 1277–1282). New York: Springer.

Visentin, F., & Bertocchi, D. (2019). *Tourism excesses in an Venice: An analysis of overtourism icon in overtourism*. Wallingford: CABI.

Wollmann, P., Kühn, F., & Kempf, M. (Eds.). (2020). *Three pillars of organization and leadership in disruptive times – Navigating your company successfully through the 21st century business world*. New York: Springer Nature.

Zimmerman, R., & Horan, T. (2004). *Digital infrastructure: Enabling civil and environmental systems through information technology*. Abington: Routledge.

Further Reading

Gainsforth, S. (2019). *Airbnb città merce*. DeriveApprodi: Storie di resistenza alla gentrificazione digitale.

https://www.youtube.com/watch?v=Uimc9PRxd0M&t=1139s

Oskam, J. (2019). *The future of Airbnb and the sharing economy: The collaborative consumption of our cities*. Channel View Publications.

Slee, T. (2017). *What's yours is mine: Against the sharing economy*. Sribe UK.

Mersida Ndrevataj is an architect and urban planner, currently attending PhD in Urban Planning and Public Policy at the IUAV University of Venice. Her professional objective is to help better shape the built environment through a multidisciplinary research-based and human-centered design process. To this end, she is involved in several academic research projects and works in the field of environmental psychology.

Peter Wollmann has been a responsible manager, initiator, mentor, and facilitator in large, predominantly global transformations and strategic developments for almost 40 years. His specialties are the implementations of the three-pillar model in organizations and focused setting checks to identify strength, weaknesses, opportunities, and threats and facilitate optimization measures. Since 2017, Peter has been working independently in organizational projects and future initiatives. After graduating in mathematics and physics from the University of Bonn, he began his professional career at the Deutsche Herold, the then insurance group of Deutsche Bank; took on strategic leadership; and most recently was program director for global transformations in the Zurich Insurance Company (ZIC). In his professional network, he brought his experience and strategic thinking to the development of various leading companies. He is the author and publisher of a number of books and articles on strategy, leadership, and project and project portfolio management. He also founded a wine business: VinAuthority.

From the Inside and the Outside: A Learning Journey to Mainstream the Digital Transformation in a Federal Enterprise

Janina Kempf

Abstract

This article illustrates the continuous development of a federal enterprise, which acts within the area of its commissioning parties and political agenda setting with employees all over the world. While adhering to sectoral structures, it is essential to connect resources such as talent, expertise, and motivation to create agents of change and enable an effective internal digital transformation. Nevertheless, all employees must be given the possibility to join the digital transformation and get the support that best suits their needs. This directly adds to the digital transformation of the GIZ's service delivery, which was mainstreamed by the implementation of the "digital by default" concept, a concept that leverages the power of digital solutions in each project to achieve its goals in a more efficient, effective, sustainable, transparent, and scalable manner. This is a challenging learning journey, which is the core of a travelling organization.

The concept of the three-pillar model (Wollmann et al., Three pillars of organization and leadership in disruptive times – Navigating your company successfully through the 21st century business world. Heidelberg: Springer, 2020) highlights these considerations.

J. Kempf (✉)
Köln, Germany
e-mail: janina.kempf@me.com

P. Wollmann et al. (eds.), *Organization and Leadership in Disruptive Times*, Future of Business and Finance, https://doi.org/10.1007/978-3-030-63034-8_11

1 Setting the Scene[1]

Before this article illustrates the digital transformation journey of the German development agency *Deutsche Gesellschaft für internationale Zusammenarbeit* (GIZ), GmbH it is necessary to scratch the surface of the structure of this organization to fully grasp the complexity of this rather uncommon construct. GIZ is a public-benefit federal enterprise, which offers implementation and consultancy services in the field of development cooperation to mainly political institutions such as the German government—in particular the Federal Ministry for Economic Cooperation and Development (BMZ)—and many public and private sector clients. GIZ works in a wide variety of areas, including economic development and employment promotion, energy and the environment, and peace and security. Thus, a connection to political agenda setting and ministerial procedures and standards is an integral part of the volatile environment in which GIZ finds itself. Currently, GIZ implements more than 1500 projects in 120 partner countries, which means that although its headquarters are in Germany, the organizations itself is highly decentralized with offices and employees all over the world. More than 20,000 people work with GIZ with roughly 80% located outside Germany and most of them being national staff in their respective countries.

In a nutshell, with its unique conditions such as the dependency on its commissioning parties, its cross-sectoral projects in many partner countries,[2] and its size and decentralized character with employees from very different cultural backgrounds, GIZ is an ideal case study.

In addition to the above, due to its strong sustainable purpose of generating sustainable change and growth together with its partner countries, GIZ maintains a common identity and belonging through all its hierarchical layers and nationalities (Wollmann et al. 2020). This is proven by an extraordinarily high intrinsic motivation, which goes far beyond the financial incentives.

Since GIZ maneuvers around international politics, with changing political agendas and world political events, it has always been, and will always be, a travelling organization which needs to adapt, reflect, and react to uncertainty.

This is a very interesting starting point to capture the very different levels of GIZ's learning journey of its digital transformation—which will certainly never come to an end.

With special regard to the VUCA world evolving worldwide, GIZ needed to ask itself two major questions some years ago:

1. How do we as an organization have to transform and evolve to embrace the global digital transformation with all the challenges and opportunities it brings?
2. And consequently, how must our services develop to react to the digital transformation of our partner countries and thus remain a preferred implementing partner in international development cooperation?

[1]The article reflects the opinion of the author. This does not necessarily reflect the position of GIZ.
[2]Namely, the partner countries of the German development cooperation

These are two big questions, which needed proactive structural changes. One must always bear in mind that GIZ is a state-owned organization, which must use its resources efficiently and is thus limited in its scope for hiring consultancy firms for restructuring and investing in risky and lengthy experiments. Thus, connecting the existing resources and using them beyond the existing silos was and remains one of the major success factors of the digital transformation journey (Wollmann et al. 2020).

Back in 2015, a small team consisting of employees from different departments wrote a framework for digital change and established one of the first cornerstones for operationalizing implementation measures. With this as a foundation and with the support of its management board, GIZ established the project "digital change" as the internal driver for the operationalization of its digital transformation. Together with all units and departments and the management board, this team designed the "target image 'digital change'" to guide the organization toward the same goal and make sure it had one sound vision of a successful transformation, because a target image is both a starting point for change and a reference point for continuity (Carr et al. 1996). This is illustrated by the following eight dimensions (Fig. 1).

All eight dimensions show the nature of a traveling organization, which proactively designs change. However, if you break down the dimensions, it becomes evident that two major distinctions can be made: first, the *internal digital transformation* of the organization and its employees and, second, the *external digital transformation*, which is concerned with the digital transformation of the development cooperation projects implemented with the partner countries. The ultimate goal of this effort is to mainstream digitalization throughout the organization and to offer relevant services to our commissioning parties and partner countries. Although the target image suggests that the internal transformation is more relevant, this assumption is not true. Additionally, it must be clear that neither of these dimensions can stand alone but rather a strong interconnection between them is essential for a holistic transformation.

The importance of a digital maturity analysis: Although this target image has been proven to frame the direction of the digital transformation of the organization, it is vital to critically reflect (1) on the progress and (2) on the perception among the employees of the organization's efforts and (3) to benchmark the organization against others. All this results in an important learning experience for the whole organization and allows for readjustments. Learning and iteration was the focus of this undertaking and lies at the core of a traveling organization.

2 Developing the Organizational Brain: The Internal Digital Transformation

The internal digital transformation has many sublayers ranging from the development and implementation of IT infrastructure to IT security. However, this section of the article focuses on *digital literacy*—the tool to self-empowerment in a

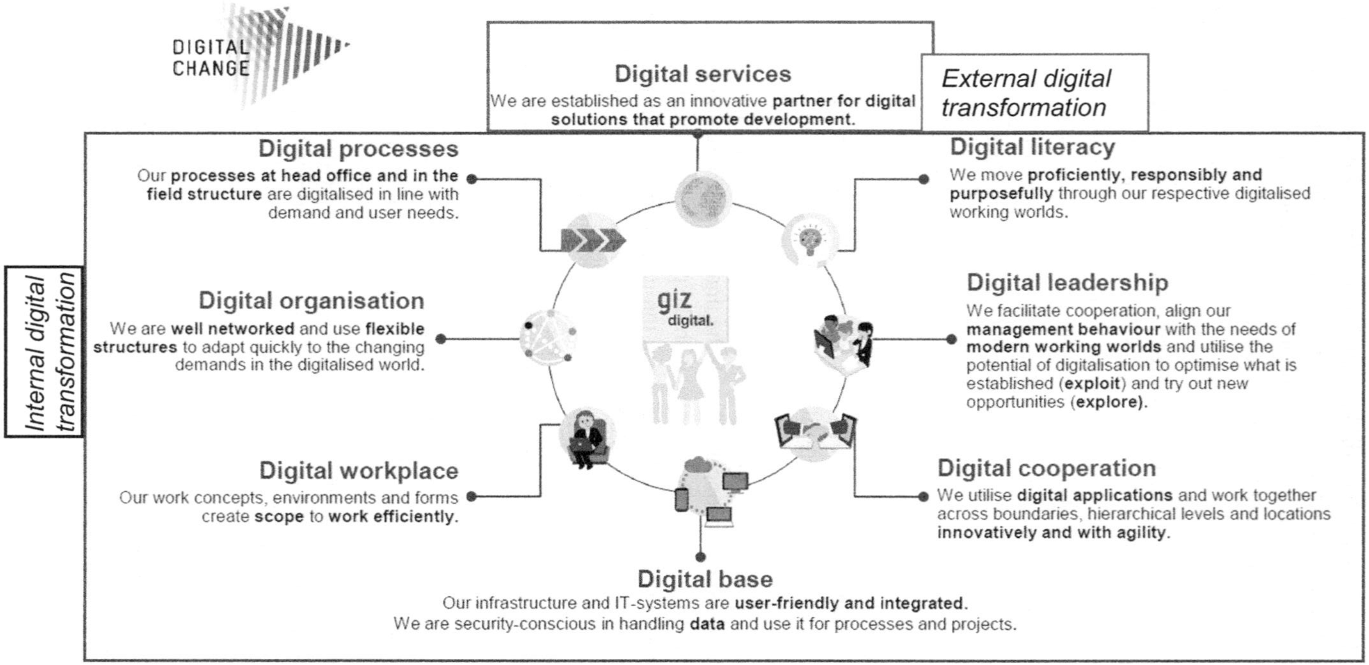

Fig. 1 Target image digital change, GIZ 2018 retrieved from GIZ internal presentation, used with permission

decentralized, connected, and global enterprise that is acting in a diverse and volatile environment.

To highlight the importance, GIZ developed the "Action Plan Digital Literacy" in 2018 and integrated it as one of the major points in its organizational annual goals. The action plan can be translated as a direct implementing measure of the target image "digital change" (see above).

Backed by human and financial resources, the "Action Plan Digital Literacy" is managed by three organizational units—the corporate academy, the human resources department, and DIGITS[3]—a prime example of successfully connecting resources (Wollmann et al. 2020) within an organization but also beyond established structures.

This shows once again that digital transformation must be a joint effort.

The "Action Plan Digital Literacy" consists of four elements:

1. Digital literacy compass (for goals and use, see below)
2. Development of training on digital skills for all employees
3. Virtual learning environment—the development of eLearning courses either as new courses or as virtual courses which were previously delivered in person.
4. The creation and support of digital pioneers, internal change agents, and colleagues ready to provide peer learning on digital skills to their colleagues

When it comes to the development of digital skills, several different roles within the organization can be identified. These findings are also in line with Vahs' (2015) observations on different acceptance levels within an organization's workforce. It is vital to point out that employees might also change their attitude and mindset and therefore need to be addressed differently to be taken on board:

Although this may seem rather black and white, let me exemplify this with very concrete personas. These personas can apply to all functional groups and hierarchical levels.

Early adopters: For an early adopter, the introduction of new software cannot go fast enough. These people require almost no training in new software or digital tools since they will either explore the functionalities themselves or will train themselves using video tutorials.

Opportunity: It has been proven to be highly effective to include these colleagues as multipliers. They can do this by supporting a colleague in using the new tool or supporting a whole team to adopt a new tool in a workshop. They can have the power to motivate others and act as a symbol for the digital transformation of the workforce. Moreover, they push for the introduction of new software and actively ask the IT department to review certain software.

Challenge: The restrictive policies and the very limited number of eligible digital tools of such companies might frustrate the early adopter. He or she might look

[3]DIGITS (Digital Transformation and IT Solutions) is an internal department of the GIZ founded in 2018. Its mandate ranges from coordinating the digital transformation and digitalizing business processes to carrying out governance work for IT security and data management.

for options outside of the realm of tested software. This could lead to data protection issues. Furthermore, as well as being a motivating force for other colleagues, they could run the risk of discouraging colleagues if they use technical jargon that only experts understand. They could also become frustrated by the fact that some tools might need a long time before they are ready for implementation.

Go with the flow: These people use the digital tools that are most helpful for them to complete the tasks required. However, they have no special interest in knowing every hack or trick to make the tools more efficient. They ask for training and are willing to learn.

Opportunity: They are content with every introduction of new digital tools that support them in their daily work, and they will use them very efficiently.

Challenge: For this persona it is difficult to see the interlinkages between the different digital tools, which make them even more powerful and useful. Thus, it is difficult to come up with creative ideas on how to optimize them and adapt them to the specific use case.

Skeptics: This persona questions the effectiveness of digital tools and is suspicious of using them. Skeptics only use digital tools when necessary, but if they can make a phone call instead, they would prefer that. They are very concerned with data protection and are not convinced that these tools are safe to use.

Opportunity: Skeptics provide a reality test and openly communicate shortcomings, which could help optimizing offers of support. Skeptics are rather obsessive about data protection. This competency can be used to raise awareness among other colleagues.

Challenge: With their constant questioning of the digital tools and their vocal concerns, they could intimidate other colleagues and establish a counterproductive environment, in which fellow colleagues do not dare to ask questions.

In addition to the different personas, GIZ's workforce has a wide variety of different job descriptions: from drivers to technical experts on water and waste management or civil engineers but also political advisors on EU-Africa affairs. Consequently, the digital skills they need to excel in their respective functional groups are very different. However, it has been proven helpful to employees to give them guidance on what is expected of them and how their digital skill set can be evaluated and how they can act accordingly.

Thus, within the "Action Plan Digital Literacy," the "GIZ Compass for Digital Literacy and Skills" was created. This is a powerful instrument which provides an overview of digital competencies within the organization.

The compass formulates digital skills ranging from digital project management and digital leadership to digital cooperation (to name but a few). Within these dimensions, a ranking is provided so that employees identify themselves according to their own digital skill set.

A self-assessment quiz measures the employee's competence level and gives individual recommendations for suitable training. It is thus the employee's decision whether or not they want to address it in their staff appraisal. This is also a condition to win the trust of the colleagues. As everyone can imagine, not having the relevant skill set can be a very sensitive topic. The management board of GIZ has taken the decision to provide learning time for digital upskilling to all employees according to the skill level identified found in the self-assessment quiz. Employees can decide individually and with their managers how to invest the learning time, from 5 (digital essentials) to 20 (digital leadership) days until the end of 2022.

Three other dimensions cannot be overlooked when it comes to the development of digital skills within this organization. All three can facilitate the adoption and development of digital skills if addressed correctly.

1. *Cultural sensitivity*: As an organization with a workforce from many different countries, it is vital to take the rules and polite etiquette, which differs from country to country, into account when training colleagues on how to conduct, for example, a video conference. Rules such as "who speaks first" and "who is allowed to introduce whom" need to be considered in the digital world as much as in the analogue world.
2. *Hierarchy*: It is mostly a wrong and discouraging assumption that people who are high up in the hierarchy are usually older and thus not as tech-savvy. However, people in leadership positions mostly have very limited time to use the trial-and-error method when it comes to the use of digital tools. Thus, customized training according to their questions and needs has proven to be a very good approach. As a side note, they can take on any of the personae described above meaning they may have questions ranging from "what is the difference between a like and a follow on Twitter" to "how do we have to react to the digitalization and automation of work in our partner countries."
   There are many motivated and digitally highly skilled colleagues in this organization. How can this potential be put to best use?
   As part of the "Action Plan Digital Literacy," the program introduced "Reverse Mentoring," a format which pairs a mentor with a mentee to answer all these questions. The most important rule of it all is that there is no such thing as stupid questions. This tandem arrangement creates a safe space to enable the best learning environment. It is a win-win situation: The mentee has the possibility to improve his or her digital skills, and the mentor can expand his or her network and get to know the reality of people in management positions. This mentoring program is a prime example for connecting resources within the organization. People who would probably never get to know each other break out of their hierarchical silos and people in leadership positions leave their comfort zones.
3. *Multipliers*: In large organizations such as GIZ, it is easy to find people who want to share their knowledge and passion and to spread the word about the latest digital tools. These colleagues are not bound by any hierarchy and contribute to the competent use of digital tools. Furthermore, they boost intraorganizational virtual collaboration. This means that they spread their knowledge in different fora, within their teams and beyond. Although multipliers can also act in rather informal networks, the "Action Plan Digital Literacy" decided to formalize this role and monetarily incentivize it. This concept goes hand in hand with the role of

agents of change. However, this is not a formal position but rather a function you fulfill within a job.

As already acknowledged by Carr et al. (1996) "no element is as crucial in an organization, as important to its good functioning, its success or failure, its survival or demise as the human one" (p. 67), it is vital to respond to all these different roles in different ways and subsequently encourage all employees to join the learning journey.

3 Digital by Default: The Transformation in Service Delivery

3.1 Why Is the Digital Transformation an Imperative for Development Cooperation and Its Service Delivery?

The answer is multilayered:

1. As witnessed by all of us, the digital transformation does not recognize national borders. In many partner countries, digital development happens at a faster pace than in Germany. If you look at the buzzing digital hubs of Nairobi, Jakarta, or New Delhi but also at the rising percentage of internet access in the partner countries, digital is an imperative for economic and human development. Thus, German development cooperation wants to adapt and offer *new modes of delivery* to be able to do meaningful work in many regions of the world.
2. Next, it is argued that digital solutions make the implementation of development projects more *transparent*, *efficient*, *effective*, *scalable*, and *sustainable*—five important indicators for successful development cooperation.
3. The Agenda 2030 of the United Nations and thus the facilitation of the *Sustainable Development Goals* (SDGs) are at the heart of GIZ's mission. Although digitalization plays a minor role in the SDGs, development experts claim that it will be impossible to meet the SDGs without digital solutions.

   Let me exemplify (and please excuse simplification):

   Education is at the very core of the development cooperation; next to the fact that 258 million children, adolescents, and youth were out of school in 2018 (UNESCO Institute for Statistics 2019), the lack of education is often argued to be the root cause of poverty. Thus, many projects focus on the delivery of quality education which, however, is impossible to access for many people. Hour-long walks to the nearest school or the need to work pose clear obstacles. However, with the spread of internet across many partner countries, access to online educational content such as books, online courses, and educational games give many children and adolescents the opportunity to have a formal education, within a constraining environment. This also supports the efforts to meet SDG 4: "Ensuring inclusive and quality education for all and promote lifelong learning."

4. *Closing the digital divide*: Although internet penetration is on the rise in many partner countries, marginalized groups such as women or people living in rural areas often lack access to information and communication technology (ICT). This means these groups risk missing out on important services, such as access to finance, news, or education, and consequently hampers development.
5. The rise of digital economies *transforms* the world we live in—and we need to act. Not only apps and 3D printers revolutionize our world. Digital transformation goes far beyond this and raises many questions to which an organization such as GIZ wants to find answers. For example, some partner countries have the textile industry as their major trade. This industry provides millions of women and men working in these factories with a regular wage.[4] However, the automation of work, especially in the textile sector, is threatening many jobs. In contrast, the rising platform economy, ranging from UBER to graphic design jobs, has the potential to create many new jobs in the so-called gig economy. However, how can this new form of economy be regulated? And how can fair wages be guaranteed? Most importantly, how can we assure that the partner countries can use the opportunities but also have the capacity to react to the challenges? All these very complex questions and global changes must be part of effective development cooperation.

3.2 Digital by Default

To respond to all these complex changes and global challenges, GIZ introduced a powerful concept—digital by default[5]:

Digital by default (DbD) argues that all projects must use digital solutions or work on the global challenges connected to digital transformation to achieve its goals—meaning that "digital is the new normal." If, however, there is a reasonable argument why the implementation of digital solutions does not contribute to successful implementation the obligation is waived for the project in question. This shift in the burden of proof aims to be a significant driver for promoting digital services.

Following the example of other development agencies, DbD was introduced in 2018 and has proven to be a powerful instrument to mainstream digital transformation in the various implementing projects of GIZ.

But how can DbD be implemented in such a complex and decentralized organization?

It needs to be said that DbD is especially relevant to all the implementing projects that work together with the partner countries, thus having the capacity to use digital solutions within their project delivery.

[4]Do not take this example as an acceptance of the working conditions in these factories.

[5]This concept was not invented by GIZ; similar models already exist in the British development agency DFID and the Belgium development agency.

The implementation of DbD starts at the beginning of each project—the appraisal of the project, the formulation of its goals and its safeguards. This created new requirements for employees involved in these processes, meaning that they had to develop their expertise in a specific sector (e.g., rural development) adding the intersection of digital development (e.g., the use of digital technologies in agriculture). This of course needs to be compensated by sufficient possibilities to develop the respective skill set.

However, after 2 years of DbD, we can already see many interesting observations[6]:

1. *Fact*: DbD was a top-down decision.
   Learning: The management board and the directors of the operational departments made DbD mandatory. On the one hand, this was helpful for the process, since projects that neglected the opportunities of digital solutions had to react to this. On the other hand, this made the process of mainstreaming not demand-oriented, and some projects that already implement digital solutions or advise on global digital questions considered this to be redundant.
2. *Fact*: the sticking point is the use of suitable resources.
   Learning: Although the organization has many employees who are eager to include digital solutions as part of their projects, time is needed to build up the relevant expertise, and this cannot be expected to happen overnight. This resulted, in some cases, on the one hand, in recruiting new colleagues who already possessed this expertise and on the other hand also in the training of specific digital skills for the existing workforce.
3. *Fact*: DbD opens silos,
   Learning: Organizations with strong sectoral structures (e.g., department 1, rural development, compared to department 2—sustainable city management) must break open these structures for a meaningful use of connecting resources. Silos need to be abolished.
4. *Fact*: one size does not fit all.
   Learning: This fact is true on various levels. First, since the projects within GIZ are diverse, ranging from purely implementing projects with the respective partner countries to projects which solely advise a commissioning party, DbD needs to be adapted to the specific context. Second, the projects had very different starting points when it came to the implementation of digital solutions—some of them used digital solutions as a basic support, but others embedded digital solutions as being essential to the project meeting its targets. This benchmarking needs to be done frequently, and DbD must account for these different starting points. Third, the country context and the user of the digital solution must be at the center of the design process.
5. *Fact*: As well as being a mainstreaming tool, DbD must also focus on the

[6]This list is not complete and illustrates a few learnings.

scalability of projects.

Learning: Within the past years the organization has put a lot of effort into mainstreaming DbD and thus making digital the new standard. However, it is also essential to not only encourage the use of digital solutions but rather to scale them and facilitate spillover effects if these prove successful. This also ensures efficient use of resources.

All in all, the implementation of DbD is a long process which requires constantly evolving expertise, leadership backup, and a cross-sectoral approach. This is a prime example of a travelling organization, which connects its resources as a condition for success (Wollmann et al. 2020).

3.3 Evaluation Means Evolution

This article began with the argument that digital solutions in the project delivery of development projects ensure more efficiency, effectiveness, transparency, sustainability, and scalability—five powerful words in international cooperation. To empirically prove this, the evaluation unit established a project which is solely concerned with measuring the development results of digital solutions. This undertaking aims to establish proof and credibility that digital service delivery is a driver for a meaningful international cooperation. Furthermore, it ensures the continuous improvement of DbD as a new methodology which is part of the three-pillar model proposed by Wollmann et al. (2020).

4 COVID-19 as a Boost for Our VUCA World?

It cannot be dismissed that COVID-19 has brought a lot of negative restrictions and unforeseen challenges to all people. Yet, it is indisputable that COVID-19 has facilitated a boost to digital transformation in many sectors, which has in turn reduced some of its negative effects. It can even be argued that the pandemic is becoming the accelerator for one of the greatest workplace transformations of our lifetime or, in other words, the concept of VUCA is becoming even more a reality. This also holds true for GIZ—again on both on the internal dimension and the external dimension of the digital transformation.

4.1 COVID-19: A Boost to DbD in Project Delivery

A pandemic in a highly interconnected world calls for innovative digital solutions to provide answers to the spread of the virus. Especially in vulnerable regions, rapid action is needed. Thus, together with the commissioning parties and other organizations, GIZ is scaling up digital tools at a fast pace. However, this rapid

Table 1 A quantitative comparison of the use of the organization's digital communication tool—count/day

	Just before COVID-19 5th of March 2020	Midst of COVID-19 20th of May 2020	Increase in %
Chat message	85.283	272.507	~310
1:1 calls	2.261	13.371	~600
Group calls	195	1.231	~630

development also poses the threat of leaving marginalized people behind. Thus, the inclusion of these people in the design process of the projects is essential.

4.2 COVID-19: Brought a Lot of "First Times" and Many Cases of "Let Us Do It"

Along with many other organizations GIZ is a decentralized organization with employees travelling to, and living in, different countries who are used to having face-to-face meetings every day. Suddenly this was no longer possible. Supported by a strong IT department, which had invested in communication and collaboration tools for the last 3 years, the organization was able to respond to the rising needs in terms of functionality and support. Although these tools were not new to the employees, COVID-19 has increased their use tremendously (see Table 1).

In addition to the fact that many employees had to leave the country they were living and working in, teams were not able to meet in person any longer and meetings needed to be via video calls, some of them while participants were taking care of their children.

This was a big challenge for all staff members—e.g., people in leadership positions, who had to lead a team digitally; new colleagues who had never met their team in person; or employees working in countries where there was no strong internet penetration or the working culture was very much based on personal relations. Nevertheless, everyone and the organization needed to find a way to cope with these new situations. New working groups beyond the department or project boundaries were formed to spread new coping mechanisms, best practices, or learnings, which is a proof of a strong connecting purpose (Wollmann et al. 2020).

Digitalization, coupled with the corresponding framework conditions, has thus contributed to the continuation of business operations.

Thus, COVID-19 showed the importance of many observations, three of which are highlighted here:

The Ups and Downs of Online Meetings Online meetings save time and money—this was traditionally the argument to opt for online meetings. Yet, if an organization must exclusively rely on online communication, as well as reliable digital infrastructure, more subtle issues must be considered. It is rather different to plan and execute a meeting online—it is worth investing in training people to facilitate online meetings—questions such as how many breaks do people need online how can it be assured that everyone pays attention and can actively participate must be answered. It becomes even more complicated if a co-creative workshop is planned. This must be addressed by people, who have developed a suitable skill set. Yet, this discipline is rather new, and training is very limited, but it opens a new and exciting world.

In contrast to the challenges, it also allows organizations to invite people to meetings who may have not been able to join because it would not be appropriate to fly around the world for one meeting. This opens new possibilities of networking. Additionally, this saves a lot of CO_2, which is not only a goal of GIZ but also the biggest challenge of our era.

Digital Empathy Empathy, in a classical sense, plays a critical interpersonal and societal role, enabling sharing of needs and "desires between individuals and providing an emotional bridge that promotes pro-social behavior" (Riess 2017). However, bringing this concept to an exclusively digital world, it requires a lot of dedication and willingness to build empathy. Nonverbal cues to better understand the people in meetings fall short—this can lead to misunderstandings, which reduces productivity and the well-being of an individual or even a whole team. Thus, it has been proven successful to turn on the camera in online meetings—this is only possible, however, if the internet connection is strong enough and the participants are comfortable with this. Moreover, many teams found their own ways to create a feeling of being together despite being physically distant from one another. Ideas like digital yoga, digital coffee corner (a digital space in which everyone can enter and have a coffee with colleagues), or a photo challenge to show the working environment of team members spread rapidly across the organization.

Improving Digital Literacy in a Fast-Track Procedure COVID-19 has motivated many employees to invest time and resources in the development of their digital skills. This has also been backed by the management board and its decision to allocate learning time to all employees. This is because it became evident that, without a suitable skill set, it will be almost impossible to achieve the same results and there is a high risk of exclusion. However, it is vital to offer different forms of training to meet the needs and deal with the fears of all employees—the ones who are at the beginning of their learning journey, already on their way, or the ones asking for the newest developments to work with.

All in all, it is impossible to say which new habits of the "new normal" the organizations will keep when COVID-19 is on the decline. However, it is safe to argue that COVID-19 will act as an accelerator to our VUCA world and, with this, to the digital transformation of GIZs' service delivery and the organization itself. We must ensure that all employees are able to join this learning journey.

Main Takeaways

- The digital transformation will be a continuous learning journey for employees, regardless of hierarchy, age, or predisposition and is thus strongly connected to the traveling organization of the 3-P-Model (Wollmann et al. 2020).
- The strong target image of "digital change" is operationalized in direct measures and supported by the management board. This offers a clear vision to employees.
- Digital literacy lies at the core of successful digital transformation. Thus, GIZ connected its resources and invested its own expertise and talent of digital-savvy employees to support and train colleagues.
- The digital transformation not only changed the way people collaborate and communicate with each other but also how an organization develops its service delivery. Digital by default was a top-down mainstreaming process, which successfully leveraged the power of digital solutions to make development cooperation projects more scalable, transparent, efficient, and effective.
- Although GIZ works in sectoral units, digital by default had a cross-sectoral approach, essential for leveraging the potential of digital solutions.
- Although Covid-19 created many unforeseen challenges for many people, it also boosted digital transformation. However, this was only possible because GIZ had invested in digital communication and collaboration tools and their roll out for a longer period and because employees see the sustainable purpose in the continuation of work.

References

Carr, D., Hard, K., & Trahant, W. (1996). *Managing the change process*. New York: McGraw-Hill.

GIZ. (2018). *Internal concept for digitalization – Target picture*. Bonn: Eschborn.

Riess, H. (2017). The science of empathy. *Journal of Patient Experience, 4*(2), 74–77.

UNESCO Institute for Statistics. (2019). *New methodology shows that 258 million children, adolescents and youth are out of school*. Factsheet No. 56.

Vahs, D. (2015). *Organisation: Ein Lehr- und Managementbuch*. Stuttgart: Schäfer Poeschel.

Wollmann, P., Kühn, F., & Kempf, M. (Eds.). (2020). *Three pillars of organization and leadership in disruptive times – Navigating your company successfully through the 21st century business world*. Heidelberg: Springer.

Janina Kempf is a young professional who explores the intersection of international cooperation and digital development. Working with the GIZ (a German development agency), she found the perfect spot to combine her drive for innovation and her passion to work with people from all around the globe, while being on the pulse of development politics. Within the organization, she works in two positions, which complement each other: First, she is an advisor to the German Ministry for Economic Cooperation and Development, advising the unit which is concerned with the digital transformation of the global south. Second, she is a so-called IT partner for the biggest department within the organization and supports the digital transformation of the department and beyond. She studied European Studies at Maastricht University and International Relations at the "Institut Barcelona d'Estudis Internacionals."

[illegible]

Scientific Guidance on Journeys in Unknown Areas: A Best Practice Example

Peter Wollmann

Abstract

Regular scientific guidance on journeys in unknown areas can give significant orientation and support reasonable decisions. It is important that the following are always transparent: what science does know, what it means and what not, which research projects are in place and when results can be expected, which results have already been accomplished and how they can be judged, where recommendations from science have their limitations, and where therefore politics has to step in.

There are a lot of valid approaches and models to analyze the COVID-19 pandemic from a medical, psychological, sociological, futurist view, etc. This article contributes some considerations using the 3-P-Model to describe a best practice example from Germany during the pandemic and deduce lessons learned for enterprises in difficult journey situations.

1 Introduction

In the worldwide COVID-19 pandemic in Germany in early 2020, the public-sector broadcaster NDR started a daily podcast[1] with one of the world's most important virologists, Prof. Christian Drosten, Director of the Institute of Virology at the Charité in Berlin with one of the largest laboratories in Germany. Each day, about one million people listened to the daily episodes, in which different aspects of the virus, its impacts and its exploration, its spread, its further development, etc., were

[1] https://www.ndr.de/nachrichten/info/podcast4684.html

P. Wollmann (✉)
Bonn, Germany
e-mail: pw@peterwollmann.com

P. Wollmann et al. (eds.), *Organization and Leadership in Disruptive Times*, Future of Business and Finance, https://doi.org/10.1007/978-3-030-63034-8_12

explained, very context-oriented, fairly easy to understand but not too much simplistic. That means that the demand for this source of scientific enlightenment developed spectacularly. The audience was very keen to understand about various linked sciences in this situation (selection):

- About virology: the origin of the new virus, how its DNA was encrypted, its relations to earlier viruses, its replication and infectiousness, its lethality, etc., what is known now, and what will be explored by when and how
- About the interface to epidemics and pandemics: which model calculation, which modelling concepts can describe the virus spread, on which preconditions are the calculations based, and how sensitive are they to assumption changes
- About the interface to mathematics: how can we understand an exponential development in comparison to a linear development
- About the interface of politics: on which scientific basis does politics have to make decisions and which risks have to be taken

Christian Drosten focused on his professional subject and refused to talk in detail about topics beyond but connected to the disciplines with interfaces and referred to their results. It was a rare situation with a large number of people listening—with an attention span of 30–45 min—to a scientist who explained the situation with all its certainties and uncertainties, trying to be understandable to a broad audience without simplifying too much. It was a moment where the work of scientists in their labs and at their computers and also their methods and their responsibility became transparent and people could get a taste of the complexity, the timespan needed for new insights and to draft measures and find solutions—and also the dilemma of politics to make decisions in a situation where only a fraction of the overall picture is clear (Fig. 1). Christian Drosten was very clear about the different roles and interactions of science and politics: what science can deliver and what not and which decisions only can be made by politics.

2 Link to the Three-Pillar Model

The three main design principles of the Three-Pillar model[2] for modern organizations and leadership can be easily applied to the scientific guidance of the journey through the COVID-19 pandemic:

- *Sustainable purpose*: The purpose of science and of scientific guidance are obvious: on the one hand, as many scientific insights on the virus, its threat, its spread, potential counteractions and medication, etc., have to be found as soon as

[2] 'Three Pillars of Organization and Leadership in Disruptive Times—Navigating Your Company Successfully Through the 21st Century Business World' (Wollmann, P.; Kühn, F.: Kempf, M. (Ed.) (2020); Cham/CH: Springer Nature).

Fig. 1 Conveying a competent, focused message in a troubled environment (Illustrated by Frank Kühn, used with permission. All rights reserved)

possible, and on the other hand, people in fear and living under restricting measures (so-called lockdown) have to understand the scientific background and the derived direction. All conspiracy theories and counterproductive activities have to be prevented. The more rationally affected people act on the basis of solid facts, the better. In addition, the purpose of this scientific guide connects with the collective, social purpose that many people develop out of the situation: to help each other and to contribute to the further development of humankind.

- *Travelling organization*: In sudden, complex, and dangerous situations, finding the right journey to identify solid facts, develop correct measures against the pandemic, create medication and vaccines, etc. is a very difficult iterative step-by-step and even trial-and-error endeavor. It is a priori clear that a significant part of previous insights will have to be corrected and that it will take a long time to reach final findings and/or an important interim target. So the people need to understand from the scientific guidance that they are, for a long time, continuously on a journey towards the best possible result and joint success, in the context of the agreed sustainable purpose to defeat or at least stanch the pandemic, coping underway with all—partly unforeseeable—influences. On the map, it will potentially have to zigzag, always exploring the best path between poles, alternatives, and options. People on this journey have been forced to accept leaving their comfort zone—so the scientific guidance gives them a modicum of certainty and orientation.
- *Connecting resources*: The scientific guidance itself is based on the collection, evaluation, and summary of the work of the global community of scientists from

different connected disciplines, from officially published and peer-reviewed studies or from prepublished documents. In the case of the COVID-19 pandemic, the whole scientific community was able to contribute and was active, coordinated by the WHO and supranational and national research facilities. This included cross-disciplinary cooperation. The connectivity became transparent in diverse reports in the media and even on talk shows and at press conferences. Interestingly, different opinions in the scientific discussion can be perceived as beneficial and not destructive as often in political or enterprise-wise contexts.

So, the scientific work to defeat or stanch the pandemic as well as the scientific guidance on the journey of the "normal people" impressively showed the applicability of the 3-P-Model and its connectivity to good leadership.

This case needs a few words about leadership

Regarding leadership, the case examined in this article is very relevant on both a social and organizational level. What we see in this case is "shared leadership" (often compared to lateral leadership, distributed leadership, collective leadership) at its best.

This means people within society, an organization, or a team who lead each other. In this understanding, real leadership is a collectively accepted task (rather than a hierarchical position) that can be split and distributed to those who are the right ones in the process, situation, and moment.

In the beginning, the case of COVID-19, virologists, presidents and chancellors, health ministers, entrepreneurs, reputable journalists, and sports coaches were involved in the right place and at the right time, taking leadership. There was no place for demagogues, know-alls, and conspiracy theorists, except in their specific echo chambers at this time. And they not only displayed leadership, they were also fairly coordinated in the first phase, had a common purpose and ensured good connectivity of information, expertise, and activities.

Each of them took on the role that people entrusted to them, and all of this arose from the needs and concerns in the situation. Otherwise, the people would not join the journey and the self-proclaimed "leader" would make a fool of himself.

This means—even though the situation changed a bit in the next phases—that everyone can lead and everyone can be led, based on one prerequisite: leadership needs followership (as a collaborative interaction) based on expertise, trust, and empathy. In our case, the scientists convince their audience with an authentic blend of well-founded knowledge and clear presentation, transparency about open questions, and a role on an equal footing: selfless, calm, and modest.

3 The Case of Christian Drosten's Podcast

As already mentioned, Christian Drosten is Director of the Institute of Virology at the Charité in Berlin and a special expert on corona viruses, especially on SARS-CoV, the predecessor of SARS-CoV-2—in this article for simplicity's sake only called "COVID-19"—but also MERS-CoV. He strongly supports full transparency of research results and very fast and free communication.

During the pandemic, Christian Drosten became an advisor to the German government, the governments of Germany's Federal States, and diverse authorities.

The magazine Stern wrote on 17 March 2020: "Covid-19 has made virologist Christian Drosten the most sought-after man in the republic. And [made him a] star . . . Since the virus has been rampant, Drosten is the man who has controlled the crisis, who has navigated us through the crisis. He doesn't gloss over anything and doesn't dramatize anything. He weighs and corrects, says if he does not know something or has thought too briefly the day before."[3]

What does this mean in detail? It seems as if we have an interesting combination of personality, expertise, clarity, openness, and authenticity:

- A well-known expert in an important discipline with a lot of research experience and success
- An internationally very well-connected research scientist with a lot of close cooperations
- A professor who is able to teach people on different levels and to enthuse people for his discipline and a really good explainer who makes science exciting and calibrates detail well
- A self-reflected person who is very clear about what he knows as a scientist and to what degree, where professional and acceptable speculation starts and where he can contribute nothing
- A self-critical scientist who has no problem to correct himself
- A narrator who sets things in contexts and timeframes, but always stays factual
- A person who is generally perceived as being very calm and collected
- A media channel that is valued for its seriousness and is easy to reach for everyone

It is interesting to see how these very personal observations correspond with a model of leadership qualities which was developed by Peter Hawkins (as quoted by Klimek and AtKisson 2016[4]) (Fig. 2).

Especially on very challenging journeys which create "big emotions" as they are existential, a neutral view of a scientist with obviously no self-interest and no drive for normal publicity is able to create trust in general and also in competence. A difficult journey the steering of which is supported or mainly influenced by a scientist with the personality and perception described above is more easily manageable—because the normal "political quarrelling" takes a step back. And people realize that they would love to know a bit of the scientific context to understand a part of the world in depth.

Certainly, there are other virologists and scientists with different opinions, but there is no mutual blame or derogation, just the clear will to bring helpful questions and insights into the journey. People recognize a certain culture of true responsibility in the scientific community, which differs dramatically from conspiracy theorists, political narcissists, and self-proclaimed futurists.

---

[3]https://www.stern.de/gesundheit/virologe-christian-drosten%2D%2Ddem-coronavirus-auf-der-spur-9184576.html

[4]Klimek, A., AtKisson, A.: Parachuting Cats into Borneo. Chelsea Green Publishing, 2016.

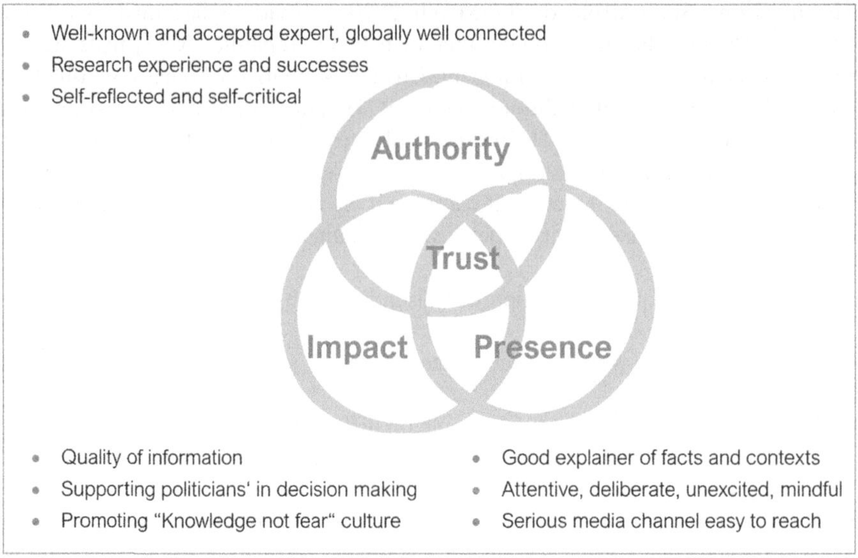

Fig. 2 Own observations connected with proven model (Illustrated by Frank Kühn, used with permission. All rights reserved)

4 Conclusion

On a meta-level the 3-P-Model can be easily and successfully applied even in the context of global and national catastrophes such as the COVID-19 pandemic and its handling. The three pillars especially help to concretely understand the challenge of the journey with a "Travelling Organization" of people who had to involuntarily join and get out of their comfort zones in a partly existential way. The clarity of the purpose creates the feeling of urgency and importance needed, and the connectivity helps to best coordinate and organize the necessary activities.

Especially putting the 3-P-Model perspective on the scientific guidance on the journey shows that the obvious honest and noble purpose and the transparent global scientific cooperation and connectivity create trust among the people affected in the scientific rationales for restricting measures like lockdowns, etc. Science is perceived as neutral, without the self-interest which is often alleged if politics decides something. Christian Drosten stressed this repeatedly in different contexts.[5],[6]

[5]https://www.spiegel.de/wissenschaft/medizin/christian-drosten-in-meinem-alltag-kommt-die-bild-zeitung-nicht-vor-a-00000000-0002-0001-0000-000171168292

[6]https://www.theguardian.com/world/2020/apr/26/virologist-christian-drosten-germany-coronavirus-expert-interview

5 Lessons Learned and Practical Takeaways

Exponential Growth

The famous anecdote of somebody winning a bet and asking for rice is helpful for understanding. His request is to start with one rice grain on the first square of the checkerboard, two on the second square, four on the third square, etc.—which add over 64 squares of the board to the volume of rice production of the whole world for more than 800 years. This is beyond the average imagination.

In crisis situations often level-headed, pragmatic people with factual and objective narratives and obviously no self-interest are able to sustainably build up trust. It makes sense to carefully check how scientific or other professional external support can be used for guidance in troubled times, especially to prevent problematic and counterproductive rumors and conspiracy theories. Trust is one of the key success factors in crisis, so something comparable to Christian Drosten's podcast during the pandemic in Germany is a very valuable tool and the time invested in it very beneficial.

As developments around it might be too complex to be understood—like exponential growth—it is important that the concept behind is explained.

Even difficult facts have to be explained adequately with the right balance between understandability and preventing too much simplification (which would make it worthless).

It is a high art but necessary and worth being intensively tackled.

It may make sense for countries and enterprises or other organizations to invest more in scientific understanding and training. As journeys in unknown areas will get more frequent, well-educated travel partners will be a success factor as they can better handle uncertainty and help the uncertainty to be gradually reduced based on real facts. Especially the ability to think in contexts is of high value in complex situations.

Peter Wollmann has been a responsible manager, initiator, mentor, and facilitator in large, predominantly global transformations and strategic developments for almost 40 years. His specialties are the implementations of the Three-Pillar Model in organizations and focused setting checks to identify strength, weaknesses, opportunities, and threats and facilitate optimization measures. Since 2017 Peter has been working independently in organizational projects and future initiatives. After graduating in mathematics and physics from the University of Bonn, he began his professional career at the Deutsche Herold, then insurance group of Deutsche Bank, took on strategic leadership, and most recently was program director for global transformations in the Zurich Insurance Company (ZIC). In his professional network, he brought his experience and strategic thinking to the development of various leading companies. He is the author and publisher of a number of books and articles on strategy, leadership, and project and project portfolio management. He also founded a wine business: VinAuthority.

5 Lessons Learned and Practical Takeaways

Experiential Gravity

Cooperation and Development in a Social Organization

Lisa Schulze and Daniel Kunstleben

Abstract

The authors underline the relevance of the three pillars as constituent factors in an organizational system and in daily work. In addition, the Three-Pillar Model in the reflection of the organizational system has significantly helped those involved to check and further optimize their work. The article describes in detail how a traveling organization is managed within an educationally, socially, and politically determined system. It reports on a municipal enterprise which offers and coordinates services such as daycare for children and family centers. The teams working there pursue a clear purpose based on an advanced educational concept. Connecting resources here means harmonizing efficient processes and daily working practice, continuously networking the expectations and participation of various stakeholders from children and parents to administration and politics.

1 Municipal Enterprise in Dynamic Development

FABIDO stands for Family Complementary Educational Institutions for Children in Dortmund and, as a municipal enterprise, runs about 100 daycare facilities for children, providing more than 8600 childcare places for children aged 8 weeks to 6 years throughout the city. More than 1100 places are currently available in daycare alone. In total, the organization has more than 2200 employees including 250 trainees. This makes FABIDO the largest provider of elementary education in Dortmund and one of the larger providers in Germany.

L. Schulze (✉)
Ennepetal, Germany
e-mail: Schulze-ennepetal@web.de

D. Kunstleben
FABIDO, Dortmund, Germany
e-mail: dkunstleben@stadtdo.de

P. Wollmann et al. (eds.), *Organization and Leadership in Disruptive Times*, Future of Business and Finance, https://doi.org/10.1007/978-3-030-63034-8_13

Due to its continuous dynamic development, the enterprise is managed in the sense of a "travelling organization" within a system that is pedagogically, socially, and politically shaped. As a growing city, Dortmund presents its largest provider of elementary education with the task of continuously securing the quantity and quality of its offerings, developing them further for the future and managing them effectively even in times of crisis.

Reflection using the Three-Pillar Model

This article underlines the factors examined in the Three-Pillar Model (Wollmann et al. 2020):
Sustainable purpose: As the *raison d'être*, the purpose describes the contribution of a company or institution to society. A good purpose gives orientation and inspiration and creates pride on the part of individuals and teams to be part of the joint journey. This is formulated, communicated, and lived in the municipal enterprise described in this article in an exemplary fashion. It includes social responsibility for diversity, tolerance, and democracy, as well as an advanced educational concept that aims to develop children's personalities as well as fostering equal opportunities.
Travelling organization: Organizations are on the move continuously and face changes, disruptions, and even global crises. The structures must be flexible, and the teams must be well prepared to meet current and future challenges. For the organization presented in this article, this means closely linking the development of services, competencies, and organizational settings with social, political, regulatory and municipal challenges, and frameworks and designing this process in an inspiring, powerful, and convincing manner.
Connecting resources: Resources such as expertise, experience, skills, and creativity on the human side but also purpose, processes, structures, methodologies, and tools on the organizational side must be well connected to become productive; resources that are not connected would not be functional. In this article, connectivity also includes networking the expectations and capabilities of various stakeholders: children, parents, educators, cooperation partners, volunteers, administration, politics, as well as the linkage of the appropriate services that have to be coordinated for quality and efficiency.

On the one hand, this is a constant strategic and perspective challenge, and on the other hand, political and legal influences must be considered immediately. In recent years, for example, the educational and childcare offer for children aged 0–6 has had to be adapted very quickly. One example is the legal entitlement to a childcare place from the age of 8 weeks, which was implemented in Germany and required a massive expansion of childcare places; the basis for this is the statutory educational mandate and the recognition of elementary education as an independent area of education.

Based on the fact that daycare facilities not only represent a microcosm of their own in society but also reflect society with all its diversity—including the social, political, and family life of the respective social space—all facilities and teams at FABIDO are called upon to develop and implement answers to current challenges, such as the following:

- Social inequality
- Medialization of the child's world
- Institutionalization of childhood
- Changed environmental conditions
- Changes in values

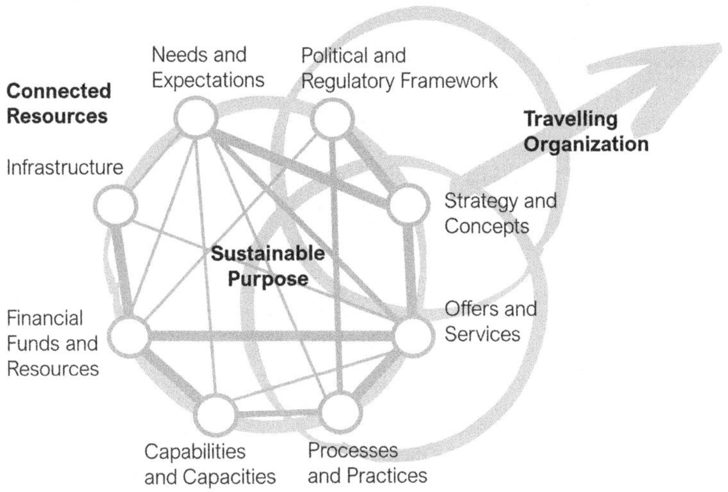

Fig. 1 General conditions of the municipal enterprise on its development journey (Illustrated by Frank Kühn, used with permission. All rights reserved)

- Globalization and internationality
- Cultural diversity

To implement these developments, all resources have to be connected as effectively as possible (Fig. 1), from the needs and expectations of children and families as well as other partners in the system to frameworks, strategies, and concepts to implementation in efficient processes and working methods. A basis is the financial resources that support the development of the infrastructure, i.e., buildings and facilities that create the conditions for advanced offers and services. None of these resources can be viewed independently of one another: they all interact more or less intensively. The constructive design and coordination of these interactions, which also evolve and develop continuously, is a challenge for management. The self-concept and purpose set the direction and provide the orientation and cohesion: what is our task and what do we stand for?

The management, the executives, and the teams throughout the company must always be aware of this dynamic and approach it as proactively as possible, each individual using his or her experience, skills, and creativity. It was therefore also highly interesting for us to review our organization and our path based on the three pillars and to take up new impulses.

In this article, after the first overview of the resources and their interactions (Fig. 2), we use a picture with three dynamic process loops in which our journey can be illustrated quite well:

- Purpose and strategy process
- Change and optimization initiatives and projects
- Operative processes and practices

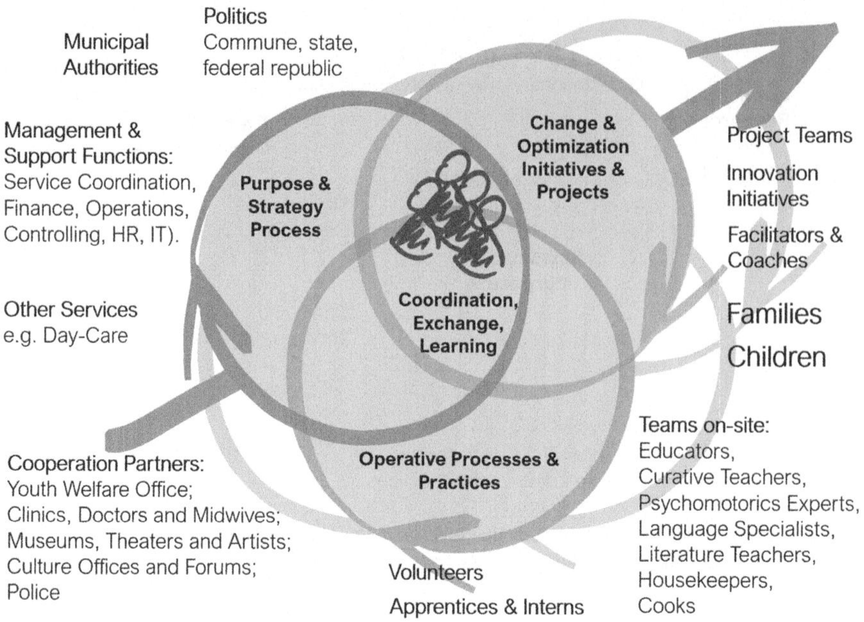

Fig. 2 Travelling organization closely connected with their internal and external partners (Illustrated by Frank Kühn, used with permission. All rights reserved)

All three processes are closely interconnected because coordination, exchange, and learning cannot function otherwise; each process needs each other. This connection is not static but should be understood as a dynamic and joint development. This is what keeps us together on our journey.

And there is something else that holds us together at the core. Each travel group has a larger, common motivation in mind. The Three-Pillar Model calls it a "sustainable purpose," as already shown at the core of Fig. 1. For us it is a social and societal contribution that we have formulated and have translated into an educational concept. Our corporate form as a "municipal enterprise" is intended to support us in implementing this claim professionally, effectively, and efficiently. This is what makes our work so exciting.

2 Decentralized Organization with Lively Networking

The pedagogical challenge—as part of the "purpose"—has to meet developments and changing requirements continuously (Fig. 1). Due to the variety of requirements, FABIDO reacts to this with a centrally developed framework concept and its decentralized adaptations to the facilities: in this way, each daycare facility works individually, has its own focal points, and lives its own character and its own pedagogical concept in order to be able to meet a wide range of families and requirements in a tailor-made way. In each facility, the focus is on working with the children of the specific social space, always in close cooperation with the parents as educational partners and experts for their children.

Besides the development of this diversity, the opportunities to connect the various stakeholders with one another must be used (Fig. 2). Some institutions are therefore grouped together and managed in a network, and others stand for themselves; accordingly, the sizes of the institutions and teams differ. Larger institutions have up to 8 groups and 40 colleagues from different professions: educators, curative teachers, experts for psychomotorics, language specialists, literature teachers, university graduates, and housekeepers. In addition, the institutions see themselves as future-oriented learning centers for trainees in all required professions and from different types of schools.

Furthermore, an extensive external network has developed around the enterprise's own operations and its facilities. These include, for example, the youth welfare office; clinics for children and youth medicine; museums, theaters, and artists; the culture office; schools, the city's environmental services, as well as retirement homes; doctors and midwives; farms; police; etc.

To ensure the efficiency of the processes—in line with daily working practice—and to receive support when needed, the family and childcare centers collaborate closely with the internal services and administrative functions.

Such a network comes alive in its communicative processes and formats (Fig. 3). This includes the active participation of parents in the parents' council, in information afternoons, in parents' cafés, or other offers. Everyone is welcome and invited to learn from and with each other.

Regular formats have been set up for conceptual work and daily and weekly exchanges within the teams on site and with cooperation and network partners. Tried and tested qualification and support opportunities, including mentoring, can also be used.

The coordination between the individual units and at management level always takes place with the aim of effective coordination, exchange, and learning to become better and better together.

3 Wide Range of Offerings

Offers must be tailored to the needs of the target group, tailored to the children and families with their expectations and needs in their social environment. This is also ensured, among other things, by parent and team surveys.

This is the reason for the diversity of the program, some of which are part of higher-level programs of the Federal Republic or the State of North Rhine-Westphalia (NRW). Thus, the "Educational Principles for Children from 0 to 10 years" are also considered. They include mathematical education, scientific and

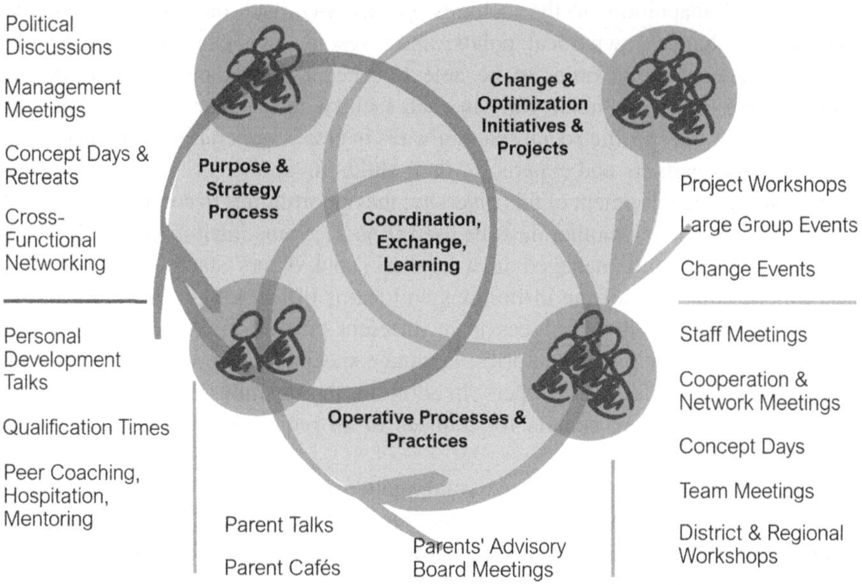

Fig. 3 Interactive and cross-structural working formats (Illustrated by Frank Kühn, used with permission. All rights reserved)

technical education, physical activity, ecological education, musical and aesthetic education, social and (inter)cultural education, language and communication, religion and ethics, physical health, and nutrition.

This range can be seen very specifically in the offering:

- "Kinderstuben" (children's rooms)—an educational offer close to home for children aged 1–4 years as part of daycare. It is aimed primarily at children and parents whose native language is not German or who have specific socio-pedagogical needs
- Large daycare homes—care close to home by trained childminders in their own or rented premises
- Daycare facilities ("Kitas") and family centers with a wide range of offers; examples are bilingual care (German with English, Turkish, or Russian), the focus on the environment (connected with the urban work area "energy management"), the focus on physical exercise (in cooperation with sports clubs), or the focus on literature and language ("language as the key to the world") with trained language specialists where reading aloud is an important part of language promotion and reading socialization. In Chess Kitas ("Chess for Kids") the children deal with the game at their individual learning pace and learning style. Culture-Kitas come within the framework of the municipal overall concept "Cultural Education in Dortmund" and are aimed at strengthening cultural, musical-aesthetic educational work, in cooperation with cultural places of learning.

- Some daycare centers are certified by the NRW Cancer Society for their sun protection measures for the children they look after. Further family centers, supported in state programs, are intended to improve educational opportunities and participation for disadvantaged families, including those caused by poverty, or in areas with inadequate infrastructure or poverty.

All institutions want to be certified as "Fair Kitas" under the auspices of "Education for Sustainable Development" by 2021. In the facilities, the youngest members of our society learn about "world issues," gain global insights, and understand the effects of their own consumption.

These examples show how the diversity of the offer is connected with many cooperation and network partners, with strong local commitment and, where necessary, support from associated facilities and central functions.

4 Implementing Sustainable Purpose

Beside the slogan "A strong offer for children and parents in Dortmund" (and this at all times, i.e., also as part of a dynamic system characterized by a diversity of interests), the claim "We live diversity, tolerance, and democracy" goes even further and forms a core of the "sustainable purpose" which expresses our societal contribution.

Through active participation in initiatives such as "DORTBUNT! One town. Many faces.," Diverse City, the Dorstfeld Democracy Conference, our commitment to children's rights, or even our help in the fight against right-wing extremism and Salafism, the organization, its teams, and its colleagues demonstrate their self-conception, experience meaningful engagement with other sponsors, and make their work known and attractive across all cities. These initiatives are carried out by the various facility teams together with the office staff. We also understand this as connectivity: the integration into democratic movements in the city.

At the same time, there are, of course, common principles and frameworks in addition to this diversity. Directly linked to the demands of diversity, tolerance, and democracy are, for example, a systemic basic idea and a development-oriented attitude, which are also reflected in the training courses offered to all colleagues, in the mission statements on leadership, and in position papers in which the teams are given guidance and safety in their work on all specialist topics.

FABIDO sees itself not only as a provider but also as a sociopolitical player; this also includes letting children participate in the sustainable anchoring of values and attitudes.

5 Educational Concept as a Core of the Sustainable Purpose

The purpose described above is realized in a progressive educational concept, which is continuously checked to see how up-to-date and forward-looking it is. Both together, purpose and educational concept, create the orientation for the organization.

The core of the educational concept is the triad of education, upbringing, and care. The educational work is intended to contribute to more equal opportunities, irrespective of gender and origin. The personality development of the children is promoted, and the strengths and interests of the children are taken into account—questions and ideas of the children are always taken up and taken seriously.

In strategic personnel development, the sustainable purpose as well as the travelling organization are realized among other things in a "phase of life and work-oriented HR policy." In addition to the everyday and situational exchange between daycare centers and office staff, staff can access a comprehensive range of training courses and a wide repertoire of professional development and support measures. These include as follows:

- Peer consulting (at any time or by appointment)
- Coaching (individually or as team coaching)
- Supervisions
- Quality circles
- Team development or training
- Leadership development
- Annual appraisals and management feedback
- Consulting and development talks on request (also before and after job interviews)
- Sponsorship for new employees
- Mentoring

6 Three Pillars in the Daily Implementation and in the Perspective Discussion

Common self-image, principles, quality standards, and educational concept connect all facilities and include daycare for children. The regular exchange of information, feedback from practical experience, and ideas for optimization are coordinated across districts and disciplines. Here the three pillars interlock: the "sustainable purpose" with the ambition of the organization sets the framework—all activities are based on this framework—and the "connected resources" in various ways provide for continuously developed professional competence, cooperation, and feedback loops, which are essential for the "travelling organization" on its dynamic and often turbulent journey.

6.1 Example 1: Initiative 40 under 40

This is the name of an innovation project which deals with new ways of leadership development at FABIDO. To be able to meet the changing requirements of social self-understanding, demographic developments, and political frameworks, attractive ways in leadership development are also necessary. The "40 under 40" initiative, for example, brings together all FABIDO colleagues who already have leadership positions, are up to and including 40 years old, and will therefore still be able to help shape the future for more than 25 years.

Quarterly events are planned for this initiative. The kickoff event took place at the end of 2019 and received a very positive response. The program was varied: getting to know each other across departments, networking, and working together on the topics of the initiative. The result: very practical work packages that will be tackled in future events, in joint activities at unusual locations in the town, with information and discussion forums on current sociopolitical issues. The aim is to experience lateral and new thinking, to look beyond the horizon of FABIDO and the individual areas of work, and to learn together: as a person, for my work and role as a manager, for collaboration, and for future topics. A new attitude should be anchored in this way: "what contribution can I make?" instead of "am I responsible for it?"

6.2 Example 2: Initiative "Mutual"

Connectivity is built into this development measure from the start.

Initial Situation

The daycare facility teams and office teams had different views. The reasons for this were too little knowledge about the others' work, different cultural and professional backgrounds, and a lack of understanding between the teams about needs, tasks, and regulations, which ultimately resulted in a lack of trust.

Initiative, Idea, and Implementation

In order to improve collaboration, "mutual" was developed: all new colleagues are offered "mutual" visits to the daycare facilities for children and to the office, in order to give and receive insights into the respective work tasks and areas, to exchange information about current projects, to get to know the work processes of the teams, and to experience everyday life in a daycare facility "live." Especially important is the insight into the connectivity of daycare facilities and office work: What works well? Where are these barriers or delays? How can we work together more reliably?

Human resource development supports the implementation in all phases, from the organization of the topics and participants to the reflection meeting with superiors.

Objectives and Results

The experience gained so far has been described by all participants as very enriching; in addition to getting to know each other, there were insights into "many new things," into a lot of knowledge, which eases the daily work routine in cooperation with each other and allows common goals to be better achieved.

These are the expected benefits:

- Knowledge of areas of responsibility and contact persons
- Avoidance of tension through early acquaintance and exchange
- Better quality of work and motivation through background knowledge
- More creativity through collaboration on complex projects
- Higher acceptance of change processes through mutual involvement
- High identification and motivation through working in partnership
- Insights into other working worlds and different ways of thinking
- New impulses for staff's own work
- Reliable agreement on meaningful standards for cooperation
- Better capacity and resource planning through better overview
- Keeping important issues alive

7 Project Work Creates Progress in Content and Collaboration

Project groups, organized across levels and departments, are also a common part of our work. A current project on "Optimizing Processes—Experiencing Collaboration" is being supported externally. Originally focused on construction activities, the project clarification and exploration revealed further topics which were clearly defined, prioritized, and included in the project scope according to their feasibility. The current focus is on the topics of personnel recruitment and deployment, construction standards and processes, and procurement.

The project procedure was presented by the management: co-creation and quick action should be the principles which are now being consistently implemented. A steering group meets regularly, supported by external consultants; they prepare topics, gather impressions, reflect, and provide a framework for the process. In a large group event, participants of all levels and disciplines—also from other areas and offices—worked together in mixed groups from the beginning to put the topics in a concrete context. In subsequent workshops and subgroups, topics and mindsets are reflected upon, further developed, and, if necessary, rethought and elaborated. There is a co-creative process throughout networking; everyone contributes his or her own competency and strength—the connectivity of resources is experienced as fruitful and fast-acting, the satisfaction of everyone increases, and there is a common perception of effectiveness.

At the same time, coordination at the interfaces and collaboration in the processes is being improved, not only within the enterprise but also beyond it with other municipal offices and partners. In this context, it is also perfectly acceptable that some areas have already developed differently in different topics. From a management perspective, a process with mutual benefit takes place here: the participants learn from each other what they need personally, in their teams or in their areas or what they can contribute, and thus take responsibility for implementation.

This creates a lively, appreciative culture and an effective working structure to solve pending issues and continue the journey together. In this way, the FABIDO team lives the modern and flexible principles that it would like to communicate to children, parents, and other stakeholders in the facilities. It is always oriented towards our purpose of providing the best possible education, care, and upbringing for our part of society and the families and enabling colleagues to work in a meaningful, effective, and strength-oriented manner.

8 Conclusion

Reflecting on the most recent stages of the joint journey, some lessons learned can be formulated:

- "The journey is the destination": the journey is work, and it must be perceived as fulfilling and at the same time demanding. It is important to remain capable of communication and action with everyone in such a big enterprise with such a diverse workforce. This requires a variety of structures and meetings within which joint reviews and reorientations can and should take place—so that all colleagues experience effectiveness and can contribute their resources and the enterprise can use this in a connected way.
- If the meaning ("what for") is understood, it must be experienced in the process, support emotional anchoring, and increase effectiveness. This is the only way to accept results and implement them sustainably. This always happens in feedback loops, with revision phases and finally a sense of achievement. These iterative loops are adjusted to the organizational rhythm and readjusted accordingly.
- Successes need to be celebrated as they give energy for the future. At FABIDO, this included, for example, the fact that the "Kinderstuben" (children's rooms) initiative was awarded the "Socially Integrative City" prize as a nationally outstanding project or our daycare facilities won the German Kita Prize and the German Reading Prize and received many certifications. This shows us: We are on a great journey! More of what is good!
- With the help of the 3-P-Model, during our work and in the evaluation, it became clear once again that the change process must be well implemented as a quality factor, as meaning, purpose, and mindset.
- Meta-competencies are needed to work on the organization, to remain sustainable, and to go on the journey together. In other words, process-related methodological knowledge and structural conditions are also needed to bring colleagues and teams from different professions and functions together again and again, to develop together, and to be able to use all our strengths in a well-connected way.
- With alternative work structures and practices, change begins immediately. This includes changing role concepts and participation in projects alongside core

business. This allows outdated structures to be "renovated" step by step and transformed.

- This results in a high demand for a wide range of competencies, learning and leadership skills, as well as speed and flexibility. This can only be achieved by conscious reflection of available resources.
- For all those involved, from the management to the individual teams, this means more than just ambidextrous acting, and this cannot be done alone, but only together. This includes day-to-day business, development, innovation work, and crisis management in the pandemic with the consolidation this has entailed. The range of leadership is correspondingly broad: from daily delegation and guidance to promotion, development, projects, thinking ahead, and working on values, meaning, and purpose.
- A process like the one described must be experienced by all participants in an inspiring, communicative, powerful, and convincing way. All those responsible must be clear from the beginning. How do we preserve creativity and energy? How do we keep the sustainable purpose present, how do we maintain the positive momentum on our joint journey together, and how do we continuously ensure that all our resources connect meaningfully and successfully to create a great experience?

We have taken up these challenges at FABIDO. In addition to day-to-day business, we manage projects, create new networks, meet milestones, experience new fields of activity, go unusual ways, and develop new cooperation models, and our day-to-day business is continued in a stable manner. We experience progress, rhythm, barriers and solutions, measures, constant communication, and subsequent steps. The process optimization project mentioned above, for example, is all about a "profound change." At the same time, however, we believe that we are courageously continuing our chosen path, a lifelong journey.

The balance between "classical, municipal organizational behavior" (long practiced and often perceived as a pattern) and competence in change (with the ability to constructively deal with a certain complexity) sets the course for the journey into the future. The experienced and learned change competence as an organization is the tool to face and cope with rapid, unforeseeable developments and disruptions.

Change can only succeed if everyone participates and if it is understood as a permanent task, together with our "clients," the children, their families, our other partners, and stakeholders. By regularly reflecting on and feeding back what our small society needs, what changes are desired.

Learning. Planning. Developing. Every perspective counts.
We live diversity as an opportunity and challenge—from small to large.

Our very practical challenges are speed, recruitment, extension, conversion, and new construction projects for further facilities—accompanied by more capacity and more childcare places, as well as more networked structures with other offices, and the expansion of the digital infrastructure.

Connectivity on a lively journey! We are looking forward to it!

Reference

Wollmann, P., Kühn, F., & Kempf, M. (Eds.). (2020). *Three pillars of organization and leadership in disruptive times – Navigating your company successfully through the 21st century business world*. Cham: Springer Nature.

Lisa Schulze worked as an educational expert in several daycare facilities of FABIDO (Family Complementary Educational Institutions for Children in Dortmund) in the care of children between 0 and 6 years, most recently as deputy head. During this time, she also completed the degree courses Elementary Education and Management in Social Economic and Diaconal Organizations as a master; one of the focal points was change management. This was followed by further training as a systemic consultant and the change to personnel development at FABIDO.

Daniel Kunstleben has been the managing director of FABIDO since 2017. After studying political science, sociology, and pedagogy in Münster and several years of professional experience in state politics, he held further positions as a personal assistant to a district manager and as head of department for central controlling in a district administration. Subsequently he worked as a deputy mayor and department head for education, youth, social affairs, sports, and culture of a medium-sized town in North Rhine-Westphalia before he finally came to Dortmund.

Part V

3-P-Model Application in the Private Sector

In this part of the book the authors focus on their various practical experiences in different industries and contexts in applying the 3-P-Model to their projects or in analyzing the outcomes by means of the three pillars. They have provided us with new lessons learned and a lot of diverse take-aways. The journey in this part goes from examples from start-up and hybrid organizations to large transformations in established enterprises.

The seven articles cover a broad field of situations, types of enterprises and industries: such as start-ups, organizations in hybrid situations, former start-ups which want to retain their original spirit despite being fast growing, of enterprises in large, significant and demanding transformations, from Finance Industry through Retail, Plant Manufacturing and Medical Technology to Agriculture.

Start-Up Development in Traditionally Operating Industries: Regional Subsidiaries of Pharmaceutical Companies

Stefan Turnwald and Julia Zirn

Abstract

The authors shed light on the particularities in the setup and the development of regional subsidiaries of globally operating pharmaceutical companies and explore the relevance of the Three-Pillar Model (Wollmann, Kühn, Kempf, Three pillars of organization and leadership in disruptive times. Cham. Springer, 2020) (abbreviated: 3-P-Model). Geographic expansion brings a multitude of challenges; various internal and external factors limit the flexibility in shaping the subsidiary organization, while the diverse workforce becomes the melting pot for different expectations, motivations, feelings, and experiences. Especially the combination of the entrepreneurial mindset that characterizes a start-up with the highly regulated business environment and the traditional way of working in the pharmaceutical industry bears the risk of confusion, conflicts, and disruption of organizational development. Navigating the subsidiary organization into a successful future requires a commonly understood direction and the full alignment of leadership team and workforce on the "sustainable purpose." The dynamic growth of the organization demands the ongoing integration of new roles and assets but also of strategic elements and processes to ensure "connecting resources." Both "sustainable purpose" and "connecting resources" require continuous updating and adaptation to the current phase of the development journey to provide consistency and clarity for the "travelling organization."

S. Turnwald (✉)
Zug, Switzerland
e-mail: stefan.turnwald@compski.onmicrosoft.com

J. Zirn
Berlin, Germany
e-mail: zirn@cidpartners.de

P. Wollmann et al. (eds.), *Organization and Leadership in Disruptive Times*, Future of Business and Finance, https://doi.org/10.1007/978-3-030-63034-8_14

1 The Setup of Regional Subsidiaries of Pharmaceutical Companies

Pharmaceutical and biotech start-ups fall into two distinct groups based on the status and dynamics of the organizational growth and development: start-ups founded in the given territory can be differentiated from subsidiary organizations of operations in the process of geographical expansion. In the following, we will focus on the latter case and analyze important characteristics:

- Progression on the start-up journey
- Growth of the leadership team and the workforce
- Archetypes of employees in start-up organizations

1.1 Progression on Start-Up Journey

While the newly established subsidiary organization is in the earlier phases of the development journey, the headquarters of the geographically expanding pharmaceutical company is in more advanced phases, already (Fig. 1).

Having advanced into the growth phase of the start-up development journey, the headquarter organization expands geographically. The newly founded subsidiary organization transitions through the same phases of the development journey at its own pace. Consequently, these developmental transitions are not in sync with the development of the headquarter organization. The lack of synchronization results in different priorities, perceived challenges, and solution strategies. Miscommunication and misalignment of activities may hinder the subsidiary organization from catching up with the parent organization.

Differences in the market environment of the headquarters and subsidiary organizations add to this problem. While the headquarter organization has adapted to the market realities in the home country, the subsidiary operation faces the healthcare environment in the new territories. The particularities of the local markets

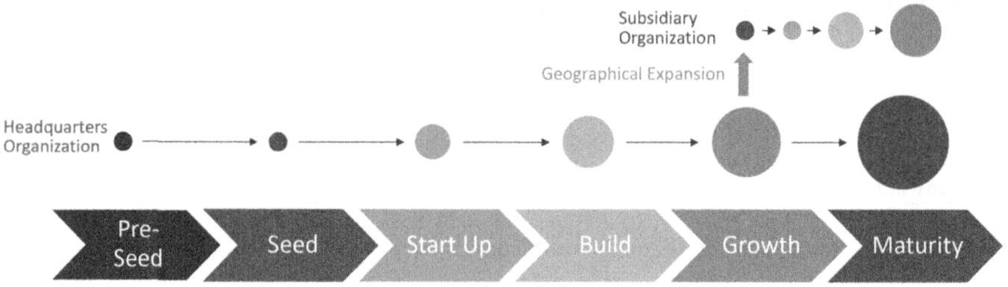

Fig. 1 The start-up journeys of the headquarters and subsidiary organizations are not in sync. The authors' own development—the phases of the start-up development have been adapted from Galadzhii (2021)

require specific attention, and any solutions may differ from the approach chosen in the home country.

1.2 Growth of the Leadership Team and the Workforce

The start-up organization is searching for talent with the specific experience, competencies, and working styles required at the given phase of the start-up journey. Over time, the diversity of employees will not only increase because of the changing selection criteria for new hires. When joining the start-up organization, new hires enter a dynamically changing environment. Onboarded to the organization at different phases of the start-up journey, the employees will enter different work environments with specific tasks, challenges, internal dynamics, and preferred ways of working. Consequently, the stage on the development journey when the new hire joins will trigger the perception of, and the adaptation to, the work environment at this point in time. As the start-up advances on its development journey, the employees may stick to the working style they have adopted when they joined the organization (Fig. 2).

Hiring the right talent at the right time is critical to the success of the operation. As priorities, challenges, and working styles change over time, it is important for all employees to continuously refocus and readapt their approach to the current business challenges and tasks. Individual employees who do not keep pace with the changes in the organizational environment have the potential to cause business disruption and hinder the start-up from developing further.

1.3 Archetypes of Employees in Start-Up Organizations

Start-up organizations in the biotech and pharmaceutical industry attract talent with different backgrounds and experience. In addition to talent with profound business

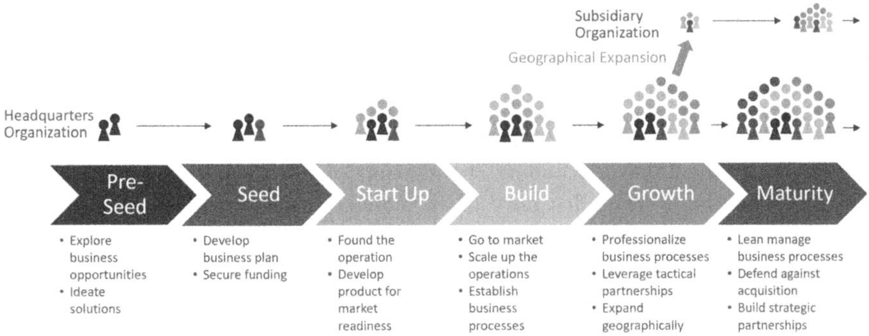

Fig. 2 Employees are joining the organizations at different phases of the start-up journey. The authors' own development—the phases of the start-up development have been adapted from Galadzhii (2021)

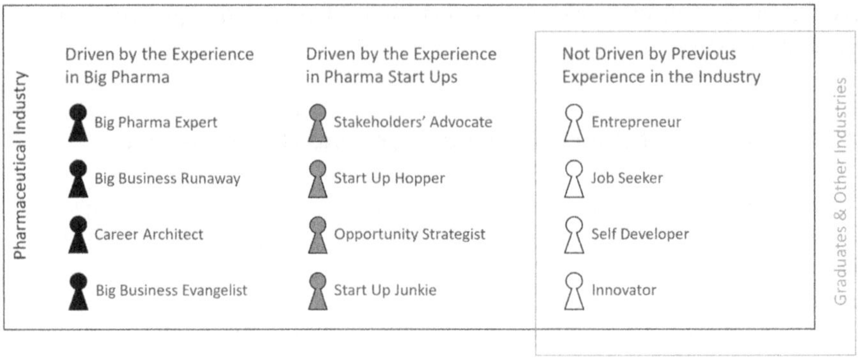

Fig. 3 Archetypes of employees in biotech and pharmaceutical start-ups. Adapted from Turnwald et al. (2021)

expertise in established mature pharmaceutical operations and candidates with experience in other start-up companies, talent is hired from other industries as well as directly from university. In geographic hot spots for biotech and pharmaceutical start-ups, e.g., Central Switzerland, job ecosystems with in-depth start-up experience have been established.

In their book *Immunity to Change*, Kegan and Lahey (2009) analyze the individual immunity to change on three levels: one's own actions in conflict with the visible commitment, the hidden competing commitments, and the big assumptions that drive beliefs, decisions, and actions. Inspired by Kegan and Lahey, the authors describe archetypes of employees in start-up organizations based on previous work experience, beliefs, and motivations (Turnwald et al. 2021) (Fig. 3).

In interviews with employees and leaders in the subsidiary organizations of pharmaceutical start-ups, a dozen archetypes have been identified. These archetypes fall into two groups depending on whether or not the beliefs, motivation, and working style of the employee are influenced by their previous experience in the pharmaceutical industry. Within the group of employees influenced by their previous experience within the industry, those primed by the environment in mature and established operations can be differentiated from those having worked in start-ups before. In the following figure, three of the archetypes are described in further detail (Fig. 4).

The above-analyzed archetypes are characterized by different beliefs and conflicting motivations for joining the start-up organization. They have hidden competitive commitments that have the potential for driving their own agenda in conflict to the needs of the developing organization.

While the new hire to a mature organization may use his or her peers for reference for good practice, there are hardly any peers to learn from, nor is there an established working style that the new starters can adopt and adhere to. Consequently, the conflicting beliefs and motivations of the different archetypes have a more pronounced impact in the start-up environment compared to the situation in established

Archetype	Hidden Commitment	Big Assumptions
The Career Architect	I will use the opportunity to complete my CV and to get myself into a great position when re-entering the established pharmaceutical business	The dynamically growing start-up allows me to take multiple career steps in a short period of time. The experience in the start-up environment complements my CV and positions me for future career steps in established pharmaceutical companies.
The Start Up Hopper	I am hoping not to be too busy before the organization is acquired and I will receive my termination package	Employees in start-ups receive significant leave packages in case the organization will be acquired. The start-up allows me to aim for the termination package with minimum effort and individual contribution.
The Entrepreneur	I am building a sustainable business	Start-ups offer the opportunity to build a successful and sustainable business. My decisions and actions are based on my unbiased professional analysis of the business situation and what is needed to steer the organization into the sustainable future.

Fig. 4 Examples of archetypes of employees in pharmaceutical start-ups: hidden competitive commitments and big assumptions. Adapted from Turnwald et al. (2021)

organizations. Therefore, the change communication in start-ups must be curated to the beliefs and motivations of the different archetypes. Seeking common ground in terms of motivation and working style should be addressed proactively.

In addition, some beliefs and motivations of the different archetypes may be beneficial at specific phases of the development journey. Archetypes who were the perfect fit when joining the start-up may not be able to adapt to the changing reality in the developing organization and hinder the start-up from progressing on its journey.

2 The Relevance of the 3-P-Model in the Management of Regional Subsidiaries

The Three-Pillar Model introduced by Wollmann et al. (2020) addresses the leadership and the transformation of organizations with regard to the three pillars of the "sustainable purpose," the "connected resources," and the "travelling organization." The three pillars represent design criteria that can be applied to the structured analysis, layout, and management of the organizational transformation in the regional subsidiaries of a geographically expanding pharmaceutical company. For further details on the Three-Pillar Model see chapter "From a Retrospective to a Perspective View".

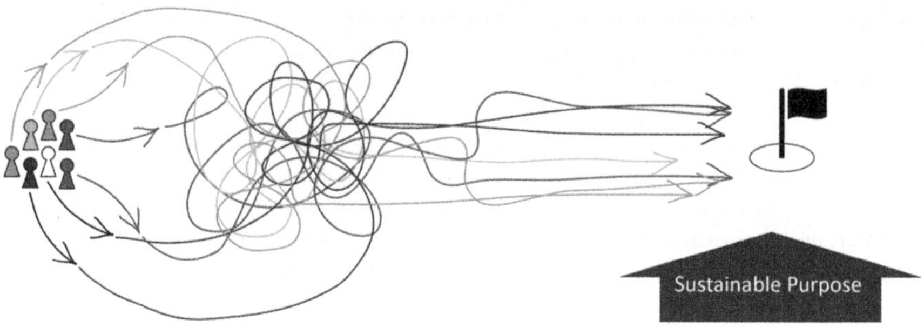

Fig. 5 Aligning the leadership team and the workforce with the sustainable purpose. The authors' own development

2.1 Sustainable Purpose

A good understanding of what the developing start-up organization stands for and the value it creates will set the clear direction for the development of the subsidiary organization. A sustainable, reliable, and consistent purpose of the organization allows teams and employees to translate it into what it means to them personally and what it means for the exchange of information with internal and external partners, as well as for priorities and tasks. When applied to the situation of the regional subsidiary organizations of pharmaceutical companies, the sustainable purpose:

- Establishes the common vision of the organization's short-, medium-, and long-term future
- Focuses on the drivers for organizational development
- Aligns stakeholders, internal functions, teams, and archetypes
- Creates a feeling of community and partnership
- Integrates individual motivations into the higher goal
- Provides the platform for the alignment of the subsidiary organization with the headquarter organization

Course corrections as well as transitional steps during the different phases of the development journey require the continuous updating of the sustainable purpose. Change communication and activities must consider the different beliefs and motivations of the heterogeneous leadership team and workforce (Fig. 5).

2.2 Connected Resources

Managing connectivity and preventing unconnected structural and task-driven silos will pave the way for the regional subsidiary to have a sustainable and successful future. The creation of an open and dynamic community of leaders and employees as well as linking not only people but all kinds of resources, strategies, activities, and information provides access to relevant assets when needed. It seeds the creative and collaborative environment that balances the various, often contradictory, beliefs and motivations of stakeholders, leaders, and employees. Connected resources allow for flexibility and successful adaptation to the continuous changes within the organization and in the environment. There are three particularities observed in the subsidiary organizations that pose critical challenges and stress the importance of the connected resources:

First, the organization mostly grows top-down. After subsidiary organization is set up, the leadership team is hired. What roles need to be filled next? Should the focus be on director and manager roles to establish the hierarchical structure? Or is it more relevant to bring individual contributors and support roles on board that will help to perform the increasing number of critical business tasks? The new hires join the continuously growing organization with continuously evolving roles, responsibilities, role interdependencies, and business processes. How can sufficient clarity on role, responsibilities, and interdependencies be provided? How can efficient collaboration and outcome driven processes be ensured if work relations are altered every time a new starter joins the organization?

Second, many of the new hires join the start-up with experience that is limited to established pharmaceutical companies. Often, a lack of awareness of the importance of some business-critical tasks is the consequence. In the start-up organization, tasks need to get done by the leader or functional expert that would be covered by the numerous functional and cross-functional support roles in large operations. Often, the new colleagues are surprised by a request to cover low-profile tasks as they have not dealt with these throughout their whole career.

Third, due to strict regulations in the pharmaceutical industry, time to market is very long. In the early phases of the development of the subsidiary, the organization does not have the possibility to get direct feedback from potential customers and other market participants. The often cited "start-up way" (Ries 2017) of producing, testing, and validating MVPs early and often and thus learning fast and in a validated manner is only possible to a very limited extent (Fig. 6).

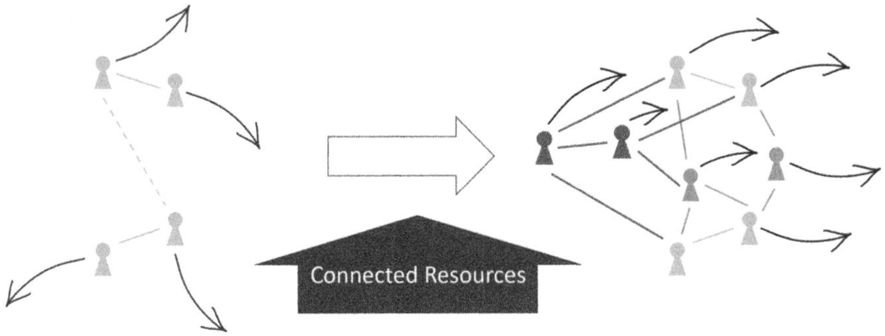

Fig. 6 Connected resources applied to people: the alignment of the leadership team and the workforce. The authors' own development

2.3 Travelling Organization

The newly setup subsidiary organization is subject to ongoing change. This continuous change happens in the transition across the phases of its development journey as well as in everyday business. For the successful leadership and management of the organizational development, the continuous change must be acknowledged and appreciated; the lack of structural clarity and operational consistency must be accepted and managed. How should this ongoing change in leadership decisions and communication be considered? What needs to be done to the needed plasticity of processes and the flexibility of collaboration networks?

The ongoing change may create feelings of uncertainty and confusion in many of the staff members: the way of working tomorrow is different from the way of working today, and what will be important tomorrow may not be relevant the following day. Some individuals even may try to use the constant change as an excuse for disengagement and low performance. Other individuals and teams may attribute the distressing situation they are experiencing to the leadership team and to their colleagues.

The pillar of the travelling organization centers the thinking in the daily work around the constant transformation process. Change becomes the norm. To navigate the troubled waters of constant change, the young and developing organization needs to set the medium- and long-term direction for the transformation. As addressed above, the sustainable purpose will help by setting the landmarks for all transformation initiatives as well as for everyday business decisions.

The organizational strategy and the tactical execution should go beyond the horizon of the current phase of the organizational development journey. Decisions should be considered in the context of the current situation but also with respect to the impact on the medium- and long-term stages of the organization's transformation journey (Fig. 7).

3 Solutions to the Challenges in Start-Up Organizations in the Pharmaceutical Industry

After outlining the impact of the three pillars in the subsidiary start-up organization, this chapter focuses on concrete measures that can be derived from these thoughts.

Before introducing specific measures for each pillar, it will focus on the selection criteria for the measures that are often more important than the measures themselves. Using a clear catalogue of selection criteria is the first useful measure.

In the case of the start-up organization, the measures must be suitable for highly uncertain, dynamic, and increasing complex environments. The Cynefin Framework (see Fig. 8) is a helpful tool to develop effective problem-solving designs and approaches as it helps to locate the identified problem and to choose an appropriate solution.

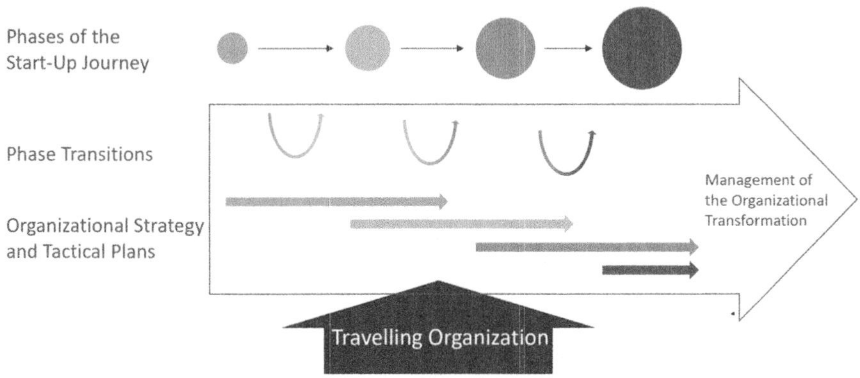

Fig. 7 Phase transitions in the "travelling organization" require special attention to the leadership and the management of the organizational development: strategy and tactical plans must aim at horizons beyond the planning horizon within the current phase of the start-up journey. The authors' own development

The Cynefin Framework distinguishes between five domains in which a problem can occur and offers a simple and clear indication of how to solve these problems effectively:

1. *Simple domain: clear cause and effect*
   Solutions can be based on experience, as phenomena can be sensed and categorized. Best practice can be applied.
2. *Complicated domain: only experts understand the problem*
   With expert knowledge, phenomena and situations can be analyzed. One of several "good practices" can be selected as an answer. A universal "best practice" is not suitable for this kind of problem.
3. *Complex domain: the problem is not clearly identifiable*
   Solutions can only be evaluated afterwards, as there is no clear cause-effect structure. Testing and experimenting are the first priority. From there, solutions can be developed iteratively.
4. *Chaotic domain: the problem is completely unknown*
   The first priority is to act in order to find out what patterns of stability are emerging and to translate the situation into the complex context.
5. *Disorder: it is unclear in which of the domains the problem lies*
   Analysis is needed to establish to which context the phenomenon/situation is to be assigned.

In the case of a start-up organization, most of the "wicked" problems originate from the complex or chaotic domain and often start in disorder. In this context, how should effective measures subsequently be selected? And what should the design look like?

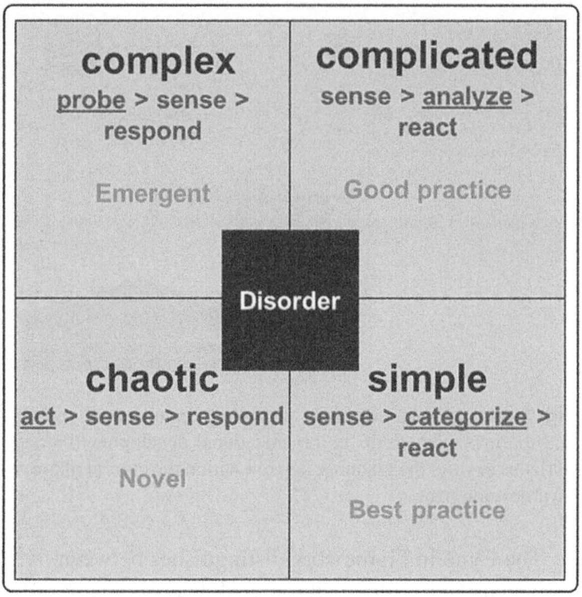

Fig. 8 Cynefin Framework, adapted from: A Leader's Framework for Decision Making; David J. Snowden (Snowden and Boone 2007) and Mary Boone, Harvard Business Review, November 2007

First, powerful measures for problems in these domains should have a high degree of flexibility and adaptability and allow for iterative approaches. As the requirements in an early start-up are highly diverse, and therefore often complex, measures must be suitable for use in highly dynamic and rapidly changing environments and, at the same time, allow for stability and safety.

Second, transparency, communication, and continuous synchronization are crucial in such a dynamic organization. Measures should be checked from this perspective too.

Third, the attitude with which the measures are selected, implemented, and applied is decisive. When a method that is designed to strengthen transparency and self-organization is used to control the team, the method will not unleash its power. On the contrary, it will produce undesirable behaviors. Decisions on measures and usage of measures in the early phases of development set the stage for the future culture of the organization.

Therefore, it is, fourth, important to review regularly whether the selected approaches produce the intended solutions. Further, in a quickly developing organization, the problems that need to be solved using a certain measure change. And thus, so should the measure. Certain approaches can be very powerful at a certain stage, but, at another stage, when the needs are different, they may not be fit for purpose. Certain questions arise. These are, for example: Is the problem that needs to be solved still virulent? Does the method reflect the level of complexity in the current situation? To ensure this reflection and review happens, retrospectives focusing on communication and effectiveness of measures can be held regularly. And at the same time, they should be done informally. Every employee should keep asking these questions and, in so doing, support the continuous development of the organization.

And finally, the meta level should be considered: Does this method provide enough stability and, at the same time, agility? Is the balance right for the phase the organization is currently in? Can needs in the next phase be anticipated? In a dynamic context of a start-up, methods should not be used with the claim to create a stable condition. Yes, they provide stability for a certain time but only in preparation for the next iteration. Methods and approaches produce a process of dynamic adaptation rather than a static condition.

In the following section, possible measures that are suitable to address typical challenges of start-up organizations in the pharmaceutical industry are outlined. Applying these, the selection criteria outlined above should be kept in mind. For further toolboxes in start-ups, see, for example, *The Corporate Start-Up* (Viki et al. 2017) or "Micro Methods for agile projects" (Zirn and Allmers 2018; Kühn and Kempf 2014).

3.1 Possible Solutions: Sustainable Purpose

Challenge for the pharmaceutical start-up organization	Impact of the pillar of the sustainable purpose	Possible measure
Asynchronous development The development of the parent and the subsidiary organizations is not in sync	The sustainable purpose of the subsidiary organization allows for transparency on the expectations as well as for the definition of the roles and responsibilities in the collaboration of both organizations	Keeping the purpose in mind and referring to it as often as possible in daily business is crucial for a common orientation and focus. To unchain the power of the purpose, deriving practices is important. For example, team meetings can be started with reference to the purpose, or, once a week, leadership can be asked to share their direct contribution to purpose during the week
Speed of transformation Rapid transition across the phases of the organizational development journey	The ongoing adaptation to the current phase of the organizational development journey and the evolution of the sustainable purpose keep the parent and subsidiary organizations focused on business-critical tasks. Course correction will be minimized if future changes in the purpose are anticipated in today's decision-making	Establishing an ongoing dialogue on purpose, goals, and strategy helps to minimize course corrections. Further, it strengthens a mindset that welcomes iterative and adaptive thinking—leadership serves as an example. Concrete measures can be quarterly goal definition workshops or a yearly purpose quest

(continued)

Variety of individual drivers The leaders and employees are driven by different or even conflicting motivations, expectations, and personal objectives	The sustainable purpose defines the common denominator of all leaders and staff members. It allows for the required self-reflection, self-positioning, and self-management of each individual leaders and employees	To serve as a common denominator, the purpose should be developed in an integrative and participative process. Involved in the process, leaders and employees start to reflect, internalize, and communicate the common vision. This personal engagement with the purpose increases commitment. During the process, the purpose should be translated into more tangible principles and practices (ask yourself: What do we see ourselves doing and not doing when we follow the purpose?). Disseminate these principles and practices among staff—for example, during onboarding, in all-hands meetings, and during everyday business meetings
High level of diversity The start-up organization is a melting pot of different experiences, priorities, and working styles	The sustainable purpose sets the North Star for the navigation of archetypes into the future of the organization. All decisions on methodologies, approaches, and working styles consider and aim at the sustainable purpose	Concrete principles derived from the purpose set the stage for the selection of concrete measures and working practices. The selection criteria outlined should support the decision on approaches and measures, backed by the purpose. It is helpful to make the different experiences and working styles (archetypes) visible and to appreciate them. This variety is extremely powerful, if it is aligned by a common North Star

3.2 Possible Solutions: Connected Resources

Challenge for the pharmaceutical start-up organization	Impact of the pillar of the connected resources	Possible measures
Limited start-up experience A critical number of new hires	Connecting resources in a start-up organization is a	Regular and ongoing dialogue on roles and responsibilities

(continued)

lack start-up experience and are greatly influenced by their experience in big pharmaceutical organizations	much different endeavor compared to a mature pharmaceutical corporation. New hires with limited start-up experience must be given sufficient clarity on their role and responsibilities. Mutual expectations should be made transparent in an ongoing dialogue on roles and responsibilities	should be institutionalized in the very early phases of the start-up organization. Uncertainties expressed by new hires are taken seriously, and the evolving corporate culture should encourage open dialogue on uncertainties concerning roles and responsibilities. For HR managers, the archetypes can serve as an effective analytical tool to obtain a better understanding of different experiences and motivations
Need to get the job done Starters joining on higher levels are focused on the leadership of a hitherto nonexistent not yet existing team without getting the job done themselves	Having clarity about which people on which level are needed for which development phase is crucial. At the same time, the individual leader or employee needs to be given sufficient clarity on the expectation of their individual contribution	The expectation of getting operational jobs done, too, needs to be transparently communicated during the hiring process and should be part of the description of roles and responsibilities. Especially when hiring experienced staff from corporates, this hands-on approach should be communicated clearly
Lack of normative power The developing start-up lacks the normative power that allows learning from observations and by good example—often there is no one to learn from	The lack of implicit and explicit rules, norms, and cultural artefacts requires the proactive communication of expectations and the management of the role in the transformation process. Every new hire becomes a role model, and this responsibility is to be addressed continuously	Proactive communication of expectations and values supports stabilization and structuration in transition phases. Leadership needs a safe space to start a dialogue on cultural topics to enable them to be a role model to their teams and to grow the new organization's culture. These cultural basics are the precondition for connected resources and sustainable growth. Investing early in these cultural building measures pays off later
Long time to market Due to the very long time to market, the organization does not have the possibility to get direct feedback from potential customers and other market participants	The time from product development to product launch is relatively long. As a consequence, experimenting, testing, validating, and improving the product and sales approach is only possible in a limited way in	"Half-open innovation" approaches allow the integration of (future) clients in product development processes. "Half" as the open innovation approach needs to be adapted to the highly regulated environment and

(continued)

	the early stages of development. The important connection of product development and market/customers cannot be established sufficiently	the thus limited possibilities of including customers in early development stages. However, advisory boards and focus groups can be used to improve fit to market and to connect crucial resources

3.3 Possible Solutions: Travelling Organization

Challenge for the pharmaceutical start-up organization	Impact of the pillar of the travelling organization	Possible measures
Ongoing change Everything within the start-up is in constant transition	Being conscious of the dynamic transformation and its impact on individuals, teams, and business processes is the requirement for accepting the continuous change which is the norm in the start-up organization	Provide tools and instruments for teams to reflect on the ongoing change and the consequences at team and individual levels, e.g., outline for short reflection workshop, moderation cards, and change canvas
Instable environment Leaders and employees are overwhelmed by the ongoing transformation and feel uncertain and insecure	Firstly, new employees should be able to handle the dynamic environment. Tolerance of ambiguity, the ability to make decisions despite uncertainty, and resilience are important skills that should be given special consideration in the recruiting process. Secondly, the effects of the dynamics should be regularly reflected on and discussed at individual, team, and organizational levels	Explicitly addressing the continuous change, and considering the impact on individuals and teams, allows for open discussion and for the path into the future to be shaped in a collaborative manner. Leaders and employees will become the architects of their present and their future. For example, "basic change in start-ups" training and targeted coaching for leadership and situational support on demand could be provided
Transformation mindset The constant change may be used as an excuse for disengagement and low performance	Considerations on the medium- and long-term impact of decisions and actions creates clarity on the value of the individual and team contribution. Performance is measured in short- as well as in medium- and long-term dimensions	"Active contribution to the continuous change process" should be part of the role description of any early employee. This expectation should be clearly formulated and required continuously

(continued)

Constant renewal Preservation of the current situation may keep the organization from developing into the future	Long- and medium-term organizational strategy and tactical plans will allow for better understanding of the impact of preserving the current situation. The impact of decisions and actions can be assessed against the impact on the current situation as well as against future scenarios	Leadership should regularly provide strategic insight and comprehensive explanations to their teams and stress the need for ongoing change. These explanations are important for the teams to understand where the journey is going and why. Comprehensive documents, clear messages, and transparent argumentation are the basis for understanding and persuasion
Asynchronous development The development of the parent and the subsidiary organizations is not in sync	Transparency of the status of parent and the subsidiary organizations allows for better understanding of the current situation and needs. Today's decisions and actions can be analyzed for the short-, medium, and long-term impact on both organizations	Including a representative of the parent organization in the quarterly strategy update helps to integrate different perspectives and sheds light on conflicting priorities

4 Conclusions

This article shows that the three pillars provide great added value when analyzing the (organizational) development of a subsidiary start-up organization in the pharmaceutical industry. The approach reveals new aspects concerning the development of the young organization that have a direct business impact when translated into practical measures.

The value of the three pillars analysis is reinforced by the specific challenges of the case. The asynchrony of the development of the headquarters and the local subsidiary adds complexity to the case. At the same time, the archetypes create a tension between start-up mentality and classical thinking, which should always be in the focus of the analysis of arising problems. And finally, the three pillars approach is valuable here since, in the highly regulated pharmaceutical industry, long time to market phases prevent the young organization of getting direct feedback from the market. In this situation, a powerful approach that identifies the central areas of action for the development of the organization and ensures continuous learning is especially important for management, HR professionals, and product development, not only for start-ups in the pharmaceutical industry but also for similar organizations starting in a regulated industry such as insurance, fintech, or crypto-industry.

References

Galadzhii, A. (2021). *Stages of startup development or seven pillars of success*. Web Blog. litslink.com.

Kegan, R., & Lahey, L. L. (2009). *Immunity to change*. Harvard: Harvard Business School.

Kühn, F., & Kempf, M. (2014). *Time flies. Integrate timelines with commitment and results*. ICG Change, 3/2014.

Ries, E. (2017). *The startup way*. New York: Currency.

Snowden, D. J., & Boone, M. (2007, November). A leaders framework for decision making. *Harvard Business Review*.

Turnwald, S., Zirn, J., & Kempf, M. (2021). *Archetypes of associates in start-up organizations*. White Paper. Zug/Berlin/Bad Honnef.

Viki, T., Toma, D., & Gons, E. (2017). *The corporate startup*. Deventer: Vakmedianet.

Wollmann, P., Kühn, F., & Kempf, M. (2020). *Three pillars of organization and leadership in disruptive times*. Cham: Springer.

Zirn, J., & Allmers, S. (2018). Micro methods for agile projects. *Zeitschrift für Organisationsentwicklung*, 3(18).

Stefan Turnwald has been an experienced functional excellence and learning and development expert for more than 20 years in the pharmaceutical industry. He started his career as a commercial representative. After switching into the learning development function, he continuously grew his responsibilities and the geographic span of his activities. Stefan is driven by the continuous transformation and improvement of the interface of the pharmaceutical operation to external stakeholders. With his holistic approach, Stefan strives for the transformation of organizational structures, functions, and business procedures for patient-centered and customer-focused way of working. He has managed and contributed to several change and business transformation projects at local, regional, and global levels. His career has spanned roles and projects in established operations of various sizes as well as in start-up organizations. Stefan studied biology at the Friedrich-Alexander University in Erlangen-Nuremberg, Germany. Currently, he works and lives in Central Switzerland.

Julia Zirn is an experienced consultant and coach with cidpartners, a renowned organizational consultancy for the facilitation and implementation of strategy and change processes located in Bonn and Berlin. Julia has been advising companies, teams, and executives from a wide range of industries, whereby "integrating perspectives" is always at the heart of her client projects. With curiosity about people and an analytical eye for processes and structures, Julia facilitates and advises on the development of powerful solutions for complex challenges. Julia studied international business administration, sociology, and cultural studies in Frankfurt, London, and at Zeppelin University in Friedrichshafen and has been published in the Journal for Organizational Development, among others.

Applying the Principles of the 3-P-Model to Build an Agile High-Performance Team Within Finance

Benjamin Rausch, John Gray, Thomas Thirolf, and Peter Wollmann

Abstract

The authors describe and evaluate an exemplary Munich Re (MR) initiative to build up a new agile unit (like a start-up) within classic Finance, using the Three-Pillar Model (3-P-Model) effectively. The project focuses on developing (individually tailored) smart, digital finance products. The development story uses, among others, communication documents of Digital Finance (DF) and their development over time. The reason why the new—virtual—unit is a magnet for global talents and why the unit has developed into a role model within MR is described, and this description is embedded and completed by two interviews (with the Head of Group Controlling and with an Application Developer of Digital Finance).

1 Recap of the 3-P-Model

The Three-Pillar Model, described in the book *Three Pillars of Organization and Leadership in Disruptive Times* (Wollmann et al. 2020), was created as an answer to the needs of a VUCA world in order to show adequate agile and flexible solutions.

The 3-P-Model is based on the following three main design principles for future organization and leadership:

B. Rausch (✉) · J. Gray · T. Thirolf
München, Germany
e-mail: brausch@munichre.com; jgray@munichre.com; tthirolf@munichre.com

P. Wollmann
Bonn, Germany
e-mail: pw@peterwollmann.com

P. Wollmann et al. (eds.), *Organization and Leadership in Disruptive Times*, Future of Business and Finance, https://doi.org/10.1007/978-3-030-63034-8_15

- *Sustainable purpose*
  The employees and teams in the organization, but also its key stakeholders in the entire ecosystem and business environment, must know what the organization stands for and what entrepreneurial value it created and what societal contribution it makes. This includes the reciprocity of enterprises, public and social institutions, science, etc.
  The purpose must remain sustainable, reliable, and consistent, supported by leaders, employees, and stakeholders, lived by important representatives of the organization. The purpose aligns, convinces and inspires the people involved in the joint endeavor, and makes them confident, proud to be part of it and contribute to it.
- *Travelling organization*
  We have to understand that organizations are continuously on a journey, experiencing twists and turns, following their purpose or even striving for survival, and always looking for the best way between poles, alternatives, and options. If the teams don't know what to expect around the next bend, they have to make smaller steps and explore the terrain. Even if they don't know in advance what the best result will be, they will achieve it: they believe in their motivation and ability to manage the journey and to rely on their agile mindset, self-reflection, readiness to embrace change, and willingness to deliver. People in a travelling organization are curious, open, courageous, and keen to experiment, and they deal well with uncertainty, stress, and unforeseen incidents.
- *Connecting resources*
  The organization has to be aware that impact, value, and efficiency but also urgent survival need multiple connectivity: between humans, organization, and ecosystem; between expertise and influence; between different political and social systems and cultures; between enterprises, scientific research, and public sector; between customer satisfaction and economic needs; between strategy, processes, and skills; and between risk management and business continuity. This means managing connectivity, preventing unconnected structural silos, boxed competencies, and echo chambers, but inspiring and supporting multilateral behaviors and initiatives in global and local professional communities, balancing the various, often contradictory interests between the stakeholders.

All three pillars are key assets of systemic dynamics and high organizational effectiveness: they provide orientation and inspiration and give fundamental impulses to start the journey and to connect the resources for joint success.

2 Analytical Report of the Design and Implementation of the Digital Finance Unit Within Group Controlling

2.1 The Structure of the Analytical Report on Digital Finance

- The article will provide a perspective on how to navigate an organization with a complexity mindset through emergent changes adopting the 3-P-Model.

- First the authors describe the initial situation when the decision to build up Digital Finance (DF) was made (interestingly DF was an idea created by employees; it was not created by a management decision), the sustainable purpose and vision; target; strategic, operational, and financial setting of the unit chosen; and preconditions at the start incl. the main obstacles. The importance of the three main players at the beginning—the sponsors (CFO and Head of Group Controlling) and the project head for building up the unit—is stressed in detail.
- Secondly the journey of the project ("travelling organization") is described, e.g., the culture (belief in people, trust, independence etc.) and the phases:
  - A first vision
  - Start small, think big but really start small
  - Fly below the radar—loose connection to the surrounding world in this phase
  - Go as fast as you can—build up key competencies away from the "normal" or classic organization
  - Have sufficient power to avoid hierarchies—keep the freedom for autonomous, self-determined focus and time for your work, stay experimental, and be aware that it is not methods that create agility but mindset
  - Chase the money and become more advanced—make sure that you are well-known inside the enterprise and that you have the connectivity to smoothly work with your real and potential clients, grow organically, and prevent overhead and bureaucracy. Foster a fast and focused development of both small and complex use cases and help to implement individually tailored solutions
- Thirdly the authors will describe and analyze the outcome so far:
  - The clients acquired inside MR and their satisfaction
  - The implemented applications and their performance
  - The high-performance team with its special culture and how this setting will be preserved
  - The role model of the unit and its impact for the rest of MR and how the experience exchange is driven**Remark**

The status of Digital Finance is discussed also from different perspectives in two interviews, documented in Sects. 3 and 4 of the article.

Finally, an overall conclusion and lessons learned/practical takeaways are documented in Sects. 5 and 6 of the article.

2.2 Introduction

Today's finance organizations must deal with digital transformation driving significant changes in their organization's business model in a disruptive environment and with new competing market entrants. At the same time, finance organizations must meet ever-increasing internal and external requirements with highly complex interdependencies.

There is a strong need for faster and more data-driven analysis as there is an increasing amount of data available. The expectation is that the use of newly available data allows for more stable forward-looking predictions, true scenario analysis, and simulations which, combined with modern artificial intelligence, support decision-making in uncertain conditions. But this growing data volume is not manageable without automation, and complex relationships between key performance indicators make it challenging to provide timely and precise decision-making recommendations for top management.

As suggested by the 3-P-Model, the sustainable purpose is one of the three key design principles of modern organizations or institutions. This calls directly for a sustainable purpose of finance organizations being part of the overall and business environment, measuring the success of the business in financial terms. During today's digital transformation, the sustainable purpose of modern finance organizations is confidently to take the best decision for their company, their teams, and their customers.

In an increasingly complex and volatile environment, it immediately follows that finance organizations have to:

- Serve and collaborate with the business units to drive customer values, taking financial needs into account
- Meet the need for faster and more effective decision-making as well as the ability to quickly change previous decisions and adapt to new information
- Use agile principles and modern leadership skills to make individuals and their teams more effective

It is important to understand that, by successfully tackling the above challenges, it is an almost inevitable consequence that the organization becomes more efficient and realizes cost savings. Even though popular amongst more traditional business models, cost savings themselves should never constitute the core part of the organization's purpose. This is mainly because cost savings are limited by their nature and thus cannot serve as a continuously remaining purpose.

2.3 The Problem to Solve

In late 2016 it all started with a single individual working in the group's central controlling division, (Group Controlling) creating first ideas on how to address these challenges. In order to make people and teams more effective for faster, more value-creative decision-making, a widespread, and mainly technical, problem that exists in almost all large organizations was identified. It is the technical separation of the data from business analyses required for informed decision-making that makes work in finance organizations laborious and cumbersome and slows down the whole organization and its people.

The lack of integration of these two components causes finance employees' time-consuming, unfulfilling, and unappreciated work, namely, to gather, prepare, structure, transform, and update the required data. Often, many process steps are still manual and labor-intensive and thus prone to errors. Therefore, comprehensive and complex test mechanisms are required to avoid errors and to ensure sufficient analytical quality for decision-making. Sometimes the integration of the required data into existing analytical models or reports can be so time-consuming that, once the results are available, they are already outdated due to, for example, market developments and they have to be updated again before they can be used for decision-making. These hurdles can obviously lead to slow decision-making—leaving the organization at risk of being unable to quickly adapt to the latest developments.

The time-consuming data integration can even prevent people from using large data sets or meaningful additional data (e.g., from external data sources) to enhance, validate, or benchmark their analytical results because they would not be able to provide their results within the required timeframe. It is obvious that this could lead to mediocre analytical results and ultimately to bad decisions with negative consequences for customers, employees, and the organization itself. In solving this problem, finance organizations and their people can become significantly more effective by enabling them to quickly provide new value-creative analytical content that was previously impossible to obtain.

Since the root cause of these issues is a technical problem, one could argue that there are already many data integration and business process automation (BPA) tools from the robotics environment available to improve process quality and efficiency. But preparation for far-reaching strategic or financial decision-making is mostly highly complex and, at the same time, relatively infrequent. These decisions are not made a thousand times a day like, for example, invoice postings using the pre-defined procedures. In addition, these decisions must be made against a background of significant uncertainty, volatility, and ambiguity, which requires meaningful scenario analyses, complex simulations, or even machine learning/artificial intelligence to support the decision-making. Finally, a significant portion of management judgement remains, but finance organizations must address the challenge to provide best-in-class analytical results to foster data-driven, well informed, and unbiased high-level management decisions (Fig. 1).

After discussing the problem with the IT department, it became clear that a different (hitherto unavailable) technical solution to the problem was required. The idea was to build the Digital Finance Platform (DFP), an open, virtual, data-driven analytics and reporting platform featuring fast, automated, and consistent data traffic from any internal and external data source to enable truly integrated and consistent analytics in a user-friendly, simple, and easy-to-use manner and to seamlessly provide mobile and web-based interactive self-service intelligence for decision-making by the Management Board.

Fig. 1 Translating business insights, enabling analyses that create true knowledge needed for effective decisions which support further business development (Illustrated by Frank Kühn, used with permission. All rights reserved)

2.4 The Technical Solution

The DFP is based on the key idea of making access to any data source system (whether external or internal) easier for people in order to render them more effective. Therefore, the focus of the DFP is completely on the people, i.e., the end users and explicitly not on the communication between IT systems as in many other existing IT solutions with similar requirements. The DFP is and must remain lean in its technical architecture for cost-effective maintenance and operation, yet flexible and easily expandable, and open in communication with various other analysis and reporting tools.

For this purpose, the DFP provides all the necessary translation services virtually (i.e., without its own data storage) as an abstraction layer between the end user and the source systems and thereby enables cross-technology standardization of the data access logic. The data is accessed virtually and in real-time directly from the data source system in such a way that it is directly pushed into any analytical model used by the end-user with the required granularity and structure at precisely the time required without any manual intervention. Thus end users can automate their existing analytical models and provide and update their analytical results very quickly to prepare recommendations for action to the management.

By querying the data in real-time from the true data source systems, it can be ensured that the end user is always using the most recent and quality-assured set of data available from the source. In order to ensure proper data governance and IT security, the DFP uses "Single Sign On" (SSO), i.e., without additional input of user data, the user is recognized with his individual authorization and permissions, for the respective data source system is taken into account and a consistent data access check is ensured.

2.5 The Evolutionary Approach

2.5.1 A First Vision

Based on the first ideas, a Digital Finance vision was developed not only to solve the problem but, even more importantly, to offer a way to implement the envisaged solution together with, and for the benefit of, the people in the whole finance organization. By sharing and discussing the Digital Finance vision with the Group CFO and Head of Group Controlling, who acted as sponsors and supporters, the vision evolved over time and is still growing.

Since the vision included the use of much modern technology which was unavailable in the market at that time, there were serious concerns about the feasibility and the suitability of the approach. The concerns revolved around the well-known observations that projects of this type can easily become much more expensive than initially expected, are finalized much later than planned, while delivering less than originally intended. In order to address these concerns, it was clear that, from the outset, a truly interdisciplinary project team was needed. Due to the extensive leeway and high uncertainty of the idea, we decided against a classical IT implementation project and resorted to agile principles.

2.5.2 Start Small, Think Big, But Really Start Small

Unlike a usual project start—typically including a lot of preparation work starting with a project charter, requirements documentation, organizational charts, and the on-boarding of all potential stakeholders and people—we decided to go for what we call an "evolutionary approach," focusing on different aspects in each of the project phases. At the beginning the project team was more a project duo that, for good reason, consisted of only two individuals—one from Group Controlling and one from IT. The duo was assigned the challenge to quickly perform a proof-of-concept and to build an initial but working prototype for key elements of the envisaged solution.

One of the key success factors in this early phase was that the duo combined strong finance and business expertise with long-term experience in IT project management as well as excellent technical and programming skills. Within 1 day the duo was able to agree on a common understanding of the problem and possible solutions. With this minimum coordination, the duo started a very simple proof-of-concept (PoC) of the idea that was pure and simple at its core: the possibility to connect various internal and external source systems. It was particularly important to keep the duo's speed high—technologies had to be evaluated and tested and, if needed, to be exchanged in very short cycles. During this phase long coordination and alignment processes between many experts and decision-makers would have hindered the team and would have jeopardized the overall success.

Even though everyone talks about "start small, think big," managers and employees may find it difficult to convey the sufficiently large relevance of an initially small topic in order to work undisturbed and exclusively on the topic. During this phase the team relied on the support and backing by its sponsors and supporters and was able to work together very closely with almost no interference from outside and to make independent decisions. Having dedicated all their resources to the development, they successfully completed the PoC and built a prototype without any external support. Due to the fast prototyping, internal funding for IT resources were not required. But at that time, and still today, the team accepted that everything they built might almost certainly have to be changed or even discarded, and they explicitly agreed to be fearless of failure in the interests of the best available solution.

2.5.3 Fly Below the Radar

After a few weeks, the team demonstrated a viable concept to the sponsor and supporters and aroused initial interest from early users in the organization. The concept not only included a working Digital Finance Platform (DFP) prototype but also described a way of working to help future users of the solution implement it into their day-to-day practice. It was clear that the pure deployment of the DFP software would fail without meaningful implementation and maintenance support provided by the Digital Finance team.

Therefore, the team focused on end users as their internal clients and started small implementation projects in nano teams, jointly with the internal clients, to digitalize and automate their use cases using a co-creation approach. Based on promising client feedback, the team iteratively improved the technology stack and connected more and more data sources to enable the digitalization of more use case and to win new clients. At this early point, the team continued to test as many different technologies as possible and changed large parts of the original architecture, still unafraid of failure and steadily accumulating small wins and beneficial changes. It became critical to increase speed and agility in order to be able to change direction very quickly. At the same time, the team grew as some of the first customers embarked on the Digital Finance journey and joined the team.

In order to get anywhere near achieving the overall concept, the team needed to fly below the radar to reduce the number of stakeholders and the number of influencers. On the one hand, critical questions, additional suggestions, or general criticism that may be important and helpful later can absorb a lot of time and energy in the early stages of the project. On the other hand, serious avoidable mistakes that could happen due to relatively broad freedom at the beginning have to be avoided. Therefore, the duo had to rely on their professional experience and, at the same time, to maintain a loose connection to the rest of the organization to ensure that the concept fitted well into other innovative projects and to avoid unnecessary redundancy.

Based on early customer success stories, the team received first small amounts of seed funding from neighboring central divisions with available internal IT budget. This informal step—the simple reallocation of internal IT budget—was very important since any further development of the DFP prototype required IT budget according to the organizations' rules and procedures. And it happened quietly. This allowed the team to silently prepare "going public" and the long-term fundraising from internal IT committees together with its sponsors and supporters.

2.5.4 Go as Fast as You Can

While still spending money but winning fans along the way, the team began marketing the concept and presented the idea and the solution to hundreds of people in Munich Re business units and central divisions and to domain experts as well as to the international organization including ERGO and MEAG. This increasing visibility brought about increasing requests and demands from existing and potential customers. To meet these requests, the team again had to increase speed and to hire new team members, bringing in the new expertise and skills needed to meet additional customer demand. Therefore, the team started its fundraising for the approval of the IT budget required to provide a business case and business plan to secure funding from the respective committees.

As in the outside world or any other start-up, the team developed its own key performance indicators such as the following:

- Number of customers/user
- Number of successfully implemented use case
- Usage metrics of the platform (e.g., data volume and number of queries)
- Enabled business growth (number of additional reinsurance deals won with business units)
- Expressed interest in the solution from external parties

to measure and to prove its success or failure. For business plan purposes, the financial values created by the DFP are based on the value of every implemented use case. Customers measure the benefits of their use case in the value of working hours saved plus any money saved that was not spent on external parties. In addition, the team and its customers try to measure any increase in effectiveness by qualitatively describing any nonfinancial indicators for improvement such as higher analytical frequency, more timely decision-making, additional previously unavailable analyses, and more profound results due to increased data usage.

When the team had to submit its request for its IT budget and to present the business case, they had very limited insight from only a few already implemented use cases. There were so many unknowns (e.g., average value of future use cases, number of potential use cases, average time for implementation of use cases) that the team had to confidently take a bold move and finally promise significant financial values as well as business and overall user growth—challenge accepted.

Based on a value-creative business case, DF was provided with midterm IT budget from the respective committees, enabling it to hire external IT developers and IT domain experts. It is important to note that the level of the requested IT budget was not chosen arbitrarily. The team could easily have asked for more but carefully decided to ask for only as much funding to hire a maximum number of new teammates before having to introduce overhead or hierarchies without compromising on achieving the maximum financial benefits from the business case.

It is important to mention that the overall team setup was not only truly interdisciplinary—in the sense that IT and Controlling experts joined forces—but also that the DF team was only convened virtually. This meant that the team consisted of two—from an organizational standpoint—completely separate teams: one IT subsection reporting to the CIO and one controlling department reporting to the Group Head of Controlling, which both have different reporting lines to the Management Board. And even beyond this, the DF team actually combines two different management levels from the IT subsection and the Controlling department. Consequently, the organizational charts of Munich Re do not show Digital Finance at all, nor is there a formal management level attached to it. And even though the formal internal procedures require the Controlling Head of Department to request IT budget in order to finance the IT subsection's work, the entire Digital Finance team still believes that these hierarchies are unnecessary to achieve great results for business, controlling, and IT as well as for the whole Munich Re Group.

In order to attract top IT talents from, or in competition with, other popular ventures, the team again followed an unconventional approach and first created competency building blocks to identify the skills needed today and in the future. Based on those building blocks, the team actively searched and approached known or referred talents and invited them to acquaint themselves with the DFP and the existing team. While getting to know potential candidates, the team received valuable feedback on the solution and understood from whose competencies the solution would benefit most and which candidate fitted best into the existing team. Along the lines of the building blocks, the team was gradually able to hire top talents in whom they believed.

In order to continue delivering on the business plan while integrating new team members, it was decided to locate all team members close to the customers. For a truly cross-functional (Business and IT) approach, this led to the creation of an island separate from existing processes, structures, or organizational affiliations, guarded against any disturbance and noise from the outside. In simple terms this allowed the team not only to maintain its speed but to increase it. In addition, the following aspects had a significant impact on the team's further success:

- Customer focus: not only was the design and the implementation of DFP and the use cases largely defined by user feedback but also the prioritization of the team's day-to-day work was primarily derived based on expected user benefits from the individual components
- Co-location: despite the different organizational affiliations, the interdisciplinary team worked in a common office space for quickly executed feedback and brainstorming sessions
- Availability: all team members worked (almost) exclusively on the DFP and use case implementation without conflicting priorities with other topics
- Technical expertise: the combination of detailed specialist business knowledge in financial models, simulations, analyses, reporting, and processes on the one hand and technical expertise on the other enabled the team to solve problems quickly and autonomously without being tied to complex and time-consuming organizational processes

2.5.5 Have Sufficient Power to Avoid Hierarchies

The team grew and prospered and stayed absolutely disciplined about avoiding traditional hierarchies within the team. A strong belief and unreserved trust in each other and the whole forms the basis of an autonomous and self-organizing team. It was very evident that the team needed to have enough power over the technology and processes to be able to avoid dependencies. The team organized itself along the use cases (in a customer centric manner) and created autonomous teams inside the team. The nano teams changed over time according to the skills needed for the use case, and at the same time the team considered due process very carefully including the ever-important requirement of compliance gates, IT security, and legal requirements. It is not methodology that makes teams agile—though it helps—it is the mindset that is key (Fig. 2).

As technologies, processes, and dependencies grew, it became more and more difficult to change direction. The team decided to have 1-week sprints to promote small and rapid releases for motion and for fun. As the innovative mindset is the foundation of what the team is doing, it is also the fuel that keeps the team going. It is important to create space by establishing (mandatory) freethinking time which allows everyone on the team to do whatever they think makes sense. It could be anything from random and seemingly unrelated experiments, training, or simply solving annoying problems for which nobody ever had enough time. There is only one obligation with the freethinking time: everybody must share their learning experience with the whole team.

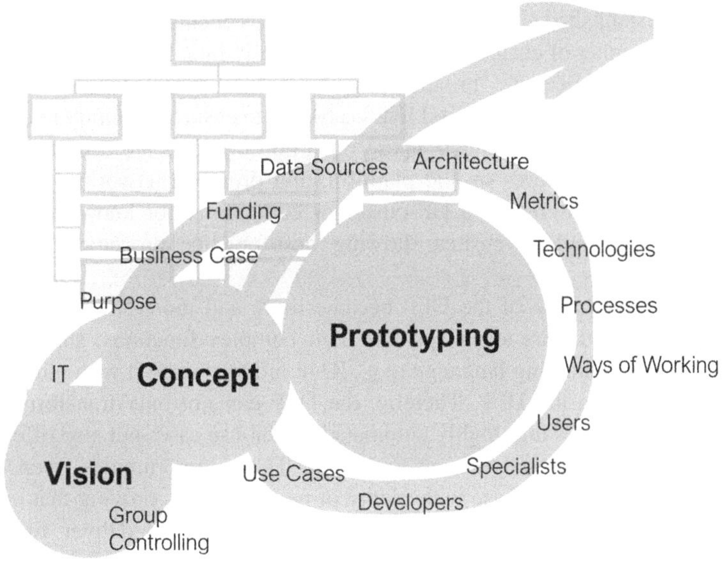

Fig. 2 Creating a dynamic of its own, connecting all resources to an evolutionary momentum (Illustrated by Frank Kühn, used with permission. All rights reserved)

In addition to the freethinking time, the team decided to present and to demonstrate the DFP solution to the outside world to obtain external feedback for further improvements. The idea is mainly to ensure that the solution not only covers Munich Re's needs but would also be able to address the challenges of a broad range of organizations across different sectors. This also includes entering awards in order to be challenged and to receive academic and expert feedback. Moreover, the team continuously invites, and is invited by, friendly colleagues from other start-ups and ventures for further inspiration. Regardless of how far the other ventures' challenges and solutions are from the DFP, there are always at least a few innovative ideas from these mutual demonstrations and open discussions that the team can use and implement into the DFP solution. This approach of continuous feedback and inspiration is precisely what is needed now, and in the future, to stay well ahead of relevant developments and to make sure that the team has all the capabilities to master future challenges on its own.

2.5.6 Chase the Money and Become More Advanced

With a smoothly operating team, handling a continuously rising number of requests, the focus moved completely to delivery of our business plan. The team was earning more and more money in terms of working hours saved for colleagues around the world. But the team was not only able to support colleagues in small- to medium-sized use cases but also in large and complex requirements saving not only time but also avoiding spending a lot of money on external suppliers for acquiring and implementing large enterprise systems. Even for those large use cases, the team encouraged and insisted on the co-creation approach to share and to maintain the digital skills acquired during the implementation.

The team established genuine relationships with its clients and partners. Due to an already high number of customers and an increasingly international community, the team searched for adequate "broadcasting channels." The team established open-house sessions that were also shared live via Skype to ensure proximity to customers and to maintain personal contact. These open-house events are used to exchange ideas, present new features on the platform, and promote networking among the users. The team also created a DF customer community for knowledge sharing, featuring, for example, websites showing best practice procedures and video tutorials.

As the technical base of the DFP became more and more advanced, the team started to help customers to encapsulate their complex functions, simulations, or analyses in a programming language (e.g., R) in order to share it with other users in the organization via the DFP. Thereby, the DFP can not only transform manual cumbersome processes into highly automated digital use cases but also offer a wide and flexible range of analytics as a service. These opportunities opened up a completely new customer base with plenty of new use cases proving that customer feedback, an innovative mindset, and the determination to deliver fuel digital transformation.

In order to meet these growing client needs and to make the platform fit for the future, the team again decided to change almost everything at the heart of the platform: its technical architecture. The team prepared the platform's migration into the cloud and split the application monolith into scalable microservices on Docker for Azure. The ability to make substantial changes in direction depends on the size of the application or how well individual components are encapsulated. From a certain critical size, it becomes increasingly difficult to make fundamental changes to an application monolith. From the beginning, the team internalized these considerations as guiding principles not only in the technical architecture and software development but also in its organization, with the aim of remaining able to implement fundamental changes at any time.

Today the DFP team has the data of the main internal and external data sources available as well as access to business domain expertise, and this logic is now available in modules. As a logical consequence, the team started working on the orchestration of this functionality for more intelligent analysis: able to use artificial intelligence (AI) such as deep learning models and stronger digital and data-driven support in the decision-making process.

2.6 Current Travel Location and the Way Ahead

Nowadays, many use cases and financial processes not only within the finance organization but also within other central divisions as well as business units have been partially and fully digitalized and automated using the Digital Finance Platform. The DF team trained many people to use its latest technology and apply digital skills and has thus contributed to the transformation of the entire (finance) organization.

The team strongly exceeded all of its business case objectives and its ambitious business plan targets well ahead of time. It also managed to support business units from a central division to create customer values and to drive business growth. This was only possible because the team grew organically and stopped growing before creating overhead. The team still resists traditional hierarchies. Decisions are made by the team, guided by the most experienced team member in quickly executed brainstorming sessions, approaching the form of a pure functional hierarchy per topic or case by case.

Admittedly, the preservation of the achieved results as well as the further development is becoming more and more difficult during these challenging times. Innovative teams must continuously justify that their value is greater than their (internal) budget requirements. Since most of the value does not simply come from working hours saved but from higher staff effectiveness, the training and application of future critical skills and a stronger collaboration across the organization will remain challenging to maintain the entrepreneurial spirit and the setup of such teams.

The Digital Finance Platform is already used by hundreds of people, part of more than hundred use cases, and applied in countless individual analyses for faster and more effective decision-making in order to create customer values and to drive digital transformation across the whole organization. Evolving technology combined with the continuous exchange between technical and business experts inspired creativity on both sides and created new digitalization ideas. Consequently, the team has already prototyped voice-driven user interaction for even greater user-friendliness and to increase the range of possible use cases. The first AI-based prototypes have also shown promising results and are being explored even further in order to manage the increasing complexity and to capture additional, perhaps unknown, insights.

It is important to mention that the application of the developed DF solution is not limited to Munich Re or the insurance industry. It is not even limited to finance. It could serve any other purpose where there is need to integrate data for better analytical results and for faster, more effective decision-making. Therefore, the team continues to gather external feedback to further improve the solution from other corporates or, for example, by applying for and being nominated for the Controlling Excellence Award 2019 of the Internationaler Controller Verein eV in Germany.

There is still a long way to travel and to explore. From the team's point of view, this is precisely what is needed for the future, not only to compete but to win. And we all agree that constantly striving to find an even better way is a noble and worthy undertaking.

3 Interview with Thomas Thirolf, Head of Group Controlling, on How to Lead a Hybrid Organization

3.1 Brief Intro

Peter Wollmann, lead editor of the book, *Organization and Leadership in Disruptive Times—Design and Implementation of the 3-P-Model* to be published at the beginning of 2021 by Springer Nature, interviews Thomas Thirolf, Head of Group Controlling at Munich Re. Thomas has been in his current role for more than 15 years, directly reporting to the CFO of Munich Re. He is the architect of a very effective and efficient controlling function at Munich Re and sponsor and supporter of the new unit "Digital Finance" in his division. Thomas and Peter have been in contact for nearly 20 years and have had many professional discussions and exchanges. Thomas knows the 3-P-Model very well, developed in the book (Wollmann et al. 2020).

3.2 Development of a Hybrid Organization at Finance, Munich Re

Question
What was the initial situation and the reason to create an agile section like Digital Finance in the Group Controlling Department of Munich Re?

Answer

The decision was based on three factors:

- The insight that the finance organization urgently needed to be more future-oriented, which meant, among other things, becoming more flexible
- The application of professional data analytics and the use of the appropriate tools is only possible if one is in command of one's own data with the ability to process it efficiently with external data
- Exactly the right person was available who had the potential to build up the new unit

In summary the realization that there was urgent need and, in parallel, the opportunity to perfectly meet it were in place, which is an ideal setting.

Question

Could you describe the development of the agile section (named Digital Finance) from the start to now? What was the sustainable purpose for this unit? What types of personalities and experiences were acquired for the team? What did the journey look like from your perspective? How is the connectivity between the unit and the "rest of Munich Re"?

Answer

There was a clear feeling of urgency in the financial organization that we needed significantly more time for analysis instead of manual data collection which would thus contribute to better steering decisions. This means lean and automated obtaining of solid, easy-to-interpret, and further evaluable data—and a conversion of the relation between data collection and evaluation from 80% to 20% today to 20% to 80% tomorrow. This describes a very sustainable purpose. By the way: an organizational increase of efficiency and reduction of costs is a positive side effect.

The decision-making and the establishment of Digital Finance did not follow traditional patterns with a detailed business plan, model for proceeding, clarification of roles and responsibilities, etc. So, it was definitively not an armchair decision but the start of an explorative journey, checking the ground step by step. Coincidentally, we had exactly the right person for such a journey—who had joined the Controlling Department for a specific temporary role and was originally already on his way back to his former position.

So we started the journey with a purpose and a high-level vision, but without defined budget, roles, and deliveries on milestones, more like a research and development venture into the unknown. The idea was, nevertheless, to come back with first insights after 6 weeks and check them against the needs of the potential clients and the probability of a sustainable installation of the concept for "business as usual." The fundamental outcome after only a few weeks was that, on the one hand, the two individuals from controlling and IT performed very well and had mastered their agile, iterative, and explorative approach and that, on the other, our potential clients were becoming more and more interested in the solutions offered as they covered urgent needs.

Question
Which are the key interfaces of Digital Finance with Group Controlling? Which fundamental decisions do you have to take and which operational decisions on a regular basis?

Answer
I would prefer not to make a distinction *or* set structural boundaries between agile and classic parts of the organization. We focus on flagging up challenges as agile or classic (e.g., using waterfall methodology) independently of where the tasks have to be performed in the organization. This means that even though—of course—Digital Finance has a larger scale of agile tasks, in other parts of Group Controlling, agile working style is on its way as well.

As Digital Finance managed early on to convince its users/clients that Digital Finance solves a lot of their problems and meets their urgent demands, Digital Finance is appreciated in the whole organization. There are no issues in cooperation at all, and all interfaces to Digital Finance work well—which is also proved by the steady increase of internal clients.

Question
To summarize: which are the key impacts for you to have agile and "classic parts" in your division?

Answer As already stressed, I don't differentiate between agile and classic parts of the Controlling Division. The organization is structurally not hybrid but the division's challenges are hybrid. The impact of this is that the people in Group Controlling have to be competent in both perspectives and flexible in their mindsets.

The decision if we go agile or classic—or something in between—is always made dependent on the specific challenge. So people have to cover both from a methodological and behavioral aspect. This means that the identification of the right people for this context is key as is the development of existing people.

In my experience, the key hiring criterion is personality—everybody can learn a new methodology. The personality "for both worlds" is flexible, thinks in scenarios, is context-oriented, is able to connect, can take responsibility, and is able to delegate. It is the personality for a journey into the unknown.

By the way, I think that I already covered the importance and applicability of the 3-P-Model for Group Controlling: the sustainable purpose giving orientation; the ability to go on an agile journey, even into the unknown (travelling organization); and the need for connectivity and thinking in contexts.

3.3 Future Challenges from the Further Development/Growth of Controlling and Digital Finance

Question
What are the main challenges for the fast-growing unit in your department and Digital Finance's increasing number of clients in the next couple of years, and what would this mean for your management and leadership concepts?

Answer To take decisions in a "VUCA-world" environment, making maximum use of different data resources in real time and consequently always thinking in scenarios in order to be able to adapt decisions very fast. This environment demands self-learning teams who act in an agile way with systematic reviews to improve their outcomes.

Question
How do you maintain the original entrepreneurial culture of Digital Finance and spread it to Group Controlling and beyond?

Answer
The most important motivation factor is success, and I completely believe in the success of this team as long as they have the possibilities (including budgets) to be innovative for their customers. As they are completely focused on their customers' needs, it is a "no-brainer" that their solutions are spread within Group Controlling and beyond.

Question
How can the travelling mindset and connectivity capabilities of Digital Finance or your whole department be maintained and further spread?

Answer
It is a bit intrinsic for Digital Finance and the whole Controlling Division to have a travelling mindset and connectivity capabilities. You approach your (potential) client and ask: "What is your problem, and how can I support you?" You have to make an advantage of cooperating transparently—and you don't know the solution in advance. You normally have to build such a solution like building up Digital Finance in an explorative journey. You have to be flexible in your mind and be capable to evaluate quickly in order to be successful. That's a travelling mindset.

In order to market the services of Digital Finance and Group Controlling, we intensively started diverse communities for professional exchange where we can advertise services. We also invite clients to get involved in our developing solutions for them so they understand what we do.

Last but not least, Digital Finance offers open-house sessions to present the latest developments and most recent features. And finally: content clients are perfect for word-of-mouth recommendations.

3.4 Your Management and Leadership Experiences and Vision

Question
Which special changes in your leadership style and your leadership principles did you have to make in order to best handle your hybrid organization? What is very different to the situation before?

Answer
I think my leadership has changed definitively over the last couple of years. I am a lot more excited to explore and invent and realize despite being aware of a certain risk. And I have a better analytical overview of the portfolio of future challenges and the options how to run them, including risk considerations, than before. It was very helpful that I already had the right setting for this as I realized with hindsight that I had the right people in the right setting and a very trusting and reliable and supportive CFO. This helped me to deploy my team members according to their strengths and give them autonomy in a defined wider framework.

Question
Which changes did you have to make in your HR management (hiring, profile descriptions, compensation, working time and places, etc.)

Answer
I have already mentioned the change to the employee profiles. Our carefully selected team therefore consists of the right talents who seem to be very happy to work in this context. We hire them not simply after one or two standard interviews. It is more like a series of informal meetings be it over lunch or by visiting the team where we get to know the individuals. We want to be as open as possible about the challenges we have, the success stories we can share, the spirit of the team, and vision for the future (Fig. 3).

Therefore, candidates we would like to have in our team have normally been in contact with us over a longer period and therefore know a lot about us in advance, which makes integration and introductory training very easy and lean. Our candidates are absolutely purpose and task-oriented, and career and remuneration volume are not primary criteria for them.

Our average age in the Digital Finance unit is not so important. What is more important is that the age of the team members ranges from the low 20s to the 50s. As already mentioned there are employees of any age who love to work in a digital and agile manner. There is even some fluctuation between "digital and classical." One last aspect: the colleagues with a lot of business experience are perfect counterparts for the newly hired digital IT experts in the team.

Question
What are your major lessons learnt from the last couple of years?

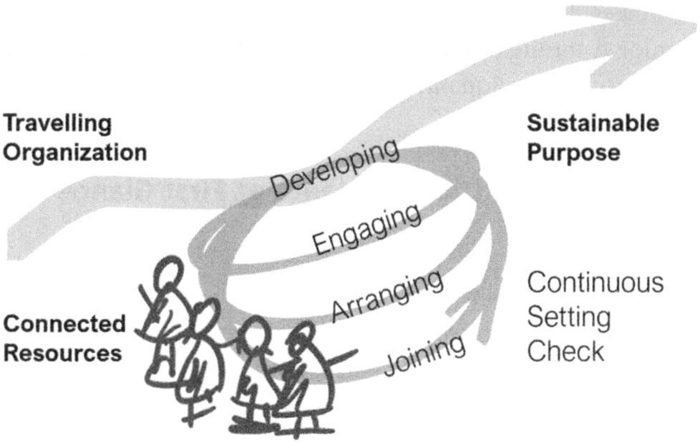

Fig. 3 Review the challenges and needs of the journey and attract the right talent and players to the joint endeavor (Illustrated by Frank Kühn, used with permission. All rights reserved)

Answer
To take some risk in running controlling and that it is a privilege for a controlling division to be innovative and to execute.

Question
How did your division cope with the COVID-19 pandemic? Did the hybrid character of your organization have positive, negative, or neutral impacts?

Answer
The pandemic turned out to be a totally unexpected scenario. The new working style and collaboration was a bit challenging, but that's not a *big issue* in a team which is on a journey anyway.

From a content point of view, the crisis made it very clear that scenario thinking has to be pushed even more. Even if there are changes of preconditions and environmental frames, the ability to think and act in scenarios is crucial to very quickly find options and solutions in a new situation. And it additionally shows that we have to act in an agile way, going step by step, not following old patterns and old rules and to be open to taking a certain risk. Quickly finding a new path in the unknown always means taking a risk. But to be slow is even more risky.

4 Interview with John Gray, Application Developer in Digital Finance

Peter Wollmann interviews John Gray, Application Developer in Digital Finance. John started leading technical accounting and business intelligence initiatives in Canada for Mozilla and Munich Re more than 7 years ago. In the past year, John transitioned into IT application development and relocated from Toronto to Munich to become the newest Digital Finance team member. John competed in ice hockey at the level of Junior A throughout Canada and the USA and has a Bachelor degree in economic and a professional qualification in risk management.

4.1 Fascination with Digital Finance at First Glance

Question

John, you joined the new unit Digital Finance at a very early stage. Perhaps you could tell us a bit about who you are, what expertise you have, where you came from, and why you were immediately so fascinated by the idea of the new unit in general?

Answer

I am a Canadian national who relocated to Munich to join the Digital Finance team. I studied economics and then risk management at university. During university and a few months after, I worked for Mozilla and then joined Munich Re in 2012 at the Toronto Office as a Senior Technical Accountant both for Reinsurance and Primary Insurance. In my time with Munich Re Toronto, I was given many opportunities, including projects for distributed ledger technology with other leading insurers, representing Finance on global reinsurance system teams as key user and on local primary insurance teams as subject matter expert.

I was immediately fascinated by the Digital Finance unit because the team is full of high-performers. At the same time, the team has lot of fun. The technology developed helps to solve a genuine problem—and this is evidenced by the rapidly growing user count and hundreds of meaningful use cases implemented around the world, despite nearly zero spend on marketing. Digital Finance job titles are just formalities. On a daily basis, each team member steps up to do what is needed. Everyone on the team was handpicked because they are extremely good at something the others are not good at. Although I don’t think I am extremely good at anything, others on the team tell me I am extremely good at the space between technical financial topics and IT. While I am an Application Developer by title, I would say that we have other much stronger Application Developers on Digital Finance. Maybe I could lay claim to being a pretty good BI developer. But I also enjoy, and am getting quite good at, leveraging the Digital Finance Platform as a means to lead digital transformation initiatives. It is very rare that I can independently start and finish a use case. In almost every case, it is a joint effort together with more experienced team members. At the same time, the whole team supports independent pursuits, and we all have the freedom to do good things. This doesn’t mean the pursuits go unchallenged—actually the toughest audience I have is the Digital Finance team, and I think there is no other better way. As well every Friday is “Fit for Future Friday” where we can independently put our daily tasks aside and research anything relevant—even slightly relevant—as long as it relates to potential future benefit for overall business values using technology.

On balance, for all of these reasons, this is why I was and always will be fascinated by Digital Finance—a start-up within Munich Re.

Question

I understand that you made a very spontaneous decision to join Digital Finance. What did this look like from a logistic and organizational aspect?

Answer

That's true. After a month or two of researching Digital Finance from Toronto, I joined the team for a 1-month project in April 2019. Part way through the month, I became aware of a vacancy, and I applied for it without hesitation. After a few weeks of working side by side with them, it was clear that this was the best team I could ever imagine being part of. And to this day, I am still surprised I got the job. I've never felt I deserve it when I compare myself to the rest of our team's super-skills.

Question

Why was joining Digital Finance so much better than other alternatives for you? Which were the key criteria for your decision? What made the setting at Digital Finance so unique for you? And what were you looking for in detail? To what extent were things like a convincing purpose, authentic agility and flexibility, and a well-connected community important?

Answer

Since first meeting Digital Finance in April 2019, I've had several other good job offers. Even some from competitors of Munich Re. The key criteria for choosing Digital Finance is because it is my life's work. Everything I've ever done in academia or professionally has been a lead up to Digital Finance. The other alternatives had low information. I got to meet Digital Finance in person for a whole month before choosing to decide. And it wasn't given to me at all; I had to chase it. I would have to move across the planet, leave behind my good friends and colleagues in Toronto, and start a new life in Munich. The Group Controlling setting allows Digital Finance to avoid a lot of distractions that other Finance- and IT-situated teams are subject to. When you combine Digital Finance team skills with Group Controlling, it provides tremendous credibility and a certain measured autonomy that just wouldn't be possible elsewhere. With the Group Controlling setting, I have the autonomy, or a mandated autonomy, to do things on a group-wide basis for overall benefit.

Question

How would you rate peers in your generation and profession, to what extent do you represent them or to what extent do you perceive yourself as part of a fundamental movement—or to be more unique—in terms of what you are striving for and how you make personal decisions?

Answer

I'm reluctant to rate or platonify peers in my generation and am hesitant to put a group of people into some neat bucket. But I appreciate the question and understand why the audience might be interested in such high-level things. In my professional career, I've witnessed many stereotypes that have proved accurate or inaccurate. We all have. I think every person has strengths and weaknesses, and we all have a duty to improve our strengths and reduce our weaknesses. Having said that, I am aware of the stereotypes, and I am aware of some of the true problems with my generation. I am also aware of some of the true problems with IT personnel, business personnel, small start-ups, large organizations, and empires too. Regarding my generational peers, I would recommend to them to listen closely to as many people as possible but only the ones that matter, to under-commit and over-deliver, to ask a lot of questions to your more experienced colleagues, and to work hard to get the best outcomes for the team and for the organization. Regarding my IT colleagues, same thing as my generational peers plus I would stress to consider that business topics are often equally or more challenging than IT topics. Never diminish business topics for they necessarily come first, for any new company must start with a business idea that helps it solve a problem and then everything else including IT is derivative.

Question
How did your friends and family "judge" your decision?

Answer
Well, my family met Benjamin and his family in a video call, and they heard how passionate and highly I spoke of him and the rest of the team. And once you meet Digital Finance leadership, it is impossible not to be very supportive. My little brother had just purchased a new home in Canada so he was very supportive, in terms of getting my old furniture.

4.2 The "Storming Phase" of the New Unit

Question
What was the official sustainable purpose of the new unit in this phase from your perspective, and how was it perceived and appreciated by the environment?

Answer
The official sustainable purpose from my perspective was to handpick a team of super-skills and develop a technology that connects to virtually any source of information for faster and more effective decision-making. And to implement as many good use cases as possible. The problem we solve is omnipresent. That is, since industry will never decide on a singular technology, it will evolve to amass an increasing number of various heterogenous sources, and so it follows that a highly flexible virtual platform is needed to bring together the most important data into one.

Munich Re has many environments and will appreciate Digital Financial more so in the future.

Question
How would you describe the journey taken in this phase? Which were the most impressive situations on the journey, the "wow experiences"?

Answer
"Wow" core work experiences are back-to-back-to-back internal demos that build on each other such as AI, chatbots, Advanced Fairness Opinion Models, and Advanced Competitor and Client Analytics Models. And generally, every time people on the team join forces to get a better outcome.

"Wow" extracurriculars are hackathons at Munich Re's country house close to the Bavarian Alps, code deployment events, and "beefer events" (barbecues) and pizza parties in our team members' homes.

4.3 Conclusions and Key Lessons Learned

Question
Which of your original expectations were realized and which not—and why?

Answer
What came true is that I am learning more and I am empowered more than I ever imagined. What did not come true is that my own personal highest-ranked use cases have not been implemented to the same extent as the ones our customers asked for. At the same time, an expectation I never had prior to joining the team is how often and fortunate we are to be unlike other teams, for example, unlike traditional IT departments where we can rather unapologetically challenge what we are asked to do.

Question
What is your professional judgement of Digital Finance and the whole overall setting of the unit within Group Controlling and Munich Re? Is this a competitive advantage and, if so, why?

Answer
It is a competitive advantage. This will be evidenced as a critical mass of people generally understand what we are doing and then get behind us to take Digital Finance to Munich Re mainstream.

Question
Why is the team so successful? What are the key success factors?

Answer
The way of working promotes a level of freethinking, and the leadership is so world-class it could lead a high-performing team in any industry. And the colleagues are all so skilled that it guilts everyone into constant improvement.

Question
What would you do differently if you could restart with your knowledge from today?

Answer
I would have joined Digital Finance earlier. I would commit to less and over-deliver more.

Question
What are your recommendations for Benjamin and Thomas based on your experience from the last couple of months? What are your recommendations for readers of this book?

Answer
Keep doing what you are doing and constantly find ways to keep the path ahead clear. Once we maximize our value within Munich Re parameters, plan what is next. It is a big world out there, and we could do this for any Munich Re environment that is ripe for digitalization.

One recommendation that could serve as a counter to an overreliance on traditional income streams is that when digitalization initiatives like ours create 1 million euros of value, these values, unlike insurance premiums or other traditional income streams, are fully earned. For an insurer, we should think of savings that are fully earned and compare them to insurance premiums that are fully earned divided by the respective average loss ratio.

Question
What do you expect for Digital Finance and yourself in the next 2 to 3 years? What are the main challenges to keep up your orientation, spirit, and agility and to digest growth?

Answer
I expect Digital Finance will continue to do very well. I think Digital Finance will evolve to become an even stronger business partner to client-facing domains. Challenges we already face and expect to continue are that we will need to avoid becoming a service desk for our technologies when in 2 or 3 years we will have five or ten times the current user count. Client-facing domains require ironclad service-level agreements and stabilities so we will have to work hard and smart to focus on things that help solve real problems from our customer perspective and that are highly scalable. As a consequence the team, we will need to be disciplined about failing faster. We will need to selflessly detach from our comfort zones, be it technology or a digitizing concept, and we will have to stay motivated to constantly find a better way.

5 Overall Conclusion

5.1 The Importance of the Right Setting

Digital Finance was decided and built up and has become more and more successful in a perfectly fitting setting:

- Munich Re as an enterprise with long-term orientation and a clear strategy
- A transparent demand for digital services in finance
- Two strong sponsors
- The right person to build up a start-up-like agile virtual organization
- A small team with different but connected expertise (finance people with strong technical interests, IT people with strong finance interests) being perfectly complementary
- A large degree of freedom for the team
- A large portion of enthusiasm and engagement in the team
- A very prudent approach with a strong communication plan
- Last but not the least, a solid base of mutual trust among the people involved

In this situation, it was accepted that at the beginning it was not known precisely what Digital Finance might become, and it is still not fully clear. However, it is irrefutable that DF has been very successful and has happened on to more good outcomes than strategized for: it is a role pattern in Munich Re, the industry, and beyond. This success might be due in part to a few guiding convictions and values. Finance organizations must forge deep and authentic team spirit as they lead our families both at home and at work.

Nevertheless, it also became transparent that there are frictions when running an agile virtual team within a traditional organization for all its rules and procedures. The situation is a hybrid between classic and agile start-up, which was brilliantly solved with solid leadership and suitable situational decisions in a flexible framework, but if the hybrid situation develops from an extraordinary to an ordinary state, sustainable systemic answers have to be found that can be applied long-term. It is crucial to preserve the "start-up setting and atmosphere" for the highly talented employees who are attracted by this—as otherwise they might leave and take with them their talent and knowledge of Munich Re. This includes taking a reasonable amount of entrepreneurial risk.

From the perspective of the editor (Peter, who spent decades as Head of Strategy and Controlling in the finance industry), it might make sense to add questions for such start-up-like units beyond the normal budget-driven query of the cost for the next planning period:

- How much investment would you need to create a competitive advantage for your enterprise, and what would it look like?
- What could you certainly deliver if you received an investment of x? Why are you sure? What is the failure risk in the investment?

- Etc.

So, the journey of Digital Finance will remain interesting and exciting and will contribute to the overall transformation of the enterprise.

6 Lessons Learned/Practical Takeaways

- Carefully design and check the setting to start an agile start-up-like unit within a classic organization (adequate sponsors and supporters, sufficient freedom to act autonomously, clear preconditions, available and engaged key persons, mutual trust)
- Invest very intensively from the beginning in communication (in unit and cross-units and functions)
- Focus on the overwhelming role of belief in persons and trust in demanding settings (like creating a hybrid organization)
- Follow the recommended phases to build up an agile organization:
  - "A first vision"
  - "Start small, think big, but really start small"
  - "Fly below the radar"
  - "Go as fast as you can—build up key competencies away from 'normal' or classic organization"
  - "Have sufficient power to avoid hierarchies"
  - "Chase the money and become more advanced"
- Be open to take reasonable entrepreneurial risk
- Focus on people: create a setting that attracts independently thinking highly talented experts—and form a high-performance team
- Stress that being a magnet for talents is important for an enterprise—and that the enterprise must do everything possible to keep the talents long term
- Leading a hybrid organization is demanding and needs behavior change—a tolerant, delegation-based, and risk-taking leadership style is successful

Reference

Wollmann, P., Kühn, F., & Kempf, M. (Eds.). (2020). *Three pillars of organization and leadership in disruptive times – Navigating your company successfully through the 21st century business world*. Cham: Springer Nature.

Benjamin Rausch started leading global M&A, equity, and corporate finance transactions more 10 years ago. For the past 5 years, Benjamin Rausch has been driving corporate performance management and developing software for financial organizations that enables faster and more effective strategic and financial decision-making. Benjamin graduated and received his doctorate in business administration on forward-looking corporate valuation techniques. Thereafter, he joined Rothschild's global advisory practice in Frankfurt and later Munich Reinsurance Company in Munich.

John Gray started leading technical accounting and business intelligence initiatives in Canada for Mozilla and Munich Reinsurance Company more than 7 years ago. In the past year, John transitioned into IT application development and relocated from Toronto to Munich to become the newest Digital Finance team member. John competed in ice hockey at the level of Junior A throughout Canada and the USA, as well holds a bachelor's degree in economics and a professional designation in risk management.

Thomas Thirolf was born in Munich in 1963. He studied economics at the University of Augsburg. After obtaining his degree, Thomas completed a trainee program at Hypobank, subsequently working in the credit and corporate banking department. He also worked in the central project office during the merger of Hypobank and Vereinsbank. Thomas joined Munich Re in 2001, becoming Head of Finance/Primary Insurance. In 2006, he became Head of Group Controlling. His main responsibilities are Capital Management (dividends, share buybacks), Performance, and Investment Controlling of the business fields Reinsurance and Primary Insurance as well as the development of economic steering methods. In this function he reports to the Group CFO and Member of the Board of Management, Dr. Christoph Jurecka. Since 5 years, Thomas is further responsible for the Digital Finance Platform, which was set up and led by Benjamin Rausch.

Peter Wollmann has been a responsible manager, initiator, mentor, and facilitator in large, predominantly global transformations and strategic developments for almost 40 years. His specialties are the implementations of the Three-Pillar Model in organizations and focused setting checks to identify strength, weaknesses, opportunities, and threats and facilitate optimization measures. Since 2017 Peter has been working independently in organizational projects and future initiatives. After graduating in mathematics and physics from the University of Bonn, he began his professional career at the Deutsche Herold, then insurance group of Deutsche Bank, took on strategic leadership, and most recently was program director for global transformations in the Zurich Insurance Company (ZIC). In his professional network, he brought his experience and strategic thinking to the development of various leading companies. He is the author and publisher of a number of books and articles on strategy, leadership, and project and project portfolio management. He also founded a wine business: VinAuthority.

Application of the 3-P-Model in a Start-Up-Like Environment of a Large Enterprise

Sebastian Kespohl

Abstract

A subsidiary of a large enterprise goes on an innovation journey developing a new business model with the focus on consumer needs as drivers for growth and success, with the aim of becoming a fast-growing European player with international market leaders as key clients. This presupposes a significant transformation in various dimensions (purpose, vision and strategy, culture and mindset, cooperation, capabilities and skills, operations and systems/tools, etc.) for which the 3-P-Model can be perfectly applied. Especially the leadership approach or mindset as requirements for a hybrid organization—an agile start-up-like unit in a classic hierarchical organization—are of particular interest.

1 Introduction

In the last 20 years, new companies, e.g. Amazon, Google and Facebook, have grown in an unforeseeable way, and, thanks to the underlying technical innovation, many other companies were started and sold for high prices. Many people love the success stories of people having a good idea and making a concerted effort to make a success of this idea. At the same time, many people struggle in even small scenarios where they could facilitate significant business growth or perhaps even more interesting grow their personal capabilities. Why? Hindsight bias is one explanation; we see the winners, but we do not see the more than 90% who failed, because they were unable to market their story properly. But this is much too simple to be the reason for not betting everything on one single idea and trying the utmost to develop it. In addition to a—certainly—fairly low likelihood of accomplishing something great, it

S. Kespohl (✉)
Verl, Germany
e-mail: s_kespohl@gmx.de

P. Wollmann et al. (eds.), *Organization and Leadership in Disruptive Times*, Future of Business and Finance, https://doi.org/10.1007/978-3-030-63034-8_16

is all the obstacles on such a journey: things you need to leave behind, things you need to change in your behaviour, the ugly truth about yourself that you need to understand and accept and the resilience to survive or become even stronger by means of serious setbacks. The essence is easy and really nothing new: Everything comes at a price.

In addition—being a manager—you need to take a second step. It is very likely that only a few people in your company will join you in trying to do something new. Most people will be hesitant, uncertain, frightened, sceptical, etc., and, in addition, their bosses might not encourage them. As a manager, you accept this; as a leader you respect this understandable human behaviour, understand the situation and choose a change. This article tries to help the latter ones to grow and be empowered. You might see your task as a leader as being how to use, and sometimes transform, your ambitions into behaviour that will facilitate companies' success and the success of your fellows and the team.

The author of this article has been responsible for some growth projects with different companies and business verticals within the last couple of years. Growth is meant as a direct and not unplanned but momentum-driven step change for the top line; it is not meant as a preparation in terms of a product development project or the like. In this article these growth scenarios will be referred to as IANS (intended and nevertheless surprising) using the example of a fintech subsidiary of a large established company. Intended means that activities have been intentionally positioned to unleash growth, where surprising means that the impact of the project is bigger than thought: from a commercial perspective as well as from the perspective what was expected related to organizational impact. In a disruptive VUCA world, growth seems to be more appealing than cost-cutting or maintaining the status quo but, in many cases, it is also the only recipe for survival.

This article will show experiences, reflections and some practical ideas for growth projects, derived from the example chosen. This includes critical closer examinations, as it has to be assumed that there is no valid navigation system for unknown terrain.

The reasoning and deducing of practical ideas are based on the Three-Pillar Model (3-P-Model) as this serves with the ultimate essence that a leader might take into consideration applying for an adventurous journey (Wollmann et al. 2020).

2 The Initial Situation in the Case Study

As a result of significant changes in the fintech market environment and therefore changes in the competitive landscape, in 2017 a decision was taken in the author's company to significantly modify and internationalize the existing business model, also against the backdrop of a newly founded subsidiary, with the aim of transforming the new unit into a fast-growing, major player in the relevant European market. This scope extension and expansion was and still is an exciting journey in the course of which substantial organization attributes had been ripe for change; some of these were successful, some failed, and some are still a work in progress.

This will be described in the article, covering a wide range of topics and additionally connected to the Three-Pillar Model (3-P-Model).

Key Topics Which Had to Be Considered During the Product Development Journey Within the New Fast-Growing Subsidiary in the Case Study and How the Topics Refer to the 3-P-Model

The new growth subsidiary:

- Had and still has to develop a new *sustainable purpose*, and design new strategies, understood as ways to utilize existing competitive advantages which allow and ensure rapid growth
- Had and still has to energize and enable the people to *go on a not plannable journey (travelling organization)* into unknown territory—which demands high flexibility, creativity and a tangible readiness to take risks
- Had and still has to re-work decision-making concepts and practices, still being in an environment which is regulated by authorities.
- Had and still has to establish a new mindset to handle uncertainty and consequently cope with mistakes[1] (more focus on learning from mistakes without losing stability)
- Had and still has to develop strong beyond-silo thinking *to connect with all needed internal and external resources* and knowledge to base the journey on the best capabilities possible
- Had and still has to anchor and execute leadership as a people-related task
- Had and still has to decide which role and personality profiles would fit the ambitious endeavour best and which capabilities, skills, etc. were crucial and therefore which talents from inside and outside were best placed to reinforce the aspiration of building up competitive advantage

In addition to the topics in the box—and last but not least—the organization of the fast-growing business has and had to be gradually recalibrated along the following questions:

- How much structure is needed in which growth phase and for which business volume?
- In detail: for which parts of the business are more 'classical' organizational attributes necessary and for which parts is the rather autonomous, agile start-up-like procedure best? (we will call this a hybrid situation)
- How can this diverse, hybrid organization be managed?

[1]Mistakes might sound like something rather small, but it is meant to be seen in a much broader sense—to the extent to accept and deal with topics that cause one to 'break out in a cold sweat'.

Interim Summary and Conclusion

In the context of growth units or projects, a focussed leadership team turns out to be a key factor to discuss and answer these crucial questions. The answers will have to cover (a) full focus on the one journey; (b) within the journey, focus on a few relevant success factors; and (c) a common understanding of how to lead.

3 Some General Thoughts on Growth and Growth Projects

Key Questions on Growth and Growth Projects

What is the difference between fast-growing and established organizations? Which parameters have to be considered for the fast-growing organization in a classic corporate environment or—more concretely–what additional/different parameters need to be considered and managed in a growth scenario compared to an established one? Do established organizations in general have limitations to grow/manage growth projects, and, if so, what are the limitations? How does it work in the given context?

We are living in special times where change is accelerating as new paradigms (like data and tech) define businesses and their success. For decades a big corporate with good management was capable of surviving and even growing with comfortable speed and a reasonably high probability that investments in business development—such as new markets or products—would be successful. In a VUCA world, comfortable speed means standing still. New developments need to be seen more as a bet, meaning an activity with a binary outcome: it will or will not work, rather than a conservative investment with stable returns. The biggest challenge for established organizations is to cultivate the mindset and the process framework that are needed by 'bet-oriented portfolio management' working on the premise that only a few bets will be successful. One precondition of being successful means accepting the following parameters:

- *Growth projects will burn money and create a lot of pain*
  In the given context, most activities have taken the journey from star to cash cow or are somewhere in between. A strong, decentralized structure enables entrepreneurship on the one hand, and on the other side, it often limits innovation to the decentralized business units. Attempts to drive common innovation between business units—which have been discussed and partially started with reasonable thinking—often failed because of early-stage discussions about profit sharing, a short-term view on cannibalizing existing solutions/products. Thus because of local optimization and therefore due to silo-like behaviour, maybe not even

thinking is possible. But in a VUCA world, you need to disrupt yourself before others do.

- *Time and time relations of corporate and growth project are different*
  The time schedule of a corporate is defined by budgeting and reforecasting exercises. Other important meetings (people reviews, strategy workshops, workers council meetings, town hall meetings, risk portfolio meetings, etc.) are scheduled (as needed) in a clear timely manner (weekly, biweekly, monthly or quarterly). This gives stability and allows the needs of information flow and decision-making to be managed throughout the year. The stability to be reached with the meeting scaffold assumes that the proven structure of inner stability can help to defy, or at least slow down, the effects of a changing world outside. One may ask if this is still the case in a VUCA world, but this will not be discussed in this article. What is relevant though is that, in an IANS growth context, decisions need to be taken quickly and also not always within the given structure since reality uncovers topics that do not find their way onto the agenda of an established decision-making forum.
- *Cultures of corporate and growth projects are different*
  Culture clashes and a permanent storming phase scenario are caused by two demanding developments in parallel: on the one hand, making something grow, especially in the given context while utilizing existing capabilities (in the sense of making use of delivery of established parts of the organization), and on the other hand, becoming at the same time much more international and doing orient thinking, product design and day-to-day decision-taking on consumer behaviour from a B2C perspective (where this was always B2B before). Becoming international and changing focus of how we go to market drastically calls not only for a different way of working and thinking, it also needs to attract new people who would normally not become part of the existing culture because of, e.g., their professional background, socialization and experience. Enabling those people to question or even provoke how business is done and how people are managed has been perceived as creating aggression. It is possible that this materializes in missing orientation and identification and less safety felt by the established organization.
- *Interfaces in the arising hybrid organization have to be carefully managed*:
  At the interfaces between the 'wild ones' and the 'corporates', there will be friction and conflict. Or as Steve Jobs called the scenario: 'Pirates in the navy' (Viki 2002) or a little more philosophically as Kierkegaard put it: 'you can make wild ducks tame, but you can never make tame ducks wild again....' (Kiergegaard 2002), seeing the wild ducks flying south where the normal ducks become fatter, unlearn flying and just a few even feel inspired by the wild ducks to go on a long journey. To manoeuvre this setup is a big challenge for an organization. One important contribution to master this challenge is to find and make use of diplomats or even 'ambassadors' within the organization. Each organization has people in management positions who are seen as very reliable, who think holistically and who always show appreciative interest in others. These people act implicitly towards a non-silo organization. At the same time, these people are

highly accepted and not doubted within the organization. These people can and should serve as diplomats. In the given context, friction and hostility is caused by the most settled parts of the established organization. In that context, it is reasonable to win also people—with the mentioned attitude—that have long experience in the company and excellent knowledge of different interests and motives for behaviour.

- *Working styles of corporate and growth projects are different*
  Established organizations tend to build their picture of working culture on the assumption that the organizational setup (defined by org chart) defines how we work. Seeing a growth project, this is conflicting. Being in an IANS growth context means focusing on growth and taking the daily surprises and challenges as they come. Handling problems or unleashing new growth steps can—at the beginning—not entail measures to lift up the maturity. The way how the growth team works can be easily perceived as chaotic, and that might be not entirely wrong—besides the diplomats you also need are chaos pilots. Expectations from the established parts of the organization are often that the growth team fits into the overall organization and makes use of the defined interfaces to other teams. Taking a technical example: there is a very likely risk that given interfaces do not fit the growth project needs:
  (a) The interfaces do not offer the right parameters within the call from growth project to the given organization and do not provide a result of the type expected by the growth project, or the pirates are/need to be on a totally different track and cannot engage with the established organization on certain topics at all.
  (b) And in general—independent of a growth project—within the VUCA world, it would cause constant reorganization while really believing that the organizational structure (in German: *Aufbauorganisation*) defines the way how work and collaboration is done.

Interim Summary and Conclusion

As an interim conclusion, it can be stated that IANS growth projects can be quite rightly regarded as start-ups. It is the nature of start-ups to be flexible, to focus on action and to be fast, whereas corporates are normally slow and complicated in decision-taking and follow a history of hierarchy and formalism. What the corporate sees, for good reason, as safety nets or elements of stability can be seen as hurdles by the start-up. Contradicting previous success of a company and the focus on the high revenue and high profit parts of the company makes them fall into the trap of being saturated.

Do established organizations in general have limitations when it comes to running growth projects? It would be unreasonable to give a generally valid answer to this question, but there is a deep conviction—based on the growth projects considered in this article—that there are no general limitations that

(continued)

could not be overcome with reasonable effort. It is key to understand and design growth projects as strategy-driven, to endow them with the right leadership and to make sure that the right change culture and risk acceptance is in place.

4 Special Organizational Change Measures Demanded by Growth Projects

In the given context of the case study, we study a successful service subsidiary to manage monetary transactions to go to market with solutions/products that can be characterized as an orchestration of the existing diverse strategic capabilities in the group.

This is somehow new for the group as those strategic capabilities had been recently packaged into own business units that run successful 'stand-alone' products in their internal and external markets, run separately and mostly independently. The mentioned orchestration strives now for a cross-unit combined service offering with added value. The difference is that the offering does not use a model akin to 'take the steak for €20 and get a Coke for €2 on top', but more in the sense of serving a predefined menu containing food and beverage and an outstanding service in a few courses with one price tag attached.

Given the described bipolar environment, strongly based on the construction of different trade-offs focussed on exploration and exploitation in parallel, there is an obvious need to understand the very complex organization and its philosophy, accept the intrinsically given bipolarity and derive the right measures to deal with it. Failure to do this cannot only cause failure for the growth project, but also damage the whole existing organization.

To manage this complexity in the given special context, certain scales for change in the context with travelling in large transformations have to be in place. They will be developed in detail firstly before connecting them with the 3-P-Model:

1. Knowledge: a broad knowledge (with linked skills and perhaps experience) is needed to manage the growth project and its outcome (product) compared to a more in-depth knowledge within the different units that are part of the delivery. This could look different in other contexts where, for example, a language or a technology not used/known by the established organization is crucial for the success of the growth project.
2. Timeline agility: established organizations map activities on a timescale (e.g. fiscal year), which gives stability and influences decision-making. In a growth project, decision-making based on predefined timelines is often not possible and may jeopardize progress. The COVID-19 crisis shows that taking

action urgently is not a limitation of corporates in general. From one day to another, it was possible for a lot of people to work from home. Growth projects identify urgency much faster and more naturally than established organizations do—they often need an external threatening trigger.

3. Risk and failure philosophy: as outlined above, seeing growth projects as a gamble, it is quite clear that this entails the risk of failure. And more precisely it is a singular approach. From a growth project perspective, failure cannot be compensated within the same context, where established organizations normally have many business activities that behave in a volatile manner but somehow tend to have a regression to average in performance. Accepting to lose the bet also means to accept failure during the journey—which is already logical in a sense that, usually, one failure does not determine the overall result.
4. People and attitude: building up something new—seen as a gamble—is also described by creativity. As there is always much more to do than reasonably possible with the given resources, there is a much lower chance to sequence things as would be done in an established organization. This calls for an attitude and people who understand that creativity means accomplishing the best with the resources available and getting things done even if it seems that the workforce is not large enough. The magic triangle of time, quality and budget is much more volatile—extent and frequency—in a start-up environment.
5. Culture: in the given context, there is a relevant difference to the established organization as the environment is quite international (many European cultures, people from the USA, South America and India within the wider team). This comes with all the differences between cultures regarding, for example, hierarchical thinking and behaviour, trust and feedback. The scale of culture could also apply within a merger where teams from different company cultures need to collaborate.
6. Decision and steering processes (stability): every system strives for stability. In the context of an established organization, this is based on predictability and on the fact that KPIs perform at a predefined level. This is also true for a growth project. But KPIs are different, and predictability is replaced by a clear indication of further growth. Stability is also reflected within the half-life of decisions. Whereas corporates take decisions that need to be valid and for a longer period of time, growth projects focus on a lot of decisions to survive the next obstacle and also need to remain flexible—doing so by revealing decisions.
7. Optimization strategies: local vs. global optimization—given the context of a highly integrated value and service chain, where each of the components has a representation in this new integrated product but also as a stand-alone product in the market, conflict in financial objectives needs to be dealt with. This is necessary to globally optimize the benefit for the company and also—as local optimization is one of the most reliable indicators for silo working—to foster cross-silo collaboration (see box).
8. Establishing new procedures: creating something new that can cause a step change will usually not work if existing procedures are used. As those processes

(like a credit approval for consumer credit) are an interdisciplinary process in the company, the established part and the growth project need to formalize collaboration.

9. Consumer focus: target group of the growth projects' products is also consumers. Doing this in a company whose purpose has always been to be a stable B2B partner in the background is innovative from different angles: more abstract in other contexts, this could be seen as a new go-to-market approach and/or change of target group, but also even more abstract as a different purpose of the company.

Interim Summary and Conclusion

The application of the scales is demanding as an IANS growth project suffers from the business being already executed, while relevant things need to be done or fixed afterwards, which means that the scale perspectives change fast. This can be referred to as: 'Paint the bus while driving'. Such a situation calls for agility in *mindset* and working, where there is a clash with the established organization as to which working processes are related to org charts, one major business process and the corresponding factory in place.

And it also calls for *focus*—people involved in that growth scenario are somehow adventurers and conquerors—as there is no alternative to winning. This requires taking *ownership* (taking responsibility for the result, regardless of what comes). Seeing the bipolarity this is extremely challenging and calls for a positively aggressive, but at the same time very reflective, approach driven by very good understanding of people and peoples' behaviour and manoeuvre conflicting situation for the good to great—trying to *be the bigger person*. This is especially important to try to *tear down parts of the silos*[2] within the established organization. Coming back to see this all as an adventure and conquest, it is likely that the conquerors influenced, educated and motivated their teams by *telling stories about* what they could expect at the other side of the world.

5 How Does the 3-P-Model Help Fast-Growing Organizations in Detail?

The following will demonstrate how the 3-P-Model (Wollmann et al. 2020) can be beneficially applied. A lot of implicit and explicit references to the 3-P-Model were made, which means that a balanced summary and completion of thoughts is sufficient:

[2]You will find some fundamental remarks on silos at the end of the article.

- *Sustainable Purpose*
  Interestingly the demand for a sustainable purpose in the VUCA world is not at all an artificial goal or constraint. It rather reflects the desire of most people to have a convincing purpose in their lives and jobs. In the case of a fast-growing organization or a growth project with its risks and uncertainties, it is crucial for the people to identify with the enterprise's purpose in the long run, also with the purpose of the unit/growth project which should clearly buy into the purpose and success of the whole enterprise which significantly increases the comfort and the motivation for the team. So, it is very probable that precisely those types of companies or projects need this well-accepted and shared sustainable purpose even more than other organizations—why else should people take above-average risks and make above-average effort?
- *Travelling Organization*
  The described fast-growing companies and growth projects are per se travelling organizations—nobody with a different mindset would survive in them for long. The need for special personalities with agile mindsets, resilience and acceptance to take risks and to frequently cope with failure is mentioned above. The perfect picture for a travelling organization is the previously mentioned 'Painting the bus while driving'. In the case of these sorts of organization, the role of storytelling is significant. Storytelling is a driver for motivation, engagement, contextual understanding and orientation (s. remarks at the end of the article).
- *Connecting Resources*
  Fast-growing companies and growth projects are mostly in contexts as described: in hybrid enterprise situations and bipolar organizations. This means a tremendous demand on connecting knowledge, resources, people, etc. across the whole enterprise and its environment (in the example of the case study, the external stakeholders are, for example, global B2B clients, global B2P clients, national regulators, etc.).

  The understanding of the importance of the connectivity—the strong ability to connect with all important parties—demands action across silos within the company. The precondition for this is—very important for fast-growing companies and growth projects—a holistic end-to-end view of all processes or activities leading to a coverage of the value proposition to the clients and, in this context, to a clear understanding of which contribution is needed regardless of where the people are located in the org chart and whether they are internal or external. The idea of connecting resources is closely connected to the full commitment to a target, performance—and to a sustainable purpose.

Interim Summary and Conclusion

The statements prove that the 3-P-Model can be perfectly and beneficially applied in the case of fast-growing companies or growth projects in general and that it was very helpful for the chosen case study. There are two additional outcomes of the 3-P-Model to be mentioned:

(continued)

- 3-P supports people to take real ownership in their big endeavour.
- 3-P significantly influences the understanding and practice of project and project portfolio management, allowing agile, flexible proceedings that are very strongly committed to the enterprise and/or growth project purpose.

6 A Collection of Highly Instructive Situations on the Growth Journey

For 2018 several marketing activities had been agreed with some merchants, to (a) boost volume and (b) attract new users to the product. Seeing the early growth within the peak season, it became obvious that some of the operational systems involved might not stand the capacity demanded—this is also applied to the central transaction approval system, meaning the heart of the product. Within 1 day a small team created and implemented a bypass (similar to critical heart surgery) considering input from all relevant departments and dealing with all risk, regulatory and compliance topics. Nothing like this had ever been done before in such short time frame with such criticality. Having a clear focus on growth and connecting the right resources gave the right impetus to take a reasonable decision.

Later the following year a configuration caused an outage of a critical online system during a marketing campaign, meaning that a lot of transactions were declined. From a contractual perspective, the downtime and the lost transactions would have been covered. But the team had focussed on reprocessing the transactions and complies with the promises that had been given to the consumer. Reprocessing declined transactions within an already critical system status is of tangible risk. A small team was convened quickly and gathered all relevant information to be able to judge any side effects and assess how to ensure that follow-up processes were connected seamlessly. A plan was defined, reviewed and documented by the small team, and a decision was taken to execute the plan in under 2 h. A prominent decision, taken with uncertainty, time pressure and unstable system behaviour, was made while connecting the right resources driven by the purpose of growing the business.

7 Overall Conclusions and Takeaways

This article shows how beneficial the 3-P-Model can be to navigate a particular part of our VUCA business world, namely, starting something new in a corporate environment. More precisely the term IANS (intended and nevertheless surprising) growth projects has been introduced. IANS growth projects are, and will be, increasingly the norm when it comes to establishing start-ups in a corporate environment. The specifics about IANS—the surprise effect of significant growth—is mainly relevant because organizations need to place a set of bets on their horizon and at the same time they do not have the capacity that—if one of those bets is as successful as expected or even more so—it can be managed in a normal and balanced way as is known for the established parts of the organization.

Thus—in a VUCA world—companies need to be fast, need to take risks with bets and prepare themselves for this becoming a change for the organization—a stretch referred to as a non-avoidable bipolarity. There are a lot of preparations that can be made from a company's perspective, and at the same time some of them will last to be theoretical until they become tangible in reality, which means the effects of an IANS project hit the organization.

Some practical ideas and impulses stand out and are worth mentioning (as takeaways):

- In a start-up-like environment, it's very likely that a lot of things will have poor maturity while going to market. It's important not to neglect these topics, but rather focus on operationally handling them as well as possible.
- Your management is your key stakeholder—be transparent and honest. This increases your support that bipolarity is accepted and wanted.
- Have an organization plan for the risk and accept it beforehand. Avoid financial control that simply inputs figures into spreadsheets until they think that these numbers will appeal to management.
- In addition, it's relevant to bear in mind that established parts of the organization might not feel comfortable if their personal success, e.g. incentive/bonus, is at risk due to the growth project. Upton Sinclair said: 'It is difficult to get a man to understand something, when his salary depends upon his not understanding it'.

In addition, and specifically, it is relevant to understand and steer the impact on purpose, mindset and spirit which needs to become obviously transparent in collective practices. Embedding the goals of the growth project into the strategic trajectory of the company is necessary to create purpose—a heroic idea alone without strategic alignment will be an even harder, most likely unsuccessful journey. With this strategic alignment, a North Star can be created that allows one to develop the story of the journey and to deduce not only where to go but also how things should be done. From the authors' perspective, it is a positive rebellious behaviour to challenge the collective practices of the established organization and maximize the stretch of bipolarity.

Friedrich Glasl (Glasl and Lievegoed 2011; Fritz 2011) separates the organizational development in four steps. It's interesting to review and apply his thinking within the given context as well. Within the initiation of the growth project, until there is proven impact of the projects' outcome, it can be seen as being in the pioneer phase. Growth, incidents, dependencies and being a system relevant for the company, it is unavoidable that the normal and corporate management instruments are applied (functional differentiation, team buildup, management attention increases which leads to more 1:1s, steering boards, etc.) which is not a problem at all, but also helpful.

It is reasonable to maintain the start-up mindset; it does not make sense to fight against the changes leading into the differentiation phase, it's more of the following:

- Take the help that is provided.
- Let additional people jump on the bandwagon.
- Focus on how to integrate processes and connect resources within the new setting.
- Directly start the next journey to facilitate further growth and expand by features, geographies, etc.

This way it is possible to shorten the adaptations coming out of a differentiation phase and create an environment that enters a new pioneer phase on a more experienced level and is actively going into the VUCA world.

Going this way is an additional stretch, because the new journey will challenge the organization especially if the prior expectations of success are high. At the same time developing out of the differentiation phase into the integration phase takes much more effort than the normal evolution from pioneer into differentiation. This is because becoming integrated means creating a common purpose, connecting resources and keeping the organization travelling—a perfect application of the 3-P-Model.

Some principles of leadership can be seen as outstanding in such a leap:

- Taking ownership and ensuring that the team can take ownership.
- Understanding, willingness and experience that taking risks is needed to generate significant success.
- In an IANS context, the world can become quite hot, challenging and confrontational. It is important not to lose your head while maintaining ownership and taking risks. It is important to stay reflective, humble and appreciative to your environment. Let the circumstances impact on the fact that you are a leader.

Remark 1 Some Fundamental Remarks on Storytelling
How can storytelling within the frame of the 3-P-Model provide a basis for success in travelling an adventurous journey? How does it work in the given context?

It has been proven that brain activities of people listening to the same story adapt on a same level, in other words, those brains enter into a homogenous vibration. In addition, it is proven that brain regions that get activated by actually, for example, smelling fresh coffee and spring air when the soil gets warmer, are activated in exactly the same way as if we just read the words explaining the smell or if we listen to someone telling us about this. This means that putting together the right words into a story constructs a complex artificial environment that causes the same perception and feeling in the recipient as if it were for real.

Thus, telling stories is a profoundly powerful tool in our lives and therefore also in leadership. And we all actually know this, as we feel how movies, sports competitions or our beloved songs change our emotions and also our thinking and attitude.

At the same time, storytelling is something that has different interpretations and acceptance throughout different nationalities/cultures and professions. For example, in German engineer-driven environments, it will likely—at least partially—be interpreted as manipulation and simplifying the truth in an unreasonable way. And yes, storytelling itself is a kind of manipulation. But 85% of anything we do that has an impact is people related and 15% is process and technically related. And how do we win people over for our ambitions? By understanding the interests of the people we want to win over. This sounds quite easy, but as long as one is not highly focused and disciplined to take the other's view, to get inside his head, being empathic, he will switch back to take care of his own interests. Good storytelling is based on very good knowledge of the audience's state and expectations. A good story combines (a) to win people over while allowing them to easily adapt and open themselves to the story and make them really feel the context and (b) convey the facts and figures. A present gains in value if it is packaged in an appealing way, and painting the new summer house works better if you apply a prime coat first.

The authors' experience is that you normally have a team who do not share a common history, experience and culture in IANS contexts. This causes a situation where you face a lot of the situations that the Japanese describe as KY (*kuuki yomenai*) which means 'one who cannot read the air'—this is due to a lack of common experience and cultural background. This means that storytelling is a powerful tool, but it is only one part of the communication tool box. If you act in western cultures, it is crucial to be precise and repetitive in your communication efforts, e.g. summarizing results or defined action items.

Remark 2 Some Fundamental Remarks on Silos

There are a lot of discussions about silos and their negative impact on companies' success. Frequently the diagnosis 'silo' is made when collaboration at organizational interface level does not work properly and might cause friction. And most likely the diagnosis is accurate meaning that challenges in collaboration can be referred to silos. However, the impacts that silos have are much more substantial than something that can easily perceived such as a fight for a plastic spade in a sandpit.

Silos are groups of people who classify the world in a certain way, which forms a mental map. This mental map gets stronger and stronger when living and executing in line with this mental map. It is comparable to well-trodden paths in forests that (a) arise literally step by step and (b) every other way that would also have been a possible path is not seen (part of the mental map) later, because it seems non-approachable. Based on this mental map, silos are merely oriented on their/by their own structure and do not pay enough attention to external relations (Fenwick et al. 2009).

Understanding and managing silos is a wide field that can be approached from different angles. For example, Gillian Tett (2016) takes a look through anthroposophical glasses showing the impact of silos and how they endanger the existence of companies from surviving very critical situations up to innovation. With our common everyday usage of the word 'silo', we would not normally associate it with such profound examples. But it is not about a terminology definition exercise, more relevant is to dig deeply and fully understand the silo effect while finding the right approach to manage them and also be precise. It's natural that people build groups to create belonging and a certain subculture—it would be wise to have a more differentiated view of silos, e.g. led by the following general questions:

- Does the group/team have negative impact on the company while showing a silo mentality?
- Is it really a silo, or is it a subculture that is open and collaborative towards its environment?
- What especially makes the silo so rigid that you tend to try to tear it down—what would be a measure to establish results-driven cross-silo working instead?

And: assuming you have no silos in your company, how do you avoid your company itself becoming a silo?

References

Fenwick, Seville, & Brunsdon. (2009, March). *Reducing the impact of organizational silos of resilience.* Resilient Organisations Research Report 2009/01.

Fritz, P. (2011, June). Retrieved from https://www.fritz.tips/entwicklungsphasen-einer-organisation-nach-friedrich-glasl/

Gillian, T. (2016, September). *The silo effect.* Abacus.

Glasl, F., & Lievegoed, B. (2011). *Dynamische Unternehmensentwicklung, Grundlageen für nachhaltiges Change Management, 4.* Auflage, Verlag Freies Geistesleben Stuttgart.

Kiergegaard, S.; retrieved from reprint 2002 by The Bruderhof Foundation, Inc., cited by IBM.

Viki, T. (2002, May). *Pirates in the navy.* Unbound.

Wollmann, P., Kühn, F., & Kempf, M. (Eds.). (2020). *Three pillars of organization and leadership in disruptive times – Navigating your company successfully through the 21st century business world.* Cham: Springer Nature.

Sebastian Kespohl has been working as project manager and project portfolio manager in different verticals, mainly telco, FMCG and e-commerce in a highly tech-driven environment. Nowadays, he is a managing director of a regulated financial institute providing payment services to e-commerce merchants, for small and medium business up to the big global players. Sebastian has an educational background in bioinformatics and holds an international executive MBA and a Certificate as an International Senior Project Manager, IPMA.

MedTech Companies on Their Growth Journey-Leadership Responses to Growth Challenges in the Light of the 3-P-Model

Marie Theres Schmidt and Dieter Fellner

Abstract

On the base of their broad industry experiences in different companies, Marie Theres Schmidt and Dieter Fellner developed a case study on challenges faced by fast-growing MedTech companies. The continuous strive for breakthrough medical innovations requires an agile mindset and the readiness to embrace change. Global demographic changes lead to a growing demand for innovative diagnostic and treatment options in the coming years inducing MedTech companies to explore the space while growing fast. At the same time, the medical device market will face increasing regulation to contain healthcare costs and safeguard patients' safety requiring companies to respond to changing conditions.

Regular assessment of the level of agility and resilience is key for fast-growing organizations to successfully manage the growth journey. Leaders of these organizations should establish reflection cycles to monitor success. As an outcome of Marie's and Dieter's experiences, the Three-Pillar Model (3-P-Model) (Wollmann, Kühn, Kempf, Three pillars of organization and leadership in disruptive times – Navigating your company successfully through the 21st century business world. Cham: Springer Nature, 2020) can be applied to facilitate the reflection cycles and emphasize challenges of the organization connected to the growth journey. This is illustrated in the interview which evaluates the three pillars based on the authors' individual leadership experience in fast-growing organizations. The interview reveals companies' persistent focus on improving patients' lives as a sustainable purpose connecting employees around the globe on their joint mission. It further highlights that the sustainable purpose becomes an

M. T. Schmidt (✉)
Bonn, Germany
e-mail: mtaj.schmidt@gmail.com

D. Fellner
Mondsee-Tiefgraben, Austria
e-mail: dieter_fellner@edwards.com

P. Wollmann et al. (eds.), *Organization and Leadership in Disruptive Times*, Future of Business and Finance, https://doi.org/10.1007/978-3-030-63034-8_17

individual and organizational compass: the sustainable purpose provides employees with a tool, or rather an ethical standard, to respond to unforeseen changes. Thereby, the organization preserves its agility to react quickly to uncertainties and remains competitive through the ability of fast adaption to change. A strong sustainable purpose that is deeply embedded in the company's DNA is key to ensure personal commitment and joint success on the growth journey—and frames cross-functional connectivity in fast-developing organizations.

Consequently, fast-growing MedTech companies should thoroughly invest in keeping their sustainable purpose present in all areas and accessible to all employees.

From a leader's perspective: the better a fast-growing company can maintain its DNA, the more successfully and sustainably it will grow.

1 Introduction

Medical device companies are constantly striving to develop best-in-class innovations. In order to remain successful, however, companies need to invest a lot in differentiating themselves from competitors who are always just a small step behind. Therefore, medical device companies are on a continuous journey to explore potential innovation based on patients' needs. At the same time, increasing legislative and medical regulation and harmonization of the MedTech sector, particularly with regard to patient safety, requires companies to react quickly to new standards and to invest in meeting these standards. A high degree of organizational agility is needed to ensure success in the face of uncertainty. Balancing unforeseeable factors by anticipating changes becomes a major strategic imperative for growth in a highly regulated healthcare market. A flexible journey mindset among employees is the key to success.

The ability of an organization to respond to volatility and environmental uncertainties is natural to smaller organizations while being more challenging for larger organizations. As long as few employees are running the business, typically also by definition of their roles, individuals' openness to freestyle in order to respond to uncertainties is high. However, when traveling organizations have successfully managed the growth journey and reached a considerable size, it becomes more challenging to maintain the original organization's resilience and agility (Fig. 1).

With growing numbers of employees and expansion of business areas as well as company hierarchies, the willingness and ability of individuals to execute strategies in a flexible manner, and thereby respond to uncertainties, decreases. Individual agility is additionally hampered by increasing role differentiation and resource separation according to technical ability and business area. Accordingly, larger traveling organizations in particular must remain agile in order to maintain growth.

Overcoming the challenge of uncertainties and agility while growing quickly is considered crucial for traveling organizations to make sure the ability to react to

Fig. 1 The three pillars have proven to be key in every phase of the corporate life cycle. The effectiveness depends on the way of implementation and communication. This must be regularly strategically reflected on and discussed (Illustrated by Frank Kühn, used with permission. All rights reserved)

environmental changes does not stop. In order to respond quickly to changes, companies establish business functions that oversee market dynamics and system changes. Entire business processes and functions (individuals) are dedicated to monitoring and communicating changes in the environment. Forecasting activities reflecting anticipated changes, e.g., changes to funding structures or the competitive environment and other business intelligence processes, is a response to the continuous uncertainties faced by larger organizations. By accurately tracking the likelihood of these uncertainties, organizations become learning organisms that increasingly perfect their response to uncertainties.

In addition to professionally managing uncertainties by integrating their surveillance in processes and functions, maintaining the sustainable purpose among individuals becomes a major driver for organizational agility. Making patients' lives better is an easily understandable, comprehensible purpose with a high ethical level. Joint success through connected resources is only possible if the sustainable purpose remains present and integrated in the company culture. Sustainable purpose is harder to maintain once the organization grows; a small character ensures intimacy and joint commitment, while traveling organizations risk losing people's commitment. From an employee perspective, sustainable purpose becomes less transparent in their daily work due to the increasing complexity of processes and tasks and increasing distance to the key customer: the patient. From a management perspective, inspiring and aligning people on the sustainable purpose becomes a major task in fast-growing companies to ensure stability and continuous growth. Navigating the journey is fundamental to management especially in smaller and medium-sized organizations with strong growth ambitions. Global companies in particular need to ensure strong alignment on the sustainable purpose across continental entities.

How do learning organizations respond to unforeseen challenges, and how flexible are they in adapting their business models and processes? Especially with the Covid-19 pandemic, organizations had to reinvent and rethink their normal business model. What happens to technology companies if their technologies are suddenly less in demand and if access to customers such as hospital staff is prohibited due to increasing infection rates and a focus on Covid-19 patients? What happens if global supply chains are suddenly impacted and availability of specific products becomes scarce?

The flexibility of a company to adapt to these changes contains two elements: first, the culture that is able to adapt to changes and second, the operative adaptation to changes and execution of quick reactions to changes. Both will be highlighted in the interview below.

2 Brief Recap of the Three-Pillar Model

The Three-Pillar Model, described in the book *Three Pillars of Organization and Leadership in Disruptive Times*, was created as a response to the needs of a vulnerable, uncertain, complex, and ambiguous world (VUCA) in order to show adequate agile and flexible solutions.

The 3-P-Model is based on the following three main design principles for future organizations and leadership:

- *Sustainable Purpose*:
  The employees and teams in the organization, but also its key stakeholders in the entire ecosystem and business environment, must know what the organization stands for and what entrepreneurial value it adds and societal contribution it makes. This includes the reciprocity of enterprises, public and social institutions, science, etc.

  The purpose must remain sustainable, reliable, and consistent, supported by leaders, employees, and stakeholders and lived by important representatives of the organization. The purpose aligns, convinces and inspires the people involved in the joint endeavor, making them confident and proud to be part of it and to contribute to it.

  The sustainable purpose is of special importance for the growth journey of medium-sized companies. It navigates and connects people throughout the organization and provides a corporate compass to react to unforeseen changes on the journey.
- *Traveling Organization*:
  We must understand that organizations are continuously on a journey, experiencing twists and turns, following their purpose or even striving for survival, and always looking for the best way between poles, alternatives, and options. If the teams don't know what to expect around the next bend, they have to make smaller steps and explore the terrain. Even if they don't know in advance what the best result will be, they will achieve it: they believe in their motivation

and ability to manage the journey and to rely on their agile mindset, self-reflection, readiness to embrace change, and willingness to deliver. People in a traveling organization are curious, open, courageous, and keen to experiment, and they deal well with uncertainty, stress, and unforeseen incidents.

At the beginning of the journey, enthusiasm is enough to drive people. However, at a certain point in the journey, structures and programs are essential to facilitate collaboration across the fast-growing organization without hampering agility. Structures need to be chosen carefully to support people's enthusiasm and ease decision-making rather than slowing it down, which can often be observed in big companies. The ability to constantly embrace change remains the major principle for growth.

- *Connecting Resources*:
  The organization has to be aware that impact, value, and efficiency, but also survival, need multiple connectivities: between humans, organizations, and ecosystems; between expertise and influence; between different political and social systems and cultures; between enterprises, scientific research, and public sector; between customer satisfaction and economic needs; between strategy, processes, and skills; and between risk management and business continuity. This means not only managing connectivity and preventing unconnected structural silos, boxed competencies and echo chambers but also inspiring and supporting multilateral behaviors and initiatives in the global and local professional communities and balancing various, often contradictory, interests between stakeholders.

  Connectivity poses a major challenge for fast-growing companies with evolving structures. Particularly, expanding to new markets and connecting globally requires a high level of connectivity and willingness to collaborate on all levels. Connected resources improve deliverables and advance knowledge-sharing and management.

All three pillars are key assets of systemic dynamics and high organizational effectiveness: they provide orientation and inspiration, give fundamental impulses to start the journey, and connect the resources for joint success.

3 Interview

The key messages and outcome of the article can best be presented in the form of an interview that Marie conducted with Dieter, who has many years of leadership experience in diverse fast-growing global MedTech organizations, aiming to discuss the opportunities and challenges of unpredictability for growth and company performance. Questions and answers aim to make use of the broad experiences of Dieter from different companies and contexts and his general conclusions made.

The questions are divided into four categories:

1. Application of the 3-P-Model to the MedTech industry in general

2. Future challenges of organizational growth
3. Leadership experience and vision
4. Company's agility and ability to adapt to changes

3.1 Interview Part 1: Application of the 3-P-Model to the Medical Technology Sector in General

Question
You know the 3-P-Model from our last book. Do you think it is—adjusted—applicable to companies in the MedTech industry and how would you "interpret" each pillar in the context of the MedTech industry and your company on a general level?

Answer
Yes, the 3-P-Model is perfectly applicable to companies in the MedTech industry, as constant and rapid change is necessary. For example, more than 90% of the turnover in successful MedTech companies comes from products and services that are not older than 3 years.

Our vocation is to help patients in a sustainable way and to save and improve their lives (sustainable purpose).

Our employees accept this challenge every day and thus master many challenges and also unforeseeable hurdles (traveling organization).

In an international matrix organization, project teams are created that contribute ideas from different perspectives. Networking and further training of employees is encouraged and a focus on inclusion and diversity is placed (connectivity).

Question
How do you specifically assess the status of the last organizations you worked for in terms of sustainable purpose, traveling organization, and connectivity? In your opinion, what is often the general level of maturity for each of the three pillars and overall, and where is frequently room for improvement?

Answer
- Sustainable purpose: mostly excellent and meaningful.
- Traveling organization: mostly the journey is exciting and great.
- Connecting resources: mostly good, but often with room for improvement in cross-functional activities. The strong growth in the number of employees in many companies is a challenge in terms of corporate culture and the need for structured, simplified processes.

Question
What is the sustainable purpose of MedTech companies (its main reason for being), and how does this strengthen personal commitment and create a sense of community among employees?

Answer

To help patients to live longer and healthier.

Personal drive, as it benefits many personal acquaintances and all heart patients, enabling them to do again what they enjoy most. So, you are working for the health and happiness of your fellow human beings.

The sense of community is strengthened by always keeping this in mind. Everyone in the company contributes in his or her field of activity, so that, in the end, sick people are helped. The gratitude of the patients is enormous and can be seen and experienced by all employees, for example, through patient days in the office or at meetings. In honor of our patients, some meeting rooms bear the names of the patients.

Question

What special characteristics of a MedTech organization prove its way of thinking as a "traveling organization?"

Answer

The aim of all organizations I got to know is to develop groundbreaking treatment options for patients together with doctors and to introduce them to the market: this is a patient-focused innovation strategy. Companies aim to be the first and offer the best solutions for patients. This innovation journey is indescribably beautiful and successful and is continuous. Unforeseen obstacles and setbacks with new product launches can pose hurdles, but are part and parcel of the work of companies that claim to be the first and the best.

Learning quickly from mistakes and setbacks gives the opportunity to improve further.

Question

What special skills make it possible to achieve the required connectivity?

Answer

I think it is the willingness of a company to invest in the personal development and advancement of its employees: here, the personality training and coaching offered to management teams are particularly worthy of mention. This links different departments from different geographical areas and inspires them to improve.

It is crucial to recruit talents who have the ability to connect to the organization and have a flexible way of thinking, broad horizons, and the courage to embrace new things.

3.2 Interview Part 2: Future Challenges of Organizational Growth

Question
What are the biggest challenges for very fast-growing companies in the years to come, and what would this mean in terms of the three pillars of organization and leadership?

Answer
In sustainable purpose:

- Maintain and promote the corporate culture.
- Select employees with regard to the vocation.

In traveling organization:

- Adapt the organization to changes in the healthcare market.
- Prepare employees for constant change.
- Train employees continuously in new technologies.
- Develop digital processes to improve internal processing.
- Place patients at the center of the work.
- Optimize patient pathways.
- Increase the use of business intelligence systems to improve and regularly adapt strategies.

In connecting resources:

- Promote interdepartmental cooperation.
- Introduce a knowledge management system.
- Use agile teams to develop strategies and tactics.
- Allow flat hierarchies and more self-organization.

Question
How to maintain the company's original corporate culture when it is growing so quickly?

Answer
Show the company's vision at the beginning of team meetings and explain and discuss one point in detail.

Employee selection according to cultural fit is a basic prerequisite. Onboarding program and an induction day for new employees, plus support from a mentor or coach, are also essential.

Question
In particular, how can the way of thinking and connectivity skills concerning "travel" be kept on the growth track, which will also have a significant impact on the requirements of the company?

Answer
Thinking skills can be developed by transforming implicit personal knowledge into explicit documented knowledge and by creating a so-called growing knowledge spiral within the company.

The freedom of the employees at all levels creates an open and inspirational climate that promotes innovation. The challenges are thus solved by the employees who induce the solutions. Personal responsibility in the interest of the patient is the highest guiding principle.

3.3 Interview Part 3: Your Leadership Experience and Vision

Question
How to make and keep the company attractive for young talents? What career, or rather development, pattern do you see for growth? And what is the connection to the 3-P-Model? Especially, what role does the sustainable purpose and attractiveness of travel in unfamiliar territories play?

Answer
A growing market and innovation leadership make MedTech companies very attractive employers because success is inevitable.

Leadership in innovation means introducing a large number of new products and services to the market. This is exactly the right thing for agile and performance-oriented people.

Companies aim to succeed in further transforming the treatment of illnesses, and the individual employee is thus involved in something worthwhile and great. The corporate community generates a lot of happy and healthy patients. This creates a high potential of satisfaction and makes many employees happy. Successes are rewarded and celebrated.

Question
What have you learned in the last few years?

Answer
A lot, because I love to learn new things, and here are my top five experiences:

1. Trust leads fastest.
2. Be humble and stand up for others.
3. People remember how they felt, not what you did.
4. EQ is important alongside with IQ.

5. Give more and you get more.

Question
What are the most important competitive advantages of MedTech companies in general?

Answer
- Striving to have the best products and services
- Having the most engaged employees
- Optimally positioned for the future
- Highly specialized, competent organizations with great expertise in specific disease areas

3.4 Interview Part 4: Agility and Adaptability of the Company to Change

Question
What skills and attitudes are needed by people within the organization as a result of increasing external changes (external effects within the organization) now and in the future?

Answer
- Willingness to welcome change in all respects (digitalization, social change, change of tasks, etc.) and to embrace new opportunities.
- The will, the strength, and the discipline to awaken new abilities within oneself.
- Live common values and always be an example for others.

Question
How do companies from your experience react to changes? Have you adapted certain processes or set up new functions to better respond to market changes in the past?

Answer
Many companies react very well and quickly to changes.
Many processes have been simplified and recurring manual tasks automated.
Digitalization is used in many areas and functional departments.

Newly acquired raw data are processed for information and to enrich company knowledge, which is transformed into imperative company wisdom and allows to derive a strategic imperative. From this, KODs (Key Operating Drivers) are created annually, which make the corporate success measurable in all areas. KODs are reviewed monthly, and the development is tracked in order to adjust tactics if necessary and to stay on course despite market changes.

Market changes are captured by the increased use of electronic business intelligence systems. Employees with customer contact, consultants, and other market research data sources provide a great deal of input here. Company's own business intelligence represents the most predictable market situation. When reality checks reveal unforeseen changes, companies react immediately: critical decisions are made using short paths and fast scenario planning.

Question
Take the corona crisis as an example. How can business be maintained in times of social distancing and difficult access to customers?

Answer
Contact via telephone and video conferencing.
Issue certificates to employees who need to travel and have access to clinics and offices.

According to § 6 of the BSI regulation, MedTech companies belong to Germany's so-called ›system-relevant critical infrastructure and thus make a significant contribution to ensuring medical care. In the event of failure or impairment, there would be lasting supply bottlenecks, considerable disruption to public safety, or other dramatic consequences for medical production and thus patient safety. It is therefore necessary that MedTech companies remain open without restrictions throughout the entire period of the pandemic and that employees are allowed to go to their workplaces and to clinics.

- Training of customers and employees via webinars and video conferences
- Coordination of online congresses
- Informal coffee teams meetings to stay in daily contact via video

More background to Dieter's statements in the interview can be taken from Reindl (2018), Malik (2006), or Sprenger (2010) (Fig. 2).

4 Concrete Case as an Example

The *sustainable purpose* is important for companies' growth journey. Ensuring joint efforts in providing innovative solutions for patients and the singular focus on the large unmet need of critically ill patients leverages the patient-focused innovation strategy that has been key to companies' success story. Patient focus is not just a theoretical concept but companies' core, which should be physically present as well to remind all employees of their joint mission. How do leaders physically establish the sustainable purpose?

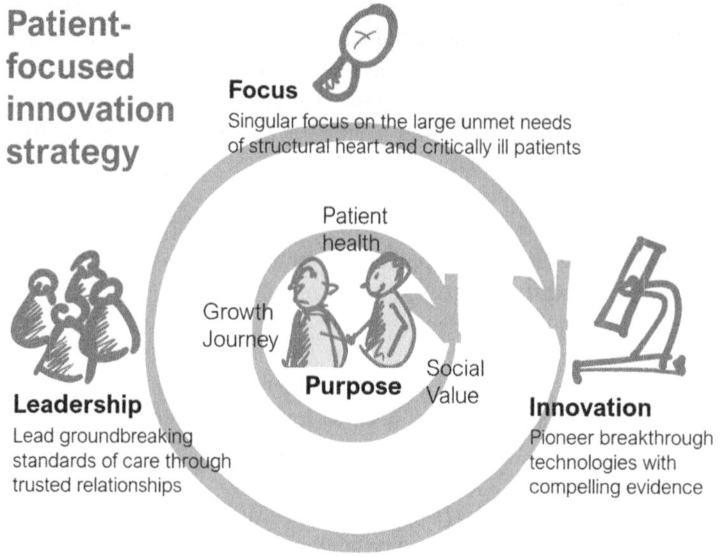

Fig. 2 The purpose is the core and one of the constituent factors of the corporate strategy (Illustrated by Frank Kühn, used with permission. All rights reserved)

1. Patients are invited to annual company meetings across the different regions to present their stories to all employees and leaders. The stories are very lively and emotional as presented by those who have lived them, and they remind employees and leaders of their joint mission and the impact that the company can have for people.
2. Meeting rooms or buildings can be named after patients to show employees and patients that each individual patient has their own story and is a unique building block of the company's journey.
3. Clinical staff are engaged to ensure each patient in need of a device receives the operation and the product in a timely manner. They travel to the clinics, ensure that the right product is available, and support the operation team however they can. This means that the company's clinical employees are available to answer critical questions and to support individual patients and physicians in the field.

5 Special Takeaways

1. The three pillars have proven to be essential checkpoints for regular management reflection cycles. Verifying the status and effect of each of them enables organizations to control their growth journey and adjust where needed. Identifying such checkpoints is a good way to evaluate short-term implementation effects of structures, processes, programs, and culture. It further provides a roadmap to achieve resilience and growth of fast-growing organizations.

2. Excellence should be targeted across all areas: the best-in-class product is complemented by the best talents. New hires are selected according to their emotional intelligence (EQ) and their personal fit with the company culture. It is crucial that employees bring the right mindset to drive agility and growth. Growth mindset includes the willingness and ability to connect across departments and the ability to adapt to constant change. Besides the individual prerequisites, adaptability also needs to be trained and lived by leaders of the organization to ensure no one is left behind on the growth journey.
3. One of the major keys to success proves to be sustainable purpose: the joint commitment to improve patients' lives creates a strong sense of community and identity for all employees. It is deeply embedded in the DNA of most MedTech company. The DNA is the key success factor, while it can also become the biggest challenge throughout the journey. From a leader's perspective, the better a fast-growing company can maintain its DNA, the more successfully it will grow.
4. New employees need to adapt quickly to the company culture, while leaders need to prominently encourage company culture. The higher the frequency of new hires, the higher the risk of individualists working in silos. Therefore, companies create comprehensive onboarding programs and an induction day for new employees at different locations to convey the company's culture, vision, and product specificities as soon as people join. New hires are further supported by mentors or coaches.
5. Special focus on cross-functional connectivity under fast-growing staff preconditions is recommended to foster planned, but also coincidental, exchange of knowledge between members of different functions, departments, or affiliates. This increases organizations' resilience and ensures active knowledge management and distribution. Thus, organizations remain more agile in responding to unforeseen change.

6 Conclusions

The Three-Pillar Model of organization and leadership helps to identify the challenges and drivers that MedTech companies face on their growth journey. They have proven to be suitable checkpoints for regular management reflection cycles to verify whether organizations are on the right track and to adjust programs and structures if needed to ensure resilience on the growth journey.

Navigating MedTech companies successfully through disruptive times requires a strong focus on community. The interview takeaways show that a major driver for the sense of community is the sustainable purpose that guides all employees in their tasks, a purpose that constitutes the core component of the company's DNA. MedTech companies strive for breakthrough therapies to improve the lives of patients. This sustainable purpose should be lived and encouraged by all leaders, conceptually as well as physically.

The challenge of fast-growing organizations with a strong company culture is to maintain that culture and joint purpose while increasing the frequency of onboarding new employees. Therefore, hiring the right talents is key: emotionally intelligent individuals with a very agile mindset and strong willingness to adjust to the company culture based on bottom-up feedback. At the same time, leaders need to ensure that the DNA of the company is present at all times to guide and connect new employees with the joint vision and to onboard them on the growth journey with top-down guidance. This process will ultimately lead to a highly agile and connected organization that can respond quickly to uncertainties arising from unforeseen changes while remaining competitive. Leaders must invest in employees' agility as well as strengthening connecting resources across the organization.

In the light of the three pillars, the sustainable purpose plays a superordinate role in safeguarding the resilience of a fast-growing organization, as it positively impacts on its agility and connectivity. Achieving connected resources without a clear sustainable purpose as part of the company's DNA is not conducive to the growth journey.

At the same time, connectivity in cross-functional activities is easy if an organization is small as everybody knows everybody else. A rapid growth in the number of employees is, therefore, a challenge for cross-functional connectivity and activities. Connectivity as a growth element may need explicit support and promotion as a counterbalance to naturally increasing processes and structures that are bureaucratic but vital. In this context, it might be important to encourage coincidental real and virtual meetings of employees as is common practice at tech companies in Silicon Valley.

When evaluating an organization's resilience, the interconnectedness of the organization's sustainable purpose and its agility and connectivity need as much attention as the status of each pillar separately. Management should carry out regular reflection exercises to adjust the organization where needed, thus enabling them to remain competitive and resilient. The ability to reflect on and react to failures and the ability to embrace change are the key characteristics to success of fast-growing organizations.

References

Malik, F. (2006). *Führen, Leisten, Leben: Wirksames Management für eine neue Zeit*. Herausgeber: Campus Verlag.

Reindl, R. (2018). *The HOW of leadership: Unleashing the capacity of your people*. Visual Insight Press.

Sprenger, R. (2010). *Mythos motivation. Wege aus einer Sackgasse*. Herausgeber: Campus Verlag.

Wollmann, P., Kühn, F., & Kempf, M. (Eds.). (2020). *Three pillars of organization and leadership in disruptive times – Navigating your company successfully through the 21st century business world*. Cham: Springer Nature.

Marie Theres Schmidt studied Health Economics at the University of Rotterdam and SDA Bocconi School of Management where she graduated in 2012. She specialized in market access of pharmaceuticals and medical devices throughout her professional career and has led pricing and reimbursement processes for innovative medicines and medical devices for global companies. As Director of Market Access and Government Affairs at Edwards Lifesciences, she is developing strategies to ensure patients' access to innovative, best-in-class medical technologies while pursuing political engagement for structural heart diseases. Her projects are driven by strong cross-functional collaboration across organizational entities and healthcare authorities, always engaging multiple disciplines in decision-making processes. With her international working culture, she effectively manages diverse teams and projects in changing environments.

Dieter Fellner is a qualified engineer for fundamental and theory in electrotechnics and biomedical engineering and has more than 30 years of professional experience in the area of healthcare market. During his studies at the Vienna University of Technology, he worked at Siemens Medical Technology in the development of the latest magnetic resonance imaging. He started his professional career at Philips Medical Systems in Hamburg and then led the development and introduction of the latest medical laser systems in Europe and Australia at Kapsch Medical Technology. He was able to further expand his leadership experience in the fields of intensive care, cardiac surgery, and cardiology at the companies Baxter and Guidant (now Boston Scientific). In his position as Country Director for Germany at Edwards Lifesciences, he experienced the intensive journey from a listed spin-off MedTech company to a rapidly growing, patient-focused MedTech company in a top 30 global position. He strives to develop employees and drive innovation.

Building a Sustainable Brand in Specialty Chemicals (Carve Out from a Big Corporate)

Jürgen Scherer, Susanne Marell, and Jutta Wenzl

Abstract

Cognis was a leading global supplier of specialty chemicals in the home and personal care, functional performance, and nutritional ingredients markets. The company was carved out as the former chemical division of Henkel AG & Co. KGaA in 1999, acquired jointly by three private equity funds in 2001, and sold in 2011 to BASF. In its 12-year lifetime, the management established a corporate culture—"We know how"—to mobilize, bond, and develop all stakeholder relationships.

This article will highlight and illustrate key components of this journey along the organizational and leadership pillars of "sustainable purpose," "traveling organization," and "connecting resources" (Wollmann et al., Three pillars of organization and leadership in disruptive times – Navigating Your company successfully through the 21st century business world. Cham, Springer, 2020). Each component represented a significant building block of the company's financial success, its reputation in the marketplace, and most importantly its strong bonding among its employees. However, "the magic glue," the differentiating DNA building element, is the combination of the three pillars via awareness, initiation, creation, and continuous learning. The mutual reinforcement between the pillars created a strong brand (identity).

J. Scherer (✉)
Düsseldorf, Germany
e-mail: chererjn@yahoo.com

S. Marell
Haan, Germany
e-mail: susanne.marell@t-online.de

J. Wenzl
Munich, Germany
e-mail: jutta.wenzl@t-online.de

P. Wollmann et al. (eds.), *Organization and Leadership in Disruptive Times*, Future of Business and Finance, https://doi.org/10.1007/978-3-030-63034-8_18

1 Introduction

Comparing the business environment of today (2020) with or without Covid-19, one might say that, two decades ago, at the birth of Cognis, the economic world in 2000 was much less stressed. VUCA was, if at all, only known to insiders as a military term describing a volatile, uncertain, often complex, and ambiguous world resulting from the end of the Cold War era.

However, Cognis' new shareholders and management had a different view and—though VUCA was not the terminology used at that time—recognized a very challenging business environment.

Being carved out in August 1999 as the former chemical division of Henkel AG & Co. KGaA, the new investors, representatives of three private equity funds—Goldman Sachs, Permira, and Schroder Ventures Life Sciences—signed the sale and purchase agreement (SPA) on September 12, 2001, one day after the terror attacks in the United States. Both parties agreed to re-evaluate the impact on the financial markets and closed the deal two and a half months later on November 30, 2001.

The relevant market segment for specialty chemicals was, and certainly remains, a very tough business position within the end-to-end B2B2C value chain. Figure 1, adapted from the Chemical Week (2002), displays the situation as "Caught in the Middle."

Upstream, specialty chemical companies like Cognis, similar to its competitors Rohm and Haas, ICI, and Lonza, source the materials typically from (crude) oil refiners (e.g., ExxonMobil, Shell, BP, Total) and various raw material companies

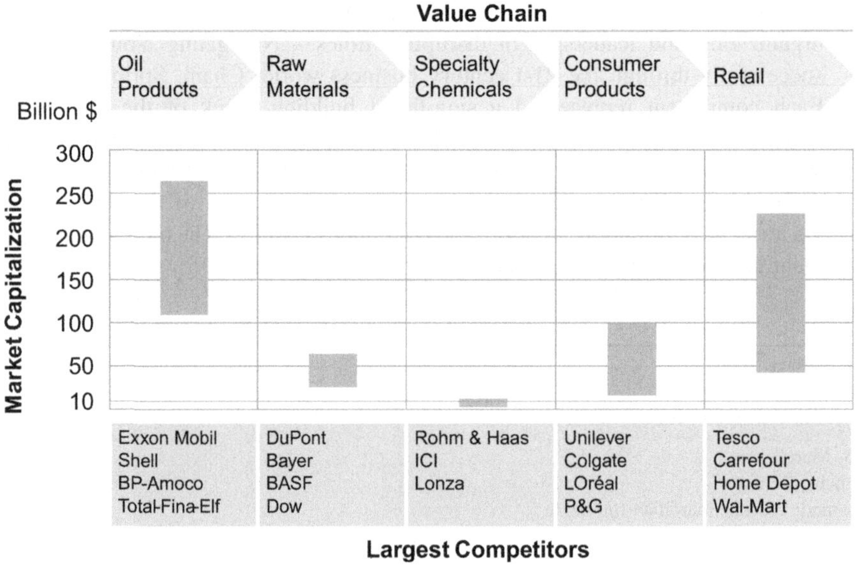

Fig. 1 "Caught in the Middle" (adapted from Chemical Week 2002) (Illustrated by the authors, used with permission. All rights reserved)

(e.g., DuPont, Bayer, BASF, Dow). After processing and conversion, downstream, they sell the specialty chemicals to the fast-moving consumer goods (FMCG) industry with customers like Unilever, Colgate, L'Oréal, and Procter & Gamble, ultimately ending in consumer (branded) products sold in retail stores such as Tesco, Carrefour, Home Depot, or Walmart. Simply comparing the market capitalization of all players in the value chain, it is obvious that specialty chemical companies are a fraction in size and power, thus best described as being "sandwiched." It is a battle of "survival of the fittest" by managing complexity, providing innovative solutions, and focusing its portfolio on profitable segments. It should come as no surprise that, two decades later, two players mentioned in this figure no longer exist: ICI was acquired in 2007 by AkzoNobel and Rohm and Haas in 2009 by Dow—as Cognis was in 2011 by BASF.

2 Sustainable Purpose

The creation of an entire new company based on an existing business history of 125 years within a large family-owned corporation (Henkel AG & Co. KGaA) provided an exciting and challenging opportunity for the management team.

From the very beginning, it was the stated objective to position Cognis as a strong and unique global brand within the market of specialty chemicals and nutritional ingredients. The management therefore defined branding and communications—both internal and external—as a strategic success factor for Cognis.

In detail, the following three objectives were defined:

- Creation of a separate company and umbrella brand with a strong position according to the company's goals
- Motivation of the employees to commit to a new company and convey the feeling of a new beginning and a visionary common goal
- Strong positioning in the different market segments and convincing presentation of the product and concept performance toward (potential) customers

"Cognis," a neologism word, derived from the Latin "cognoscere"—to recognize, to learn, and to know—and the visual translation into the blue iris of a human eye, formed the company logo. The central message of the Cognis brand was expressed by the claim "We know how."

This reflected the unique expertise available at Cognis for the development of intelligent solutions for its respective markets. Five *key values* were defined to tell the target groups what Cognis stood for:

- Strategy nature.
- Innovations are our business.
- Intelligent chemistry solutions.
- We take care.
- Sustainability.

Accordingly, two decades before Greta Thunberg initiated the "Fridays for Future" movements and BlackRock CEO Larry Fink stated: "Ultimately, *purpose* is the engine of long-term profitability" in his famous CEO letter "A fundamental reshaping of finance" (Fink 2020), Cognis created a sustainable purpose by design.

The first Cognis Sustainability Report in 2001 clearly signposted the way forward:

> Naturally, it is our top-most priority to be successful as a company. But it is for this reason in particular that we also intend to maintain an equilibrium between economic, ecological and social responsibility. We also want to ensure that the generations to come have every opportunity to determine their own future. The demand for environmentally friendly products and manufacturing processes is growing steadily. With our natural raw materials, we are excellently positioned and can actively shape this market.

With around 60% of its raw materials portfolio based on renewable natural oils and fats from vegetable sources, Cognis focused its entire product and service portfolio by serving the two megatrends "Wellness and Sustainability." Cognis' objectives were aligned accordingly: Penetrate existing growth markets and open up new ones; recognize trends at an early stage; and quickly bring new ideas and concepts to market. Therefore, creating an extremely marketing-oriented and customer-centric company was the driving force: "Think B2C—Act B2B," based on a deep understanding of its customers' markets unlike most competition in a traditionally research-driven and product-oriented chemical industry.

The creation of the uniform—purpose-driven—corporate brand started during the carve-out process from Henkel in 1999 with the comprehensive internal motivation and communication concept called "Open your eyes." Around 500 top managers were invited to a global kick-off meeting in Cannes, providing the opportunity to understand and discuss the strategy and goals of the newly formed company and, more importantly, to experience the Cognis spirit and vision to become the first choice for employees, customers, shareholders, and the community. More intuitively than strategically planned, the "Golden Circle of why, how, and what," later defined by Simon Sinek (2009), drove important parts of the initial communication cascade.

In a second step, all 10,000 employees around the world raised their glasses to the future success of Cognis on the occasion of the first "Cognis Day Celebration." The core objective was to create a very symbolic and historic moment that employees would love to remember. "Think Cognis"—be one team, drive one dream—was the global message. Everyone was asked to contribute to the creation and positioning of Cognis as a leading supplier of specialty chemicals.

Externally, the birth of Cognis was accompanied with a series of concerted actions worldwide to rapidly build up a distinct and unique identity for Cognis. Advertisements, image brochures, standard presentations, banners, customer letters, and PR measures were launched to send a self-confident and clear message to the market: "Dear Customer: The good news is, Cognis is here, there's no bad news!" and shortly after "Dear Competitor: The bad news is, Cognis is here, there's no good news!".

The management unswervingly believed in the success of using renewable raw materials and innovative technology to transform natural oils and fats from vegetable sources into intelligent solutions. With a high sense of its customers' needs and a feel for markets and trends, the central promise was to create a competitive advantage for all partners across the various industries, such as:

- "In chemistry, the formula nature is developing into the formula for the future. Cognis has chemical solutions based on natural raw materials today to match the demands of tomorrow."
- "Successful companies put their customers' needs first. We think on a larger scale. To provide the best service to our customers, we focus on the demands of their customers."

These messages were constantly spread to decision-makers, marketing and production managers, product developers, and purchasers worldwide and to all other important stakeholders such as journalists, financial analysts, and key opinion leaders across the whole value chain.

The corporate brand also served as an umbrella brand for the business units and product areas from the outset. The motifs of the first target campaigns highlighted values and competencies such as "innovative strength" and "chemistry from nature." In the media, the topics "Sustainable Development" and "Wellness" were consistently placed and got a high share of voice over time. Fresh and innovative divisional campaigns followed over time, entitled: "Feelosophy," "Greenovating," or "Newtrition," built on (eye-)catching plays on words.

Without being legally obliged to, Cognis published annual and sustainability reports on a yearly basis to showcase the vision and brand promise by innovative products, concept developments, and corresponding market successes. All corporate and marketing communication concepts were developed from a single source, and, as a consequence, all positioning activities complemented and supported each other. Today, this is known as "360-degree campaigning." A globally unique and outstanding profile as an innovative and sustainable specialty chemical company was the result.

It is important to point out that the journey to build up a purpose-driven corporate brand was not a smooth and easy one. Not every single step was outlined when Cognis was founded, and many ideas and initiatives were developed along the journey: Success breeds success in a learning organization. In the beginning, the number of doubters was probably significantly higher than the number of supporters. And there were many valid questions and arguments:

- Would it be possible at all to build on one common brand promise but serve heterogeneous industries such as cosmetics, detergents and cleansers, nutrition and health, as well as industrial markets like coatings, textiles, agrochemicals, etc.?
- Would Cognis have problems if it promoted natural resources in a very prominent way while 40% of the portfolio was not based on renewables?

- Would it be possible to adjust the brand promise to the different regions?
- Should all money be put into branding and communications at all?

However, gradually, more and more colleagues recognized that the Cognis brand promise (purpose) was providing a clear, convincing, and inspirational orientation internally. It helped to align and motivate people across all countries and business segments. And it underpinned the general resilience to keep going even in the deepest economic and emotional troughs of the 12-year change process of Cognis.

The clear purpose and targeted branding were key success factors to carry management and employees through the challenging and troubled period of being carved from Henkel, sold to investors, numerous restructuring and redesign programs, and finally the sale to BASF.

Building a sustainable business model was an encouraging goal giving a "Why" beyond private equity ownership, financials, multipliers, and exit attempts. The identification with Cognis and its goals grew over the years and welded the team together. The Cognis glue was probably at its most effective during the sale to BASF, and, for many former employees, the alumni community is still a close and important business network. A certain pride is attached to having been a part of the Cognis story. And, according to Larry Fink, the purpose was definitely one engine of driving the multiplier for the investors (Fink 2020).

3 Traveling Organization

The Cognis story started and ended with disruptive change. The carve-out from Henkel and the acquisition by BASF in 2011 created the most unstable and unsettling working environments in a corporate life, involving major change efforts.

There had been many operational activities during the carve-out from Henkel, i.e., setting up new IT systems and redesigning processes and structures while stabilizing day-to-day business operations. However, the most radical change was the emotional separation from the old identity—both for managers and employees. It was about cutting the umbilical cord without really wanting it, becoming somebody new, and creating a separate culture, thus facing contradictory dynamics.

Driven by the carve-out and the aforementioned business environment, management set up a clear strategy to reach the defined Cognis objectives: strong sales growth, increase in profitability, and cash flow. The strategic objectives cascaded into continuous improvement programs. Six *Corporate Improvement Programs* were initiated: "Business Excellence" and "R&T Efficiency" (growth), "Purchasing Optimization," "World-Class Manufacturing," "Fixed Cost Reduction" (profitability), and "Cash Flow Optimization" (cash).

These programs were followed by the so-called Business Model Redesign (BMR) a few years later: setting up clear responsibilities, sharpening P&L responsibility for the top and bottom line, and "redimensioning" the organization. All initiatives were managed and steered in a stringent and consistent manner, promoting high performance and discipline. Though initiated by the shareholders in the beginning, continuous improvement and innovation became a natural part of day-to-day business, combined with the strong will to succeed.

Communication was a strategic success factor in this context: Management provided continuous orientation by communicating constantly and consistently.

Cognis focused early on leadership, culture, training, and development in order to strengthen the organization's ability for change—knowing that, above all, it is about people turning plans into real-life actions.

4 Leadership

Execution is about human behavior. Strategies succeed, thanks to people. If they fail, it is because of people. The Cognis success depended strongly on the leaders of the company. From the very beginning and throughout the whole Cognis journey, the strengthening and enabling of the leadership team was vital. As CEO Antonio Trius stated: "We can only win if we love our work and develop a passion for our company. We will only succeed if we believe wholeheartedly in our projects."

There is magic in every beginning. The special kick-off event created an opportunity for our global leaders to outline the strategy and the way forward, to express the expectations, and to celebrate—planting the seeds for a new era by encouraging an optimistic spirit and the joy of shaping something new.

This, of course, was not enough. Central to the successful Cognis journey was selecting the right leaders, enabling them, and creating a high level of commitment and consistency in management.

From the beginning, programs were set up to build strong competencies among the management and leadership teams, accompanied by training the global Human Resources community in change management and consistently developing these measures over the years.

Cognis encouraged its leaders to get involved as "entrepreneurs in their own right" and to take the initiative and responsibility for their own professional and personal development. In particular, enabling the leadership team to manage change throughout the Cognis lifespan and to learn how to coach and help others adapt to change effectively. Different platforms were developed to share challenges, best practice, and knowledge and create space for personal reflection.

5 Culture

The Cognis culture was based on an interesting mixture: a tradition of chemical competence paired with the adventure of a start-up seeking ambitious business objectives for the future. In several global, interdisciplinary working teams, six core *Cultural Principles* were jointly defined, reconciled, and calibrated against the corporate strategy and amended over the years where necessary. They served as the cornerstones of a performance culture, aligning the interests and guiding all actions toward the common objectives:

- We at Cognis value a passion for customer success.
- We at Cognis value one team—one dream.
- We at Cognis value exceptional performance.
- We at Cognis value an empowering and rewarding work environment.
- We at Cognis value change and innovation.
- We at Cognis value personal leadership.

With a focus on driving business results, Cognis implemented a simple but effective annual review process to ensure the entire organization was committed to improving business outcomes. It took 2 years until the process for goal setting and reflection worked properly and developed into a powerful ongoing review cycle. Based on this, Human Resources augmented the process using team calibrations among the leadership teams to understand how talent was performing in the organization, using the calibrations to make better and faster talent decisions.

In addition, the compensation and benefits management systems were aligned along more stringent lines with performance-based salary reviews and performance-based salary bands. People were expected to perform, and it paid off.

6 Training and Development

It was clear: Cognis would be only as good as its employees. The "4C Competency Model" had been adapted several times to the developing needs during the Cognis lifespan. The 4C model summarized the core competencies reflecting the Cognis mindset: Focus on Cognis results, communication, change, and commitment. Described in more detail, they were the basis for the recruiting processes as well as training and development and internal promotions.

All learning activities focused on the needs of the business, characterized as pragmatic and based on measures that could be quickly implemented and adjusted to different situations. Gaining the necessary qualifications and continuous lifelong learning was the underlying philosophy of the Cognis College and later the Cognis Sales Academy, offering tailor-made training modules.

Training and development activities not only aimed at gaining skills and methods but at personal development and building a global network among the employees. Cognis offered international onboarding seminars for new leaders, promoting self-reflection and learning how to give and receive feedback. Personal reflection was key to leadership development as were international exchange programs.

The Cognis Acceleration Program provided new and extended learning and development opportunities by creating experiences that "got under the skin." Selected top performers with a high potential were given the opportunity to develop and grow by working together on strategic topics in cross-functional international teams. Avoiding formal bureaucratic processes, the team members were asked to organize themselves in virtual teams. This was "action learning" at its best: pragmatic, business-driven, and on-the-job-learning combined with opportunities to reflect and increase one's set of competencies.

Strong leadership and clarity provided psychological safety as well as strong bonds, the "magic glue" among leaders and employees—many of them always ready to go the extra mile. Short paths and flat hierarchies smoothed the way to establishing a culture based on trust and delegation, the freedom to act, and true collaboration. There was a willingness to address conflicts openly in order to solve them. Overall, Cognis was successful in combining dedicated work and a strong focus on results with fun and quality of life at the workplace. Cognis was driven by its products and solutions, by an expression of the life and soul of its employees, and by an expression of the corporate identity.

By the time Cognis was acquired by BASF, both leaders and employees had experienced a unique journey to become an organization with a strong culture, with people who were proud of the achievements and working relationships that turned into friendships around the globe—and then the journey started all over again!

7 Connecting Resources

Key to success in any organization is its ability to connect resources effectively and efficiently. This predominantly relates to its own employees and the workforce and applies to the entire organization, i.e., the divisions/business units, the business functions, and the various geographical regions.

Cognis started in 1999 with five Strategic Business Units (SBUs) and, after being carved out from Henkel, had the opportunity to set up all core business functions in an unconditional way.

Especially as the core principle of the organizational setup had been maximum empowerment to the operational units in the local legal entities, while allowing only a minimum of inevitable corporate structure, it was vital to still capture as many synergies as possible in the chosen matrix organization. That was ensured with three initiatives over time.

Firstly, as mentioned above, the implementation and execution of the six *Corporate Improvement Programs* started immediately after the acquisition by the new shareholders in 2002. The programs set the tone for the entire organization in terms of cross-divisional, cross-functional, and cross-regional cooperation. Internal resources were focused on the biggest improvement areas for Cognis, i.e., on top-line revenue generation, bottom-line cost reduction, and cash flow optimization. At shareholders' request, one of the leading business consulting firms managed the central program office for approximately 18 months. However, the management of the programs themselves was done entirely using internal Cognis resources. That ensured a strong buy-in and commitment, particularly for the rollout beyond the initial phase. All six programs established ongoing processes and procedures. They became the backbone of all core business activities.

Secondly, by 2004, Cognis had streamlined its organizational setup with a *Business Model Redesign (BMR)*, together with the implementation of a standardized ERP system. At the center of this reorganization was the conscious decision to further "divisionalize" certain functions. Thus, the entire R&D structure was dissolved and integrated into the SBUs. All production sites, including multi-purpose plants, were assigned to the SBUs, as was the operational part of the Supply Chain function, especially Sales and Operations Planning (S&OP). As a consequence, the Business Units developed a very strong "silo-busting" Operations function, including Asset, Inventory, Margin, and Value Chain Management. Finally, the role of Managing Directors in the various local legal entities was dissolved, and so-called Legal Representatives were appointed. These were members of the Senior Management Team (Executive Committee) taking on a "second role" besides their core business role, e.g., as a global or regional SBU head.

All these organizational changes led to fully fledged P&L responsibility within the SBUs. The local country organizations served fundamentally as "Service Centers," covering the remaining functions, such as Finance and Controlling, Supply Chain Services (essentially Purchasing, Transportation, and Warehousing), Information Technology, Human Resources, and Safety, Health, Environment, and Quality (SHEQ). Key Performance Indicators (KPIs) were introduced to set clear targets for the legal entities ensuring and/or improving the respective Service Level Agreements (SLAs) toward the Business Units. The dual role of the Legal Representatives served as a mediating factor, as "bridge builder" in case of different expectations and conflicts.

Thirdly, the financial crisis of 2008/2009 forced the organization to initiate further steps of stretching the business toward a leaner structure. Cognis had undergone a concentration of its business activities from originally five to three global business units. In preparation for a potential exit by the shareholders and different buy-out scenarios, various (mostly regional) *Shared Service Center* concepts were evaluated and gradually implemented. This provided an opportunity to adjust the workforce without drastic measures according to the requirements of a reduced divisional diversity and span of activities.

In summary, the Cognis matrix organization achieved its ambition to be decentralized and efficient. However, thanks to the various programs it was well connected, utilizing its resources effectively. Furthermore, active *Knowledge Management* was institutionalized in one division, based on individual or team debriefings of major (customer) projects, (product) launches, or (technical) initiatives. Thus, key learnings were captured and documented, in order to apply the intrinsic knowledge gained to future activities and build a wider group of subject matter experts across divisions, functions, and regions.

Connecting resources certainly has another very important element—the cross-boundary aspect of reaching out and integrating the external side of the business. This means for instance customer and Supplier Relationship Management, benchmarking via independent industry associations with competitors, collaborations with research institutes, universities, start-ups and the like.

Some of the most impactful initiatives were the customer (satisfaction) surveys in cooperation with specialized B2B market research firms. While the first survey in 2005 was mainly focused on identifying improvement potentials across divisions and regions based on customer feedback (Scherer and Kühlborn 2008), the second

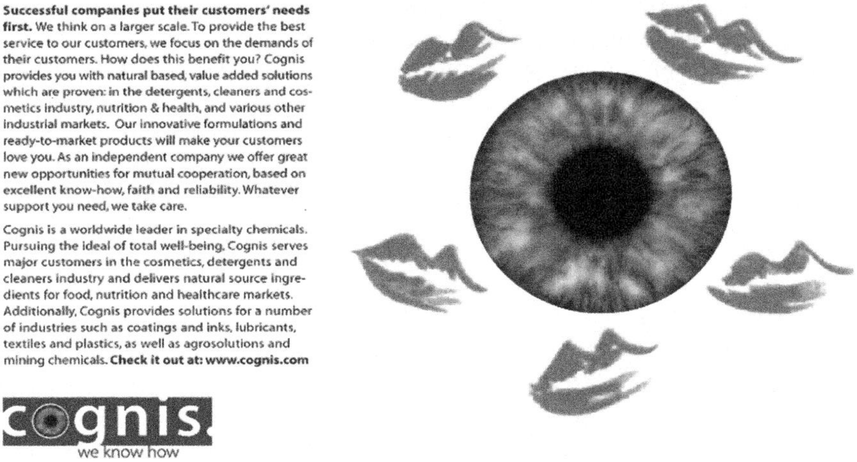

Fig. 2 How to make your customers love you (own source of the authors)

survey in 2008 provided a very insightful aspect of the Cognis business model, as an acting B2B2C company.

As much as overall customer loyalty is driven by customer satisfaction in terms of "hard facts" such as quality, service, delivery, and price, it is equally driven by the overall company image, i.e., the "soft facts" of reputation, authenticity, sympathy, or technical know-how (Becker and Daschmann 2015). In other words, from a customer perspective, it is as important "how you sell and serve" as it is "what you sell and serve." Or, from a supplier (Cognis) point of view, the positioning and the strong branding of the company contribute equally to its (financial) success versus the ongoing performance of supply and service. Disproportionate efforts on performance improvements are "flogging a dead horse," while too little efforts devoted to branding and positioning are "forgetting a hidden gem."

The image campaign "How to make your customers love you" addressed this soft side, the emotional bond in a B2B2C environment and the Cognis ambition that its innovative formulations and ready-to-market products would assure the customer's customers benefit (Scherer et al. 2008; Fig. 2).

The 2008 survey unveiled a distinctive ability of Cognis, a Unique Selling Proposition (USP) differentiating itself from the competition by means of its established company image. The aforementioned efforts devoted to Sustainable Purpose, Cultural Principles, Leadership, and Development were clearly mirrored in high ratings when it came to positive customer experience and loyalty (Marell and Borgards 2008).

Cognis was a board member of the Institute for Market-oriented Management (IMU) at Mannheim University, Germany, joining top listed DAX and Fortune 500 companies across all leading industries such as Audi, BASF, Deutsche Bank, Deutsche Post, Deutsche Telekom, E.ON, Google, IBM, L'Oréal, Microsoft, Nestle, Pfizer, Procter & Gamble, RWE, and SAP. The cross-industry network with these co-members fueled numerous benchmarking initiatives and continuous learning how to better serve customers in the B2B2C markets.

A further spin-off was the membership of the Corporate Executive Board (CEB), an independent global benchmarking organization, meanwhile a subsidiary of Gartner. In both core functions, Sales and Purchasing, the modular multicomponent assessment of a "World-Class Sales and Purchasing Organization" helped Cognis to continuously advance its go-to-market functions based on best-in-class cross-industry examples and resources.

8 Summary

According to the Three-Pillar Model (Wollmann et al. 2020), firstly, Cognis was driven by a very strong *sustainable purpose* serving the needs of its customers for products and services around "Wellness and Sustainability" based on renewable raw materials. Secondly, it was the ability of the company to be mindful; to adjust its portfolio focusing on fewer, but important, activities; and to become and develop a speedboat-like, agile *traveling organization.* And, finally, a culture of constant learning, of *connecting resources* internally through knowledge management and externally through market penetration and relationship management. These three organizational and leadership pillars assured the required robustness and resilience to successfully operate in increasingly volatile, uncertain, complex, and ambiguous (VUCA) market conditions.

References

Becker, R., & Daschmann, G. (2015). *Das Fan-Prinzip: Mit emotionaler Kundenbindung Unternehmen erfolgreich steuern.* Wiesbaden: Springer Gabler.

Chemical Week. (2002, December 30). *Caught in the Middle.*

Fink, L. (2020). *A fundamental reshaping of finance.* Retrieved January 14, 2020, from www.blackrock.com

Marell, S., & Borgards, A. (2008). Spin-off. Cognis GmbH & Co.KG. Die Chemie-Sparte von Henkel entwickelt eine eigene Unternehmensidentität. In J. Pfannenberg (Ed.), *Veränderungskommunikation* (pp. 173–188). Frankfurt: Frankfurter Allgemeine Buch.

Scherer, J., & Kühlborn, S. (2008). Management von Kundenzufriedenheit in der Spezialchemie: das Beispiel der Cognis Gruppe. In C. Homburg (Ed.), *Kundenzufriedenheit* (7th ed., pp. 461–481). Wiesbaden: Springer Gabler.

Scherer, J., Marell, S., & Wenzl, J. (2008). How to make your customers love you. In *Image campaign Cognis* (own source).

Sinek, S. (2009). *Start with why – How great leaders inspire everyone to take action.* London: Penguin Books.

Wollmann, P., Kühn, F., & Kempf, M. (Eds.). (2020). *Three pillars of organization and leadership in disruptive times – Navigating your company successfully through the 21st century business world.* Cham: Springer.

Jürgen Scherer holds an MBA and PhD from University of Cologne in Germany. He has 30 years spanning broad industry experience in executive positions for global corporations, namely, FMCG company Henkel, specialty chemicals company Cognis, and industrial packaging company Mauser. He was part of the Cognis Executive Committee; was the Legal Representative of Cognis, Germany; and has led as Cognis Group Vice President the Sales/Key Account Management as well as the Supply Chain Services organization. He has published various papers in academic journals and readings and has presented business-to-business management topics at leading business schools and international conferences. Since 2019, he is a Business Consultant and Coach with www.bxb-exchange.com.

Susanne Marell is the CEO of Hill+Knowlton Strategies in Germany. Before joining H+K, she was Managing Director at JP KOM, and prior to that, she served as CEO of Edelman for 6 years, overseeing the acquisition of and merger with ergo Kommunikation. After her studies, she started her career as a consultant with the agency Kohtes and Klewes (now Ketchum). In the following years, Susanne worked for companies such as Schering, Hoechst, and Aventis CropScience. As Head of Communications and Market Services, her responsibilities included strategic communications support for merger and acquisition activities. In 2000, she moved to the chemical company Cognis and, as Vice President of Corporate Communications, took over the management of worldwide corporate and sustainability communications. Following the acquisition of Cognis by BASF in 2010, Susanne was responsible for the global brand management as Vice President of Corporate Brand Management at BASF in Ludwigshafen. Susanne is a certified systemic consultant and change expert. She has many years of international experience in communications, marketing, and sustainability, both on the corporate and agency side. In addition, she is co-founder of the German network "Global Women in PR" and has built up the initiative "Next Gen Leadership" as a member of the extended board.

Jutta Wenzl is the Head of Global HR at KraussMaffei Group, a manufacturer of machinery and systems for the production and processing of plastics and rubber. After her business studies, she started her career at Henkel and joined Cognis right from the start, when it was carved out from Henkel. During her time with Cognis, she held several operational and strategic HR roles. After the acquisition by BASF, she supported the Cognis integration being responsible for the Global HR integration before joining H.C. Starck, a leading supplier of technology metals, as Head of Global HR. Jutta is a certified systemic and hypno-systemic consultant and change expert. She has many years of international experience in HR, particularly in personnel and organizational development.

[illegible]

[illegible]

[illegible]

Climate Change and Winemaking: A Significant Transformation in Agriculture

Christal Lalla and Giancarla Domini

Abstract

Climate change is impacting agriculture more and more—and impacting winemaking in particular more and more quickly. People can observe the changes almost every year. To understand the dramatic situation and to develop successful measures to cope with it, the Three-Pillar Model (3-P-Model), developed in the book *Three Pillars of Organisation and Leadership in Disruptive Times* (Wollmann et al. 2020), is extremely helpful. Keeping the sustainable purpose of winemaking in general and of ambitious wineries in particular unchanged—to produce a set of remarkable wines of best quality—it is necessary to have the mindset of a long and challenging journey (travelling organization) and to connect with a broad network of scientists, sommeliers, winemakers, etc. in different countries and regions. It is crucial to understand the journey and the network as an exploration setting foot on—in places—hitherto unknown territory. The article describes and evaluates significant examples of successful development journeys from different perspectives: for one famous grape variety and in some of the most important wine regions of the world—Tuscany and Piedmont—and also explores an interesting case in New Mexico. The journeys are different from grape variety to grape variety and from region to region—but they are ultimately based on comparable principles which can be best described by the 3-P-Model.

C. Lalla (✉)
Bonn, Germany

Montalcino, Italy
e-mail: vinauthority@gmail.com

G. Domini
Montemagno, Italy
e-mail: giancarla.domini@lamondianese.com

P. Wollmann et al. (eds.), *Organization and Leadership in Disruptive Times*, Future of Business and Finance, https://doi.org/10.1007/978-3-030-63034-8_19

1 Initial Situation

There is no doubt that climate change is a reality which is increasingly affecting all parts of our lives. Thus, winemaking is now also significantly impacted. These days, grape varieties are growing where they were never able to grow before, and, conversely, grape varieties are having more difficulties growing where they do now or might no longer grow where they have grown for centuries. The characters of wines are also changing, for instance, regarding alcohol level and tasting profiles. The winemaking industry and scientific institutions are worldwide intensively working on issues like this. Fast solutions are needed since the whole wine regions with a high reputation and high quality, combined of course with high prices, are—in the worst case—at risk of vanishing from the winemaking map altogether due to climate change. In this context, wineries are "wandering up the hills," if possible, or new wineries are being started north of the better-known wine regions (in the northern hemisphere); Scandinavia and England are prominent examples. And in the old wine regions, grape varieties are becoming indigenous which could not be grown there previously. For example, German consumers, who were focused on Riesling wines and Pinot Blanc or Pinot Gris (Grau- und Weissburgunder), are now finding more and more local Chardonnay and Sauvignon Blanc wines of a reasonable quality.

And the changes described above have accelerated in recent years and cannot be ignored even by those consumers with no special wine expertise. What this means for winemakers, wine experts, and consumers will be shown in the next paragraphs.

It is easy to comprehend the ongoing development caused by climate change if one looks at the following graphs which give an overview of global temperature increase over the last 130 years and the increase of days with temperature above 10 degrees in Piedmont (Figs. 1 and 2).

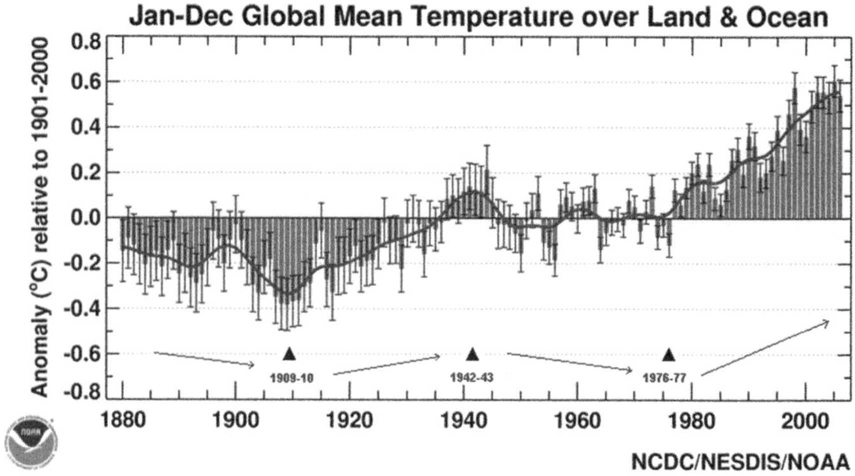

Fig. 1 Overview of average temperature increase between 1889 and 2010. Retrieved from "Viticoltura e cambiamento climatico" ©Maurizio Gily 2016, www.gily.it, used with permission

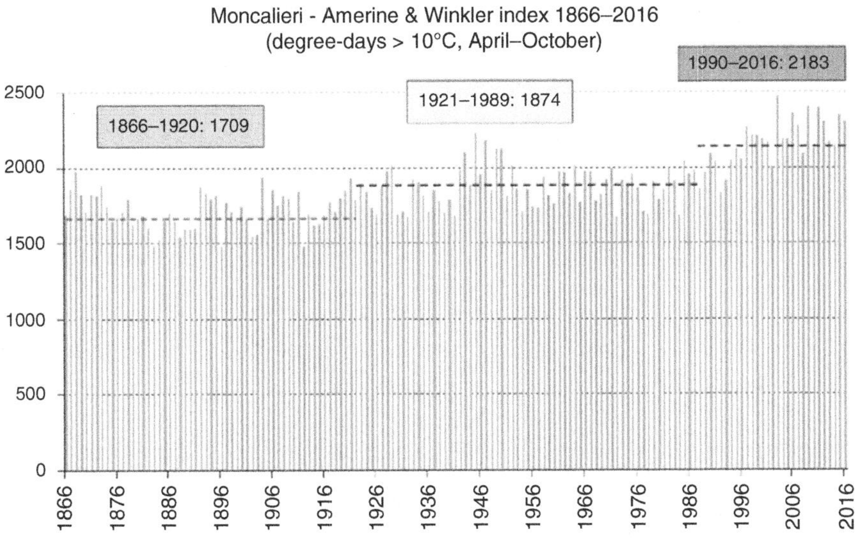

Fig. 2 Development of the Amerine and Winkler index, 1866–2016, in Moncalieri (Piedmont). Retrieved from "Viticoltura e cambiamento climatico" ©Maurizio Gily 2016, www.gily.it, used with permission

Also analyzing the temperature increase in some selected famous wine regions such as Burgundy or the Rhine Valley, Barolo, and Bordeaux shows exactly the same tendency in the past (1950–2000, first four graphs)—and also expected in the future (2000–2050, last four graphs) (Fig. 3).

The impact of temperature and temperature development on the attributes of the wines is significant (in terms of acid and alcohol degrees, color, tannins, etc.)—which means that wines change when the temperature changes (Fig. 4).

The graph says that we have to consider, on the one hand, two weather situations, cold weather and hot weather (and respectively early and late harvest), and, on the other hand, the development of key attributes of wine taste: acidity, alcohol, color, green unripe tannins, ripe smooth tannins, green sensation, and round ripe fruit. Normal acidity and alcohol (dependent of the sugar level of the grapes) are inversely proportional, so a good balance is needed.

The color increase follows ripening but not for the entire period as we see in the graph.

The green tannins became round and smooth with ripening, and all the green sensation turns into hints of ripe fruit, but only for a certain ripening period, and then starts to decrease.

Thus, we see that the winemaker has to be careful because extra ripening can lead to a loss of freshness, deep color, and feeling of fullness.

Reflecting the above, a first conclusion is—in simple terms—that in the multidimensional factor system of wine production, one key factor (temperature) influences

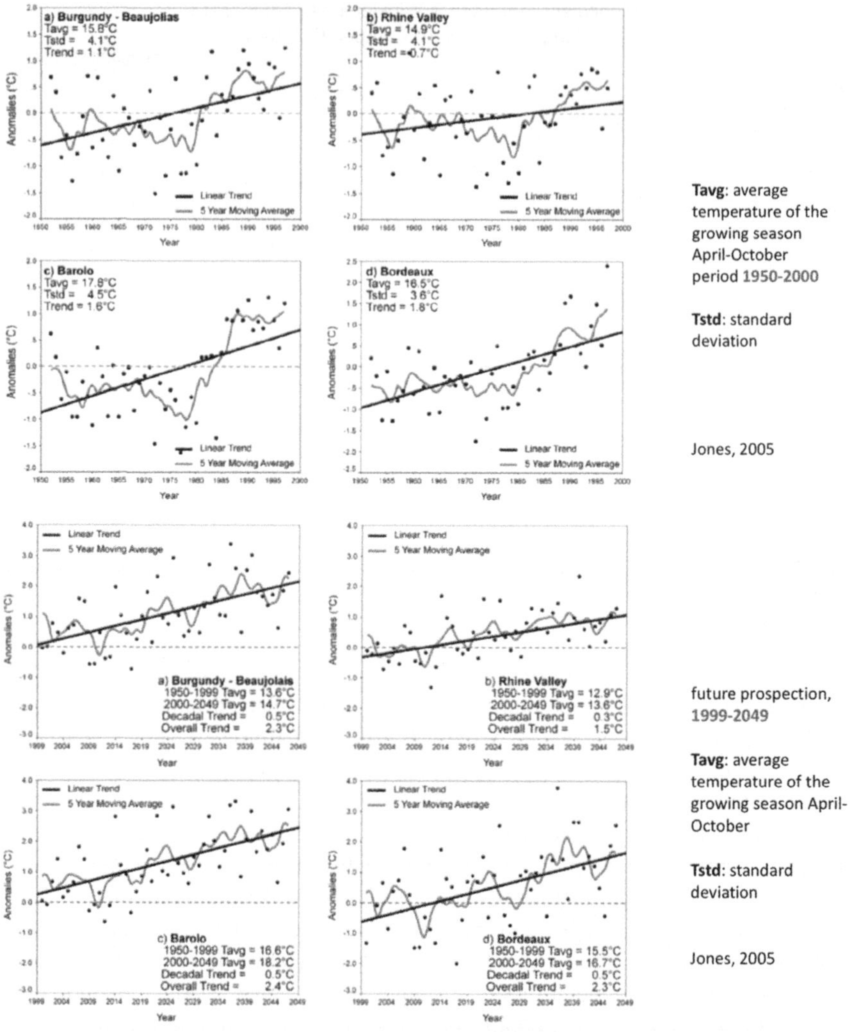

Fig. 3 (**a** and **b**) Overview of temperature increase in selected wine regions in the past and future. Retrieved from "Climate Change and Viticulture," LinkedIn slideshare.net' ©Maurizio Gily 2017, www.gily.it, used with permission

a lot of other factors, so new solutions will have to be developed, either by exploring or experimenting or by scientific research.

We will now go into more—but not too much—detail in some small case studies of regions and wineries, but we will try to stay on a meta-level as we want to describe the underlying "mechanisms and trends" rather than t teaching winemaking in detail.

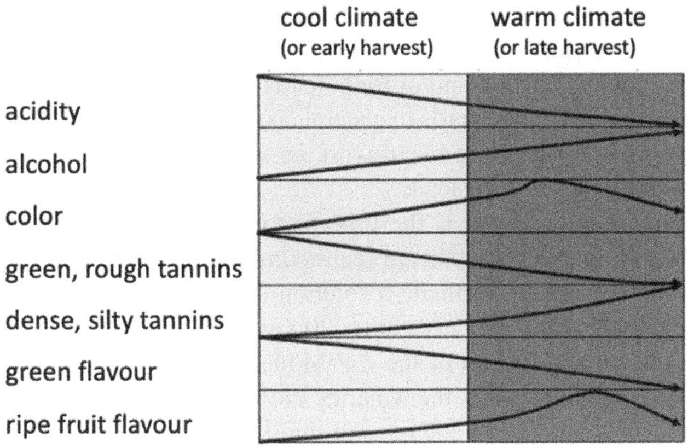

Fig. 4 Climate and wine attributes. Translated and cited from "Viticoltura e cambiamento climatico" ©Maurizio Gily www.gily.it, used with permission

2 First Case: The Issues for Making Merlot

At present, Merlot is a significant and special example for the impact of climate change. The Merlot grape normally needs muddy soil and free-flowing nutrition and a reasonable balance of vitamin reception but also reasonable temperatures and not too much sun. The gradual disappearance of sufficient natural irrigation, too much sun and heat, and too many vitamins in the nutrition are causing problems.

We will have a close look at two famous Merlot regions: Bordeaux in France and Maremma/Bolgheri in Italy. Both regions are affected; in both regions, Merlot is a key building block of great wines, composed of Merlot, Cabernet Sauvignon, and Cabernet Franc. In both regions, winemakers and scientists are very concerned about what the future will bring—successful winemaking over centuries or at least decades is at significant risk. Therefore, in both regions, many of the best wine scientists are working on solutions which involve moving vineyards uphill, changing the work and treatment in the vineyard, relocating vineyards, using different grafting styles, planting wines lower or higher from the ground, building on more intensive soil analysis, and also finding alternatives to traditional grape varieties. One of the most interesting concepts after visiting Bordeaux and Bolgheri came from Professor Attilio Scienza, the Chief Scientist of the Vinitaly International Academy who is working on the special situation of the grape variety of Merlot in the context of the soil situation and climate change.

The key coping strategies for Merlot are, among others, systematic irrigation (which means certain places might need changes in their regulations) and leaf protection for the grapes to prevent them from being burned by planting crops at a higher or lower elevation depending on the wine and grape varieties.

This means that it is key to understand the soil situation in the wine region in detail (based on scientific measures) and to explore which opportunities the soil offers in detail for the existing and/or for potential new grape varieties. It also means changing the work in the vineyards in general and at the vine. It means changing, for example, the famous Bordeaux blend working with less or without Merlot and/or adding other grape varieties instead.

A challenge in this context is the time factor: on the one hand, the climate is changing quickly and so solutions are required quickly. On the other hand, it often takes a long time to finally evaluate a solution (e.g., when the wine has to have a longevity and so the final test only comes 20 years later).

This is a classic application of the 3-P-Model (Wollmann et al. 2020): with an unchanged sustainable purpose, the wineries and winemaker have to go on a journey which is partly in the unknown and have to significantly intensify connectivity, from a content base connecting and newly combining the multidimensional factors of producing great wines—and from an interaction base connecting with experts, scientists, peers, etc. to exchange experience and knowledge. It is a lot more important than in the past to be flexible and to have the mindset for the explorative journey into the unknown. It is also important to be able to connect the past with the future, earlier wine traditions with new methods and procedures, etc.

3 The Second Case: The Situation in the Piedmont Region

The situation in Piedmont is comparable to other regions: climate change is obvious.

This will be discussed using the example of La Mondianese, a medium-sized winery north-east of Asti, in the middle of a region with very special autochthonous Piedmontese grape varietals such as Ruché and Grignolino and in which La Mondianese has particular expertise.

For this, the co-author of this article, Giancarla, answers the same interview questions which were put to two other winemakers.

Question: What is your special ambition in winemaking, the sustainable purpose of your winery, and the reason why you make these daily efforts?

Answer: For me, it is the opportunity to live outdoors, to see how nature changes with the season, and to do a job where not only knowledge but also sensitivity is needed and to have a deep intuitive understanding of nature, terroir, the soil, the weather, the plants, etc.

Question: On a scale of 1 to 10, with 10 being the most severe, how would you rate the impact of climate change on your winery?

Answer: I think we are now at around 3 or 4. At the moment, we are trying to start from the vineyards, intervening with appropriate pruning and cleaning at the right time. We check the characteristics of the grapes several times before harvesting, and we will try to arrive at the right time in the cellar, preserving the aromas and trying not to have too high sugar degree in the grapes, which is a real risk in these days.

Question: Has climate change been tangible for your winery and how?

Answer: Yes, it has. The flowering period of the grapes has changed, the growth of the branches is gastropods-like, and the ripening is faster and therefore earlier than in the past.

Question: How is your winery adapting to the climate change? What is your winery doing to mitigate climate change?

Answer: For now, we have not implemented a fixed irrigation system, but we have provided irrigation in the new plant areas. It's possible that, with increasing temperatures, fixed irrigation systems will have to be installed everywhere.

In the new planting, it's possible to have more space between the plants, with longer pruning and higher shoots from the ground. For all vineyards, it will be important to have a good leaf wall that protects the fruits, topping, and leafing later.

Question: Has climate change affected your winery's purpose and your special ambition?

Answer: No, not much. The goal has always been to get the best out of what we have available and to produce amazing wine for our clients.

Question: Has climate change affected the competition and the markets for your wines? And what is your forecast for the future?

Answer: Certainly, not only climate change but also globalization has brought many changes. I believe that victory or success in the long run is always aimed at quality as a competitive advantage. People are a lot more interested in something special, in the philosophy of the winemaker and his or her special methods. People like a story around the wine, covering the whole experience of the terroir, the history, the improvements and developments over the years, the exploration of something new, and the whole journey of the wine. That's the reason why La Mondianese offers the experience to stay at the winery, in the middle of the terroir, and experience the work in the vineyard and cellar.

Question: How has climate change changed your way of working?

Answer: We are now acting in an even more timely manner in the vineyards, paying greater attention to the weather forecast and, above all, to the right time for the ripening. And this is more different from year to year than it was in the past.

Question: To cope with climate change, do you get support from colleagues/peers, scientists, etc.? What knowledge, resources, etc. are important for you?

Answer: The exchange of information between producers and researchers is very important.

In the territory, the work of the associations of the production areas, the so-called "Consorzio di tutela delle Doc," is supposed to manage this exchange, follow new insights, and give advice. All these institutions are getting more important—and more challenged.

Question: How will climate change impact on regulations in the future in your opinion?

Answer: I think we should review the guidelines, the so-called "disciplinari di produzione," especially for some selected items and have support from the regions for wineries to adapt to new climatic challenges.

I have already mentioned irrigation. For some production zones of DOC and DOCG, irrigation has been forbidden so far. It should be carefully discussed whether change is necessary and possible. But there are many similar items to be checked, not only irrigation.

4 The Third Case: The Situation in the Montalcino Region, Tuscany

One of the most famous red wines in the world is produced in Montalcino: the Brunello. It is a DOCG wine subject to very detailed regulation. Brunello is produced from a Sangiovese clone, developed at the end of the nineteenth century by Biondi Santi in order to have a grape varietal perfectly suited to the especially demanding terroir. Wines named Brunello can only be produced in the clearly marked area of Montalcino. Brunello wines are very complex, structured, and elegant and have a special longevity.

Climate change is also tangible in Montalcino, and limiting alcohol levels in parallel with keeping the unique structure of the wine has become more demanding. The different areas of wine production—in terms of the four cardinal directions and elevation levels (between 200 and 600 m)—all have their different microclimates and should therefore be treated individually. This interview is with a young wine-maker from Podere Il Cocco, whose vineyards are in a special location (Fig. 5).

Fig. 5 Podere Il Cocco (Photo by Peter Wollmann, used with permission. All rights reserved)

Fig. 6 Giacomo Bindi (Photo by Christoph Betz, used with permission. All rights reserved)

Interview with Giacomo Bindi, Winemaker of Podere Il Cocco, Azienda biologica (Fig. 6)

Giacomo Bindi (photo) is one of the young winemakers of Montalcino with a very explorative and experimental mindset. He started winemaking in the year 2000 on the grounds of the old farm, which had been owned by his family for centuries. Il Cocco is a small organic winery with less than 3 ha situated at between 500 and 600 m attitude on the southern slopes of the Montalcino region. The vineyards are among the highest ones. Giacomo produces a remarkable Brunello di Montalcino, Rosso di Montalcino, and some IGTs.

Question: What is your special ambition in winemaking, the sustainable purpose of your winery, and the reason why you make these daily efforts?

Answer: The idea of organic and the desire to go on come from discovering new things every day, being surprised by nature and having customers who appreciate your every effort. In 20 years, many things have changed and I, too, have changed. First of all, my approach to agriculture is changing: I firmly believe in an archaic agriculture, made of alternations, of different varieties, and of nonindustrialized times. The evil of modern viticulture is to see and want only profit from what you do. Let's be clear, I also need profit, but when you get to have an activity that meets your primary needs, expenses, and some investment to improve, why do you have to grow to have even more?

(continued)

Question: Has climate change been tangible for your winery and how?

Answer: The climate is essential in having developed a unique microclimate in every area of the world, and there are major changes that affect the balances hitherto found and discovered. The Il Cocco farm is 600 m above sea level on the hilltop. There are winds that come from the Apennines, winds that come from Mount Amiata, and winds that come from the sea . . . all this makes this place, combined with its soil, a more unique than rare microclimate.

Question: On a scale of 1 to 10, with 10 being the most severe, how would you rate the impact of climate change on your winery? How is your winery adapting to climate change? What is your winery doing to mitigate climate change?

Answer: Climate change is a challenge that forces us to use our experience and to learn every year from farmers all over the world. The challenge is to produce quality grapes and from them to produce our wines. I remember a visit to a winery in Las Cruces (New Mexico), where the owner explained that due to the night frosts in the spring period, in which the vines sprout, he had to do a double pruning: the first at 5/6 eyes at the end of winter and the second with 2 eyes once the risk of frost in the spring had passed; well this year, after about 10 years on from that meeting, I implemented this technique due to a winter and a spring with temperature changes that could cause early budding and a high risk of freezing.

Question: Has climate change affected your winery's purpose and your special ambition?

Answer: Climate change has not changed my wines but only the attention I place on them once I enter the cellar. My idea is to produce indigenous and non-native wines "written and directed" specifically for the public. Of course, the levels of attention have risen, in the vineyard and in the cellar, but at the same time, we have a niche of loyal customers (we call them "the Apostles of the Coconut") who support us annually with purchases of wine and free advertising among their friends.

Question: Has climate change affected the competition and the markets for your wines? And what is your forecast for the future?

Answer: The work has become much more meticulous. In 2016, we installed a weather station in the vineyard to keep every detail under control, and for over 5 years, we have been experimenting with new organic products for the fight on the field, from actual microorganisms to wood distillate . . . old and new discoveries that carry us forward in biological experimentation.

Question: How has climate change changed your way of working?

Answer: Experimentation in the vineyard and in the cellar is the spice of life . . . always producing the same would mean not being ready for change. Life is made up of changes and changing means smiling at the future. In the cellar, every day is a challenge to improve and improve your wines but also to

(continued)

experiment with new techniques. The latest challenge is the "vinification" of rosé wines (already on the market for over 9 years) from unripe Sangiovese grapes to produce a wine to be fermented in the bottle. The idea is to not use anything from outside the company (such as MCR) but only own products (we freeze a small part of the must during the harvest, which is then used to have bottled sugar for the second fermentation).

Question: To cope with climate change, do you get support from colleagues/peers, scientists, etc.? What knowledge, resources, etc. are important for you?

Answer: Certainly, as already mentioned, it is essential to collaborate, speak, and share experiences. Only by comparison can agriculture of the future be born free of the hypocrisy that many producers have in selling themselves as organic/biodynamic and then behaving as in the 1970s where the only goal was to produce a lot by any means possible.

5 The Situation in the New Mexico Wine Region

New Mexico is the oldest wine region in the USA which people don't usually know. Wine production started in the seventeenth century—which means before New Mexico came from Mexico to the USA. The first winemakers were monks who needed altar wine for the Holy Mass. They firstly planted a grape varietal named Listán Prietro of the species *Vitis vinifera* in the Rio Grande Valley. New Mexico has a very long wine tradition and has built up a lot of experience. Many key wineries were founded by Europeans coming from Italy, Spain, or France. Today, New Mexico has some top wineries with excellent reputations in the USA, but compared to, for example, California, it has very limited production (around 0.1% of the total US production).

New Mexico's climate is very dry and alternates between extreme temperatures (very hot in summer, cold with snow in winter). Thus, it is obvious that global climate change impacts on New Mexico and its wine industry. However, water has been an even bigger issue than temperature thus far.

Interview with Gordon, Winemaker of Rio Grande Winery (Fig. 7)

After 10 years of intensive planning, Gordon Steel (photo) started building a great New Mexico winery together with his wife Sandi in 1995. Gordon studied vineyard management and winemaking at UC Davis and Washington State University and additionally took the chance to visit important wine regions of Germany, England, Italy, France, Spain, Washington, and California while with the US Air Force. Gordon's and Sandi's Rio

(continued)

Grande Vineyards/Winery are located in the historic Mesilla Valley in New Mexico where vineyards were initially established by the Spanish priests in the late 1500s to early 1600s. In the winery's tasting room, Gordon and Sandi offer a taste of New Mexico's historical Spanish past with a New Mexico twist. The Rio Grande Winery offers about 25 different wines.

Question: What is your special ambition in winemaking, the sustainable purpose of your winery, and the reason why you make these daily efforts?

Answer: Well, it is my intensive love of wine and of people who love it as I do. It is great to be in such a community. Wine is a very special good with an exciting history and a cultural role. Wine contributes to the well-being of people.

Question: Has climate change been tangible for your winery and how?

Answer: I would summarize like this: bigger and more intensively red grapes, higher alcohol level.

Question: On a scale of 1 to 10, with 10 being the most severe, how would you rate the impact of climate change on your winery?

Answer: Up to now, it is about a 3. It is getting hotter here which means picking the grapes earlier and also an increase of sugars which could change the character of the wines. So, we have to change something.

Question: How is your winery adapting to climate change? What is your winery doing to mitigate climate change?

Answer: Well, we are going for different styles of wine and reaching out to different markets than before. It is quite a significant change.

Question: Has climate change affected the competition and the markets for your wines? And what is your forecast for the future?

Answer: Yes, the market has changed and is moving slightly toward dryer wines. But I am not sure that this has mainly to do with the climate change but more with younger drinkers. So, there might be different factors coming together.

Question: How has climate change changed your way of working?

Answer: We need to get up earlier to be able to cope with the heat. Work in the vineyard does not make sense when the temperature is too high.

Question: To cope with climate change, do you get support from colleagues/peers, scientists, etc.? What knowledge, resources, etc. are important for you?

Answer: We have a good community here; we all try and work together. This is really very helpful.

Question: How will climate change impact on regulations in the future in your opinion?

Answer: There are changes to government regulations which have had more impact, some very positive and a little negatively, but much more than climate change in terms of temperature so far. Our big issue in the future will be water—which is—of course, also impacted by climate change.

Fig. 7 Gordon and Sandi Steel (Photo by Gordon Steel, used with permission. All rights reserved)

6 Recap of the 3-P-Model

The Three-Pillar Model (Wollmann et al. 2020) was created to address the urgent need of global institutions in the current volatile, uncertain, complex, and ambiguous (VUCA) world, in order to provide adequate solutions to how enterprises and institutions should be organized and managed in a dynamic way in a dynamic world. Applied to the agricultural industry, this includes how to get all stakeholders of farming committed to a clear direction and belief. This includes going on the necessary journey in the climate change situation by experimenting, prototyping, and piloting approaches to find the right step-by-step development path and products of a high quality. And it also involves how to develop and connect with all necessary information and support needed.

The three main design principles for this type of modern organization leadership in agriculture can be described as follows:

- *Sustainable purpose*: The people in the company but also its key stakeholders such as clients, neighbors, associations, scientists, etc. need to know the mandate and philosophy of the organization and the sustainable value it is creating. The mandate has to remain very stable; be supported by leaders, staff, and stakeholders; and be inspirational. Key representatives of the organization have to "live" the mandate.

Or in other words, the mandate gives clear and convincing orientation on the right level that aligns and inspires people to go for a joint endeavor, which makes the people involved confident, inspired, and proud to be part of, and contribute to, it.

- *Travelling organization*: The organization needs to understand that it is continuously on a journey toward the best possible result and joint success in the current challenge of, e.g., climate change, in the context of the agreed sustainable purpose, coping with all—partly unforeseeable—influences. On the map, it will potentially have to zigzag, always exploring the best path between poles, alternatives, and options. Sometimes, the people in the organization don't know the whole environment and thus have to take smaller steps and explore the terrain. Even if they don't know what they will have to face around the next bend and what the best result will then be, they believe in their motivation and capabilities to manage it. People in a travelling organization are curious, open, and impartial, have the capacity for self-reflection, are experimental, and cope well with uncertainty, stress, special challenges, and unforeseen obstacles.
- *Connecting resources*: The company has to be aware that impact, value, and efficiency need connectivity between individuals; between geographies to learn from each other; between people and organizations or institutions such as associations, universities, and scientific boards; between diverse global experts and influences; between different political and social systems and cultures; etc.

Based on the aforementioned three principles, the Three-Pillar Model (3-P-Model) was built, and application tested and described mostly in, or with reference to, the private sector. But it is striking how well the model can also be applied in industries such as agriculture and here for wine producers, as shown in the article.

7 Conclusion and Lessons Learned

The wine industry is an interesting case study for the 3-P-Model, as the products and the whole outcome are something very tangible, also from a sensory perspective. Changes are very concrete to people, so the impact of climate change on this industry might be perceived as more real than in other industries where the change is more abstract and intellectual.

In terms of the 3-P-Model, the journey of the industry, partly into unknown territory, is significant and demands a "travelling organization mindset." This situation gives rise to new generations of winemakers and wine scientists. In this context, the sustainable purpose profile is sharpened (not only production of the best wine but also, e.g., in terms of reinventing special old autochthonous grape varieties, becoming a biological winery, experimenting with blend changes and grape combinations, using special production methods, etc.)—and a lot of winemakers are keen to communicate their philosophy. The environmental changes trigger the sharpening of the purpose profile—at least with all winemakers using artisanal production.

The connectivity demand covers, on the one hand, the need to have a holistic approach, meaning that all items in the big puzzle of factors relevant for winemaking have to be regarded. On the other hand, connecting with peers, experts, associations, and scientists, and also from other related fields (e.g.,, biochemistry, pedology—the study of soils in their natural environment—or physics), is absolutely necessary.

The—connected—journey needs a good balance between unique own long-term philosophy and new beneficial developments, between tradition (incl. old and forgotten procedures) and modern scientific methods, and between personality with intuitive experience and scientific outcome.

And last but not the least, climate change is real, is accelerating, and urgently needs suitable solutions; the fascinating world of wines has to be preserved and be made more diverse.

8 Takeaways for the Reader

- Climate change is real and is affecting the wine industry with increasing speed.
- The wine industry has to embark on a journey which will impact on unknown areas—this is inevitable, so winemakers and vineyards have to accept and prepare for it.
- Climate change—like all crises—gives wineries the chance to sharpen their sustainable purpose and profile so as to be unique.
- The situation is complex—more pieces of the puzzle have to be regarded if good wine is to be produced.
- Exchange and networking with peers, experts, scientists, etc. is crucial.
- At the end, everybody has to decide which individual setting to choose.

Reference

Wollmann, P., Kühn, F., & Kempf, M. (2020). *Three pillars of organisation and leadership in disruptive times – Navigating your company successfully through the 21st century business world*. Cham: Springer Nature.

Christal Lalla is a certified sommelier, working in Italy, Germany, China, France, and the USA since 2010, frequently as an international judge at tastings. She has established a fast-developing, innovative business around wine, wine services, and wine education under the name VinAuthority and The Wandering Sommelier as well as providing out-of-the-box leadership training. Her approach is grounded on the premise that wine drinking is a holistic experience and event for all of the senses, including the winemaker's philosophy, motivation, and techniques, the visual and haptic sensations of the vineyards and the cellars with their barrels, and the taste of the wine combined with food pairings—and with well-fitting music or acting. Christal is also an author of several manuscripts describing the connections between vinification, wine, spirits, and food pairings.

Giancarla Domini is an oenologist who has worked in famous wine companies in and outside the Piedmont region. She initially started working in industries unrelated to wine, e.g., in the arts and communication such as jewelry, radio, and other related industries until she decided to follow her primary instincts and focus on the science of wine. Her broad experience and knowledge of the wine business covers several regions, beginning from the center of Italy, through the Piedmont hills to

Virginia, USA. Through this intensive journey, she has been able to gather different scientific experiences and insights worldwide. Now she works very closely with the well-known winery, La Mondianese, trying to create the perfect balance of wine and terroir. Her dream is to make a harvest in Australia before retirement.

Trapped in the Bermuda Triangle Among Project, Process, and Line Organizations: Accelerating Complex Tech Development Projects

Markus Beer and Philipp Bosselmann

Abstract

This article describes an organizational development program deployed to stabilize and accelerate new product development projects in a high-tech industrial company. Initially, functional egoism, conflicts between project and line organizations, and inflexible processes frustrated the ambitions of all concerned. Within a year, many of these chronic issues were resolved using an approach aimed at clarifying the reason for action and promoting cross-functional collaboration among project and line organizations. Within the program, simple and hands-on solutions were developed that facilitated task execution and increased the transparency of project progress and fulfillment. A set of shared guiding principles was formulated, which served as a foundation on which to establish a robust and sustainable cooperative work culture. The new solutions significantly helped to deliver the next new product on budget and on time. We retrospectively evaluated the program using the Three-Pillar Model (abbreviated 3-P-Model; Wollmann et al., Three pillars of organization and leadership in disruptive times, Springer, Heidelberg, 2020).

1 The Starting Point: Operations Under Pressure!

Late again! And too expensive!—Dieter Müller (name altered) heads the Operations department of a leading global photovoltaic system technology manufacturer. He is under pressure from within his organization. His core responsibility is to ensure the

M. Beer (✉)
Kassel, Germany
e-mail: Markus.Beer@sma.de

P. Bosselmann
Frankfurt am Main, Germany
e-mail: pb@sprout-consulting.de

P. Wollmann et al. (eds.), *Organization and Leadership in Disruptive Times*, Future of Business and Finance, https://doi.org/10.1007/978-3-030-63034-8_20

production of photovoltaic inverters, but his department is also closely involved in the company's Product Development Process (PDP). Resources under his command qualify—that means specify the properties that the sourced items should have (including price)—and make sure that the supplier is able to fulfill the specification and procure all critical materials from international markets, organize supply chains, and engineer the lean production lines enabling competitive manufacture of advanced electronic subassemblies and inverters in a high-wage country. This is a challenging mandate considering that both prices and margins of photovoltaic inverters delivered by the world's former market leader have been spiraling downward for years in the face of growing global demand. Chinese competitors are relentlessly capturing market share, and the company has already carried out several rounds of restructuring in recent years. And the Board of Directors expects the company's new class of inverters will herald a turnaround. But the prospective manufacturing costs of the new product are still too high, and, above all, time is running out. But this situation is not new. Previous new product launches rarely met expectations. Müller is painfully aware that each week that production start is delayed has high five-digit financial consequences. To make matters worse, important product component specifications are not yet mature enough to begin sourcing the manufacturing stocks. Worse, in the wake of the automobile industry's switch to producing electro-mobility models, global procurement lead times of critical components are stretching to 9 months.

2 Distress in the Bermuda Triangle: We Need to Do Something Differently!

Müller summons his management and the team responsible for the launch of series manufacture of the new product. In a perturbed voice, he describes the overdue status of the project and questions whether cooperation among the various operational areas is working. He asks why things aren't running smoothly despite the recent update of the PDP, where the descriptions of project work packages have just been updated yet again. In his view, it is now crystal clear what needs to be done. Frustration provokes accusations—project managers defend their rationales. The crisis meeting concludes with a clear realization: things cannot go on like this; a new approach is needed. Müller delegates an assignment to his organization developer: "Find an experienced external person who understands something about launching products. Get someone with a talent for connecting and motivating the different project disciplines. And while they are at it, they should set up the whole process anew. But remember, we're putting our own house in order first. We're not going to simply shift responsibility onto the Development department."

Let us go—two external consultants from Sprout Consulting, the same pair who led and supported harmonization of the company's internal Product Development Process years before, come to mind. The Sprout crew became acquainted with the corporate culture when playing a pivotal role in helping structure and enhance the company's innovation and operations capabilities. For the members of the internal project core team to be set up, there are clear favorites: the recently established global project representatives of the different functions. Without exception, these dedicated professionals have in-depth methodological and technical knowledge, and they are trusted by their divisional managers. Reciprocally, they are interested in participating in the program and it is possible to get them on board at short notice. The Head of Operations Engineering assumes responsibility as project sponsor.

Initial considerations of the core team signal that new process designs, more KPIs, further standardization, more detailed task descriptions, and more RACI matrices would not help to solve the problem.

The problem rather lies embedded somewhere among the Development Project execution procedures (process dimension), the cooperation between various project disciplines (project dimension), and synchronization among the line functions of procurement, supply chain management, quality management, and production (line business dimension), a dangerous triangular territory where projects can potentially lose direction and sink. The new initiative is christened, "Bermuda," which is also a group of islands in the Caribbean, blessed with summer, sun, and holidays and which also gave its name to a style of knee-length shorts. In this respect, from the very beginning, the Bermuda program stood for both management overcoming a crisis and the destination of smooth-sailing and friendly collaboration.

3 Detailed Diagnosis: Understanding the Problem

At first glance, two main aspects are clear: we are late with every development project and we fail to achieve its targeted production costs. But why? The Bermuda program management team, consisting of the internal organization developer and the two external consultants, decide to start with a broad-based diagnosis to identify hot topics and fields of action that would be effectively optimized in the course of a subsequent improvement process. During hour-long one-on-one sessions and, as appropriate, group interviews, about 50 people, i.e., employees in the organization who are closely involved in the series introduction of new products, from line and project, are interviewed about the situation. Statements are logged and sorted, and some problems noticeably arise again and again and gradually crystallize around a few key issues. And it becomes clear that, apart from factual topics, questions of responsibilities and competencies are enduring concerns: who tells whom what to do and when to do it? Who is in charge of what? Who delivers what to whom?

In order to illustrate the landscape of the players involved in a way different from that of a traditional hierarchical line organization chart, a circular organization chart is created, which displays project and line functions as concentric bands encircling the Launch Manager. The Launch Manager is responsible for coordinating the four operations functions in an industrialization project and is the go-to person when any doubts about meeting the project goals arise. During the course of the diagnostic phase, it becomes clear that clarification and strengthening this key coordinating and controlling role is paramount to finding new effective solutions (Fig. 1).

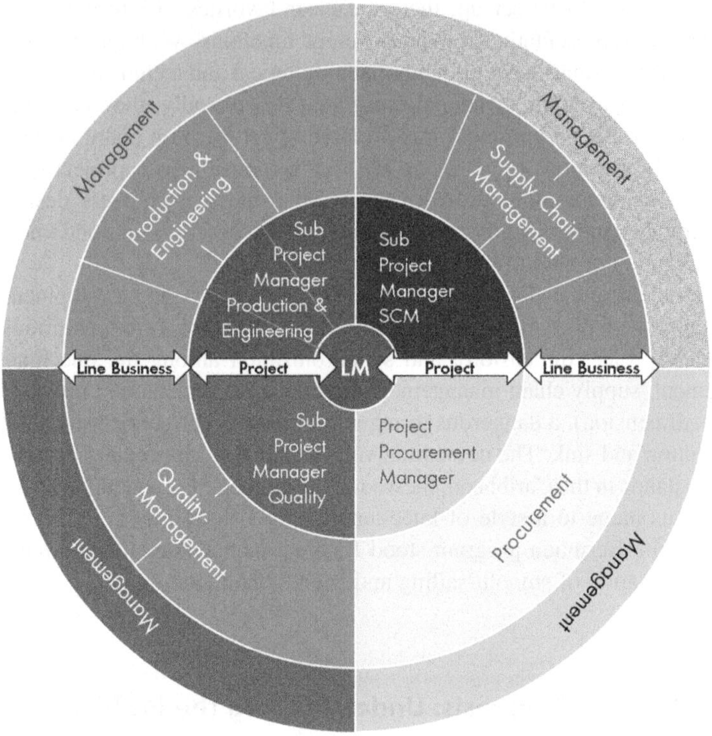

Fig. 1 Bermuda organization chart—project and line functions at a glance (Illustrated by the authors, used with permission. All rights reserved)

In order to confirm the results of the semi-structured interviews, online surveys of all players directly or indirectly involved in Launch Projects are conducted. From the 150 asked to participate, 130 actually take part. In this survey, the employees are asked to position themselves on key success factors of the Launch Projects. The structure is a project maturity model which the core team had compiled previously. In a second round, the survey is extended to the management team, yielding very similar results and further validating the key findings. The management team is also assessed which results in further validation of the key findings (Fig. 2).

The interviews are conducted rather openly allowing specific problem areas to quickly surface. And the high response rate of the online survey validates the results and shows the extent of the problem areas. In this respect, the two diagnostic instruments mutually complement each other to an exceedingly high degree.

The results of the individual diagnostic steps are reviewed, ordered, and discussed in the project core team on several occasions. From the six essential core topics that emerge, three involve tangible content and relate to Product Development Process deliverables.

Fig. 2 Success factors for Launch Projects (Illustrated by the authors, used with permission. All rights reserved)

- Risk Management: systematic and regular collection, evaluation, and mitigation of the relevant project risks in the Launch Team
- Technical Change Management: recording suggestions for technical changes to the product in the course of development, as well as their evaluation, decision-making, and follow-up
- Material Availability: creating transparency in the bill of materials across all subprojects in order to procure long lead time items in time

The other three action fields address management and leadership issues.

- Project Management: systematic planning and coordination of deliverables and work packages in the Launch Team
- Interface Management: identification, processing, and resolution of potential or existing conflicts between organizational areas
- Leadership and Collaboration: clarification of the target vision "how we want to work together" and reflection of the underlying leadership behavior

Confidence is growing in the core team: if we can get a grip on the above six key issues, the Launch Project's objectives with respect to time, costs, and quality should then also move in the right direction. Joint calculations with the accounting department had additionally revealed that, due to the delayed market launch of the most important new products, the company was annually losing double-digit millions of euros owing to lost sales and excessively high manufacturing costs. It is becoming increasingly clear to everyone involved that Bermuda could make a significant contribution to the company's economic success. This leads to a perceptible motivation boost for the project, for the core team, and for the management team. The amounts—extrapolated into millions of euros—may seem somewhat abstract, but for the first time, everyone recognizes that, with manageable means, there is something to be gained that can make a real difference for the company! Everyone has agreed on an attractive goal that can only be achieved together—the common purpose has emerged.

In order to have everyone on board when moving from the diagnosis results to precisely demarcated fields of action and then to specific project assignments, the Bermuda core team and the extended management team retreat for one and a half days to a hotel on the Edersee in North Hesse.

Together, the results of the diagnosis phase are examined and evaluated, and specific assignments for concrete improvement projects are formulated. This workshop ensures commitment and involvement of the management team for the inevitable follow-up efforts. In the course of discussions, it becomes clear to everyone involved that if we want effective change, supplementary key performance indicators and adjustments to the process manuals and work instructions would not suffice. Rather, a fundamental realignment of the collaboration across project workstreams, a reduction in divisional egotism, and substantial support of projects from line functions would be necessary.

In order to bring expertise and perspective from project and management together in the best possible way and to ensure strong management involvement and commitment, teams of two are formed for each of the six improvement projects: one Bermuda core team member as project manager and one divisional manager as project sponsor. For the tandem matchmaking, close attention is paid to the chemistry between the two and their respective content expertise and preference.

To ensure that the improvement projects deliver solutions that are as practical and useful as possible, it is decided to pilot them in a prominent and economically important Launch Project code-named "Stormtrooper" to demonstrate impact and generate further support with a concrete example of success. The fact that the Launch Manager of the pilot project is also a member of the Bermuda core team proved to be very helpful in the consecutive rollout of the solutions to five more Launch Projects.

4 One Year of Bermuda: Careful and Tentative Steps to Success

4.1 Diagnosis

The Bermuda initiative launched in January is initially scheduled to last only 3 months since the management wishes first to observe results of the diagnostic phase and only then release decisive further steps. However, after the scheduled March management workshop, it becomes clear: we are on the right track; we have addressed the right fields of action; the solution procedure seems appropriate; and the iterative approach permits sufficient inclusion and adjustment to authorize the next steps and proceed.

Conception, piloting, and multiplication of the solutions to five further Launch Projects are scheduled for the end of the year, leaving 9 months to demonstrate tangible results. In retrospect, this detailed diagnosis paid off—the six Bermuda projects referred exactly to the statements retrieved from the surveyed employees. In this respect, the program team was able to emphasize that—at all times and in consideration of all activities—key topics addressed originate from the employees themselves: "We aren't doing this for the gallery or for the management, and we do not follow fashionable management method trends—we only tackle what bothers you." This approach has been very helpful in generating support and energy for Bermuda. The fact that we were building and improving the solutions feeding back from the organization and that the team worked toward a common vision kept the shared purpose alive and up to date.

4.2 Program Setup and Project Planning

The team chooses a lean program setup that includes weekly program round tables with the core team to share progress, to advise one another, and to coordinate activities of the six projects. The Bermuda project managers are middle managers from the various functional areas, all of whom are well-known and well connected in the Operations area, the Development departments, and among the Business Units. On the one hand, this helps to underline the seriousness of the Bermuda mission; on the other hand, it helps to strengthen the cooperation between the line functions of the divisions. Thanks to their high level of credibility in the line organization, the Bermuda project managers are also entrusted with mandates to develop the Bermuda solutions and institutionalize them within the project work. The program management is handled by the internal organizational developer together with the two external consultants. This trio also provides support and coaching for the six project managers; here too, the best suited resources and their skills and strengths were deliberately brought into play: the internal manager takes care of the two soft topics ("Interface Management" and "Leadership and Collaboration"), while the two externals take care of the other more tool-heavy and process-intensive projects.

A manageable five- to six-member project team is put together for each of the six Bermuda projects. Particular attention is paid to attracting committed representatives from the respective organizational areas who have a high potential and whose capacities are not being fully used for other high priority projects. In this way, qualified resources with a strong commitment to the Bermuda program are connected throughout the organization.

In order to ensure that the members of the Operations management team actively support the Bermuda program, beyond their role as sponsors of the individual Bermuda projects, the progress of the program is monitored, conflicts are resolved, and critical decisions are taken jointly in so-called Mission Control meetings. The high priority of the Bermuda program also made it a regular agenda item in the biweekly Operations Management Meeting.

The regular exchange with the management team is very helpful in ensuring close management involvement and keeping the program on track.

Employees of the organization who are not directly affected by the Bermuda program, in particular employees with a line function, are regularly updated on progress through short briefings during the monthly divisional meetings.

Key stakeholders, like the chairman of the board responsible for Business Units, Development, and Operations, as well as the senior managers of the functional areas, are kept abreast of program activities in individual meetings (Fig. 3).

To be able to quickly react to any operational problems coming up in the Launch Projects, a weekly half-hourly stand-up meeting called "Operations Project Board" is established. This regular meeting replaces a monthly briefing (feared by the Launch Managers), at which Operations Director Müller asks challenging questions to gain a comprehensive overview of project progress and, at the same time, does not skimp on "juicy" criticism and helpful advice. With the new format, the divisional managers take over the steering wheel to gain a better overview of the operative project activities and learn to be able to jointly intervene earlier and in a coordinated way. At the same time, they are better prepared for discussions in the higher-level steering committees of the Development Projects with Business Units and Development divisions. And Müller no longer finds it necessary to intervene in any of the Launch Projects across several hierarchical levels. A new format for exchange and

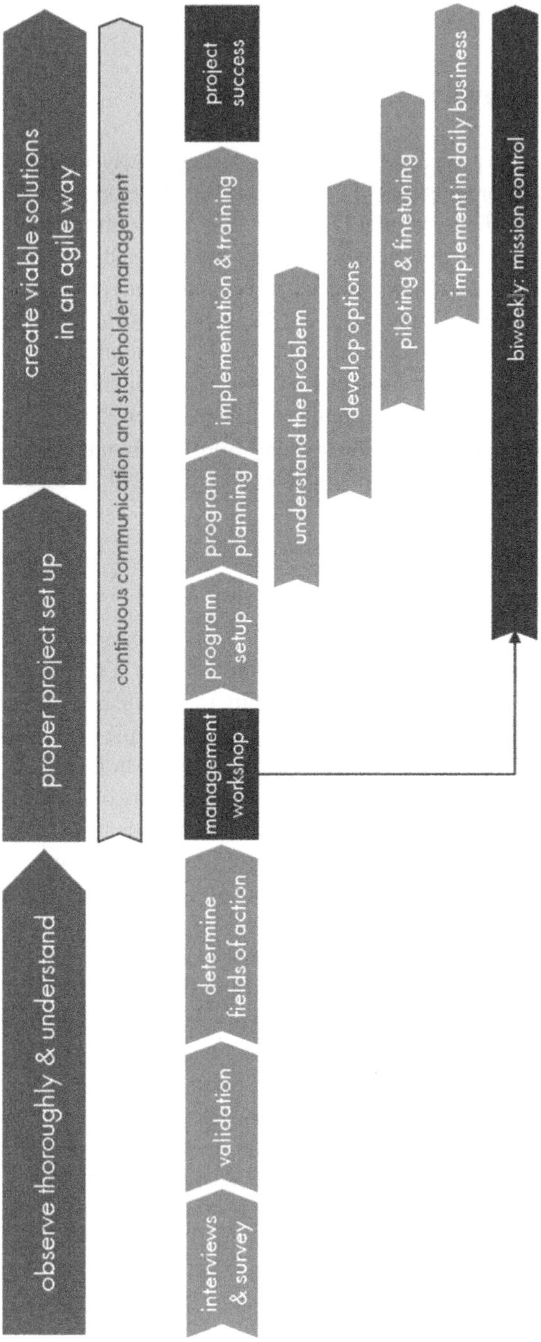

Fig. 3 Bermuda process model: diagnosis—solution development—implementation (Illustrated by the authors, used with permission. All rights reserved)

cooperation is found, which creates significant added value for line and project organization.

4.3 Solution Development and Piloting

The six improvement projects are set up in an agile way to actively search for available solution approaches in the organization, develop them iteratively, and apply and improve them in the Development and Launch Projects. Solution approaches are tested early on, so failures are detected as early as possible. Approaches that have already been tried out by individual players in projects or in the line business are deliberately taken up. Thus, the concept of "Technical Change Management" is essentially based on earlier ideas and attempts by one of the core team members. Similarly, the concept for "Material Availability" had already been drafted by a line manager from the purchasing department before the program was started. Both players can now use the tailwind from the Bermuda program to further develop their ideas in a cross-functional team and establish them in day-to-day business.

4.4 Drivers for Project Success

Even at an early stage of the program, it would not be a question of developing groundbreaking new instruments, because many of the ideas for effective solutions already exist and only need to be put together. The example of the Bermuda project "Risk Management" shows that beneficial leverage lies in increasing the transparency of project activities and in the intensity and continuity of collaboration between the subprojects: one key result in the Product Development Process is a listing of relevant project risks that needs to be produced at defined stage gates. Common practice for the project teams, which are already working to full capacity, is to compile these risks quickly, just before the deadline, and present them to the steering committee. Usually, their reaction, in order not to jeopardize the project's time to market, is to wave the project through with conditions. Risks are neither systematically attended to nor actively managed but simply accepted based on the principle of hope. As a result, the responsibility for the risks remains with the project team, but, for them, dealing with the risks is not an attractive task. The Bermuda project recognizes this and tries to break the pattern. The tool and process for recording and assessing risks is basically kept the same, but the way to handle the risks is changed. In the pilot project, risks are identified, recorded, and evaluated regularly in moderated short workshops, together in the cross-functional project team. Only the top risks are escalated to the steering committee, but only in conjunction with proposals for countermeasures that specifically mitigate risks. For the implementation of the approved measures, specifically named line function experts are obliged to implement them and are thus actively involved in the project. This adaptation aligns the organization to a more entrepreneurial way of managing risk. Regular updates of the gradually shrinking list of risks to the entire project team make the effectiveness of the new, iterative approach visible and tangible.

A similar procedure is used in the "Technical Change Management" project. For the first time, all technical changes throughout the entire product design process are systematically recorded, evaluated, prioritized, and decided upon by a mixed team of operational and development functions. Here too, short, joint, and regular meetings of the responsible project functions ensure that important changes can be implemented smoothly and efficiently. The pilot project has shown that far more changes than expected were necessary, but that, in contrast to earlier projects, these changes could be managed in a controlled manner with the new approach. In the "Technical Change Management" project, the program is deliberately expanding the scope beyond the Operations area. Since most technical changes in Launch Projects are initiated by the Development departments, the pilot project consciously and successfully sought to close ranks with the technical disciplines. The positive experience and the effectiveness of the approach in the pilot project are jointly presented to the Development management—and are positively received there. "That's how you do it"; the *eminence grise* of Development ennobles the approach of the Bermuda team and thus marks another milestone in the cooperation between the organizational units. It is a "knighthood" for the guys from Operations—and a boost for the systematic application of the approach in further projects.

In the "Material Availability" project, an IT tool is being established using internal resources, which brings together information on the development status of bills of material from different IT systems on one uniform interface and thus provides up-to-date and consistent data for the different project players. In this way, numerous individual Excel lists that required painstaking manual maintenance and were never fully up to date can be replaced. And procurement can use a sound database for sound sourcing decisions.

4.5 Attitude and Behavior Explicitly Addressed

In addition to working on tools for process improvement, the diagnosis phase reveals that the "human factor"—and which experienced organization developer would be surprised?—plays a not-to-be-underestimated role in navigating the project through stormy seas. Here, deficits are revealed both in regard to hierarchical cooperation (i.e., between managers, project managers, and their subordinates) and horizontally among colleagues and team members and within departments. In order to make the management aware of the problem, quotes from some 100 original interviews are printed on cards for the management workshop at the end of the diagnosis phase. Each individual statement is comprehensible and not surprising, but the collective impact of the ensemble of statements induces enough momentum to spawn a separate project dedicated to this purpose. The 100 statements are later condensed and prioritized in several processing loops in various target groups. Ultimately, 12 critical behavioral patterns hindering project cooperation were identified for immediate treatment. The collection of behavioral patterns culminated in the

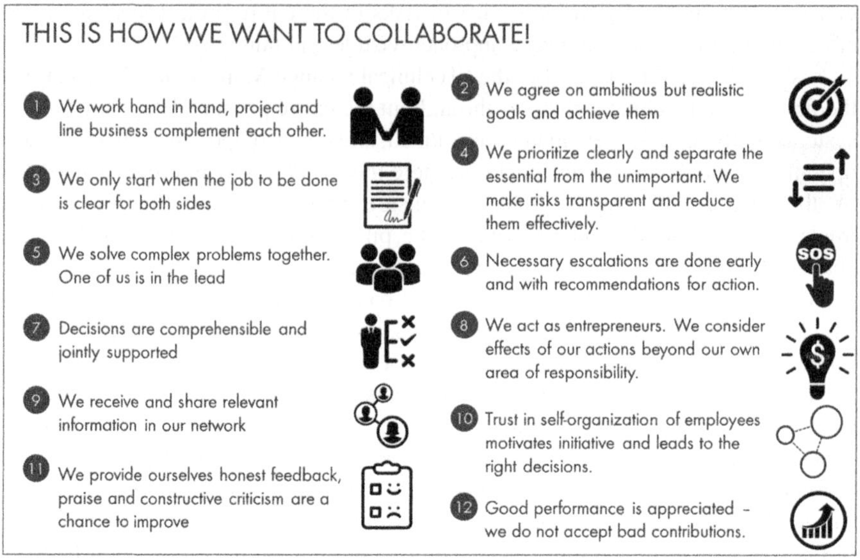

Fig. 4 Bermuda principles of collaboration (Illustrated by the authors, used with permission. All rights reserved)

creation of guidelines distributed to the whole Bermuda organization intended to promote beneficial, and thwart toxic, behavior (Fig. 4).

The formulated principles are approved across all levels and units without exception. Some departments and project teams begin to reflect on the principles in workshops and in light of participants' own individual realities and put new ways of behavior into practice. Working on attitudes and habits demands patience, perseverance, and a willingness for critical self-reflection, and, unfortunately, sustainable implementation of the principles across the broader organization remains a work in progress. Nevertheless, the momentous progress achieved convinces the management team of the human and business virtues of instituting Bermuda behavior principles. They now strive to institute the guiding principles across the organization. Devoted disciples, even one and a half years after program completion, retrieve the laminated cards from their briefcases to draw attention to some or other principles or admonish delinquencies. All those originally actively involved in formulating the principles remain passionate practitioners.

4.6 Program Completion

After 12 months of Bermuda, the key players take stock. Not every high-flying plan has been fully deployed, but the results of the six Bermuda projects have measurably energized all important Launch Projects and facilitated easier project navigation across the board. A further multiplication of the Bermuda solutions into more

Launch Projects is planned for the following year. In a final workshop with the Operations management team, progress and tangible results of the Bermuda projects are assessed and contemplated, and the program team is discharged. To ensure continuity of further implementation, the management and project team jointly decided to retain the core team, which now forms a "Bermuda Community," beyond the end of the program. Thus, an initially temporary element of the program organization has become a useful and integral part of the organization.

A few weeks after the official end of the program, the results are presented to a larger audience of Business Units, Development, and Operations managers—the subsequent barbecue with the entire program team marks a perfect conclusion to an extraordinary development process.

5 Key Results and Takeaways

Over the past 20 years, the company has run through a fast motion development, parallel to the development of the worldwide photovoltaic industry: coming from the pioneering phase of the industry in the years around the turn of the millennium, the worldwide solar boom led to considerable growth toward the end of the first decade of the twenty-first century. From 2012, the company went through several waves of consolidation and restructuring and numerous approaches to differentiation and professionalization of the organization. The Bermuda program revealed aspects from several of these phases: the desire to achieve joint success together across structural boundaries and away from the hierarchy ("as we did before") was just as noticeable as the drive to create significantly more orientation through manageable and modern tools and processes.

It was clear to everyone that commitment, passion, and team spirit alone would not be enough. Just as important was the disclosure and handling of conflicts and the orientation toward measurable and concrete goals. The result was an adequate balance of soft factors (agile approach, bottom-up approach, orientation toward shared values) and hard factors (hard goals, data transparency, standardized and uniform tools). However, key to success of the program was certainly the smooth and uncomplicated cooperation within the entire core team. Micropolitics played almost no role; there was a constructive struggle for the common purpose.

The Bermuda initiative was a rather unusual program for the Operations function as no clear result was specified from the onset—it was not about introducing an IT system, no fundamental process reengineering was tabled, it was not concerned with setting up or dismantling a production site, nor was it a systematic management development endeavor. The only clear motif to emerge was the organization's floundering performance regarding the project business—this needed to be improved significantly. The management agreed to an open-ended organizational development process, without anything having been explicitly drafted. And this plan could only succeed because the program addressed accelerating performance on several dimensions: processes, system, structural, and cultural. All of this was possible because the weaknesses revealed at the start were nearly unanimous. The joint and broad quantitative and qualitative problem analysis attests that the program was never fundamentally questioned. It was clear to everyone that there was something to be gained, that it represented a pressing objective, and that the undertaking would succeed only if everyone joined in. The common goal, which was perceived as desirable and achievable, created a strong sense of purpose for the Bermuda team and for the whole organization. A further success factor was the shared internal and external program management. Different consulting approaches, different expertise, and different project experience, but a similar view on successful change management and dealing with people, were debated in intensive and fruitful program management sessions which, in turn, fostered effective and well-coordinated program management.

From the very beginning, Bermuda was consciously limited to the Operations area. In the course of the program, it became increasingly clear that the upstream Development areas had to cope with comparable problems in terms of good interaction and collaboration of the project disciplines. And regarding individual cross-functional issues such as risk management and technical change management, elements of the Bermuda solutions could also be integrated into the company-wide Product Development Process. In the final "Bermuda unplugged" presentation of the program, the responsible Executive Board member recommended that the company's Development departments take up the program's impetus for the benefit of their organizations. However, this has not yet come to pass.

The program focused on the project business of the Operations organization. It was possible to emphasize the importance of the project organization more strongly and to find a better balance with the traditionally dominant series business of "buy, produce, and deliver." One of the articulated Bermuda principles sums this up: "we work hand in hand; project and line business complement each other." Both parts of the organization being on eye level are necessary because the line functions make important contributions to the fulfillment of the deliverables of the Launch Projects—without the line, there are no successful projects. And vice versa: if there are no successful Launch Projects, there is no food for future series production. In complex Development Projects, it is always necessary to enter a new territory, which always presents challenges for the organization. These challenges can be surmounted best when people from different parts of the organization jointly strive to find solutions that work for all and, where helpful, change the organization itself.

The Launch Managers were successfully strengthened in their coordinating and steering role between the Operations functions within the launch process. Their role as "team captain" and spokesperson for the Launch Team in the direction of the overall Product Development Project is now accepted and appreciated. The organization has recognized that leadership is necessary also in the project; in line with the Bermuda principle, "we solve complex problems together, but one person is accountable." At the same time, the Launch Managers have become guarantors for the continued implementation and application of the Bermuda tools.

The program was initiated to avert an existential threat to the Operations area—the new product class had to be launched into the targeted market on time and within targeted manufacturing costs. The focus shifted to achieving tangible economic

Fig. 5 Company-wide "Leadership Fundamentals" (Illustrated by the authors, used with permission. All rights reserved)

goals. Parallel to these, however, it became increasingly clear that a breakthrough leverage would lie in better collaboration between the players in the various project functions. In retrospect, it is striking that the "Principles of Collaboration" formulated for this purpose looked very similar to the company-wide "Leadership Fundamentals," which were developed at a later stage. With principles such as "Collaboration," "Entrepreneurship," and "Customer Centricity," these also emphasize values that were already addressed in the Bermuda program (Fig. 5).

Of course, there were also difficulties in the program which had to be circumnavigated. Even though most of the relevant players from the project and series business were happy to get involved in the team play in the Bermuda Triangle, some managers nevertheless maintained a cautious stance. The attempt to clarify and harmonize problematic interfaces between divisions and departments was not successful in all cases. In the course of the discussion, structural conflicts were sometimes reduced to personal conflicts between individual players. On the other hand, the application of procedural Bermuda solutions led to a situation where the influence of personal animosities faded.

From the beginning, the program was designed to develop and establish solutions together, regardless of membership of a specific (line) organizational unit. However, this also meant that it was not suitable to produce individual heroes who could proclaim success for themselves or their area. This may have been one reason why not all line managers could be fully won over to the program. In general, the support of the management in the Operations functional area was available throughout the duration of the program. Sometimes, however, a rather indifferent attitude could be observed—not all line managers actively promoted the program, but the majority at least cleared the way for the commitment of those involved in the project. Unfortunately, the widely expressed desire to specifically promote changes in attitude and behavior in accordance with the newly formulated principles of cooperation was only partially successful. Here, too, more conviction and impulses from the hierarchy would certainly have helped. Presumably, the program's impact beyond the Operations function would have been more effective and sustainable if the Operations management team had been even more proactive and top-down in promoting sustainable implementation of the solutions and measures.

The bottom line, however, is that the program demonstrated a perceptible positive impact. Solutions developed in the program complemented each other and helped Launch Projects to reach their goals faster and more reliably, thus ensuring an effective contribution of Operations to a timely market launch of new products.

In the "Stormtrooper" project, which was running parallel to Bermuda, and where most Bermuda solutions were first implemented, the planned start of series production was achieved 3 months after the official end of the Bermuda program.

Dieter Müller was no longer in the firing line of his critics—and was able to turn his attention to other challenges in the Operations business. The Operations ship weathered the storm in the Bermuda Triangle. Not every high-flying goal was met in full, and not all the players in the Operations project organization are walking in shorts in the Caribbean sun. But big steps have been taken, and a solid foundation is built to take further steps in a continuous development process.

6 The Three Pillars of Bermuda

Even though the 3-P-Model was not used in the initial design of the program, it has proven very helpful for our retrospective assessment. We found it especially insightful to analyze the program approach along the three pillars.

6.1 The Bermuda Purpose

A desirable and achievable target picture was developed and formulated with the involvement of all project participants. It included:

- Tangible financial benefits.
- Greater transparency concerning the status and risks of the projects.
- Continuous cross-functional collaboration.
- Establishing the Launch Manager as the coordinator and "steerer" of the Launch Project and helping Operations to "speak with one voice."

- Operations area makes valuable contributions to the Product Development Process and is on an equal footing with other participants.

6.2 The Travelling Bermuda Organization

In the 1 year of the Bermuda program, the existing organizational procedures and structures were questioned many times, sometimes slightly adjusted and sometimes more. Thereby, we observed (and accomplished) the following:

- The program consistently considered the different realities of line and project and tried to integrate these.
- The broad-based diagnosis meant that all players in the Operations area found themselves in the derived fields of action and improvement projects. The solutions developed were appreciated.
- With the "Operations Project Board," an agile format for the operational deviation management of Launch Projects was established, in which both line and project functions could coordinate and jointly solve "hot" issues. This made line power usable in projects.
- The cross-functional Bermuda core team continued to work together in a community even after the program was completed.
- The program made implicitly known weaknesses in the organization explicit, especially at the interfaces between different areas of responsibility. It was possible to conclude viable agreements between the interface partners.
- An agile program setup made it possible to take advantage of opportunities arising during the project period. Continuous exchange within the program management team and close contact to the key players in the organization were essential.

6.3 Connecting the Bermuda Resources

The Bermuda program directly or indirectly involved 150 employees from the Operations organization. In order to serve the Bermuda purpose and jointly reach our program targets, key resources were connected in the following ways:

- Project and line managers assumed joint responsibility for the development and implementation of the Bermuda solutions.
- A cross-functional core team jointly represented the full package of different solutions coming out of the six Bermuda projects.
- Bermuda project managers and sponsors regularly met in the biweekly Mission Control meeting.
- Quarterly joint assessment of the current situation and coordination of further action between the core team and management.

- Solutions already available from experienced experts were taken up, professionalized, and implemented.
- In the course of the program, synergies between the individual Bermuda projects became visible—success in one project benefited other projects—this was taken up and reinforced through project communication.

Further Reading

Coyle, D. (2018). *The culture code: The secrets of highly successful groups*. New York: Random House Business.

Doppler, K., & Lauterburg, C. (2019). *Change Management: Den Unternehmenswandel gestalten*. Campus.

Glasl, F., & Lievegoed, B. (1993). *Dynamische Unternehmensentwicklung. Wie Pionierbetriebe und Bürokratien zu schlanken Unternehmen werden*. Bern: Haupt.

Knapp, J., Zeratsky, J., & Kowitz, B. (2016). *Sprint: How to solve big problems and test new ideas in just five days*. New York: Simon & Schuster.

Laloux, F., Appert, E., & Kauschke, M. (2014). *Reinventing organizations: A guide to creating organizations inspired by the next stage in human consciousness*. Nelson Parker.

Oestereich, B., & Schroeder, C. (2017). *Das kollegial geführte Unternehmen: Ideen und Praktiken für die agile Organisation von morgen*. München: Vahlen.

Sagmeister, S. (2016). *Business culture design*. Frankfurt: Campus.

Timinger, H. (2017). *Modernes Projektmanagement: Mit traditionellem, agilem und hybridem Vorgehen zum Erfolg*. Weinheim: Wiley-VCH.

Wollmann, P., Kühn, F., & Kempf, M. (Eds.). (2020). *Three pillars of organization and leadership in disruptive times*. Heidelberg: Springer.

Markus Beer has been supporting managers and their teams in complex change processes as an internal and external change manager for more than 20 years. In doing so, he draws on his experience in different sectors (retail, industry, and consulting) and different corporate functions (supply chain management, operations, human resources) and positions (project manager, manager, consultant). Markus is convinced that organizations and their members are successful when they continuously challenge their strategies, structures, and processes while trying out and practicing new forms of leadership and collaboration.

Philipp Bosselmann has been an experienced Management Consultant for over 15 years. Being trained as a physicist, he started his professional career leading product development projects in the semiconductor industry. Working as a Management Consultant since 2004, he first took a deep dive into process improvement, coaching projects, and managing efficiency programs in various industries. In the past 10 years, he explored the emerging new innovation methodologies and ways of working and co-developed a unique innovation project management approach. Following the mission "help making good ideas change the world for the better," he in 2014 co-founded Sprout Consulting, as an innovation platform for entrepreneurs from small and large technology companies. Philipp has been deeply involved in over a hundred innovation projects, providing focused acceleration and steering support, introducing new ways of working on project team and management team level, and improving collaboration across the organization.

Part VI

Helpful Design Concepts to Best Use the 3-P-Model

The authors show in this part of the book helpful concepts that are closely interlinked with applications of the 3-P-Model. Some concepts are new, some other concepts are well-proven but unfold new meaning in their interlinkage with the 3-P-Model.

These five articles cover different conceptual ways of applying the 3-P-Model. The broad range of topics covered goes from sophisticated ways of designing organization along the product life cycle to fast product development redesign, change management design in complex situations, creating and using a compass for entrepreneurial journeys and to crisis management with 3-P-using the example of the pandemic.

Organizations Meandering in the Product Life Cycle

Lilian Matischok and Frank Kühn

Abstract

This article describes the consistent connectivity between organization, product, ecosystem, and markets. If companies want to be successful, they have to pursue a sustainable purpose that creates value propositions, contributes to societal development, inspires people, and gives them clear orientation. Following this idea, companies need to adapt and interlink their structures, processes, practices, and teamwork to the architecture and life cycles of their products so that their overall performance meets customer requirements and market developments. Since different products are in different phases between genesis and commodity, a multiple organizational setup is required to connect the resources in a challenging journey of the company. The concept of the Three-Pillar Model underlines these considerations very strongly.

1 Start a Hero's Journey

What triggers a company's transformation? And what triggers the insight that a traveling organization is needed to survive in the future? What should the organization orientate toward? Only one thing is certain: It is not just about a new organizational form or figure, but it is also about change itself, and it is always even more about being in the right place. Structures are only snapshots that will be rethought in the next moment. Only a sustainable purpose (and sustainability can also have an

L. Matischok
Stuttgart, Germany
e-mail: post@lilian-matischok.com

F. Kühn (✉)
Dortmund, Germany
e-mail: fk@kuehn-cp.com

P. Wollmann et al. (eds.), *Organization and Leadership in Disruptive Times*, Future of Business and Finance, https://doi.org/10.1007/978-3-030-63034-8_21

expiry date) and the common will to connectivity provide support; everything else is adaptable at any time.

So, it will be exciting. And I am the hero of this story: the organization. I follow the call to adventure; that is what heroes do. Always!

My Executive Board discussed the realignment of our company in its annual strategy meeting: we must expect that our market will be shaken by disruptions and that our business model will no longer be profitable. Customer requirements are changing rapidly, leaps in technology are emerging, geopolitical upheavals such as the energy transition and trade embargoes are already challenging us.

As an organization, I am still rigid due to my high level of internal complexity and stability. This is because my figure is designed for division of labor and specialization. I am tuned for efficiency, sometimes flat, sometimes slim, but always highly dependent on each part remaining in place and doing its job. If nothing changes, everything is fine. But even with small changes, I get out of step; and my heart stops when customer requests come in that are outside our standard range.

Confirming the Approach of the Three-Pillar Model

The three pillars (Wollmann et al. 2020) support the ideas and concepts presented in this article very clearly.

- Sustainable Purpose: This creates alignment, inspiration, and the pride in being part of a company and contributing to both customer success and societal requirements. The purpose is particularly important when a company tries various organizational approaches to best meet market opportunities.
- Traveling Organization: This means adapting the organization to volatile markets, uncertain business dynamics, and product innovations with their specific life cycles. They have to pull and determine the appropriate organization designs, not the other way around.
- Connected Resources: Businesses, product architectures, processes, structures, knowledge, the teams' experience, competencies, and creativities must be balanced and connected with each other; this is even more complex in hybrid organizations that correspond to the diverse product life cycles and have to allocate their resources optimally.

Nevertheless, I am still fine. Why change? Our sales and profit figures are great. Our order books are so full that I really do not know how to find time for "fun and games" in addition to our daily business. This would cost us efficiency and defocus our employees. We have trained the employees on efficiency and quality for years; they are just as innovative and agile as I am.

But the Executive Board says we have to use the time now to prepare for big changes—develop new strategies, transform our business model, push new products to market; in short, as an organization, I have to be faster and more flexible. Apparently, this no longer works top-down, so I should be redesigned for decentralization and self-management. For this I will get a comprehensive fitness program, all of me must slim down and become more agile.

2 When an Organization Starts to Ponder

These huge expectations overwhelm me. It is so easy to say: "Be more flexible, adaptable, faster, and more innovative." I have not done that since my youth. I am feeling too old and lazy for such a big change. Agility is something for young start-ups, software companies, etc., not for such a long-established industrial company like I am. Please show me how to do it!

A beginning . . .

Our "Organization Development" department organized a trip to various companies that stand for agility and self-organization. I was really impressed: beautiful modern offices, happy employees, and great products. Connectivity between space, products, and employees. My CEO then approved the project, including the budget, for the organizational development: We are launching a broad-based "Agile Transformation" initiative, and, in addition, we are modernizing the offices of our Development and IT teams. We want to make the specialists of tomorrow happy. And I think to myself: It looks easier than I expected! Could even be fun for people. Let us give it a try . . .

. . . practical test . . .

Time is our enemy! So, while we practice agility and self-organization, the disruptive forces work faster and stronger than ever on the market. New competitors are faster than we are. Our previous cash cows are increasingly becoming "poor dogs." Profits collapse; first locations have to be closed.

> At the last Board meeting they decided to cancel all initiatives that do not contribute to cost reductions or sales increase. And since they have not seen direct results from the agility program (the agile units are not visibly more productive than the "non-agile" ones): further rollout stopped for now . . . So, I cannot expect any support from here.

At least we can switch quickly to a "shared desk" concept to save rent, thanks to our modern office environment. And I already feel a little more flexible than before the agility program and will continue to do so unobtrusively. The hero continues his journey in secret.

Time Is Our Enemy?

It is nonsense to try to compete against time! Because unfortunately, time is stronger than we are. Always. So, let us turn this thought around: Time is our friend! Because the urgency of the change gives us the arguments: Let's make the organizations fast and agile. Let us use rapid practices.

A case study: The new 4.0 business unit is to be organized, which wants to deliver technical solutions for digitalized industries. The idea: Rapid prototyping and minimum viable product practices are to be applied not only to the range of services but also to the organization itself. The management team is flexible and agrees to regularly review and, if necessary, adjust the strategy and roadmap as well as the definition and distribution of roles among them. Weekly and monthly stand-ups and workshops are to be used for tactical and strategic reflection and adjustments.

A nice example of the pragmatic procedure is the "marketplace of roles." It is a simple method for clarifying roles in the management team. The setting consists of a circle of flipcharts. The space in between is free, or there are tables with materials (sticky notes, pens). Depending on the maturity

(continued)

of the team, the process can be moderated by a team member or an external facilitator. The process takes between 2 and 4 h.
The procedure in detail:
1. The participants agree on the following procedure (10–15 min).
2. Each team member describes their understanding of their role in terms of approx. 10–20 technical and collaborative tasks on a flipchart (and which tasks they do not see in their role) (15–30 min).
3. The participants go through the flipcharts created by their colleagues. They mark points where they see a need for clarification. This step still contains no discussion (15–20 min).
4. Together, the participants go through role by role, clarifying questions and controversial points. Each team member adjusts their role description if necessary (30–90 min).
5. More complex questions are collected in a "management backlog" for clarification in the next meetings (10 min).
6. Common "rules of the game" are agreed and recorded on a separate flipchart (10–20 min).
7. A process for regular retrospectives and feedback on roles is agreed. This also includes an "expiry date" for the agreements made (10–15 min).
8. The results of the meeting are agreed (5 min).
9. The team coordinates the communication of the results in the organization (10–20 min).

3 Connect and Harmonize Product and Organization

Recently, a new consultant started to support our company. She was not too surprised that we had not become more profitable with "agile." They had only experimented on me as an organization, on my structures and processes, but not on our business strategy and value proposition. She recommends the BAPO model to us (Fig. 1) (Van der Linden et al. 2004).

BAPO or ESAO: The Ecosystem Is Always Involved

The BAPO model is based on a simple premise: The starting point for every organization is the strategy (business) and the innovations that define the future of the company. The way we shape our value creation and business model should be the starting point for all further decisions. The next step is to define the architecture (A) for our products and value propositions and the underlying decisions on technologies. This then shows how we have to define or select our processes (P) including effective methods and tools. Finally, the organization is defined based on B, A, and O (Fig. 1).
Based on the BAPO model, the ESAO model is now also proposed (Bosch and Bosch-Sijtsema 2014). It makes it even clearer that all elements have a strong connection to the ecosystem. Neither strategy nor architecture nor organization and processes can be discussed regardless of what is happening in the company's environment. One example is currently—and this emerged during the Covid-19 pandemic—global supply chains or the new sensitivity to good organization or architectures for collaboration tools. However, we continue to prefer the BAPO tool because of its immediate coherence, always with a view to its connectivity with the ecosystem.

This is a completely different quality of connectivity between entrepreneurial design elements; their connection is given a direction, a logical order, and a direction of thinking and discussing. This is not linear, because loops are also part of it, but the

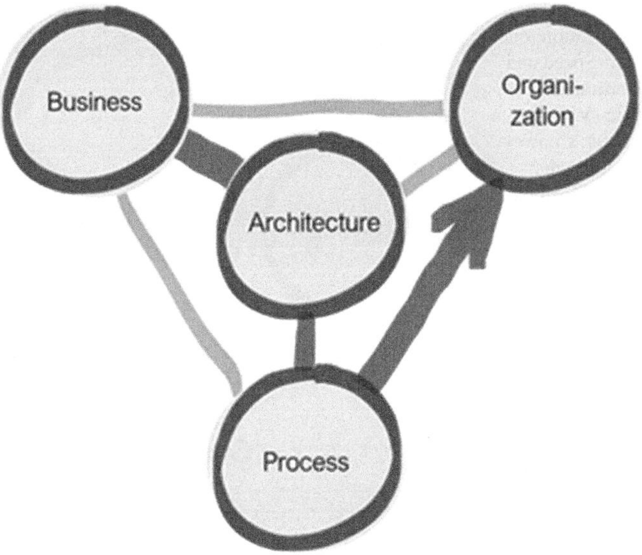

Fig. 1 BAPO stands for the connectivity between business, architecture, process, and organization; business pulls architecture which pulls process which pulls organization (Van der Linden et al. 2004) (Illustrated by the authors, used with permission. All rights reserved)

priorities must be clear. Agreeing on such an explicit discussion path is a first step toward a good, common outcome.

That sounds reasonable to me as the organization. We have already worked on the strategy; it seems to be almost finished. We already know the big profit pools of the future. Now we only must align our product architecture (and later the processes) with these new business ideas. It cannot be that difficult! And I like the structured procedure anyway—that is in my DNA.

4 OPAB Instead of BAPO or Conway's Law

In practice, we often observed the opposite. They built me, the organization, around the interests and profiles of existing people. This established my structures and the interfaces for the processes along them. Ultimately, the structures and their areas were reflected in the product architectures. And without being aware of it, they have developed products and value propositions that result from my shape and not from the corporate strategy or market needs. "Many companies block the path to innovation by starting from existing organization and processes instead of their future business and the architectures derived from it. What is done? OPAB. The right thing would be BAPO" (Van der Linden et al. 2004) (Fig. 2).

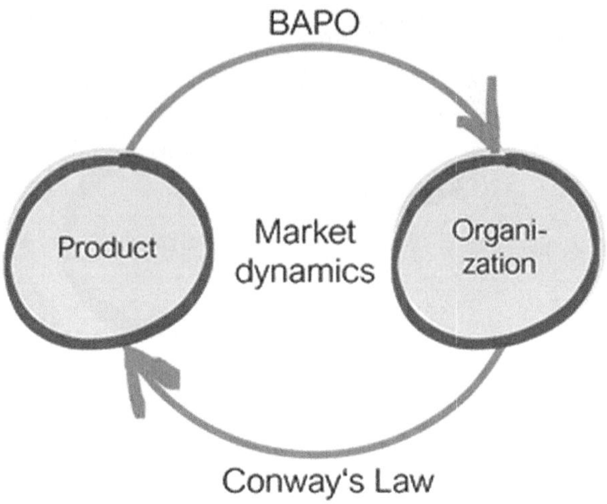

Fig. 2 Connectivity of product or organization: one pulls each other. Speed and timing are determined by market dynamic (Van der Linden et al. 2004; Conway 1968) (Illustrated by the authors, used with permission. All rights reserved)

Conway's Law
Conway (1968) describes the dysfunctional relationship between organization and product, which can be seen particularly well in the development of software products. The system architecture, i.e., the structuring into modular components and the interfaces between the components, follows the communication relationships and the organizational structure of the organization(s) that designed it (Fig. 2). Studying software in relation to product life cycles is like studying the fruit fly *Drosophila melanogaster* in relation to genetics. Unlike the development of mechatronic systems, where the system design has to be consistent from the beginning due to the high dependencies and the associated effects on production and assembly, software can be easily changed or adapted to new interfaces using adapters. It is therefore not uncommon for software system design to be "sloppy" and collect "technical debt," be it due to a lack of awareness of the long-term consequences or due to tough schedules (I say: Time is our enemy!). When different teams or even individuals work independently on similar issues, software modules with redundant features emerge (Fig. 3). The structure of the software modules often shows where communication was hampered by organizational, spatial, or interpersonal boundaries or how collaboration was prevented by different programming languages and development tools. For example, a software system for warehouse automation is developed or purchased several times, or there is a Frankfurt and a Berlin ticket management system.

5 Product and Organization Put to the Test

Back to our company and me as an organization!

> We are working hard to find our new digital unit, adapted to our strategy and our promise of performance. Two organizational units that are working on comparable offerings are to merge. As soon as the first draft is completed and approved by my Board, our customers and we notice at a large international trade fair that other business units in our group are working

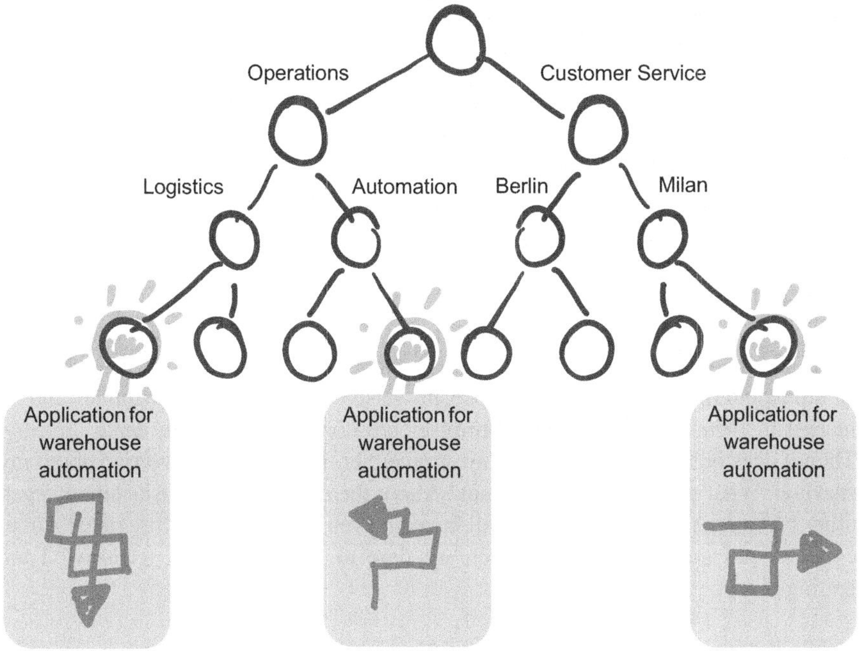

Fig. 3 Effective solution suffers from organizational separatism: Organization determines solution (Illustrated by the authors, used with permission. All rights reserved)

on the same topics. "Competitive products" have arisen both in one of our foreign branches and in a subsidiary. Probably Conway's Law was at work.

Our customers are confused by the visits of 3 different sales teams from our company presenting similar topics within a week. Of course, the products are not compatible with each other, and some of the teams were not aware of the overlap.

The Chief Sales Officer, to whom customers complain, brings the topic to the next Board meeting and calls for a joint sales organization, of course under his leadership. The Chief Product Officer suggests integrating the other organizational units into the new organization to prevent further proliferation in product development. The CFO disagrees. This would be far too complex and expensive, especially across national borders. In addition, none of these activities actually had any sales. Our CEO is very relaxed about the situation. Does it matter? Remember, we wanted decentralized responsibility and self-organization. Competition stimulates business, also internally.

And me? Who will ask me? Isn't that a too simple way of thinking due to the time pressure and the attempt to avoid complexity and the claim to keep one's own influence? And isn't the well-thought-out approach of personal responsibility and self-organization being neglected too quickly to leave connectivity behind? I feel misunderstood and torn apart: Autonomy, cooperation, and responsibility belong together and only become productive in their connectivity! Just as a role is only effective through its working relationships.

It becomes clear. There will be no agreement. It is not the right time to structure our organization according to the BAPO model, in a consistent way and around the globe. And the right time will probably never come. Time is our enemy! If time were our friend, we would act now.

6 Market and Customer Orientation

Since the Executive Board does not agree, on an ad hoc basis, which perspective is the right one, they set up a strategy team and instruct them to analyze the current situation with regard to "who does what" and to work out a proposal for a customer and market orientated approach and relevant business potential.

Market and customer orientation. Bliss at last! I had already wondered when the Board would finally look at my purpose, my raison d'être. With no customers and no market in focus, all performance promises are doomed to a quick death anyway. Then it does not need me as an organization either. I am seriously worried about my survival. What are they thinking about? About the distribution of tasks among each other? About a new structure that will have an even shorter best-before date? About experimental approaches with which we dare to enter unknown territory? I am getting dizzy.

The strategy team starts work. A few insiders who know the internal situation, as well as some external consultants, analyze the portfolio and assess the market potential. There is a lot of discussion: Who are the target customers? What do customers want? Which activity best meets customer needs? How do we segment the market? By region? By industry structure? How mature and scalable are the "products"? How can we do profitable business? What should we avoid?

What I would now also find important as an organization is that they include me in the discussion. My question would point to the future. How do we not only want to create clarity about the current market situation, but also be organizationally prepared to ensure that this orientation not only remains an episodic undertaking, but is also installed as a permanent task? How can I position myself as a traveling organization to continuously synchronize with the customer journey? Then, however, a new mindset is required: radical from the outside in. What is developing in the markets and customer needs; how do we perceive this through our outer skin, our periphery; which solutions are in demand; and how do we develop them in a creative partnership with our customers? (Fig. 4)

Oops... brooding ... the common purpose has apparently taken a back seat, now the internal competition, own ambitions, status thinking, and personal KPIs count; this has nothing to do with local market and customer orientation, which can make perfect sense. But why don't we combine the competencies, the creativity, and the experiences that we have distributed in the company around the world?

Firstly, it requires a pull from more than one customer so that we can identify an attractive market. Secondly, an internal pull of more than isolated perceptions, competencies, and interests is required to create a common focus and to blend our strengths. We not only have to understand what connectivity is emerging out there in

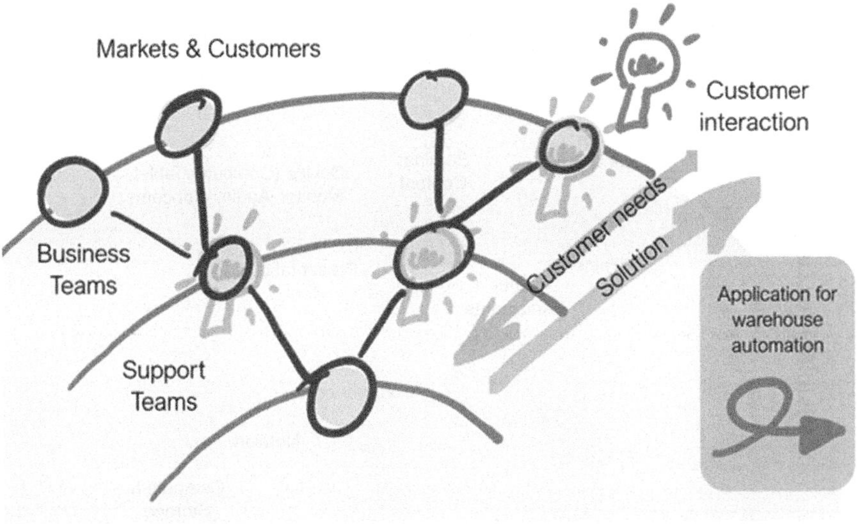

Fig. 4 Customer needs and customer interaction pull and create solutions. This means connectivity of needs, impulses, and competences in the ecosystem (Oestereich and Schröder 2017) (see also Fig. 3) (Illustrated by the authors, used with permission. All rights reserved)

the markets, but we also need to make sure that we respond to it in our own connectivity. And to make it even more demanding: Connectivity doesn't just happen outside and inside (Fig. 4); we even have to connect the two—connectivity is required in the ecosystem as already explained above in the context of the BAPO and ESAO approach; as an organization, I'm excited: This is new thinking and fresh wind!

> There is confusion in the strategy team. How do we make a meaningful proposal? How do we advance a new understanding of organization that runs counter to many previous organizational experiences and individual interests and long practiced silo thinking? With our internal organizational discussions, we slow down further. None of us are clairvoyants; the future is uncertain. Nevertheless, we have to start and to see.

If time is to be our friend, we must have the courage to start. Somehow. With the clear awareness that no solution will be without new problems. But that is called entrepreneurship.

7 Value Chain Mapping

I am the organization, and I sink into self-pity. I was dreaming about a new self, what I could have looked like: confident, young, lively, and enterprising. But I can no longer imagine that we will succeed that quickly on the market. Time is my enemy …

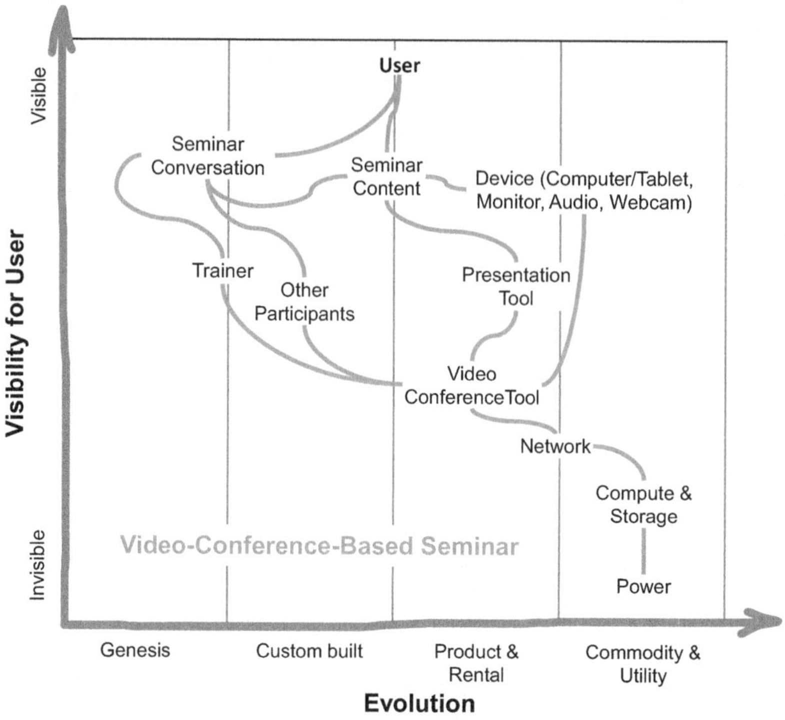

Fig. 5 Example for value chain map to visualize and manage the interrelationship between value chain and evolution phase (Wardley 2016) (Illustrated by the authors, used with permission.)

The feeling of helplessness spreads. Until one of the strategy team says: "Can we take a few hours today and pretend that we are clairvoyant? And write down our hypotheses about how which activities will develop?" And another says: "Wait a minute . . . I recently saw a talk by Simon Wardley in which he claims the future is predictable! I believe that the underlying systematic in the development from Genesis via Custom Built to Product etc. could help us on our journey towards clairvoyance. . ." And a third one intervenes: "The company where I worked 15 years ago has also started with customer projects. They now have a very mature product portfolio and are market leaders. The initial situation here was very similar, only that it was a 'start-up'".

Value Chain Mapping in Strategic Product Development

In his "value chain mapping" approach, Simon Wardley (2016) refers to the typical development steps during a product life cycle (Fig. 5). First, an idea for a value proposition is created (Phase 1: "Genesis"). This idea is then implemented as a customer-specific solution (Phase 2: "Custom-Built"). If this solution fits enough similar customer problems, i.e., if supply and demand develop accordingly, the solution will, over time, result in a product/product-like service offering that is replicable and sold to many customers in the same way (Phase 3: "Product"). If a very large number of customers buy the product, the resulting competitive and price pressure will drive forward the standardization of the product. Then there are also many competitors who offer

(continued)

comparable, standardized products (Phase 4: "Commodity"). The commodity phase is typically followed by a new genesis, which generates more complex service offerings (product service bundles or systemic solutions) based on the commodities to differentiate themselves from the competition and achieve higher margins.
Even if one does not know how long each respective phase will last, one can be sure about the direction of evolution. In this respect, one can use this development sequence to make strategic deductions about the next steps.
Wardley uses this dimension on the x-axis of the Wardley maps. The y-axis shows the value and visibility to the customer.

Using the Wardley method to visualize value chains (Fig. 5) helps us to understand where the different components of the business are today and where they will move to in a successful future scenario. And it helps to differentiate between the management methods and process standards that are appropriate to the different components in evolution stages between genesis and commodity and between exploration and exploitation. The more a component is on the right-hand side, the more stable and mature the corresponding organizational structure and processes are. Components in genesis need, e.g., cross-functional teams with an explorative working style. Product organizations are often based on a stable functional architecture of the product and stable organizational interfaces. An organization for a business in commodity stage will be very focused on efficiency, quality, and costs.

The team creates an overview of the ongoing activities and places them in the Wardley Map Logic (Fig. 5) on the evolution axis. Which activities are still in the early phase of development and first require validation as to whether they will work at all and are viable as a business model? Where are there specific projects with paying customers who are even involved in development? Are there any new topics that already boast a stable product architecture and ongoing product business? What about the topics that overlap in content? Are they all in the same phase or are they at different stages in their maturity? And which long-running existing business has already reached the rear end of the product life cycle as a commodity and should therefore be checked?

The logic of the BAPO model can then be used to further discuss and decide which type of business fits into the overall strategy and which does not. The team also looks at what the common denominator is. Is the service promise aimed at customers of the same type? Are there building blocks in the product architecture that can be reduced to a common basis? Are the necessary business models and processes such as sales channels, customer service, and operations similar enough to connect them synergistically? Or do you need parallel lines to cover everything? And what are we able to, and what do we want to, afford in terms of complexity and diversity in business?

In my mind, a picture emerges of how many variants of me there should be to cover all requirements. It is therefore decided to focus only on selected customer segments and business model patterns. More exotic topics are discontinued or released for spin-offs. Perhaps there are young entrepreneurs who are keen on dedicating their lives to exciting subjects and starting a new venture for this.

The strategic questions that need to be answered are challenging enough for me. After using my right hand for exploitation for many years, my left hand is now also needed for exploration.

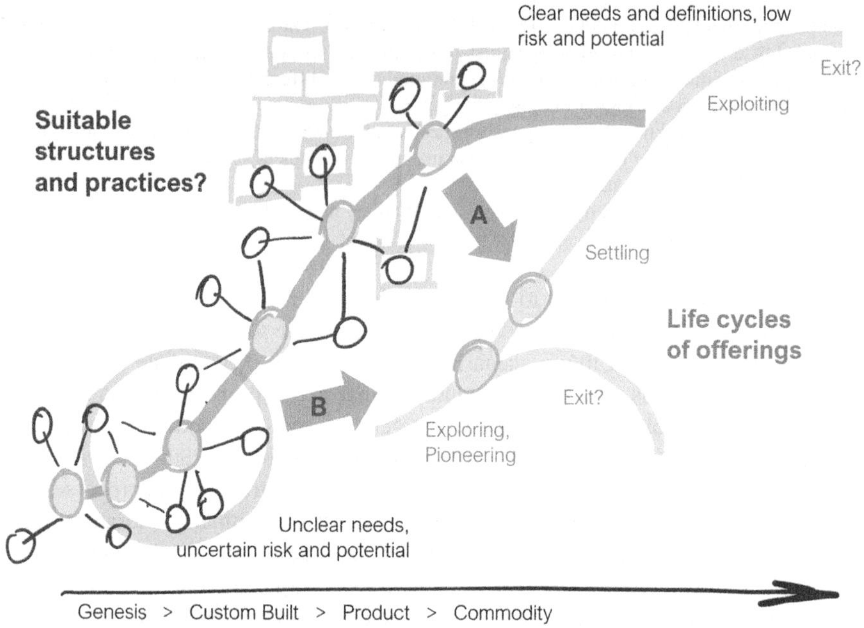

Fig. 6 The development of the offer on the timeline determines the requirements for the suitable organization. The transition to the development of new offerings means transforming the set organization (A) or commissioning an experienced development team (B) (Illustrated by the authors, used with permission. All rights reserved)

The magic word is ambidextrous. What does that mean specifically? For me and for the management?

It means letting go of the idea that there is an ideal and stable organization that fits everything equally. We are and remain a traveling organization. Activities in the early stage of maturity are in the wilderness or on trails (Genesis and Custom-Built), the middle ones on more or less paved roads, and the mature activities on railway lines. And little by little, trails become roads and roads become railway lines. And in between, grass grows over the paths again and railway lines are shut down because no train travels from A to B . . . This creates certain organizational archetypes that are designed for pioneering, settling, exploitation, or even exit (Fig. 6).

This can also be described as follows:

Use the beaten path The young topics that are in Genesis and Custom-Built mode are given a temporary organization: flat hierarchies, small teams with generalists, and temporary experts. There is neither time nor opportunity to get used to the role, its security, and its status. Why? Anything that does not evolve toward the next maturity level within a reasonable time window will be stopped. Success is not measured by sales and profit, but by the learning results that are collected during validation and in customer projects. In this environment, completely different people are suddenly more successful than in our long-established core organization. Diverse knowledge, ability to learn and adapt, and a willingness to experiment are more important than years of functional expertise. Teamplay is more important than exercising power, and networking is more important than management experience.

Paving roads Then there are the topics that are in transition to products and stable product architectures. Associated with this is also a more stable organizational structure with a more stringent division of labor. Painful change processes are pending, because wherever you must agree on common architecture, someone has to say goodbye to the work results they love. And it also means making human resources decisions and putting teams together. In spite of our appreciation of the individuals and their performance, it really makes no sense to set up functions redundantly and staff them twice. That would only reactivate Conway's law and lead to an uncoordinated product landscape.

Railway lines at the right end of the scale I am doing what I have already perfected in recent years: reducing costs, achieving efficiency gains, and continuously improving timing, products, and processes. And occasionally, one or other business model or product is "composted." After a long and productive life, it is time to make way for something new.

The development and different maturity of offers or products on the timeline determine the requirements for the suitable organization between pioneering and settling. Offering pulls organization. The diversity of the development stages of different offerings inevitably leads to a diversity or hybridity of the organization, which has to be managed with at least two hands (ambidextrously). The transition to developing a new offering can mean that an established organization is engaging with the new exploration (A) and giving up management practices that were designed for exploitation. Or for a development team that is set up for exploration, it means transferring its mode of operation to a new range of offerings (B), provided that the skills are available (Fig. 6).

What sounds so easy here is a huge change and effort for me. Mastering the work with both or even more hands with virtuosity, paying attention to all phases at the same time, and making decisions in the logic of the respective phase stress my brain and body far beyond my comfort zone. Fortunately, I had already practiced agility. The learning curve now required can only succeed because our Board is aware of the importance of this common task and has supplemented and reorganized themselves into strengths, skills, and attention. One is left-handed, the other is right-handed, and the third can juggle and manage transitions. The team's reflection on when which logic is the right one and where that changes has become a standard item on the agenda to establish ambidextrous awareness and learning loops permanently. Inevitable conflicts between the different operating modes are perceived and negotiated.

At least as important is the fact that we have taken all employees on the journey, explained the strategy to them, and "operationalized" it. They understand why different approaches are needed in parallel and are of the same value for our company, even if they follow different logics. That may even be the greatest challenge as an organization: to give all my parts equal appreciation and to cultivate connectedness between them, although in everyday life, in the subcultures, and in the management there are specific differences, even sometimes a feeling of injustice.

When I look back at my development in recent years, I am amazed at how much I have changed, even if it is not so obvious from the outside …

Regardless of whether and for how long the current business models function on the market, the meta-competence needed to recognize the maturity of the various activities and how they are successfully managed in the ambidextrous spectrum makes me more flexible, resilient, and robust to tackle disruptive developments and crises and more able to respond to new customer needs and requirements.

Speaking of crises, facing the Covid-19 pandemic, we now have a challenge on the table that concerns the Board day and night. They have no time for anything else. They even ask the strategy team to devote their resources to this urgent issue. Until a Board member intervenes: Dear colleagues, now we have exactly the situation that we have to master different operating modes in parallel, at the same time connecting them due to our limited resources. This is also connectivity!—It has now been decided to map the different modes with their short, medium and long-term backlogs on an online platform; so, they always have everything to hand and can prioritize the necessary activities. The Board is learning on the job how to use agile steering and collaboration.

Time is our friend: It gives us the chance for a different way of thinking. No more misery—now we need commitment to work hand in hand with time.

8 Final Thought

The process has progressed: The Board and the strategy team are working on the issues; and they are constructively unsettled and confused about the old and new normal. Only one thing is clear: that are on a journey together with me, their traveling organization, and that we are experiencing unforeseeable twists and turns in crisis-ridden times. But now they have models that give them the logic for the further management and development, in constant loops of reflection and renewal.

The Board has been through a fundamental learning process; new thinkers have joined the team; they have been brave enough to build a hybrid organization, the parts of which have progressed differently; and sometimes they have outsourced parts with their own organizational form to protect and secure their development. On the one hand, it means being fast, on the other, taking the time to experiment, not stopping too early, avoiding frustration and loss of credibility. The Board agreed to this path and placed the challenge on the agenda with sufficient frequency, seeking a balance between the time required, personal impatience and current urgencies.

As an organization, I like this development. I have become supple, although in the past, I have often been reduced to rigid structures. Now the end is open, there is actually no end—because then we would have got a lot wrong. We have started to change into a traveling organization, have got to know the connectivity of important resources, and have the necessary maps in front of us. And with all this dynamism, one thing keeps us on track: the sustainable purpose that gives us our direction, inspiration, and energy.

9 Lessons Learned/Takeaways

1. Developing new capabilities such as agile working or cross-functional collaboration should start in times of good economic conditions, but they are pressurized when the going gets tough.
2. Organizational development and the design of organizational structures are strongly tied to the architecture of business and products. This includes shaping the future of business by designing the organization coherently to your strategic plans. Otherwise, it is quite sure that the architecture of your products and offerings will follow your as-is organizational structure.
3. It is crucial to create a common understanding of the future of business and products first and then to discuss how processes and organizational design should address the targets. Create a continuous learning and development loop process that connects and reflects your organization to your offering.
4. Consolidating innovation activities in an early stage of product evolution is like herding cats. It is difficult to resist the temptation to merge early-stage teams or to create stable organizations before the innovative offerings have demonstrated traction via real customer projects and market pull. Closeness to customers with fast market feedback is more important at this stage than organizational synergies.
5. As the parallelism of established business and the genesis and evolution of new products will be the new normal, there are some insights: Focus on how to synchronize your organizational setup continuously with the developments in your ecosystems and offerings. Stick strictly to this pull principle and avoid any overdetermination of the organization. Get rid of the ideas "One size fits all" or "We will implement this change and then stick to it." Instead, develop a "traveling organization" mindset and culture. Add an expiry date to your org charts.
6. Known patterns of evolution can be used to predict the future and to manage ambidexterity. Tools like Simon Wardley's value chain mapping help to understand where and when to stick to the well-known management method of "exploitation" and when to start with "exploration mode" and the corresponding tools and methods. Most tricky seems to be the transition in between.
7. We have to learn how to establish and maintain a culture where the coexistence of the new and the established is acknowledged, and both sides, and the scale in between, are valued equally but not made equal. A diverse skill set and mindset is needed to handle the differences. Each person has their "zone of best fit and performance." It is helpful to foster collaboration and connectivity not only on a working level but also in executive management.
8. Paths arise when walking: If we stay in motion, the paths our organization follows will evolve over time.

9. And finally: Share these ideas with your people. They will understand and welcome you.

References

Bosch, J., & Bosch-Sijtsema, P. (2014). ESAO: *A holistic ecosystem-driven analysis model.* In C. Lassenius & K. Smolander (Eds.), ICSOB 2014, lecture notes in business information processing (p. 182).

Conway, M. E. (1968). *How do committees invent?* In F. D. Thompson Publications, Inc. (Hg.): Datamation. Band 14, Nr. 5, 4/1968.

Oestereich, B., & Schröder, C. (2017). *Das kollegial geführte Unternehmen*. München: Vahlen.

Van der Linden, F., Bosch, J., Kamsties, E., Känsälä, K., & Obbink, H. (2004). *Software product family evaluation.* In R. L. Nord (Ed.), Software product lines. SPLC 2004. Lecture notes in computer science (Vol. 3154). Berlin: Springer.

Wardley, S. (2016). *Finding a path*. Chapter 2 of https://medium.com/wardleymaps/

Wollmann, P., Kühn, F., & Kempf, M. (Eds.). (2020). *Three pillars of organization and leadership in disruptive times – Navigating your company successfully through the 21st century business world.* Cham: Springer Nature.

Lilian Matischok is a mechanical engineer by university degree and a systemic thinker and developer by vocation. Her favorite professional "job to be done" is connecting the dots of business strategy, product architecture, and organizational development to holistic transformational programs. She worked over 20 years as a manager, engineer, and internal consultant at Robert Bosch GmbH in the automotive and in the industrial technology business area. Since 2020, she supports as a freelancing consultant manufacturing companies in transforming from a brick and mortar business with tangible products toward digital and service business models and in collaborating successfully in platform-based ecosystems.

Frank Kühn has been supporting companies and institutions for many years in the areas of organization and leadership, change, and project management. He brings his experience to developments such as the Three-Pillar Model and systemic setting checks. Frank has a doctorate in work science. After leading positions in research and industry, he was a partner at HLP in Frankfurt and the ICG Integrated Consulting Group in Berlin and Graz. Today, he is an independent consultant, business partner of ICG, and associated with other project partners and think tanks. He has published numerous articles in management journals and books.

Transformation in the Field of Product Development: A Five-Day Micro-Project

Frank Kühn and Michael Kempf

Abstract

The product development process of a company working in the automotive industry is to be reinvented. The Three-Pillar Model provides the key questions: the sustainable purpose that is crucial for aligning and energizing the company and its project, the connectivity of key actors and capabilities for a true co-creation, and building a flexible process to support the traveling organization. The micro-project format supports the structural and cultural shift: cooperative, creative, fast, and result oriented.

1 Situation

The company is a global player and leading manufacturer of automotive components. A critical review of the success factor "time-to-market" has shown significant competitive disadvantages. The development of e-mobility and hydrogen technology is having a massive impact on production processes in the automotive sector, which is why rapid product development is strategically important. Thus, the management team initiated the redesign of the "product development process" toward more comprehensive "solution development activity" which should include not only the process but also leadership principles, roles and capacities, and collective tools and practices.

F. Kühn (✉)
Dortmund, Germany
e-mail: fk@kuehn-cp.com

M. Kempf
Bad Honnef am Rhein, Germany
e-mail: michael@kempf-cp.com

P. Wollmann et al. (eds.), *Organization and Leadership in Disruptive Times*, Future of Business and Finance, https://doi.org/10.1007/978-3-030-63034-8_22

The first diagnosis using the Three-Pillar Model (Wollmann et al. 2020) resulted in the following findings:

- Sustainable Purpose: Being a leading company can not only refer to the quality of the technical product but must also include fast and reliable delivery, appropriate service, and standing also for the company's contribution to societal and ecological challenges. All of this means creating comprehensive solutions, as formulated in our case by the management team.
- Traveling Organization: This means understanding the organization as no longer being a stable constellation. When the discussion about resilience intensified during the financial crisis, there were warnings that crisis-proof and flexible organizations need redundant resources.
- Connected Resources: This is one of the biggest challenges—to overcome the vertical and horizontal hurdles and silos in organizations. Several "missing links" were found in our case: the knowledge, capabilities, and tools of the diverse functions were not interconnected. The stakeholders were not yet reliably collaborative with one another.

To tackle these issues, we apply the approach of "activities" (Türke 2008). It is based upon the understanding that the purpose of any organization is the collaboration of people in entrepreneurial activities that are crucial to deliver the solutions that companies want to contribute to the world. Thus, each activity "pulls" the people needed to contribute their experience, skills, and creativity to the activity. Together, they define efficient processes, effective roles, and collective practices to manage the activity (Fig. 1). There is multiple connectivity: the activities must be connected to make up the traveling organization, and most people will connect a variety of roles in themselves. Finally, the activities may pull supportive structures if necessary.

To date, this activity has been limited to a sequential procedure with changing responsibilities; some key players were involved late and then questioned the results developed so far. Even the project managers changed from project phase to project phase; especially the handover from "Project Manager Development" to "Project Manager Production" had proven difficult. In the course of the process, additional functions were included, such as purchasing, who checked the availability of raw materials and supplier parts relatively late, sorted the possible suppliers, and—along with other functions—had become one of the bottlenecks. Finally, the product was delivered after 2–3 long years, and the initial business case could not stand the subsequent review or had to be rewritten with respect to the latest developments in the market and customer needs.

The challenge was now how to better connect all the necessary resources from product management, sales, development, supply chain, production, controlling, and purchasing in an activity that is more than a process in the sense of a workflow or a value chain, namely, part of an organizational system? How should collaborative co-development be started?

In the past, efforts to renew the process had failed due to missing priority, but this time, the management team was consistent. They reminded everyone of the

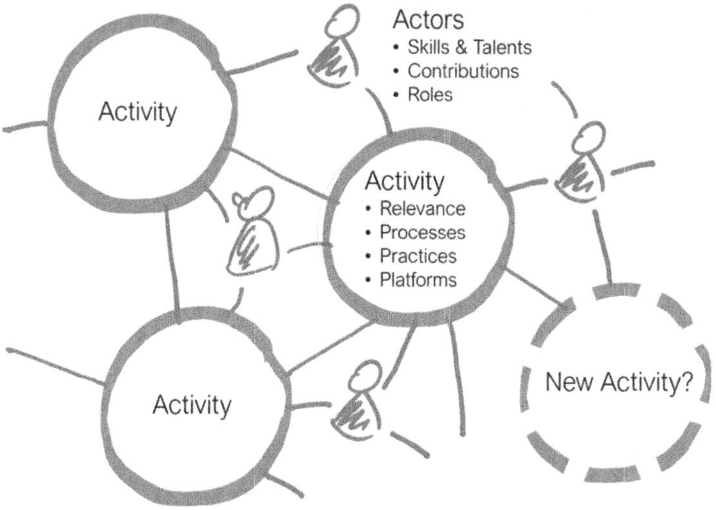

Fig. 1 Activity-based organization emerging from market dynamics and entrepreneurial needs instead of hierarchical structuring (Illustrated by the authors, used with permission. All rights reserved)

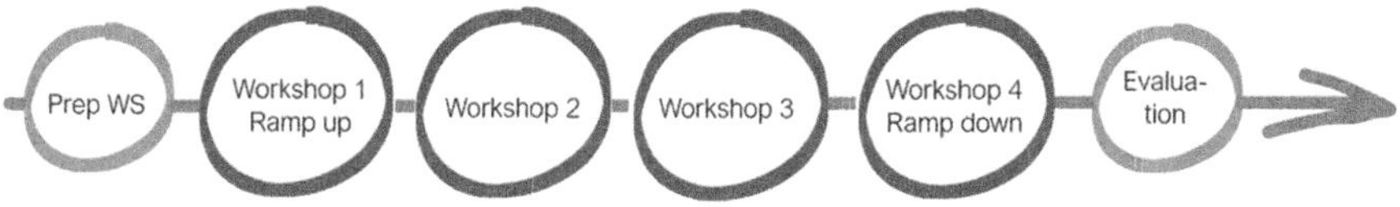

Fig. 2 The core elements of a micro-project. In its "pure mode," everything is done within the workshops: working, decision-making, starting action, and implementation. The "extended mode" may allow additional conference calls, face-to-face talks, or decision-making meetings (Illustrated by the authors, used with permission. All rights reserved)

corporate purpose, i.e., to serve their customers with co-created, innovative solutions; they asked their experts to join the collaborative development from the beginning, to ensure quality and save time and money; they underlined the relevance for the corporate journey. And they chose the micro-project method (Kühn and Kempf 2014; Fig. 2) for practicing collaboration, co-creativity, and speed.

2 Challenge

As one consequence of the current sequential approach, the communication effort had been minimized, which seemed to accommodate the time pressure of everyone involved; but at the same time, the potential for conflicts had been maximized due to a lack of early coordination. This is a classic situation in the world of organization, which has established itself in corporate culture. The proposal to exchange know-how and experience about the process right at the beginning—involving the functions mentioned above—met with a lack of understanding. How expensive would that be? How should we organize a joint appointment? "All of us have a lot of other things to do." Previous efforts to renew the process had already stalled several times under these conditions. After initial euphoria, participation had quickly waned.

The following questions can create shared insights at this point: Did the last reorganization of product development bring about lasting improvement? What expectations were thwarted? How do you rate the efficiency of the newly organized process (0, excellent; 10, bad)? What would be necessary to get a better rating? What is preventing your team from achieving top performance? Which specific behaviors have become established (collectively called "culture") that make success difficult?

After all, this fundamental problem was not only understood but came with a clear statement from the top management and an equally clear setting of priorities: an agreement was reached that:

(a) The sequential product-oriented process had to change fundamentally toward a more collaborative solution-oriented activity
(b) The project should already practice the new quality of collaboration in the understanding of an "organizational prototype"

3 Solution

Three approaches were combined: "Three-Pillar Model" for focusing on three essential levers, "activity-based organization" as an approach for highly effective organizational design, and agile "micro-project working" as a format for rapid implementation, which also supports the two models mentioned above.

Firstly, the approach of "activity-centered organization" proved useful: the view was expanded and focused on the entrepreneurial "activity" of product development or rather solution development. According to the holistic definition of an "activity" according to Türke (2008), this included all critical aspects; this meant not only checking and updating the process but also reviewing and developing principles, roles, skills, collaborative culture, collective practices, and tools in product development.

This holistic view could be interlinked with the Three-Pillar Model: the development of the activity had to follow a "Sustainable Purpose" aiming at customer needs and market opportunities. This proved to be a successful way to align the development with inspiration and effectiveness. The "Connected Resources" approach included the stakeholders with their skills and, as already mentioned, processes, roles, principles, and tools. The claim "Traveling Organization" was based on the desired acceleration and a more efficient way of working; only in this way could the company become more agile and expand its fitness for the future.

The "micro-project" method was chosen to tackle the challenge. This method accepts tight time budgets, which means time is set as the priority. Time over

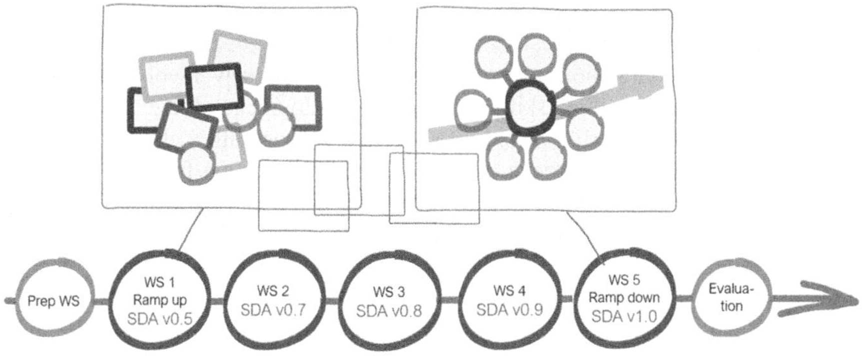

Fig. 3 Micro-project application to the solution development activity. In this case, five workshops were planned. Workshop 1 was to deliver a first draft of the new "solution development activity" (SDA) (version 0.5). This early version was further developed toward version 1.0 finalized in workshop 5 (Illustrated by the authors, used with permission. All rights reserved)

content—what can we do in the given time? It forces creative focus and workshops that include everything that needs to be done: reflection, elaboration, decision, and implementation. This can only happen quickly and together—which immediately started the journey to becoming a more agile company.

The project started with a strategic mini-workshop in which the priority of the activity "solution development" and its processing was determined and the procedure was planned. As a prerequisite, the active participation of all relevant functions and actors was agreed. In view of the tight schedule, five 1-day time-box workshops were scheduled at monthly intervals, in which the activity was to be processed holistically, co-creatively, and iteratively from the start. Everything was connected immediately, from the first time-box. It was further agreed that the goal of time-box 1 was version v0.5 of the new activity to be designed, the goal of time-box 2 was version v0.7, etc. Between the time-boxes, the participants had to do "homework" as needed. After 5 months, a collaborative activity concept v1.0 should be finalized (Fig. 3).

The following example from the case shows how different competencies and strategic aspects and responsibilities (as "Connected Resources") were interlinked from the start. In the strategic mini-workshop, a common understanding and statement was created in the management team, which was fundamental as the basis for the further proceedings: "(1) The purpose of organization is to enable people to collaborate in entrepreneurial activities which determine the corporate journey. For every activity, it is important to secure and blend the required contributions and skills in effective roles and collective practices. The collective solutions create the basis for a highly effective and flexible organization. (2) In reflecting on our weaknesses, barriers, and bottlenecks, we see the relevance of the Three-Pillar Model for the future viability of our company: a strong purpose, the connection of our resources, and the mobility of our organization. (3) Time is not—as we like to say—our enemy, but our friend and partner, because it forces us to new ways of working, which we want to practice here in the form of a micro-project."

4 Implementation

The setting of the time-boxes was designed to immediately involve the people expected to contribute their skills for the co-development of the activity. The workshop room was clearly divided into two halves: one with a circle of chairs, a projector, and a screen to retrieve any background information from the corporate intranet and to share it in the group and the other half as a free area with free pin boards and flipcharts. This kind of joint development was new to some of those involved but was promoted by the facilitator and quickly accepted by the participants. Over time, this personal responsibility of those involved became established and was also focused on by the participants.

The development began with an initial, complete mapping of the process with cards on six pin boards, which stood for the process phases, from "ideation" to scale-up to "large-scale production." From their point of view, the participants had to formulate, write down, and explain value-adding process steps, relevant outcomes, and decisions to be made in the process. In addition, the participants were asked to mentally detach themselves from their organizational function (e.g., "Controlling") and, instead, to take a holistic view of the solution and, for this reason, to formulate their items in an object-oriented way (e.g., "Business Case" to be delivered and monitored).

When developing the future process, it was also the facilitator's job to be aware of faint hints and signals, which are often omitted in subordinate clauses, but which may provide clues for the roles, principles, and collective practices to be clarified. ("We need training for this first," "Can't you involve colleagues from other teams if necessary?", "It's not that easy for us . . .," "But it would be an excellent idea for future collective practice?", etc.). This resulted in "loops of dialogues" about collective practices, which could also lead back to the process design having to be checked and readjusted again. From time to time, the crucial question was: "What is still missing to ensure that the solution development works perfectly in the future?" This has repeatedly resulted in relevant aspects being considered in the process and in role definitions, principles, structural requirements, or quick coordination requirements.

With the growing attention of the participants for all aspects of the activity "solution development," a purpose-oriented, holistic, and increasingly sorted and interconnected picture emerged that would not have been possible without the connection of experiences and ideas in the room.

At the end of the first workshop, we had achieved a so-called initial filling, i.e., version 0.5. The homework was to reflect on the results and review them with other colleagues and, if necessary, make suggestions for additions.

In the further time-box workshops, the way of documentation gradually developed. The initial results were successively transferred early to the collaboration and presentation tools already used in the company, where they were further specified. The exchange of ideas and experience was increasingly captured and recorded on large projection screens.

5 Results

The following insights were formulated in the evaluation workshop:

The challenge (the need for orientation via an entrepreneurial purpose and for the flexibility of a future-proof organization) was basically clear to everyone involved, but so far there has been no consistent implementation. Explicit support from the top management was crucial for this success.

For the first time, there has been an activity that was relevant to, and accepted by, all concerned. From now on, it should be reviewed regularly.

The view on all the involved resources has, for the first time, led to a holistic view with a shared understanding of their interconnectedness. The crucial factor here was the joint effort of joint collection and sorting; it held the activity together.

In the future, there will be an end-to-end project manager who will take responsibility for leading the solution development process and the team. Everyone in the team is co-responsible for the success, points out (weak) signals for risks and deviations, and actively participates in problem-solving.

The priority of each solution development and the time required by the stakeholders have been clarified with the top management. Priority and progress have become transparent in a new project portfolio management. The top management will receive a regular report.

In regular, stringently moderated, 1-hour meetings every 2–4 weeks, the stakeholders will agree on progress and need for action. Deputies are only accepted if they are "up to date" regarding technical and decision-making competence.

The future business case will be more comprehensive and regularly checked during solution development. Everyone must contribute. This can be, for example, information from sales about declarations of intent from customers or information from purchasing on procurement risks due to the political situation in the countries of origin.

A peer feedback practice on personal behavior in the activity was agreed between the participants. Everyone will invite two other people to give personal feedback once a quarter.

After the experiences in this project, new workspaces were provided for more effective exchange and co-creative design. The advantage was immediately apparent: results are now being processed more quickly, and the more effective involvement of the various functions leads to greater acceptance. Finally, the provision of the rooms was perceived as an explicit commitment by the management team to the new way of working.

Status: The solution development time is expected to be halved and the costs to be significantly reduced through early coordination and the avoidance of wasted work. The effectiveness of the team will be monitored and further optimized if necessary.

6 Transfer

With the fifth time-box workshop, the new "Solution Development" activity was finalized and documented in the systems. From the start of the micro-project, the wider communication (beyond the circle of participants) had been agreed in every time-box and carried out between the time-boxes.

Two further activities, including a deepening of the "Ideation" activity, are pending. Some of the participants involved so far are also needed here; they have agreed on the same procedure and invited other colleagues whose skills and contributions are needed.

In the meantime, the procedure has developed as "good practice" in the company. Some people have already taken on their role in various activities and network with each other across different activities.

The extent to which this networking of activities and roles can be a future organizational model is currently being discussed. The core question is how acceptance and effectiveness can develop in addition to the existing hierarchical pyramid, whether it can work as an isolated way of working in the technical area, or whether there must be a commitment by the top management for such a hybrid organizational development.

7 Evaluation and Takeaways

With the procedure presented in this article, a quick focus on the challenge was achieved, combined with the activation of the responsible players. With the Three-Pillar Model and the activity-based organization approach, the project was designed to combine all resources for common problem-solving from the start.

The format of the micro-project allowed for a very quick start, requiring the immediate connectivity of all functions and resources involved—i.e., it was also a pilot and prototype for the future type and quality of the collaboration.

The holistic approach was helpful from the start, which also prevented fragmentary solutions. All facets of the subject were immediately discussed and developed. This ensured connectivity of all problem dimensions across all workshops from the start.

The "Three Pillars" have proven to be the success factors of the development: the "Sustainable Purpose," a reliable and future-oriented partner of the automotive industry also beyond the combustion engine, aware of its ecological responsibility; the "Connectivity" in the interlinkage of strategy, activity, skills, prioritization, roles, and tools; and the "Traveling Organization" in the ongoing discussion of the extent to which the new organizational experience around activities and emerging roles and networks should be the primary direction for working procedures and organizational transformation as a whole.

There is a strategic process underlying the case presented above.

1. Identification of the entrepreneurial activities that need redesigning and updating
2. Listing and ranking them in a strategic backlog, which ones must be solved first, second, etc.
3. Applying the corporate purpose for justifying the ranking and creating a deeper commitment
4. Transferring the priorities into the corporate project portfolio and roadmap
5. Creating and sharing a holistic view and understanding of the focused activity, which includes:
   (a) Involved and affected processes and their connectivity
   (b) Capabilities and contributions needed
   (c) Key players and functions to be involved
   (d) Their roles and responsibilities to be defined regarding the activity
   (e) Collective practices and tools to be applied
6. Using customer-centered "solution" thinking (instead of self-centered "product" thinking)
7. End-to-end management of the activity, i.e., consistently following the purpose and connecting the resources during the joint journey
8. Demanding all participants' co-responsibility for the activity's success
9. Providing the team with the workspace, tools, etc. that they need for their (co)working

References

Kühn, F., & Kempf, M. (2014). *Time flies. Integrate timelines with commitment and results.* In: ICG change, Graz 3/2014.

Salovaara, P. (2015). *Leadership in spaces and places.* Cheltenham: Elgar Publishing.

Türke, R. E. (2008). *Governance – Systemic foundation and framework.* Heidelberg: Physica/Springer.

Wollmann, P., Kühn, F., & Kempf, M. (Eds.). (2020). *Three pillars of organization and leadership in disruptive times – Navigating your company successfully through the 21st century business world.* Cham: Springer Nature.

Frank Kühn has been supporting companies and institutions for many years in the areas of organization and leadership, change, and project management. He brings his experience to developments such as the Three-Pillar Model and systemic setting checks. Frank has a doctorate in work science. After leading positions in research and industry, he was a partner at HLP in Frankfurt and the ICG Integrated Consulting Group in Berlin and Graz. Today, he is an independent consultant, business partner of ICG, and associated with other project partners and think tanks. He has published numerous articles in management journals and books.

Michael Kempf has been an experienced Management Consultant for over 20 years. The driving force of his professional activities is his strong ambition to design processes and organizations in a sustainable manner. He relishes identifying key challenges, diagnosing complex relationships, and assisting in shaping the future. Gaining experience and learning something new are indispensable parts of his life, which is why he likes to seize new chances. He began his career as a carpenter before studying social work, education, and business administration. His career has spanned various jobs in social work, 10 years as a manager (HR and logistics) in industrial and retail companies and, since 1998, in advising people, leadership teams, as well as working teams and organizations that are all very different. Michael has co-authored numerous publications in the field of leadership and organizational development.

Emergent Change: Embracing Complexity as a Key Challenge in a Travelling Organization

Nicole Hoenig de Locarnini and Frank Kühn

Abstract

The article provides a perspective on how to navigate an organization with a complexity mindset through emergent changes and even crises adopting the Three-Pillar Model. The authors show approaches, practices, and tools on how to deal with "emergent elements" within an organization and how these will be ideally addressed in a "new" organizational setting that is characterized by transparency and connectivity and guided by a clear purpose since the traditional elements of an organization no longer provide the previous stable structures and mechanistic problem-solving procedures.

The universe is not made up of atoms; it's made up of tiny stories. (Joseph Gordon-Levitt)

1 Framing Today's Realities for Organizations in a Complex World: Why Do We Need New "Mindsets and Tools?"

How can organizations free up business-as-usual ("BAU") time to focus on strategically relevant projects and organization development processes which ensure a thriving organization and not just a surviving one? These new projects, processes, and practices are characterized by agile ways of working, cross-functional collaboration and can be used as "test balloons" to co-create new thinking and to identify organizational impediments which are based on past

N. Hoenig de Locarnini (✉)
Zürich, Switzerland
e-mail: nlhoenig@gmail.com

F. Kühn
Dortmund, Germany
e-mail: fk@kuehn-cp.com

P. Wollmann et al. (eds.), *Organization and Leadership in Disruptive Times*, Future of Business and Finance, https://doi.org/10.1007/978-3-030-63034-8_23

mechanistic views (bureaucracy, slow decision-making, power games, lack of a holistic picture, lack of common purpose, siloed thinking) and help to produce both incremental change and even larger transformation throughout the organization. In this way, organizational thinking connects to individual and societal thinking and acting, for solving complex issues that unfold new experiences and resist well-planned, linear (cause-and-effect) approaches. At present, the Covid-19 pandemic is increasing complexity and bringing a new work mode (in addition to the BAU mode and the development mode) with new schedules and new insights into opportunities, limits, overcoming structural and cultural barriers, and, at the same time, a wide range of behaviors between political and organizational cooperation.

The topic of this article closely relates to the Three-Pillar Model (Wollmann et al. 2020):

- The "sustainable purpose," which formulates the company's raison d'être and its contribution to the world, must provide guidance and inspiration, which is all the more crucial when we have to navigate our organization through the complex and volatile requirements and conditions of the markets, our ecosystem, and even crisis-ridden times.
- The "travelling organization"—which no longer subscribes to the illusion of stability—has to master complexity and volatility via agile working methods, incremental changes, and experiments if tasks can no longer be planned linearly. This requires a high level of awareness and a dynamic "map" of the issues to be solved, as well as the appropriate mindsets and methodologies to tackle them.
- "Connecting resources" in this period means cross-functional collaboration, overcoming obstacles and barriers in individual and team behavior, and interlinking strategies with processes and agile practices as well as effective tools. Finally, the connectedness of the resources creates a real boost in their joint productivity.

When we look at mature organizations today, many of them will not have much longer to live—the average age of an S&P 500 company is under 20 years today down from 60 years in the 1950s (Corporate longevity report, Credit Suisse 2017). The disruptive force of technology is killing off older companies earlier and at a much faster rate than decades ago, squeezing employees, investors, and other stakeholders.

Everything is speeding up—innovation cycles are increasingly accelerating because costs and impediments to experimentation are falling continually as technology is changing. As a result, product and company life cycles are shrinking. We can argue that disruption is nothing new but that the speed, complexity, and global nature of it—whether we speak about innovation or crisis—are something we have not experienced before and are not prepared for in terms of structures and methodology. All sectors are currently being impacted by multiple disruptive forces simultaneously.

"Understanding Complexity"

The leadership team discussed how to make a difference in their future-oriented organizational journey. They explicitly decided to include all strategic initiatives, independent of their categorization to date (as strategic or innovation project, etc.). Thus, they set up a new kind of entrepreneurial portfolio (Fig.1), which forced them

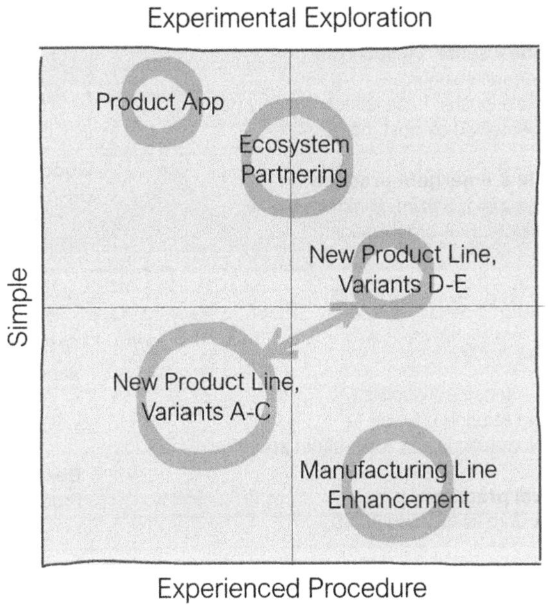

Fig. 1 Re-understanding the landscape of current and planned initiatives in terms of complexity and adequate practices and procedures (Illustrated by the authors, used with permission. All rights reserved)

to discuss the complexity of their issues and where to apply known procedures or where new thinking and collective practices were required to break new ground.

It became apparent that their understanding of complexity was different. Therefore, they started their work on a common understanding and terminology using the so-called Cynefin model (Fig.2). Then they tried the approaches together with their facilitator, walked through their various initiatives, and simulated the approaches.

What we observe in most sectors is that the classical 10-year, 5-year, and 3-year strategy planning horizon is dead. It is important to have a long-term view about how the world is changing if an organization wants to place some "big bets"—yet there is no certainty on getting this right. If an organization is small, nimble, and more agile, it can change faster—which is a major competitive advantage in today's world. Larger organizations which are like supertankers need to get these bets right with greater certainty as it matters disproportionally more because they cannot change course and align their resources fast enough. Getting these big bets right is often no longer the job of one person making decisions and dictating them to the organization as is (still) the case in more traditional, hierarchical organizations.

Today's most successful organizations crowdsource ideas—not to seek consensus but rather to collect multiple data points and views. This is guided by a joint purpose and a common understanding. Conversely, they create transparency and enable their experts on site to make decisions faster than would be possible along the hierarchical lines, based upon the common understanding and inspiration given by the joint purpose.

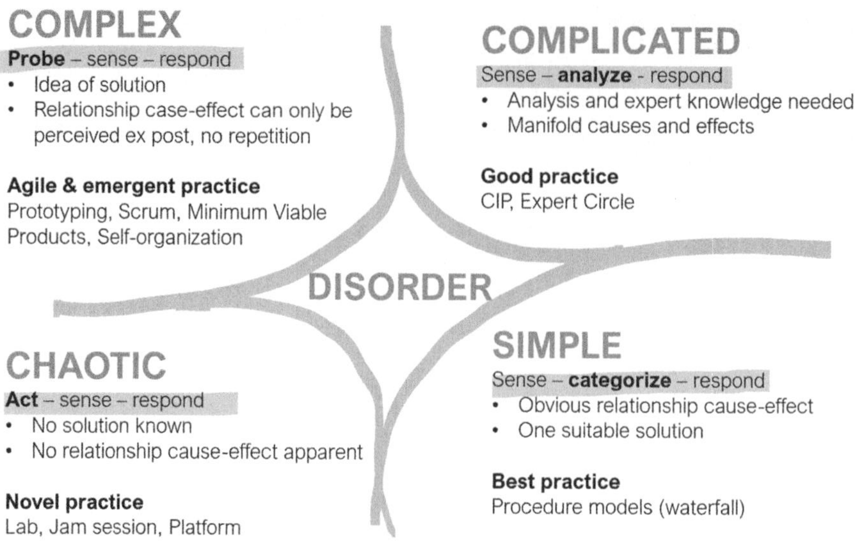

Fig. 2 The Cynefin model displays different issues and recommendations, proposing experimental procedures for complex challenges (Snowdon and Boone 2007) (Illustrated by the authors, used with permission. All rights reserved)

Change of paradigm

"From sophisticated separation to lively interconnectivity"—On the one hand, there are enthusiastic discussions about the Internet of Things (IoT) where everything is connected and transparent and each part can act autonomously. On the other hand, many companies are not able to co-create an organizational awareness that goes hand in hand with this technological mindset, i.e., connecting their resources and providing the transparency, autonomy, and space for individuals and teams that bring in their creativity, experience, and engagement. Instead, they are used to separating whatever they can separate into vertical and horizontal silos. To become faster in acting and decision-making, the cultural and structural transformation is fundamental, changing managers' power play and silo-mindset into enabling, empowering, and encouraging the experts' autonomy.

"Joint Strategizing"

The CEO of the engineering company defined a new strategy, supported by a consultant team. Then, the consultants advised him to communicate the strategy in the company. He used the next leadership meeting (with about 50 managers) and gave an impressive presentation, and the participants applauded. Some days later, he was invited to an internal "marketplace" event where the latest management concepts should be shared; he was offered the opportunity and a "stand" (arranged as a discussion corner) to consider the strategy with the same participants. He presented his ideas once again, and the participants admitted that they didn't understand him at all and, furthermore, would like to contribute their own ideas. After overcoming the CEO's disappointment, they decided to implement a joint strategy process. The evaluation of the marketplace led to some lessons learned: a continuous common process is more important for a travelling organization than any perfected strategic top-down statement. The key is to share and connect the ways of complex thinking between the individuals; from an individual view, each one exercised complex thinking in their individual way, struggled with the need to make it understandable, retired to the silo, and was frustrated due to the waste of their talents and ideas. This all needs more time, space, and mutual openness. Their latest activity was to design a process with practices that combined such requirements with speed and effectiveness—Epilogue: In the impending crisis, they experienced enormous benefit from their well-exercised teamwork and started a triple process: first, to manage the urgent crisis-ridden activities; second, to maintain the strategic perspective, which included continuous evaluation for future business models, strategies, and processes; and third, to prepare the transition from crisis mode to future mode.

Change of paradigm
"From hidden strategy to joint momentum"—For many companies, it has even seemed challenging to implement a rolling strategy process; in addition, they were told to share the strategy with their people in order to coordinate the shared endeavor. Now, they have to learn how to open up their strategies and organization to the ecosystem to co-create true joint momentum beyond their structural silos and boundaries. This will lead to more effective strategies and a higher commitment in the ecosystem.

"Organizational Openness for Shared Solutions"

An automotive supplier was confronted with their customers' demand for predictive maintenance solutions. In their first management workshop, they discussed questions such as how to understand the challenge, how to create the engineering knowledge in the company, how to develop a well-designed system, and how to turn it into a competitive advantage? The facilitator asked them to reflect on their questions, and they saw that they had considered and formulated the issue from an internal view; this would not suit the idea of a cross-company integrated 4.0 system. That is why they also discussed it with their customers, and their demand was different (what they could have expected): how should they connect the resources across the suppliers and further external business partners in terms of knowledge, creativity, and technologies in order to co-create an interlinked system (and not to follow separate approaches)? The customers were pretty clear: they defined the openness and connectivity of their providers as preconditions to take part in a shared process and true partnership—or to leave it.

In order to be able to deal with this complexity, we need to create a new environment that nurtures the ability to innovate—trusting empowered networks of small teams who are connected through a joint purpose and relevant tools to solve an organization's challenges in a cross-functional interdisciplinary way. In order to develop this, we need new "tools," "concepts," and "mindsets" as well as "leadershifts" (Maxwell 2019) in order to not only survive but to thrive—as a travelling organizational with the mindset and the certainty that anything can be managed that may come their way through connected resources and a holistic transparent perspective on the organization's realities. The classic management theory worked for organizations in times of stability and predictability; when faced with more innovative tasks, they set up projects and closed them after delivery.

But in today's uncertain, ever-changing, and even crisis-ridden world, it seems that leadership counts more than management. The three most desirable attributes for future leaders are "the ability to motivate staff, the ability to work well across cultures," and "the ability to facilitate change." These attributes depend on another vital trait: adaptability, which is "the ability to change (or to be changed) to fit new circumstances. . . . Good leaders adapt. They shift. They don't remain static because they know the world around them does not remain static" (Maxwell 2019). This applies to leaders who are appointed to a leadership function or position, but it also applies to everyone who assumes leadership as a role that arises from a situation or a current need (Oestereich and Schröder 2017). This situation may be a conflict in a meeting that needs to be solved, or a crisis in which people take leadership based on their medical expertise or their empathy, which makes them start civil initiatives.

The "leadershift" messages (Maxwell 2019)

The most critical change-management tactics in today's world are "leadershifts"—dynamic directional changes that have a positive impact on your organization and employees. To be an effective leader, individuals must deliberately undergo "leadershifts" in several ways, always with an emphasis on focus, continuous personal development, an abundance mindset (Covey 2004), personal impact, and passion. The "leadershifts" identified by Maxwell include moving from "positional authority to moral authority," from "directing to connecting" and focusing on "ladder-building" for others instead of "ladder-climbing" for oneself.

"You cannot be the same, think the same, and act the same if you hope to be successful in a world that does not remain the same."

"Leadershift!"

In the team's latest review meeting, they faced a lot of new tasks to handle on their journey. To date, all the coordination work had been done by the team leader. Now, they started to distribute more and more leadership tasks among the team members. They defined tasks such as performance review, technical coaching, or meeting management and delegated the lead of each task to pairs of team members. In this way, they reduced the individual uncertainty of how to deal with this new kind of responsibility. Finally, they created a true shift in the room; in the checkout, they appreciated this substantial development as inspiring, animating, and fresh thinking.

In the face of increasing global changes and crises, they started to use their experience to assume responsibility and set up a management marketplace. It consists of three physical or digital pinboards—for short-, medium-, and long-term view—each with an evaluation and a backlog area. They use this transparency to keep an eye on all views and to distribute the tasks and responsibilities with a comprehensive and contextual understanding of the overall complexity.

Latest thinking provides us with effective approaches (e.g., Oestereich and Schröder 2017; Huschka 2020; Türke 2008) that make a significant difference, disrupting classical ways of leadership and management:

- *Managing ambidexterity has become fundamental and must be developed* (which means much more than just using two hands)—how to deal with the parallelism and tension between long- and short-term focus, solid and quick decision-making, experienced and new workforce generation, and "fail fast and learn fast" with long-term value creation and purpose?
- *Organizational consciousness is described in various stages of development and growth*—from survival characterized by the pursuit of profit and shareholder value toward transformation and travelling organization which focuses on adaptability and continuous learning resulting in the most conscious state of a service organization working and connecting its resources with other organizations. The stakeholders of the organization and its ecosystem pursue societal objectives that enhance the sustainability of humanity and the planet while deepening the level of internal connectivity inside the organization by fostering compassion, humility, and forgiveness.
- *Leadership as an adaptable term, distributable task, and joint process*—instead of hierarchical position (e.g., Huschka 2020). The development of leadership ("leadershifts") with new skills is necessary to deal with these changes. This requires future-oriented patience beyond the hustle and bustle of everyday life.
- *Strategic reflections and decisions must be made and committed throughout the company*—how can organizations enable new elements to "emerge," and how can they ensure that these "projects 4.0" can be brought to life without being killed by the traditional organization?
- *Transparent, issue-centered decision-making practices*—instead of power play. Decisions have to be made where the relevant information and true know-how are located. This practice needs trust and transparency and, based on these preliminaries, creates better decision quality and high speed.
- *Activity-based organization*—instead of top-down structures. The question of how to embrace complexity thinking in day-to-day business or project situations is too "small." The challenge is to be aware of and avoid oversimplification as a well-exercised reaction to complex issues. Working on concrete entrepreneurial activities with a need for development leads to practical solutions instead of discussing highly sophisticated categorization in terms of small or big project, process, or function.
- *Multiple, networked backlogs and sprints*—instead of inflexible roadmaps. Some key principles of Scrum (Schwaber and Sutherland 2017) can be transferred to the organization as a whole. For example, development processes cannot be predicted any longer; their speed and effectiveness depend on transparency, review, and adjustment and are driven by qualified, interdisciplinary development teams who know best how to organize themselves and achieve good results. The coordination needs high frequency and disciplined communication. What is delivered is

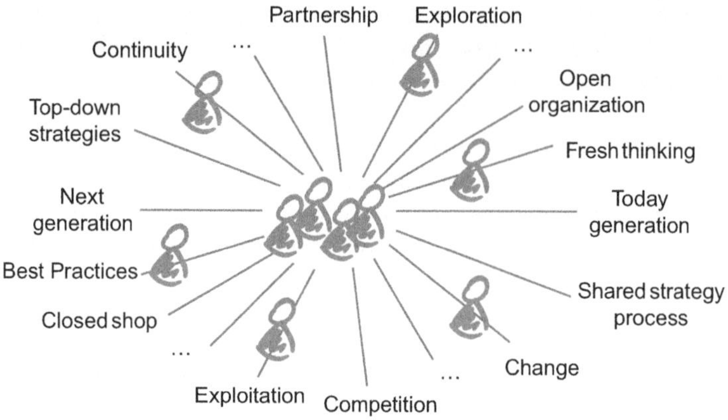

Fig. 3 The multi-view exercise: the participants collect the polarities, dissonances, and varieties of beliefs and views they experience in their organizational practice and future-oriented discussions. Then they approach a specific high-priority question, e.g., how to achieve a new product quality. Pairs discuss the question from different views (as displayed) and bring their results back to the plenary session in order to reach a joint result. If there are dissonances left, the procedure is repeated (Illustrated by the authors, used with permission. All rights reserved)

business functionality—no ppt presentations—at intervals of 1–4 weeks, which also means that the risk of misunderstanding and failures is significantly reduced.

Regarding the first of the above statements: is it about ambidexterity or multidexterity? We have seen it in the following case.

"Exercising Multidexterity"

*The leadership team started a strategic program on how to shift the organization in order to face the VUCA business. One remarkable discussion was about ambidexterity and the inherent risk of black-and-white thinking. They discussed the value of differences and polarities—or even more precisely: the variety between them, not understood as a difficulty but as an opportunity to change and vary their professional view on entrepreneurial issues. They used two exercises: (1) the multi-view exercise (Fig.3), which helps peers mutually understand different beliefs and perspectives, connect their ways of thinking, and co-create an outcome of this variety (see also the approaches ofDe Bono (*1986*)or the Walt Disney tool (Martin et al.*2000*)), and (2) the complexity-travelling exercise which helps the participants to "travel" together into the different worlds of simplicity, complicatedness, complexity, and chaos and to build efficient ways to powerful solutions (see Fig.2).*

Travelling through the four worlds as displayed in Fig.4, the participants arrived at a variety of results. They concentrated their creativity and discussion on the urgent question of how to get into good connectivity and interaction with the partners in their ecosystem (which was new to them due to the multitude of stakeholders including providers, customers, professional associations, antitrust authorities, etc.). The "simple" approach was to take the well-exercised way and

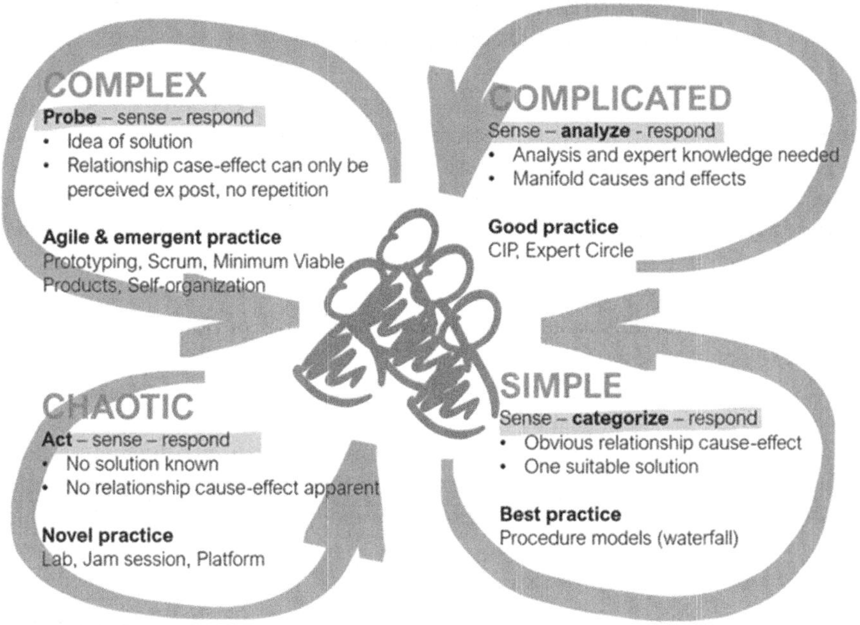

Fig. 4 The complexity-travelling exercise: the participants go on a journey through the worlds of simplicity, complicatedness, complexity, and chaos and try to find solutions based upon the different practices (Snowdon and Boone 2007) (Illustrated by the authors, used with permission.)

categorize the issue as a cooperation project, i.e., getting in contact and signing letters of intent with their counterpart, e.g., beginning with sales or R&D. The more "complicated" way was to analyze the multidimensional issue, i.e., to internally practice the partnership that was intended with external partners, to explore the challenge, and to commit to a well-planned and coordinated way. The more "complex" approach was to select some activities (such as predicted maintenance), assign teams staffed from all participating organizations, and agree on an iterative development procedure with rapid learning and adjustment loops. The "chaotic" approach was to spread the idea and see what would happen—At the end, they agreed on the complex way that seemed the most appropriate one. In addition, they learned how to differentiate between the different approaches offered by the model and, especially, how to embrace complexity.

2 Facing Complexity and Uncertainty with Emergent and Evolutionary Development

Today's world is too complex to be managed with the traditional tools and techniques known in the business environment—the old mechanical view of an organization is dying and organizations are developing to become living organisms that are tied to (a) a common purpose which appeals to something bigger than the core organizational purpose and (b) have a travelling mindset and the certainty that challenges on their journey can be best managed through (c) connecting the resources that are available in the ecosystem.

In order to find the way through this complexity, it is a "journey" to embrace complexity as a mindset—by accepting one's own limits of beliefs and knowledge and acknowledging that whenever we think about any kind of actions, it depends on the perspective the individual takes and what is made out of it (see Fig. 3).

In our projects, we have seen many executives "socialized" through years of management literature and ideas that have been taught in MBA courses for decades based on a mechanistic view of the organization and recipes for top-down leadership. However, most of them were willing and open to review their personal experiences and resource-oriented approaches.

"Dissonances in Management"

The manager tells her story: on the one hand, some of our experienced colleagues are used to a mechanistic understanding and struggle with emergent and agile approaches; other colleagues welcome them as new tools in their hierarchical power play; others understand the relevance of the approaches, incorporate them in their management repertoire, and combine them with their long professional experience. On the other hand, we experience some next-generation colleagues who love these new, vivid approaches, but don't have a professional background to integrate them into a bigger, organizational picture and to give them their appropriate place in it. So we suffer from the dissonance between such attitudes—careful integration or enthusiastic going ahead—as fundamental conflict, often without the readiness to solve it. The multidexterity exercise (Fig. 3) helped us to advance the openness to discuss this dissonance and how to cope with it via mutual support.

For a long time, departments and tasks in institutionalized organizations have been run like machines with predictable cause-and-effect links. Therefore, processes could be standardized, planned, controlled, and executed and continuously be improved by adopting leadership practices resulting (in best-case scenarios) in greater economies of scale. This has given a perceived feeling (or illusion) of control by running organizational operations. It is still the common belief (or illusion) that, when following the above described mechanistic steps, the results will be improved organizational outcomes. This is the same with change: there are well-exercised linear procedures that are to be applied and followed by the staff members. Defreeze—change—refreeze! (Lewin 1947).

However, it can be observed that these "old recipes" do not provide (and most likely never have provided) the intended results. According to the research of Jean Boulton et al. (2015), only 20% of managers admit that their strategy has gone according to plan.

Change of paradigm

"From illusion to truth"—Most of us know that a lot of projects don't meet their goals (as mentioned, 70% of project fail or do not meet their goals). However, we continue to agree such goals and expect best-case fulfillment. And we feel good, because we are "socialized" in a community of illusionists. We agree on project goals—and know that we will never achieve them. Going into battle with the project sponsor would need more energy, and our nature tries to prevent us from doing so, on both the project manager's side and the sponsor's side. Illusion of feasibility (we can make it) meets illusion of power (what I say will be done). In our experience, asking the experts for their professional experience is a proven better way. Pushing them doesn't help; they have the time they have—there isn't more time. In this way, the agile pull principle is a realistic approach: the experts decide what they are able to achieve within a specific time span. This way appreciates their expertise and responsibility and connects it with the joint journey.

This means not only offering tools and practices for handling complexity, such as scrum or autonomous teamwork, but also interlinking them with the rest of the organization and managing the differences and dissonances toward a pluralistic setup; putting all the facts, feelings, and conflicts on the table; and coping with them (Fig. 3).

"Self-Organization?"

(1) The young IT team was applying a scrum-sprint when a senior manager entered their room and asked them to prioritize another task which he wanted to give them. He continued this behavior, and the top management didn't back up the team. Some of the agile key players have now left the company.

(2) Teamwork and self-organization were introduced in one department as a pilot—and it worked well. But the head of the department next door tried to sabotage the new way of working by reminding the pilot-team members of their hierarchal trauma: "Aha . . . self-organization all day? . . . If I were your superior, I would ask you to work hard. . . . Always remember!"—In this case, the conflict was escalated to the Management Board, and the superior was asked to make a decision: support the pilot initiative or leave the company.

> When people work in small teams of trusted colleagues, when they have all the resources and power to make the decisions they feel are needed, extraordinary things begin to happen. (Frederic Laloux 2014)

Many people take little satisfaction in their jobs and managerial efforts to fix corporate culture often create problems. But companies can make life more gratifying for their people by reaching for a new developmental stage based on trust and collaboration.

Organizational expert Frederic Laloux explains in his book *Reinventing Organizations* (2014) how organizations have evolved over time in line with seven historic stages of human development, the "paradigms." He outlines two modern paradigms as models for creating a supportive corporate culture and earning solid profits as well. His paradigm on "evolutionary-teal" focuses on self-management which is replacing the hierarchical pyramid with organizations seen as living entities oriented toward realizing their potential. The teal stage corresponds to the "self-actualizing" level of Abraham Maslow's "hierarchy of needs" (which comes from a different approach, but actually ends up on the same level).

Teal organizations make decisions based on trust and collaboration instead of on ego-driven "fears, ambitions, and desires."

Teal organizations are characterized by three distinctive characteristics:

1. "Self-management"—Hierarchy isn't relevant, nor is consensus. Teal organizations manage their processes through "peer relationships." Most of these firms provide employees with special training, so they can manage their own work.
2. "Wholeness"—Most organizations believe rationality matters above all. Anything related to the "emotional intuitive and spiritual" side is not as important. Teal organizations want evolved, aware employees.
3. "Evolutionary purpose"—Purpose matters most in teal organizations: what they do, whom they serve, and how they want to evolve.

Change of paradigm

"Reliable behavior is more fundamental than organizational structures"—Structures can be changed quickly, behavior not. People trust other people due to their competencies, empathy, and behavioral reliability. Such behavioral patterns can be described as culture or even a new quality of structure.

In today's increasingly complex business environment, the managerial dilemma is not just to understand or even recognize what is happening but to have the ability to take the "right" decisions on what to do next—and to re-understand decision-making as a professional task instead of a hierarchical act of power. When trying to implement any kind of change today, there is not necessarily a thorough consideration of the circumstances or the historic developments within the organization. Considering evolutionary science and taking a Darwinist view, any kind of "destruction" enables the development of new "things."

In general, new "things" emerge when something changes that has suited the local conditions; that is why, in order to enable change and adaptability, a certain level of diversity and messiness is required. The chemist and Nobel laureate Prigogine was intrigued by the question "why does physics not accord with biology?" In 1947, Prigogine showed that for open systems order, patterns or newness can emerge which is seen as the start of science of complexity (Boulton et al. 2015). Today's organizations (e.g., in the financial sector) can be seen as open systems with multiple influences within and outside of the organizations.

It could be argued whether or not the "wrong" science with the Newtonian mechanistic worldview has been chosen to understand human and natural systems and that an evolutionary approach would be more suitable. With the complexity of today's organizations, it can be observed that innovation or change is rather emergent and evolutionary than planned—with understanding organizations as living organisms.

Today's management is faced with two options: (1) pretend that the world is more certain than it actually is and impose a Newtonian, mechanistic, controllable, and predictable approach or (2) take the perspective that the world is chaotic, too complex, and uncontrollable and leave the development to the market to get sorted or hope that things sort themselves out. The mechanistic "business worldview" is well-known, described as predictable, standardizable, and controllable with clear cause-and-effect chains. The "chaos theory" claims that the world is radically changing and is entirely unpredictable and uncontrollable. Not considering extreme events, the likelihood of complete chaos and unpredictability is highly unlikely. Today, we experience the Covid-19 pandemic and its influences, but we must not forget climate change, migration, etc. with their global impacts as well as other influences that we can't imagine today. Such risks or crises are so-called Known Knowns or Known Unknowns, but what about the Unknown Unknowns?

What is the solution for these two opposite 'mindsets'? Control versus chaos? Processes and procedures versus random behaviors? Or something in between? Or both together? (Figs. 1 and 4)

3 Complexity Thinking: Accepting the Middle Ground between Whatever It Is

The "middle ground" can be described as the "complexity view." Jean Boulton et al. (2015) describe "complexity theory" as systemic, emergent, unique, and nonlinear. Complexity "is a middle ground theory between saying we know everything, and we know nothing ... It's about learning to be comfortable with uncertainty, because inevitably things will not go according to plan."

More than a theory, it is, from the business perspective, a state of mind on how to approach today's challenges. In general, the world is connected and interdependent and shaped by history and (local) context with a future that cannot be predicted. Past developments do not shape the future—moreover, the past set the conditions for the things that might happen in the future. New things can emerge when some elements change in the local conditions.

Coping with complexity means connecting views
The complexity view, in comparison to the traditional views of management, requires a much higher degree of sensitivity to context. Take, for example, the "I-C-A-R-E" model: it is based upon the connectivity of intentions, context, actions, regulations/rules, and evolution. This model considers, as described above, the overall context (a given element such as resource constraints) as well as the evolutionary element (e.g., various different outcomes based on the other four elements)

(continued)

It follows that connectivity, as one of the three pillars, is not only focused on how people are connected or whether strategies are connected with processes and skills, etc. In this article, we demonstrate an additional quality of connectivity, namely, how views and aspects are linked to better understand a complex situation or challenge. Facts can never be understood in isolation. This is not easy, especially in times of crisis, when we see both: temporary shifts in empathy and collaboration, but also trends such as singularization and separatism, echo chambers, and nationalism.

To embrace complexity in a complex business environment, e.g., a major business transformation program, new ways of "management" are required. A program manager is merely an "orchestrator" rather than a day-to-day "manager."

And he or she has to face a double challenge: firstly, explaining and driving an iterative, experimental approach that makes a difference compared to programs that people have experienced to date as linearly planned procedures and secondly, in terms of the travelling organization, the transformation itself is a double one: it is the transformation to a transformative organization.

In such kinds of program, instead of "doing things," the focus is on firstly observing (new) emergent patterns. Rather than constantly measuring results and outcomes, enough time for reflection on progress and potential upcoming risks and issues but also future potential chances should be taken. This also requires a reframing of existing processes and procedures and an expansion of mindset.

"Transformation Forum"

The program manager and her team proposed a very different approach that should stand for the complexity that could not be managed using linear procedure models. Instead, they implemented a "Transformation Forum" (Fig. 5) that was both physical and digital. They organized it as a collaborative marketplace, for professional exchange, co-creating solutions, and starting teamwork on defined topics. Facilitators went around, listened carefully, gave impulses, encouraged exchange, and supported discussions. Thus, the transformation emerged from shared interests, creativities, and experiences and became a joint movement. At the same time, it was a fundamental learning process for the future organization, which meant sticking to the sustainable purpose as a joint direction, understanding the program's (and future organization's) journey character, and the need to connect all individual and organizational resources. The participants experienced an open process that made all this possible.

"Virtual Transformation Platform"

Due to different working models with remote working, off-site working, people travelling, or people not always working at the same place (e.g., desk sharing, factory workers, mining workers), it is sometimes difficult to create a physical space for people to interact and meet within a certain time frame. One company therefore decided to experiment with and deploy an interactive app that all employees were asked to install on their work phones. Employees without a work phone received one, which was very well received. Within the app, employees could select certain

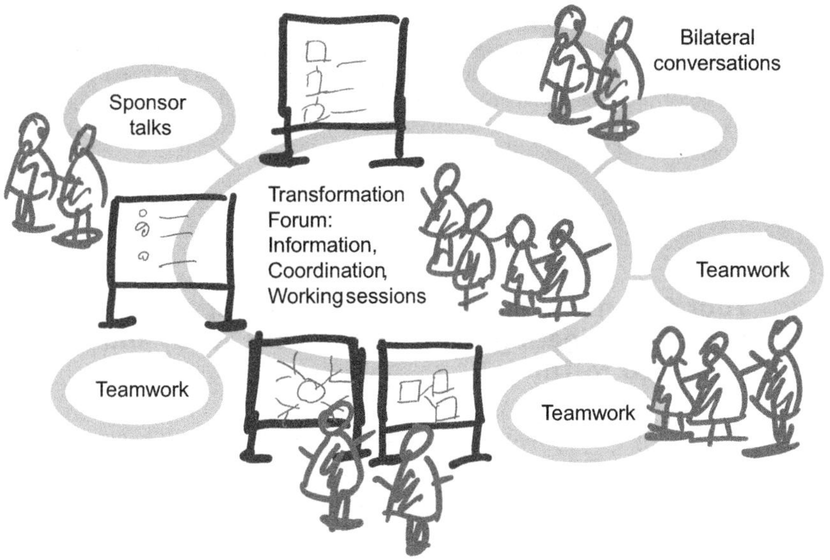

Fig. 5 Organization driven around a Transformation Forum (Illustrated by the authors, used with permission. All rights reserved)

pathways to contribute and co-create content based on certain criteria e.g., their expertise, functions, location, and level of engagement they wanted to bring to the transformation. The app also offered "nudges" for trainings which might be of interest for them or activities which were needed to anchor the required changes within the organization. The idea of "nudging" here was to inspire people to think about questions, issues, and opportunities and to make the appropriate decisions themselves instead of pushing them forward. Furthermore, every 2 weeks, they received a so-called "pulse check"—this was a very simple questionnaire consisting of few questions such as "Do you feel well informed by your manager on the transformation activities and next steps?" or "Do you feel the time you spend on learning 'agile ways of working' is valuable?". With these insights, the central program office was able to tailor the transformation journey with "emergent" new patterns—instead of following a classical transformation plan, they were able to tailor and adjust the transformation activities according to the immediate bottom-up feedback of the organization. The app was not the only communication and engagement tool used, but it was a critical success factor in getting immediate feedback and therefore enabled the leadership team to anchor the required key changes in a much faster way within the organization while, at the same time, regularly measuring their own organization impact and transformation effectiveness via the biweekly pulse-check results.

Change of Paradigm

"Starting is the key with complete transparency—instead of isolated conceptualization"—Many initiatives are well prepared—and encounter considerable resistance. This is because people want to be taken seriously, respected, and involved in the development of their professional lives, i.e., the company. The more comprehensive a critical concept is developed, the greater the risk of resistance from noninvolved stakeholders.

4 Your Organizational Map and Your Compass: How Well Are You Navigating Your Environment Today and What Do You Need to Thrive?

The approach of "systems thinking" has a long tradition in research and practice in organizational change. Recently, complexity theory has become a major influence on organizational development. When designing change interventions in today's business environment, the focus should primarily be on complexity and its implications across the organization. The complexity perspective can also be used to frame large-scale programs, which involve multiple stakeholders, dependencies, connections, and uncertainties and ultimately lead to change.

Change of paradigm

"Don't bring me just any answer, bring me a relevant question"—We are often asked to offer a stringent development model that helps to create and communicate together how organizations can adopt resilience based on the Three-Pillar Model and feel comfortable in the VUCA reality. But instead of offering clever and obvious or even expected answers, the question about the questions is a much more powerful way of approaching complexity. In order to simplify business life, we are used to welcoming recipes and appreciating people with answers—but too often we have forgotten to clarify, sort, and map our questions, assumptions, ways of thinking, and finally organizational territory.

Putting the theory and the provided context and content into practice, we developed an organizational map that you can use to determine where you are on your journey and which "regions" you still need to explore to master the "territory" in order to move ahead more assertively (Fig. 6). Key questions are the following:

- What does your organizational map look like?
- In which areas do you believe you have mastered the environment?
- Where does your organizational map still have unknown territories?
- How is your map changing?
- How are you moving through the map—as a group, individually, or with small teams?
- How do you intend to use the map within your organization?

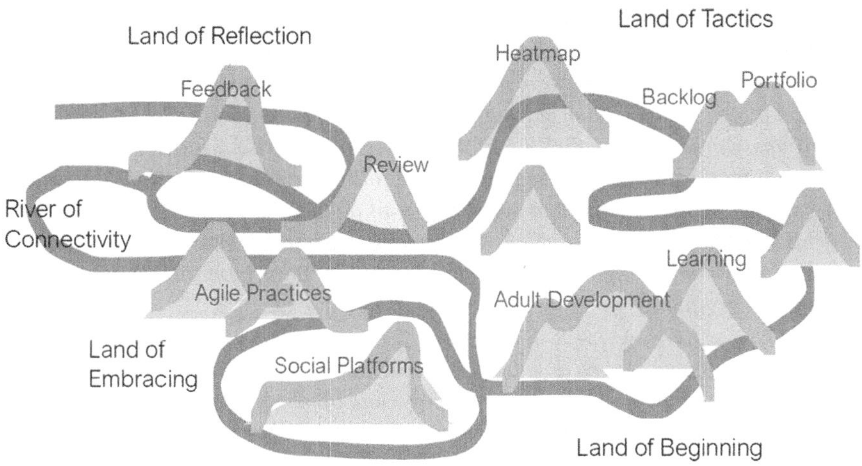

Fig. 6 Example of an organizational map displaying regions, mountains to climb, and the river of connectivity (Illustrated by the authors, used with permission. All rights reserved)

5 Not Only Surviving but Thriving: The Travelling Organization with Its Inner Compass "Purpose"

In the past, leaders of an organization would make a 10-year long-term plan, a 5-year medium-term plan, and a 1- to 2-year short-term plan. In today's world, a long-term plan might look ahead for no more than 2 years. Using the idea of an organizational map and regularly revisiting one's journey helps us to frame well which are the next steps we want to take as an organization and where we want to place our focus with our current actions—discovery, learning, reflection, or necessary revisits of our portfolio. Although many people, especially in the business environment, are used to Gantt charts, KPIs, and budget plans, we are better at problem-solving or being creative when we take different angles and approaches to look at a topic—be it a challenge, a way ahead, a new strategy, or an organization that is constantly evolving and "travelling" in a creative way, e.g., with such an organizational map. Due to the increasing level of complexity within organizations and the external world—and therefore the ecosystem they are part of—it is often exceedingly difficult to keep an overview like this on a map. As we have learned, nothing is static and everything changes constantly—like the seasons, the climate, or the circumstances in our environment. This sometimes happens quickly, e.g., in terms of a crisis or more slowly, like the case of global warming. What these things have in common is the ability of the organization to adapt as quickly as possible to these new circumstances. This can be achieved by well-connected resources working toward a common goal—a joint purpose.

"First Management Experience of Co-creating a Map"

Inspired and excited by the idea to embrace complexity and add complexity thinking to other, long-practiced ways of thinking and problem-solving (Fig. 4), a cross-functional management team started to co-create a map for their organization. Two subgroups worked in parallel, one formulating profound questions and the other drafting a map with strategic regions. In the following plenary session, they mutually enriched their ideas and co-created a joint picture.

This was the final result which was implemented and is now subject to further development, monitoring of agreed activities, and regular monitoring:

Land of beginning

- *Adult development: How do adults learn? What hurdles do we have to overcome? How can we apply leading research and a mix of personalized online and offline training? Do we develop further critical business skills or focus more on personal development?*
- *Continuous learning: What are the skills that we need to survive and thrive in these new times? How can we embed learning and real-life application into day-to-day working life?*

Land of reflection

- *Feedback/feedforward: How do we provide candid open feedback? How can we use strength-based feedback and feedforward? Which peer practices can be helpful?*
- *Review: Is an annual review process still state of the art? How can we truly assess individual contributions in an era of collaboration? Is there a way to focus on output and general performance?*

Land of Tactics

- *Heatmap: Where are the threats and opportunities? What are their origins, dynamics, and sustaining forces?*
- *Backlog: What are the objectives our organization wants to achieve and how do we achieve them? What are the skills and organizational resources we have to develop to achieve them?*
- *Portfolio: What does our portfolio look like? What are our factors for prioritization? What are the priorities and do we agree on them?*

Land of Embracing

- *Agile practices: Can everything work in an agile way or only certain parts of an organization? If yes, do we apply agile working methods, or do we truly work in agile cross-functional teams? How much external support do we want to get adequate training and coaching?*

– *Social platforms/connectivity: How do we create connectivity? Which platforms and tools do we use? How do we build online and offline connectivity and ultimately trust? How do we involve our partners in the ecosystem?*

6 Lessons Learned/Takeaways

- How we embrace complexity thinking within an organization can be developed and practiced in day-to-day business as well as in project situations. The challenge is to be aware of and avoid oversimplification as a well-exercised reaction to complex issues. Therefore, it can be helpful to co-develop a common understanding of the differences between simple, complicated, complex, and chaotic: what they are and how to deal with them.
- It is necessary to develop leadership with new skills needed to deal with these changes. This can be done very practically and less influenced by hierarchical thinking by understanding leadership as a task that can be distributed in the team, too. So the team members get the immediate opportunity to experience what complexity and leadership means.
- From hidden ambition to joint momentum: strategic reflections and decisions must be made, understood, committed to, and connected throughout the company. A continuous common process is more important for a travelling organization than any perfected strategic top-down statement. This needs top management clarity and consistency; otherwise, it is easily killed by the traditional organization and long-exercised behavioral patterns.
- Managing organizational pluralism becomes fundamental and must be developed. How do we deal with the parallelism and tension between short-term and long-term focus, quick and solid decision-making, experienced and new workforce generation, and "fail fast and learn fast" with long-term value creation and purpose?
- A shared development model helps co-create and communicate the emergent transformation and organization. A sustainable purpose, the understanding of the joint journey, and the need to connect all resources will help a company to be a successful player within the ecosystem and VUCA reality.
- A substantial precondition is complex thinking, openness for understanding how others think, complexity, and mindful exchange: in the team, the organization, and the ecosystem. On the one hand, this a personal learning opportunity; on the other hand, it is a necessary step for joint development and true communication.
- Emerging change needs appropriate platforms that allow rapid communication, understanding, and co-creation. Such platforms can be understood as prototypes for future collective practices.
- The emergent transformation can be very pragmatically applied to entrepreneurial activities (such as order processing, product creation, etc.) instead of redesigning or updating top-down or position-oriented structural organization designs.
- The development can be updated via strategic and operative backlogs. Some key principles of scrum can be transferred to the emergent change and to the

organization as a whole: transparency of issues, clear ranking, experts estimating the resources needed and organizing their work, fast-acting reviews, and adjustment.

- A new quality of trust in individuals' and teams' competencies and behavioral reliability is key. Courageous trust will replace controlling mechanisms standing for mistrust, as developed over decades.
- From illusion to reality: cope actively with conflicting interests, opinions, and estimations instead of postponing the disaster and wasting energy and time. Involve people who are able to connect realism and enthusiasm for the shared journey.

References

Boulton, J. G., Allen, P. M., & Bowman, C. (2015). *Embracing complexity: Strategic perspectives for an age of turbulence*. Oxford: University Press.

Covey, S. R. (2004). *The 7 habits of highly effective people* (15th ed.). New York: Free Press/Simon & Schuster.

Credit Suisse. (2017). *Corporate longevity – Index turnover and corporate performance*. Retrieved from https://plus.credit-suisse.com/rpc4/ravDocView?docid=V6y0SB2AF-WEr1ce

De Bono, E. (1986). *Six thinking hats*. Boston: Little, Brown & Co.

Huschka, I. (2020). *Leadership creating organizational, interactional and individual impact.* In P. Wollmann, F. Kühn, & M. Kempf (Eds.), Three pillars of organization and leadership in disruptive times – Navigating your company successfully through the 21st century business world. Cham: Springer Nature.

Laloux, F. (2014). *Reinventing organizations*. Brussels: Nelson Parker.

Lewin, K. (1947). *Frontiers in group dynamics.* Human Relations 1/1.

Martin, J., Bell, R., & Farmer, E. (2000). *B822-technique library*. Milton Keynes: Open University.

Maxwell, J. C. (2019). *Leadershift*. New York: Harper.

Oestereich, B., & Schröder, C. (2017). *Das kollegial geführte Unternehmen.* München: Vahlen.

Schwaber, K., & Sutherland, J. (2017). *The Scrum guide*. Retrieved from https://www.scrumguides.org/docs/scrumguide/v2017/2017-Scrum-Guide-US.pdf

Snowdon, D. J., & Boone, M. E. (2007). *A leader's framework for decision making.* Harvard Business Review, 11/2007.

Türke, R. E. (2008). *Governance – Systemic foundation and framework.* Heidelberg: Physica/Springer.

Wollmann, P., Kühn, F., & Kempf, M. (Eds.). (2020). *Three pillars of organization and leadership in disruptive times – Navigating your company successfully through the 21st century business world.* Cham: Springer Nature.

Nicole Hoenig de Locarnini is an executive consulting professional with one of the leading strategy firms focusing on organizations for the future and enabling lasting change. To date, she has devoted her professional life to developing deep technical insurance/reinsurance expertise at a major global insurance company (she originally trained as an actuary) and later leveraged this, matched with a diverse skills set in strategic transformation architecture and execution, operations, innovation, digital enablement, and people and organizational design within the management consulting industry. Her work spans companies and business units within the financial services, life sciences, and producing industries. To satisfy her continuous passion for learning and growth, she graduated Consulting and Coaching for Change Specialized Executive Master/MBA Program at Oxford Saïd Business School and HEC Paris.

Frank Kühn has been supporting companies and institutions for many years in the areas of organization and leadership, change, and project management. He brings his experience to developments such as the Three-Pillar Model and systemic setting checks. Frank has a doctorate in work science. After leading positions in research and industry, he was a partner at HLP in Frankfurt and the ICG Integrated Consulting Group in Berlin and Graz. Today, he is an independent consultant, business partner of ICG, and associated with other project partners and think tanks. He has published numerous articles in management journals and books.

Building and Using a Compass for Travelling Organizations

Frank Kühn and Georg Wiesinger

Abstract

A compass for the travelling organization helps to keep an eye on the resources and their connectivity inside the company, but also includes the connectivity with the ecosystem and the wider environment; both are described in this article as multidirectional connectivity. A collaborative process of building and using the compass ensures a shared entrepreneurial mindset and supports the commitment to the joint journey, which is here understood as organizational transformation toward a transformative organization—far beyond any well-known experiences of continuous improvement or episodic change traumata. The Three-Pillar Model proved helpful to understand and frame the considerations in this article.

1 Navigating the Transformation

A management compass for the travelling organization is proposed. It displays the most important resources and success factors of a company and their interlinkage. The compass can be used as a management and monitoring tool for both transformation projects and as a collaborative approach to continuously check the position of the joint journey, to develop and embed visions and perspectives, to identify the need for action, and to initiate interventions.

F. Kühn (✉) · G. Wiesinger
Dortmund, Germany
e-mail: fk@kuehn-cp.com; gw@bpe-wiesinger.de

P. Wollmann et al. (eds.), *Organization and Leadership in Disruptive Times*, Future of Business and Finance, https://doi.org/10.1007/978-3-030-63034-8_24

Beyond well-known "cockpits" and "canvases," the proposed compass includes not only the connectivity of the resources in the organization itself but also their connectivity with the ecosystem and the wider environment, so to speak; we can call this a multidirectional, at least circular and radial, connectivity. See, for example, "management concepts": Where, in comparison to good practices in the ecosystem, do we need a shift in our management proficiency? Or "technology": How does our own digitalization approach fit into the digitalization strategies in our ecosystem and how well are we connected with global developments? Or "purpose": How does it fit to the societal expectations of a responsible company?

To ensure the consistency, acceptance, and thus effectiveness of the compass, collaborative processes are proposed which involve all relevant teams and stakeholders and follow a sustainable purpose which may make the journey unique. This creates a common understanding of the transformation and the entrepreneurial journey and involves experts' experiences and profits from their feedback. Practical examples are described for application of the model.

Using the Three-Pillar Model

The Three-Pillar Model (Wollmann et al. 2020) proved helpful to understand and frame the considerations in this article.

- The sustainable purpose, which is crucial to provide any organizational development and transformation or even cope with disruptions and crises with orientation and inspiration, is the basis for any compass which is to be applied to steer the organizational journey.
- The travelling organization is the main subject of the compass. Since no organization has ever been a stable constellation (even if hierarchical structures pretended this), the challenge is to reflect, align, and control the journey in its ecosystem.
- Connecting the resources means networking all resources that are relevant to follow the purpose and master the corporate journey in the best way possible. This includes people, competencies, strategies, processes, products, etc. even beyond the organizational boundaries, i.e., the ecosystem. The compass presented in this article supports this explicitly.

Improving, Changing, Transforming, Travelling . . . The change in organizations through digitization, globalization, and other drivers is omnipresent. Diverse change categorizations may help to find the most effective approaches, e.g., gradual "improvement" within the framework conditions of the company, or more fundamental "transformation" that changes an organization in terms of its basic assumptions about paradigms, its nature, and how it is related to its environment.

The compass proposed in the following makes a difference. It supports the transformation of an organization toward a transformative organization with transformation as core competency, offering a big picture that mirrors the corporate journey networked with the wider ecosystem and business environment. The compass interlinks these dimensions and relates them to the factors and resources that are important for the journey, which may result from inner insights, developments in the ecosystem, or disruptions in the VUCA business world. Thus, the factors themselves are always changing and continuously struggling for a better understanding of what is happening, what is expected to be relevant in the future, and where to navigate the journey.

Three applications of the compass are presented. The first application relates directly to the three pillars and the resources to be connected. The second shows how the concept of purpose and connectivity is applied to the definition of a strategy in an engineering company. The third case uses a bottom-up, pars pro toto approach: It shows how a future-relevant technical component helps to reveal and specify the need even for organizational transformation.

2 Building the Compass

Coming from the navigational challenge (Fig. 1), different questions can be helpful to create the compass; they also offer different entry points to the discussion depending on the thinking culture in the company (scenario- or experience-oriented, opportunity- or risk-oriented, deficit- or strength-oriented, big picture- or detail-oriented, etc.):

- What are the future developments in the environment and in the ecosystem?
- What is our success in the market and with the customer, and how can we advance our success?
- What are typical pitfalls, risks, and hurdles in business, and what do they mean for the definition of the challenges and resources we must develop?

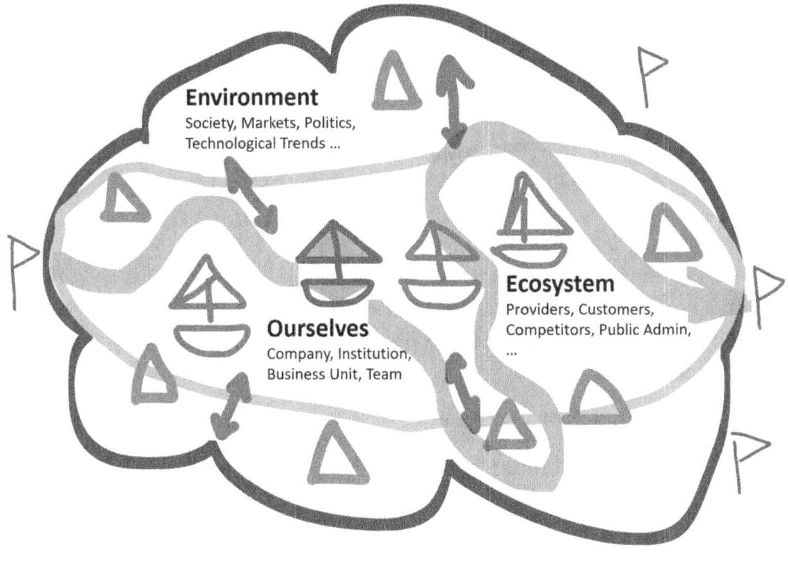

Fig. 1 Navigating our transformation (the boat in the middle) connected with the ecosystem (including the other boats) and the influences and challenges of the wider business environment (Illustrated by the authors, used with permission. All rights reserved)

- What is important in the creation of our services, and which representative products are suitable for this investigation?

Typical or company-specific pitfalls can serve to identify success factors for the travelling organization. The following examples may be familiar to many readers; nonetheless, they are unsolved in many organizations and cost a lot of energy and effectiveness. A courageous deep dive and open discussion is needed to understand such cultural and structural patterns and identify the true issues of any transformation.

- *The scope of a project is not clarified*—Is this down to the lack of courage of project managers or a lack of patience on the part of the sponsor, or even a lack of knowledge of how to approach projects in unclear conditions?
- *The team succumbs to the illusion of planning and feasibility*—Is the reason a hierarchical culture where the top management accepts nothing but best-case planning (and no contradiction), denying any possible technical or social risks and barriers?
- *It should be quick and cheap*—Do time and cost pressure dictate quality? All parties know about the conflict but are not willing to cope with it?
- *The goal is assumed to be correct until the end*—And nobody is willing to question the aim, even if it no longer fits business needs and opportunities? Because management decisions must not be questioned?
- *The loudest speakers have the floor*—Those who take the lead do not always have the best ideas but are preferred. And the others aren't brave enough to intervene?

Such exemplary pitfalls not only waste energy and damage engagement, but they are fundamental barriers to any transformation. Analyzing patterns as exemplified above will reveal the real challenges that we can then reframe into a positive future vision, e.g.:

- Close connectedness with the business environment, market, and customer needs
- Regular setting-check of the impact and efficiency of projects and processes
- Active involvement of courageous experts, even if this not always comfortable
- Application of agile practices and protecting them against hierarchical sabotage
- Immediate coping with conflicts (even with weak signals) in a constructive way, etc.

Thus, we can derive—even from a deficit-oriented discussion—hints to crucial resources and success factors that should be part of our compass.

The three pillars help to check the quality of the success factors:

- Do they support the sustainable purpose?
- Do they challenge and inspire the travelling organization effectively?
- Are they connected and consistent with each other?
- Are they relevant and consistent with regard to the ecosystem and business environment?

And finally, the compass itself must be checked again and again: are the success factors still up to date and future-oriented?

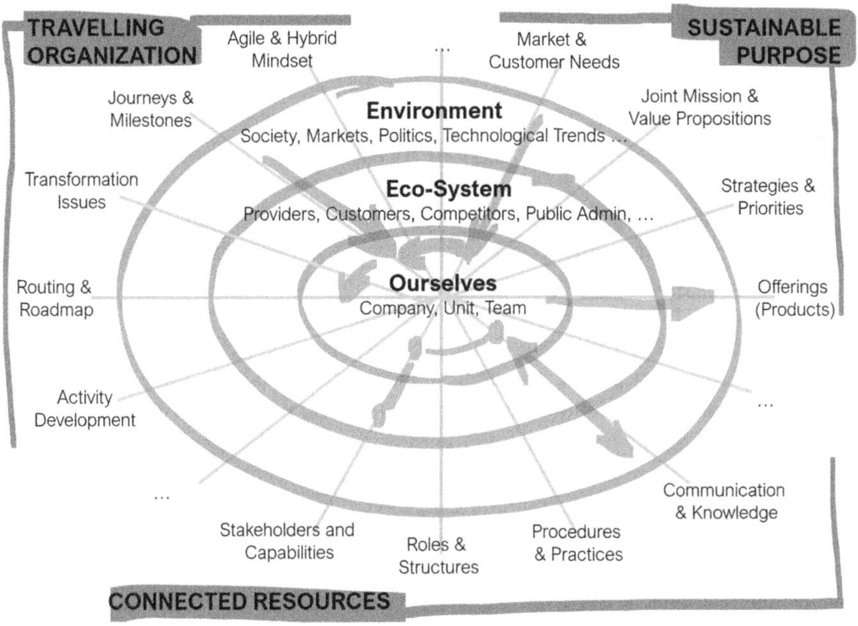

Fig. 2 Example of a compass, based upon the three pillars (sustainable purpose, travelling organization, and connected resources) and some typical factors. In this case, the outside-inside connectivity is more emphasized (Illustrated by the authors, used with permission. All rights reserved)

3 Generic Example: Using the Three-Pillar Model

A generic concept of the compass is useful, for example, to connect it immediately to the three pillars. This enables the management team to find out which success factors they can use to lead their company toward a sustainable purpose and how the success factors or resources must be connected to each other and which connectivity is required within the ecosystem and with the wider environment. Thus, they can immediately see the systemic and contextual relevance of the success factors and how the travelling organization is reflected in the set of identified success factors.

Figure 2 shows a compass in which a company explicitly uses the three pillars for orientation, defines its challenges, and ascertains the relevant relationships; in the next step, assessments and measures can be discussed.

In this case, the discussion is mainly focused on the connectivity of market, ecosystem, and corporate journeys and needs (outside-inside or "radial" connectivity): How to understand and connect market and customer needs and journeys, how to market attractive offerings, how to exchange knowledge with the wider system (e.g., via involving experts in communities of practice), how to involve players and capabilities from the ecosystem in our own journey, and how to synchronize our journey, roadmap, and milestones with the dynamic development of the ecosystem and business environment?

4 Case: Strategy Discussion in an Engineering Company

In this case, the company provides engineering services. The structures of the company are set up as a matrix according to technical competencies and customer groups. The project teams are made up of both structures.

The company has been successful so far, but can success be sustained? In view of new technical trends, more aggressive international competitors, growing uncertainty in the company, and demographic-related resource bottlenecks, it is necessary to set clear strategic guidelines for the orientation and navigation of the company.

When asked about the company's current strategy, the employees shrug their shoulders. Either there is no strategy, maybe it is only related to marketing or sales, or it has simply not been communicated. The people do not see any explicit connection between a strategy and their daily business. This is where the work starts: The compass model is used to name the strategically relevant factors, to ensure their connectivity with each other, and to put them in context with developments in the ecosystem and in the markets.

The management board initiates a survey on the positioning of the company. A first analysis from our discussions with project managers already delivers some essential criteria. Our questions are simple: Why do customers hire you? If we asked customers, what would they say? The answers provide information about competitive advantages, which can be confirmed in further discussions.

The experienced (or desired) customer statements are best gathered in the customer's language. They can be weighted to strategically focus the further discussion. In this case, the customer statements were the following:

- "We feel in good hands with the service provider."
- "The team of our external partners works reliably."
- "They have smart ideas."
- "We always have a good overview."
- "We can always ask our questions."
- "The collaboration is refreshing and fun."
- "Their pricing is appropriate."

The evaluation leads to success factors with specific explanations that ensure a common understanding. The success factors are evaluated to set priorities for the measures to be derived. Success factors in this case were:

(+) *Customer focus:* Understanding of customer development, situation, and needs
(+) *Management quality:* Reliable and transparent planning and control of the project
(o) *Reliability:* Punctual delivery of the project results of the agreed quality
(o) *Partnering:* Accepted as preferred partner for cooperation in the ecosystem
(+) *Solution quality:* Proposal and delivery of good approaches and solutions
(+) *Information:* Ability to inform about project progress and forecast at any time
(+) *Accessibility:* Project team's availability for the clients, their concerns, and questions
(+) *Service quality:* Immediate support in all project-related questions
(o) *Cooperation:* Trustful collaboration with internal and external project participants

---

(continued)

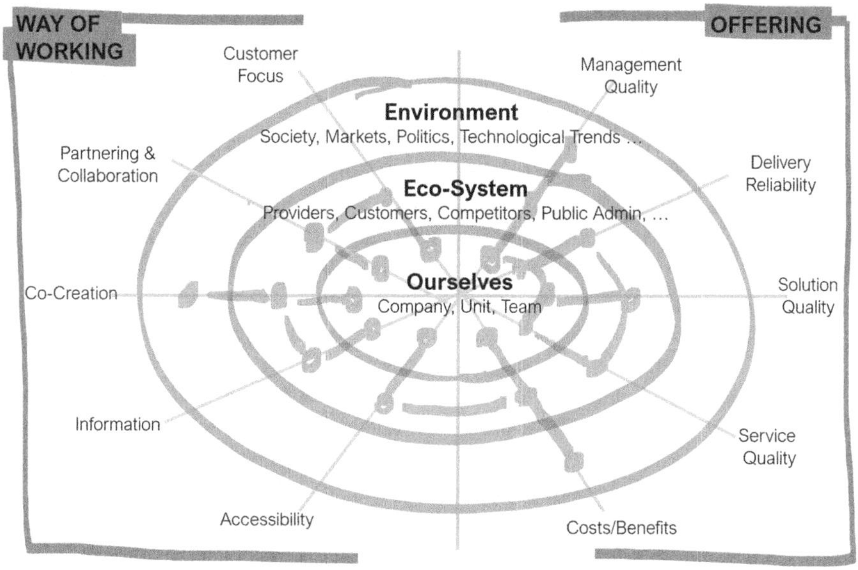

Fig. 3 In this example, the success factors are seen in two fields: Offering (*what*) and Way of Working (*how*). The discussion led to an opening for partnerships, e.g., co-creation as an important connective item in the ecosystem and with the environment. Circularly, the connectivity of solution quality, service quality, and delivery reliability seemed to be relevant items in the ecosystem (Illustrated by the authors, used with permission. All rights reserved)

(+) *Costs/benefits:* Calculating an appropriate fee
Finally, measures are agreed:

- Expansion of agile management approaches
- Comprehensive learning platforms with partners in the ecosystem
- Weekly reviews of project progress and customer feedback
- Collaboration in communities of practice and internal sharing of knowledge
- Mutual participation and learning in projects
- Defined hotlines for the customer as part of the service
- Offering and pricing including quality management and cooperation model
- Co-creation approach for the development of customer solutions

The measures are aimed at further developing the competitive advantages and connecting relevant internal and external resources, focusing on opening to an inspiring collaboration in the ecosystem.

A management team strategy workshop is used to evaluate these results and to define the compass (Fig. 3). The current as-is situation is then assessed using the compass: Where do we see the positions of our company, the ecosystem, and the environment today? What has to be our goal, and where do we set priorities? What measures are to be taken? The results are communicated, discussed, and evaluated in all departments and teams, translated into action plans for the departments and teams, and further developed at monthly project forums and annual project conferences. The partners from the ecosystem and other corporate fields are also invited to these events. This procedure creates an important additional effect: The company's reputation as a hub for engineering expertise significantly strengthens its position in the market.

The three pillars are used as meta-criteria for this discussion. Our considerations must focus on the motivation to act through our (1) sustainable purpose, on the dynamics and adaptability of a (2) travelling and transforming organization, and (3) on the connectivity of our resources with each other and with our environment. As a result, it becomes clear that the corporate purpose has to be supplemented by the topic of collaboration; here the company seems to have more or less consciously gained a competitive advantage through a highly accepted quality of its cooperation. Following on from this, connectivity with partners in the ecosystem is to be strengthened. The opening of the organization to customers and partners for the co-creative development of solutions is understood as a prerequisite for the travelling organization. It enables continuous synchronization regarding technical trends and demanding customer requirements.

The compass is now consistently used for quality assurance and control of the project processes. Together with the departments and teams, it serves the continuous professional qualification of employees, practices, and processes and sets the guidelines for the culture of collaboration in the company.

This development has the character of a true transformation. Working together on the compass has led to a high level of commitment. The entire discussion of further organization design has made an objective leap in quality, even if it has not become less emotional. However, the emotions are not so much determined by abstract arguments and personal preferences, but rather by trying out and co-creating organizational concepts and project practices that can be combined with the findings from the compass.

Takeaways from this case

- There is enough knowledge about the success factors in the organization and the people. It just needs to be made explicit and connected.
- From this knowledge, an appropriate compass can be derived and give orientation for daily work.
- The compass thus provides good information and reasons for the development and transformation of the organization, expanding the entrepreneurial and strategic thinking of the employees.
- To do this, the success factors must be explained (why they are important and what they mean exactly), and the derived measures must be transparently related to them. This connectivity and consistency between experience and future thinking, success factors, and measures make them credible for the employees.
- The company's connectivity with the ecosystem and environment supports the strategic positioning as a trustworthy and attractive partner.

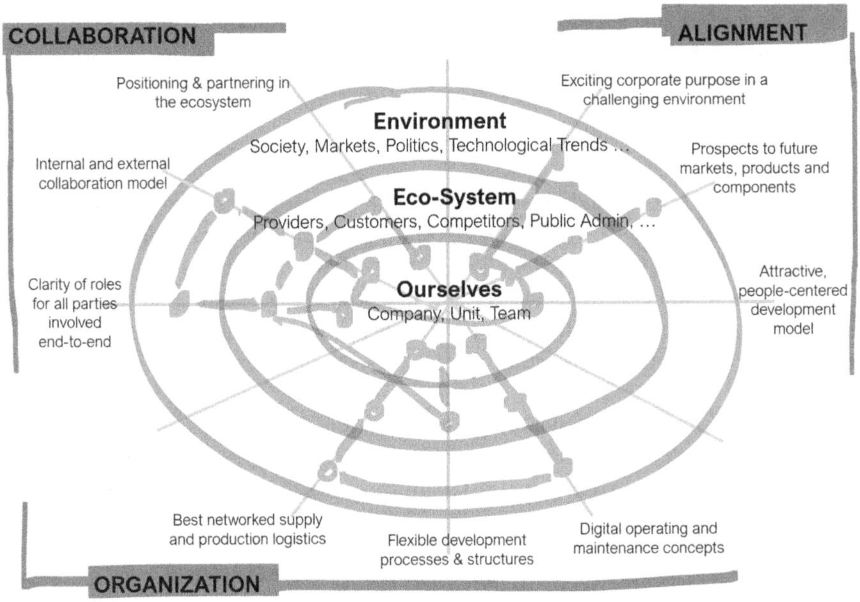

Fig. 4 Practical discussion of the success factors based on a representative, exemplary component, a modular ceiling covering with requirements for fire protection and sound insulation. Which success factors are expressed in the component? Which challenges and opportunities become clear, e.g., co-creating digital operating and maintenance concepts together with partners in the ecosystem, based upon latest technological trends? In addition, the clarity of roles involved—in the company, ecosystem, and wider environment—emerged as key items (Illustrated by the authors, used with permission. All rights reserved)

5 Case: Bottom-Up Discussion on a Critical Component

The company delivers a modular building system whose products are tailored to the requirements of use. The market is very competitive, and the company wants to find a way to discuss its challenges and capabilities on a regular basis. From this, effective steps of transformation are to be defined and its future fitness to be secured for the coming years.

For this, a bottom-up approach is chosen. Based on a critical component of a strategically important product, which represents the company's range of services, technical potential and organizational needs are to be analyzed and realized.

For the selection of the component, the criteria of the compass defined in the company are applied. Which component most likely represents the challenges in the organization, in the ecosystem, and in the competition, as listed in the compass? In our case, the following are named: exciting corporate purpose in a challenging environment; know-how for future markets, products, and components; supply and production logistics; flexible development processes and structures; digital operating and maintenance concepts; positioning and partnering in the ecosystem; internal

(continued)

and external cooperation model; clarity of roles for all involved parties; and people-centered development model in a difficult job market (Fig. 4). Whoever is at the top here has clear competitive advantages in the industry.

The following steps are agreed for the project:

1. The success factors are defined together with the top management and according to the dimensions of the compass. They relate to the environment (society, markets, politics, technical trends, etc.), to the ecosystem (competitors, suppliers, etc.), and to the corporate targets and resources (Fig. 4). Market analyses and discussions in the communities of practice underline the internal assessment. This also defines a strategy: What are the key resources that we have to develop and connect?
2. A component is selected for the examination, on the basis of which the abovementioned factors are put to the test. Potentials, opportunities, risks, and development of transformation tasks are to be worked out as examples. In our case, it is a modular ceiling covering.
3. The processes and activities connected with the component are recorded. They usually determine the scope of the examination.
4. Following from this, the skills, partners, and roles in the company required for the manufacture and operation of the component are defined.
5. Based on these requirements, the current situation is analyzed and a goal for the next stage of the entrepreneurial journey agreed.
6. Measures are defined and implemented. The three pillars are used to ensure the quality of the measures, i.e., every measure must contribute to the sustainable purpose, it must connect and integrate the resources available, and it must support the dynamism of the travelling organization.

In our case, the scope of analysis was determined by the value chain with the following activities:

- Research and development (technical requirements, tests, approvals, design to cost, easy-to-assemble design)
- Planning (BIM[a] model as a digital twin, collision check, connections and interfaces, built-in material properties, transfer of BIM to CNC[a] data for production, construction of CAFM[a] model for operation)
- Logistics (ordering from suppliers, materials management and flow at in-house operations, transport from production to construction site, construction site logistics)
- Manufacturing (at suppliers and own companies)
- Assembly (rough assembly, fine assembly, final assembly: wall, ceiling, floor, electrical, TGA)
- Interfaces and connections (interior walls, ventilation grilles, recessed lights, smoke detectors, sprinklers, etc.)
- Operating concept and documentation (quality data sheets, maintenance and defect management including predictive maintenance concept)
- After-sales service (maintenance contract for the critical connections, ventilation, etc.)

[a]BIM, building information modeling; CNC, computerized numerical control; CAFM, computer-aided facility management; TGA, technical building equipment

In a first workshop, the needs of the customer and the resulting structurally and technically feasible requirements are determined and discussed. The requirements are weighted in terms of their cost/benefit effects (value added) and compared with the current version of the component. The scope of investigation relevant to the requirements is determined and initial potential identified, e.g., in the activities of manufacturing process, logistics, and assembly construction process.

In workshop 2, all roles and responsible persons to be involved in the project team and the further project are determined based on the scope of analysis and the planning documents for the selected component. The essential activities with requirements, process steps, and dependencies are determined. In a first approach, methods and tools, resources, and time requirements are modeled and displayed transparently. The aim is to clarify the requirements for the next workshop. What are the main questions? Who has to participate? The aim is to completely rethink and try out the previous process. Approaches such as rapid prototyping and minimal viable products help here, which are applied to both the technical product and the organization.

In workshop 3, the internal and external value-creation partners are involved. Several workshops are often necessary for this step. Process walk-throughs by the participants serve to understand and question the activities: What are the value drivers? What are the cost drivers? Which questions and challenges must be clarified? Using a zero-base approach would be even more radical: How would we rethink the activities associated with the component "on the greenfield?" For these workshops, it makes sense to visit the current suppliers and production facilities, to work there together, to understand processes and ways of working on site, to discuss the supply chain, and to learn from them; ideas for the future solution will be noted.

In workshop 4, the results are compiled and evaluated. Which strategic, technical, and organizational insights and ideas have been found? Two approaches are possible: The participants relate closely to the results and recorded change requirements, or they create ideas for a future component and the necessary organization, which means fresh thinking—free from any existing concepts.

A prototype will be built in workshop 5. Simple tools can be used for this, for example, cardboard available in every company. The creation can also be used to specify the question of what a minimum viable product could look like in both technical and organizational terms.

The technical and organizational skills are examined again and again. This also includes the discussion of alternative manufacturing processes, alternative suppliers, and assembly processes. The component (in its role as the representative of the overall development of the company) is always in the foreground.

This step is also to check once more: To what extent do the proposed solutions match the three pillars? Do they serve the purpose? Are they flexible enough for the travelling organization (i.e., is it possible to create a smaller minimum viable solution [MVP] and rather rely on further development)? Does the approach connect and use our resources? And is there still a need to develop technical, organizational, and personnel capabilities?

The compass serves to understand the resources—analyzed via the representative component—in their connectivity with each other as well as with the ecosystem and the wider corporate environment.

Results can therefore be of technical and organizational relevance for the company, but also provide findings for networking with partners in the ecosystem and positioning in the markets.

For the minimum viable solution, the following is determined for the ceiling covering:

- Ceiling bulkheads (e.g., F90 test, implementation of ventilation ducts with fire damper, ventilation grille, etc.)
- Connection of the inner walls under the ceiling case (introduction of horizontal forces in the ceiling construction or cladding)
- Support structure for carrying the pipes and ducts and for fastening the substructure of the casing

The analysis of the selected component results in findings that can be transferred to the procedure for other components. This includes, for example, an expanded understanding of a component in terms of related manufacturing technology, logistics, organization, documentation, and communication (assembly instructions, instructions for maintenance, operating concepts, maintenance contracts with service-level agreements, and key performance indicators). This also confirms the relevance of factors in the compass as defined at the beginning.

A roadmap for the travelling organization will be drawn up at the latest in workshop 6: What have we learned from the results for the development of our company? What resources do we need to expand? The participants in the project are asked to reflect on their lessons learned for the further development of the organization—what are the most valuable findings?

A transformation has also taken place in the way the organization is seen and discussed in its effectiveness. The result is astonishing: A concrete, small component opens the eyes to a new quality of organization design and gives the discussion a clear direction. The compass acts as a catalyst and provides the arguments for the discussion.

Takeaways for similar projects and organization design
• Define a compass that is relevant for navigating the activities of the travelling organization and use it as a vade mecum for the transformation process in strategic, technical, and organizational terms. • Use the compass to examine which cultural prerequisites must be developed in the company. Experience has shown that this often affects openness to new technical and organizational solutions, the trustful internal and external cooperation, as well as readiness to take on relevant roles and responsibilities. • Select a strategic component that is representative of the company's future offering. Check the relevance and representativeness of the component (and further products and services) for the company's purpose, the travelling organization, and the connectivity of all relevant resources. • Examine the critical component as an example regarding strategic, technical, and organizational questions that are relevant for the company. Use the connectivity with the ecosystem and the wider environment to expand the perspective from within the company. Which trends are foreseeable, for example, in building information modeling (BIM) or in the

(continued)

development of integral components with hybrid parts that work synergistically for structures, building equipment, and cladding or partitioning?

• Thinking in connectivity categories also helps with technical questions. What are the risks or difficulties of the component with regard to connections, interfaces, assembly, and multi-functionality (e.g., the supporting structure of the paneling of the component also supports the supply lines and channels and should absorb the horizontal loads from the partition walls).

• Involve all internal and external partners relevant for product development and product operation in the design. Set up workshops in which situations are analyzed in an appreciative manner and solutions developed in a co-creative way.

• Agree professional rules of cooperation, communication, and documentation in the workshops. Practice future cooperation and commitment here and now.

• Use the discussion on a specific component to strategically sensitize employees even at the operational level. How well is the company positioned to deal with future challenges? Where does the company have to go?

• Check the relevance of the success factors in the compass. Care about a shared understanding of the factors because they should also be used in follow-up projects and be the benchmark for the transformation of the organization.

• Compare the methods, tools, procedures, and rules developed in the bottom-up analysis to existing top-down approaches in the company, and further develop the corporate toolset.

6 Lessons Learned

- The compass is the result of a discourse in which the relevance, quality, and acceptance of the defined success factors are presented in relation to the sustainable purpose, the connection of the necessary resources, and the corporate journey. Otherwise, the compass runs the risk of being unclear, incomplete, and lacking future orientation.
- Vice versa, the compass forces us to communicate the company's purpose, connectivity, and travel. Otherwise, it has no basis.
- A process must be agreed for the use of the compass. The success factors themselves have to be checked again and again in terms of relevance and acceptance.
- The analysis of the various success factors is very valuable for most participants and creates a common understanding of the situation, the goal, and the need for transformation. For example, how good is our positioning in the ecosystem (actual), how good do we want to be (should), which trends do we see in the ecosystem, and to what extent are we involved in the information flow? How do we create future connectivity in the ecosystem by getting involved in social discourse, working in communities of practice, and creating forums?
- All of this cannot be planned, perfected, and secured. We just must start. Information is always incomplete, uncertain, and changeable. A lot of information is only created en route. The compass is the platform for identifying, assessing, and discussing impressions, assessments, and contexts.
- The open discourse is the most important step. It leads to a common understanding of success in the organization as well as the need for transformation. Its

openness will provide us with insights about the transparency and communication in the company, too.

- If the top-down application of the compass seems too abstract, you can start with concrete examples, with a representative product, a component, or an activity that must work.

Reference

Wollmann, P., Kühn, F., & Kempf, M. (Eds.). (2020). *Three pillars of organization and leadership in disruptive times – Navigating your company successfully through the 21st century business world.* Cham: Springer Nature.

Frank Kühn has been supporting companies and institutions for many years in the areas of organization and leadership, change, and project management. He brings his experience to developments such as the Three-Pillar Model and systemic setting checks. Frank has a doctorate in work science. After leading positions in research and industry, he was a partner at HLP in Frankfurt and the ICG Integrated Consulting Group in Berlin and Graz. Today, he is an independent consultant, business partner of ICG, and associated with other project partners and think tanks. He has published numerous articles in management journals and books.

Georg Wiesinger develops and realizes innovative products for interior design. His focus is on integral, synergetic solutions for acoustic, lighting, and cooling in rooms with special challenges, e.g., for open plan offices. He has extensive project experience as an engineer, architect, and facility manager and is an all-rounder for the special challenges of holistic solutions along the property life cycle. He has a doctorate in mechanical engineering and is a specialist for process-oriented planning and quality management. After leading roles in research and industry, he founded his own company BPE GmbH.

If Not Now: Then When? Learning from the Pandemic for the Application of the Three-Pillar Model

Frank Kühn and Michael Kempf

Abstract

The authors examine the relevance of the Three-Pillar Model regarding the Covid-19 pandemic. They found that the model even works in a global context; it demands a sustainable purpose that takes the global community on a journey that is more turbulent than ever, connecting all available resources. At the same time, we experience the crisis as a pacemaker and trigger for rapid learning, communicating online, organizing ourselves, and questioning the social purpose of organizations. Two practical approaches are presented, which are based on the Three-Pillar Model and can be used in a process that helps understand the complexity of what is happening and draws conclusions for the further development of the "travelling organization." They support teams in creating an overview which individual, group-related, organizational, and social aspects are relevant and how they can be better connected and what this means in the different phases of a crisis and finally in the "next mode." All of this requires considerable learning and development work. How can this be done? Are we ready and able to develop? The article offers questions to test this by looking back at the 2008/2009 financial crisis and the discussion about resilience at the time.

Now, all of a sudden, we go around a bend and here it is. We stop, hardly able to believe that now it is happening, hardly able to believe, after years of confinement to the road of our predecessors, that now we finally have a choice.—Charles Eisenstein: The coronation (2020)

F. Kühn (✉)
Dortmund, Germany
e-mail: fk@kuehn-cp.com

M. Kempf
Bad Honnef am Rhein, Germany
e-mail: michael@kempf-cp.com

P. Wollmann et al. (eds.), *Organization and Leadership in Disruptive Times*, Future of Business and Finance, https://doi.org/10.1007/978-3-030-63034-8_25

1 How Does the Three-Pillar Model Fit the Situation?

In January 2020, we had to face the Covid-19 pandemic, and we found that the organizational journey was much more disruptive and turbulent than expected, even though this could have been expected after previous pandemics. So we learned that there are influences that disrupt our "travel mode", introducing the need for extremely short-notice measures; rearranging our lives in terms of physical space and communication technology; creating new experiences in leadership, collaboration, and self-organization; and questioning our balance between health care, democracy, and economic growth.

We examined the applicability of the Three-Pillar Model (Wollmann et al. 2020) in this situation, found that it has become even more relevant, and updated our understanding of the model:

- *Sustainable Purpose*: With crises (such as pandemic or climate change), people's sensitivity to the extent to which companies have committed themselves to their purpose and their actions on their social responsibility is likely to increase. There are dilemmas to deal with: on the one hand, to better support people's expectations, concerns, and issues, and on the other hand, many companies are struggling to survive. How can different interests, risks, and opportunities best be balanced? What does this mean for the formulation of sustainable purposes that must be perceived as valid and responsible for the development of our planet?
- *Travelling Organization*: The possible twists and turns are more unforeseen and more dramatic than often assumed, which initially makes us dizzy. We perceive different concepts for the necessary journey, which reveal culturally different approaches, e.g., on the one hand, the Asian countries with a more collective culture, significant discipline, and openness to digital solutions and, on the other hand, the more individualistic culture in "the West," which focuses on personal freedom of thought and action. Social distance? I am a party animal! On the other hand: the "old world ends," but we are still there; it is a new beginning with new expectations, mindfulness, perceptions, connections, and paradoxes. Triggered by a virus that travels across all social, ethnic, and religious borders.
- *Connected Resources*: In a crisis, we learn what the right blend of resources such as experience and expertise, creativity and knowledge, and best practice and technical devices can mean and how important well-functioning global and local communities are, especially in science and politics. A well-established connectivity works even when the borders are closed and people are in quarantine. It is a mindset that forces interpersonal connectivity to find new ways and to rebalance the connectivity of strategies, entrepreneurial activities, and supply chains. This way of balancing connectivity brings new continuity. On the other hand, authoritarian systems reveal and isolate themselves in such situations: greetings from the "Society of Singularities" (Reckwitz 2020), Facebook profiles, narcissists, and nationalists.

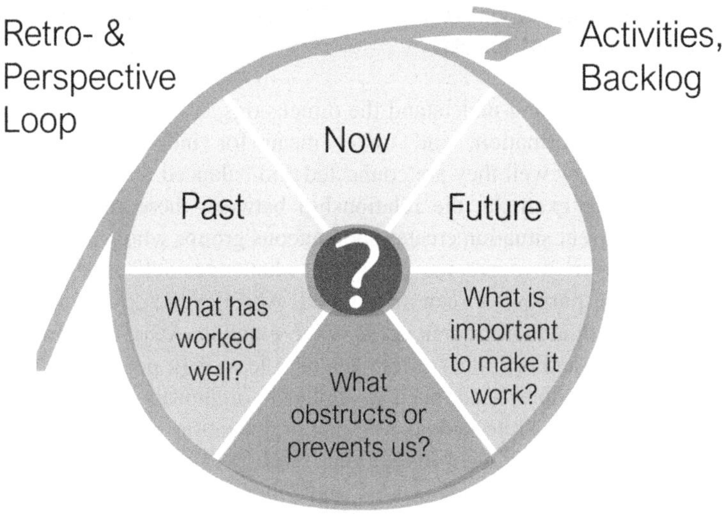

Fig. 1 A kind of learning loop or travelling "wheel": learning from what we have experienced and what it means for the future (Illustrated by Frank Kühn, used with permission. All rights reserved)

Three pillars showing their connection to one another
When taking a closer look at the crisis and its effects, we see many people on the global journey who lack the imagination or courage to deal with future scenarios and complex challenges. They limit themselves to their individual world of experience, perception, and language, meet in echo communities, distrust the rest of the world, and create their own theories—lacking a vision or belief that is strong enough to contribute all their energy to and to connect with. This underlines the need for a really sustainable purpose, for creating the feeling of togetherness especially on challenging journeys and the will to connect our resources on this planet to master this huge hurdle.

Researchers conclude that the coronavirus can be a trigger for learning and an accelerator, a pacemaker: We experience how to make decisions faster, set priorities, solve problems in a simpler fashion, care for transparency, cope with uncertainty, and keep connections and relationships without physically meeting. In any case, it is interesting to consider now and in the future what effects the pandemic will have on ongoing change and development processes, how it will influence the balance between physical and virtual collaboration, and which behaviors, practices, and new tools will be accepted and will remain after the pandemic has subsided or even be further developed (Fig. 1).

2 Gain Insights, Examine Relationships, and Identify Development Needs

To meet this challenge and understand the dimensions, we propose to differentiate what change, transformation, and travel mean for individuals, groups, and organizations and how well they are connected and balanced.

We can see, for example, the relationship between these dimensions in the pandemic: The current situation creates spontaneous groups who want to contribute empathy and support to overcome the global challenge. Self-organization arises whenever a crucial purpose is seen and shared. And flexible companies align and adapt their organization to the urgent needs of the situation. All of this corresponds to the needs, attitudes, and priorities of humans or at least their potential: Crises show the true abilities of people—and this also applies to organizations.

What about the concrete effects on the organization of companies, public administrations, and government institutions? How will we face it and what will we learn from this in psychological, social, and cultural terms? What do we learn for our processes, practices, and structures? How can we re-understand the phases of travelling organizations and ecosystems, for example, as (1) "crisis ongoing," (2) "consolidation," and (3) "next mode?" Incidentally, we suggest avoiding the term "new normal," which may renew the illusion of an overall stability instead of a travelling organization with changing milestones and adaptive operating modes.

The definition of these phases is also relevant because they differ in terms of acceptance: Given the "crisis ongoing," there is no choice; "consolidation" means tackling change, i.e., co-creating acceptance of what the next mode and the transformation process will look like; finally, the "next mode" means that the organization and teams are on their journey which now includes continuous awareness of acceptance.

Based on these considerations, we have developed and applied two matrices to support the discussion of these questions in the organization and its teams. The items in Tables 1 and 2 are only examples (selected from some of our experiences and observations) so that the teams in the organizations are free to use it to evaluate their specific situation. In the end, they themselves have to identify the elements and interrelationships relevant to their challenges, based on their current experiences and supported by latest research results and scenarios (Bauer 2018; Sixtus 2019; Zukunftsinstitut 2020).

So, the best effect of this approach can be achieved if the structure is used for a qualified dialogue that must take place in the organization and its teams in order to create a common understanding of the need for action.

The first matrix (Table 1) deals with questions and insights at the level of individuals, groups, organizations, and society, structured according to the three pillars. It helps to understand where the different aspects or resources fit together and are in harmony, where relevant gaps, differences, or even dissonances occur, where we see the need to better connect or balance the aspects or fill the gaps. To give an example: How does the item "Proactively run self-organization with new timeframes" (level "person"/pillar "travelling organization") match on a personal

Table 1 The levels of person, group, organization, and society related with the three pillars: Where are differences or even dissonances to cope with?

Pillars level	Sustainable purpose	Travelling organization	Connected resources
Person	• Recalibrating what is "really really" important (Bergmann 2019) • Reflection of own purpose in the context of society's purpose (e.g., to help society, groups, and organizations cope with the crisis) • Self-awareness and self-confidence in own role, e.g., as a helper • Recalibration of own values (e.g., accepting even restrictive rules that serve the purpose)	• Accepting a journey through unknown areas, step by step, based on volatile expert input • Increase agility, e.g., higher frequency (day or week) of key information and decisions • Rapid acceptance of new tools such as digital media • Proactively run self-organization with new timeframes • Setting new priorities (and rearranging them if necessary)	• Virtual connection with newly needed and existing resources by using digital collaboration tools to take part in the development • Striving for new experience with virtual connectivity in private rooms • Connecting (and differentiating) private and professional capacities and communication channels
Group	• Strong purpose of groups that emerge from a situation that the participating people perceive and experience in a similar way • Feeling the power of a common purpose—even if it is temporary	• New experience on an agile journey when participating in a spontaneously co-created group journey • New experience of mutual trust on a journey into the unknown • Shared development of online and virtual communication skills	• Connectivity inside and outside the group using common digital tools • New interaction, e.g., through more direct communication inside the group • Privacy of people to be fixed and agreed, which requires acceptance and trust
Organization	• Recalibrate and enrich purpose by evaluating experiences (check, adapt, etc.) • Regarding the sensitivity of people about sustainability linked to social needs • Experience of temporary change of purpose, e.g., manufacturing face masks instead of automotive parts	• Review of business models and strategies • Thinking in different options • Readiness for gradual exploration of unknown areas • Experiencing shared leadership, e.g., digitally experienced people who moderate online meetings or run virtual teams • Individuals taking new roles • Faster decision-making practices • Continuous prevention	• Reaching out for more external expertise and cooperation • Integrating critical incident management as key capability • Deeper understanding of connectivity in ecosystems and supply chains • Professionalized digital connectivity • Virtual meeting structures • Connecting new competencies created during the crisis from

(continued)

Table 1 (continued)

Pillars level	Sustainable purpose	Travelling organization	Connected resources
		of reverting to previous patterns	inside and outside the organization
Society	• Re-understanding the purpose of global society and shared responsibility • Uncovering different political perspectives on society (e.g., nationalism vs. global community) and sharpening profiles • Sensitivity about economic models, e.g., sustainable capitalism practices	• Increased awareness of the global journey and its crises such as climate change, migration, etc. • Acceptance of step-by-step approaches in unknown areas • Lessons learned from global development, its opportunities to co-create a better future and risks, e.g., abuse for power games	• Establishment of more professional communities globally • Linked self-organization of people all over the world • Need of restructuring regional and international service and manufacturing lines in terms of global continuity and risk limitation • Decision-making on level of risk taking

and organizational level the point "Connecting new competencies that were created during the crisis from inside and outside the organization" (organization/connected resources)—which would fit very well for the implementation of agile or collective practices that meet individual and organizational requirements. Another example: How will the increased societal sensitivity about economic models, e.g., sustainable capitalism practices, be regarded in the organization's sustainable purpose and in designing its journey?

The second matrix (Table 2) shows the questions and insights that are assigned to the three pillars and the phases that can be defined in the context of the crisis or the journey in the crisis, respectively. In the matrix presented here, we start with the "preparation" phase (which has not previously been the case in some organizations, as the pandemic has shown) and then continue with the three phases introduced above: "crisis ongoing" (if it happens, which can be divided into panic, confusion, realization, and action), "consolidation" (exploring and implementing new organizational ways), and "next mode." After new continuity was found based on an updated sustainable purpose, a newly defined travelling organization, and reconnected resources, this mode also includes new practices and competencies to cope with the "unexpected" (Weick and Sutcliffe 2001). The application of this matrix is like the matrix described above: How well are relevant items connected, where do they need to be better interlinked or balanced, or which gaps have to be closed? For example: With regard to the connected risk and business continuity strategies in the ecosystem (being prepared/connected resources), how well did the switch to crisis mode work (crisis ongoing/travelling organization), and how were the experiences anchored in the connected coping mechanisms of the ecosystem (connected resources/next mode)?

Table 2 Here the crisis is understood in four relevant phases and related to the three pillars that show their relevance in each phase

Pillars phase	Sustainable purpose	Travelling organization	Connected resources
Being prepared	• Declared responsibility concerning current crises such as climate change, etc. • (Defined) Contribution to a world that will face further crises in the future • Self-understanding as resilient, crisis-proof organization	• Continuous scenario work • Teams ready to cope with unforeseeable developments, disruptions, and crises (emergency plans) • Exercising cross-functional cooperation, distributed leadership, and agile decision-making practices • Exercising fast priority-setting, learning, and development loops	• Body of internal and external experts for regular setting checks • Frequent information sharing incl. weak signals • Connected risk and business continuity strategies in the ecosystem • Support of mindful and trustful collaboration • Recruiting and connecting people that bring in fresh thinking
Crisis ongoing 1. Panic/ confusion 2. Realization 3. Taking action	• Quick-check and pursuing the purpose as main guideline (after potential recalibration) • Commitment and communication of an entrepreneurial message	• Shifting to crisis mode • High-frequency management with development and crisis teams • Installing strategy and/or R&D (research and development) team for learning and future development	• High achievability on agreed channels • Connecting teams and daily exchange • Connecting information lines and agendas within the ecosystem • Highly linked management of the portfolio of initiatives/ projects
Consolidation	• Adaptation and acceptance of the sustainable purpose • Collecting feedback about the purpose (and its compatibility with the organization) from the ecosystem • Resulting purpose as stringent guideline for the further development of the organization	• Multiple relevance of this phase: coping with the crisis, exploring the future organization, accepting the necessary change • Testing new business models and strategies • Piloting new roles and interactions • Monitoring, incl. risks of reverting to previous patterns	• Anchoring critical incident management • Rebalancing the connectivity of strategies, processes, supply chains, information in the ecosystem • Implementation and continuation of proven collaboration tools and formats
Next mode	• Purpose applied to (re-)frame and monitor the travelling organization and all activities • Regular feedback and check-up	• Even higher flexibility of the travelling organization and its teams • Increased awareness of the global journey incl. its crises and changes (known	• Connected coping mechanisms as key capability in the organization as well as in the ecosystem • New understanding of ambidexterity and hybridity, connecting

(continued)

Table 2 (continued)

Pillars phase	Sustainable purpose	Travelling organization	Connected resources
		knowns) • Crisis indicators (known unknowns) are part of the joint "cockpit"	management systems for daily business, innovation, and crises

Fig. 2 Backlog with activities for coping with the different phases, to be prioritized, organized, and tackled with micro-projects (Illustrated by Frank Kühn, used with permission. All rights reserved)

We assume that many things may or should be different after the crisis. To take this into account, it is important to examine future scenarios and to collect, evaluate, and transfer the hundreds of "little stories" and human practices from crisis mode to new work mode. This must happen every day or at least every week from the start; otherwise, the stories and experiences will get lost in the dynamics, turbulence, and complexity of these days. And they have to be transferred into backlogs, priorities, and activities (Fig. 2).

3 Travelling Includes Learning and Development

On the one hand, we tried to make a positive prognosis about learning and development opportunities. We have created support structures and online channels to gather knowledge and experience, to relate them to each other, and to develop potential that has not been seen in this way before (see Tables 1 and 2). If we want to benefit from such insights, we have to be able and willing to learn, develop, and change. So far, however, this has gone 70% wrong. This is explained by studies that, e.g., about the influences on change: 23% ratio, 28% politics (tactics), and 49% emotion (CapGemini 2012).

This result underlines that learning needs an emotional connection—how can this be achieved now? We have never learned on this scale. What is the future like? We

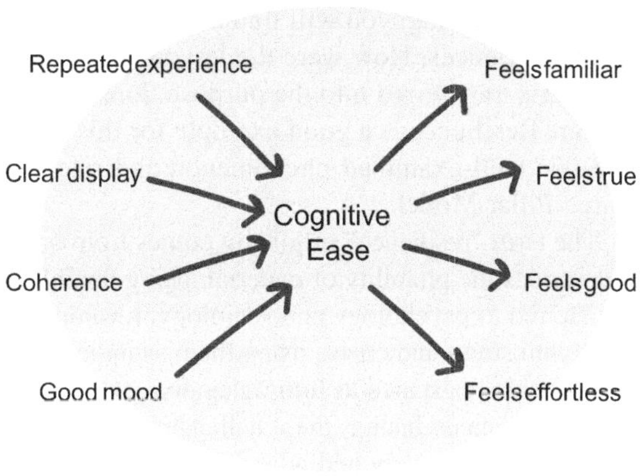

Fig. 3 Cognitive ease: How to create access to another individual's perception? (Kahneman 2011) (Illustrated by the authors, used with permission. All rights reserved)

have never been able to predict it, but at least now we are open to admitting it. How can we take the opportunity?

Unlike children, adults have already gained experience, acquired concepts, developed expectations, learned to set problem-oriented priorities, and developed a self-image. All of this can be useful to select information that I want to take in and process. Conversely, knowledge about it can also be used to prepare information so that others can more easily accept it. Kahneman (2011) summarized the main aspects in his model of "cognitive ease" (Fig. 3).

On the other hand, many filters and individual ways of perception are no longer helpful to deal with a new situation. So, a concrete personal experience is needed, which means a rational and emotional involvement in a previously unknown situation and how to deal with it or the ability for radical openness, lively imagination, and abstract thinking. This seems to be a challenge as learning content meets worldviews and self-images that are increasingly shaped by digital media and are sometimes quite flat or narrow due to the flood of information.

Taking time to reflect

Let us remember situations in which organizational development or even transformation seemed difficult because of people's resistance. How did the difficulties correspond to the aspects listed below? They have been identified as aspects that facilitate (or hinder) adult learning. Can you imagine that some of them played a role in the situation?

Some typical learning requirements for adults are:

- Respect for my self-image and self-concept
- Compatibility with my experience
- Matching my skills and expectations
- Learning purpose esp. for solving my problems

In general, people tend to observe and adopt behavioral models of others when they seem useful and easy to adopt. Such criteria are:

- Personal similarity with the behavior model
- Emotional relationship with the model
- Model that seems helpful for problem-solving
- Higher social status when using the model
- Inspirational opportunity to practice new behavior

(Bandura and Walters 1963; Knowles 1973; Hehn et al. 2016)

In the following, you will find a quick learning test that you can apply to your own experiences. How were the lessons learned about resilience from the financial crisis transferred into the purpose, journey, and connectivity of your organization? Resilience is a good example for this exercise because it is crisis-related and is a well-examined phenomenon and relevant parts of it correspond to the Three-Pillar Model.

The term "resilience" originally comes from architecture and construction where it describes the pliability of material, being flexible instead of breakable. It was then transferred to psychology and sociology, meaning the positive capacity of people to cope with stress and crises, using them as indications and triggers to further develop and provide resistance to future negative events. Today, in organizational development, it means facing the challenges of the volatile world successfully and profitably: proactively and adaptively, flexibly and robustly, learning and developing, and self-confident and open. Sometimes, this development was described as a transition of organizations from a business world managed via sophisticated structures and workflows to an amoeba-like reality flowing and changing, pulling organizational development with it, based upon a continuous understanding of what is happening in markets.

What specific lessons have been learned and how have they been transferred to organizational and leadership development? Which essential aspects of a retrospective are part of the future perspective? What experience from operational crisis management was used for the strategic alignment? Discuss the results in the box about "Lessons Learned from Resilience" with your team:

- Which of the findings summarized there are relevant for our organization?
- What has prevented us from implementing them in our organization?
- What is to be done differently so that it will work this time?

To give an example: In one of our projects, we found strict internal rules that prevented the teams from using an effective cloud meeting system. The internal system administration was not prepared for quick reactions, tests, or implementation. They had had some business turmoil in the past few decades, but not a crisis like the current one that required new collaboration tools. For this reason, they missed several lessons from resilience discussions that were virulent in connection with the 2008/2009 financial crisis and are relevant again today. A cross-functional team has now been set up to propose and implement solutions in iterative steps using the so-called micro-project approach (Kühn and Kempf 2014). First results are expected to be implemented within the next 2 weeks.

Lessons learned from resilience experience
After the financial crisis in 2009, principles of companies that had shown resilience were analyzed (Excerpt from ZEIT, 17 Feb 2011): • Do not want to be winners, rather avoid mistakes. • Keep core competency in the company. • Be willing to give up routines that have been successful to date.

(continued)

- Make tough decisions based on strong values.
- Develop strong identity and commitment.
- Always focus on the right things.
- Address challenges and improvements every day.

Further evaluation of 16 organizations delivered a list of factors standing for resilience vs. vulnerability (Bodingbauer et al. 2010):

- Reflected identification vs. blind obedience
- Entrepreneurship and leadership vs. dictatorship or "administratorship"
- Committed management team vs. pursuing interests separately
- True partnership vs. restriction to own capabilities and advantages
- Future-oriented capabilities vs. remedies that have worked to date
- Available resources vs. overloading people and organization
- Vivid organization vs. paralysis via regulation
- Agile thinking and acting vs. management by structures and templates
- Direct communication vs. formal reporting lines for massaged figures
- High attention vs. neglecting weak signals and information
- Always movable vs. fixation on space and time
- Everything simultaneous vs. strategy, organization, and operations waiting for each other

4 Conclusion

After testing the Three-Pillar Model during these times, we have found that it is even more relevant to future-oriented organizations. The sustainable purpose, which gives energy and orientation, is more than ever the heart of the joint journey. After a lot of new experiences during this time—e.g., with using online media, taking quick actions and decisions, and civil initiatives—the travelling organization has to adapt its collaborative structures and working methods. This also means integrating new crisis management skills into their resources and, on the other hand, not resorting to previous patterns that are no longer functional for travel, twists, and turns. One main concern remains: In addition to all these experiences and expectations—like the resilience discussion after the financial crisis—how can learning and development practices be made a real success factor in the travelling organization?

The following takeaways emerged as the most important:

- We can understand the crisis as a pacemaker and trigger for learning and development of agile practices, digital processes, and online communication.
- The experiences in these turbulent times should be evaluated daily or weekly (real-time evaluation). Otherwise, there is a risk that they will be lost.
- Companies have to question not only their risk and crisis management skills but also their future mode of work if they want to maintain, develop, and combine the capabilities and motivations that people are showing when coping with the crisis.
- If not now—then when? Now is the right time to assess and estimate challenges, risks, and opportunities; apply appropriate decision-making practices; review and correct decisions if necessary; and include them in corporate planning and controlling processes.

- Sustainable purpose is a core element that the organization needs to review and develop. Is it strong and convincing enough to take people on the journey? People have understood that the planet is part of the ecosystem, including Covid-19, climate change, scarce resources, wars, and migration.
- Learning and development require much more entrepreneurial readiness than ever before. The greatest challenge will be to combine the relevant experiences in a common vision of the future. People have shown that they strive for it.
- A quick approach to getting started is to gather and sort the insights (as exemplified in Fig. 1, Tables 1 and 2) and be open to discussion at all levels and in all teams. The results will be good, even if they are unexpected by those looking for the "new normal." For this reason, we prefer to call it the "next mode" because it should make a significant difference.
- Initiatives for the short-, medium-, and long-term perspective of the organization must be started here and now.
- Once the priorities have been set, implementation can be managed by cross-functional teams that work in micro-projects and deliver initial results very quickly.

References

Bandura, A., & Walters, R. H. (1963). *Social learning and personality development*. New York: Holt, Rinehart & Winston.

Bauer, T. (2018). *Die Vereindeutigung der Welt*. Ditzingen: Reclam.

Bergmann, F. (2019). *New work, new culture: Work we want and a culture that strengthens us*. John Hunt Publishing.

Bodingbauer, D., O'Callaghan, E., Kempf, M., Kühn, F., Kuth, C., Marth, D., & Lames, G. (2010). *The Trier whitepaper on resilience*. Munich: Ressential/ICG.

CapGemini. (2012). *Digitale Revolution*. Munich.

Eisenstein, C. (2020). *The coronation*. https://charleseisenstein.org/essays/the-coronation/, March 2020, and https://charleseisenstein.org/essays/die-kronung/, 4/2020.

Hehn, S., Cornelissen, N. I., & Braun. (2016). *Kulturwandel in Organisationen*. Berlin: Springer.

Kahneman, D. (2011). *Thinking, fast and slow*. New York: Farrar, Straus and Giroux.

Knowles, M. (1973). *The adult learner*. Houston: Gulf Publishing.

Kühn, F., & Kempf, M. (2014): *Time flies. Integrate Timelines with Commitment and Results*. In: ICG Change, Graz, 3/2014

Reckwitz, A. (2020). *The society of singularities*. Cambridge: Polity Press.

Sixtus, M. (2019). *Warum an die Zukunft denken?* Berlin: Duden.

Weick, K. E., & Sutcliffe, K. M. (2001). *Managing the unexpected: Assuring high performance in an age of complexity*. San Francisco: Jossey-Bass.

Wollmann, P., Kühn, F., & Kempf, M. (Eds.). (2020). *Three pillars of organization and leadership in disruptive times – Navigating your company successfully through the 21st century business world*. Cham: Springer Nature.

Zukunftsinstitut. (2020). *The corona effect – four future scenarios*. White paper. Frankfurt.

Frank Kühn has been supporting companies and institutions for many years in the areas of organization and leadership, change, and project management. He brings his experience to developments such as the Three-Pillar Model and systemic setting checks. Frank has a doctorate in work science. After leading positions in research and industry, he was a partner at HLP in Frankfurt and the ICG Integrated Consulting Group in Berlin and Graz. Today, he is an independent consultant, business partner of ICG, and associated with other project partners and think tanks. He has published numerous articles in management journals and books.

Michael Kempf has been an experienced Management Consultant for over 20 years. The driving force of his professional activities is his strong ambition to design processes and organizations in a sustainable manner. He relishes identifying key challenges, diagnosing complex relationships, and assisting in shaping the future. Gaining experience and learning something new are indispensable parts of his life, which is why he likes to seize new chances. He began his career as a carpenter before studying social work, education, and business administration. His career has spanned various jobs in social work, 10 years as a manager (HR and logistics) in industrial and retail companies and, since 1998, in advising people, leadership teams, as well as working teams and organizations that are all very different. Michael has co-authored numerous publications in the field of leadership and organizational development.

Part VII

Resume

In the two chapters of this part of the book, the editors consider the key outcome of the articles in the book and analyze which fundamental results are common in the articles, which exciting and surprising additions or new facets to complete the 3-P-Model or make it better applicable were developed, which new 3-P-perspectives are worth to be regarded more in detail in the future and how the diverse articles are linked with each other.

Finally, the part contains a detailed questionnaire which is intended to help running a careful setting check of which maturity level an organization has in terms of the 3-P-Model and which also gives recommendations for activities to get more mature.

Conclusions and Takeaways

Peter Wollmann, Frank Kühn, Michael Kempf, and Reto Püringer

Abstract

In this chapter, the editors consider the key outcomes of the articles in the book and analyze which fundamental results are common in the articles, which exciting and surprising additions or new facets to complete the Three-Pillar Model (abbreviated: 3-P-Model) or make it better applicable were developed, and which new 3-P-perspectives are worthy of further more detailed consideration in the future. The chapter contains both a cross-chapter section with general and fundamental results at a higher level and a part containing the most striking results per chapter.

P. Wollmann (✉)
Bonn, Germany
e-mail: pw@peterwollmann.com

F. Kühn
Dortmund, Germany
e-mail: fk@kuehn-cp.com

M. Kempf
Bad Honnef am Rhein, Germany
e-mail: michael@kempf-cp.com

R. Püringer
Ebertswil, Switzerland
e-mail: rpueringer@hotmail.com

P. Wollmann et al. (eds.), *Organization and Leadership in Disruptive Times*, Future of Business and Finance, https://doi.org/10.1007/978-3-030-63034-8_26

1 General Evaluation

- The 3-P-Model was first developed in the previous book *Three Pillars of Organization and Leadership in Disruptive Times: Navigating Your Company Successfully Through the 21st Century Business World*[1] which aimed to provide orientation in the current volatile, uncertain, complex, and ambiguous (VUCA) world. The reflections and cases used in the current book show the strength, the power, and the special ability of the 3-P-Model in a broad scale in different contexts in the new book:
  The 3-P-Model can be beneficially applied:
  - On diverse levels, from a meta-level of understanding general coherencies to giving orientation to a method for concrete action, for retrospective analysis or to design and plan future developments, etc.
  - For the public and the private sector
  - In a wide field of different industries
  - In different development states of organizations (start-up to well established)
  - For fundamental thoughts on leadership and management as well as for concrete design proposals
- The current book covers 3 continents and 10 countries and more than 20 concrete cases, which underlines its importance across geographies, across industries, and across types of organization.
- In some important contexts, it becomes obvious that the number of hybrid situations that we find in the same company or institution is increasing, e.g., classic and agile units; traditional and start-up business; organic and disruptive development (e.g., excessive growth); strong entrepreneurial needs and strong regulation; focus on line management and also, in parallel, on project management; etc. The systems of organizations (including planning, budgeting, controlling, decision-making, reporting, risk management, remuneration, roles and responsibilities, etc.) have been developed and refined over decades and have been underpinned with detailed IT and data management systems.

  So, they are, on the one hand, very mature and sophisticated, but on the other hand, they are increasingly producing suboptimal results in new hybrid, agile, disruptive environments—or are even hindering or preventing companies from transforming to a next organizational level or phase. This means they have to be changed and/or complemented appropriately; and at the same time, the organizations have to ensure business continuity, follow (or question) their purpose and success, and develop their connectivity within their ecosystem. To become even more concrete: It has been obvious for a longer period that the sophisticated systems of organizations in Finance/Accounting/Controlling (especially cost and profit center management, budgeting), Project and Project

[1] "Three Pillars of Organization and Leadership in Disruptive Times: Navigating Your Company Successfully Through the 21st Century Business World" (Wollmann, P.; Kühn, F.: Kempf, M. (Ed.) (2020); Cham/CH: Springer Nature).

Portfolio Management, HR (job position/post management, MBO management/remuneration systems), Organization (line vs. project vs. process management, solid vs. dotted vs. blurred reporting lines), etc. are producing suboptimal results in an increasing number of cases—or are even hindering the companies on their journey to future fitness.

Following from this, a fundamental question arises at the top level: What are we open to think about—e.g., system optimization, integration, disintegration, next-level solution, or even zero-base renewal? For instance, it can mean that those systems do not have to be abolished but perhaps to be combined with new and more flexible ones. This will be one core aspect to be intensively worked on—it is one key item on the list for our next book.

In this context, it is important to have a very careful and analytic glance at the whole setting and what the purpose and objectives of this setting are. A company, which, for example, offers sustainably high dividends to its shareholders (acting like a bond), might have a product/market mix that is mature and delivers constantly the required cash flow—based on an established setting that knows how to be successful in the market and repeat the success. If demand from customers or market rules change, then this company has more problems to temporarily transform this than a more experimental company where shareholders expect more volatile results and trust in long-term development if the story is convincing. A company with, for example, a lot of experiences in successful transformations and handling hybrid situations can afford more to experiment with system extensions and modifications than an unexperienced company—which does not only depend on the conceptional and intellectual knowledge but also on the existence of the right people for a new development, etc.

The best situation is when it is possible to connect and balance "old world" and "new world" in an organization with their different modes, between experimental and established, hierarchical and evolutionary, crisis and consolidated, etc.—in a synergetic way—and create a higher maturity level and an organizational setting that makes a difference in terms of performance and resilience. This synergetic way requires change also from the "old" which means that a setting is required that is willing to give up some existing habits and behaviors in favor of future promises. Therefore, a setting change would be necessary to be able to set up a business model that is able to constantly transform. The best situation is when it is possible to connect and balance "old world" and "new world" in an organization with their different modes, between experimental and established, hierarchical and evolutionary, crisis and consolidated, etc.—in a synergetic way—and create a higher maturity level and an organizational setting that makes a difference in terms of performance and resilience.

- In the articles, we saw how the Three-Pillar Model inspired the authors to reflect more deeply on their experiences and situations, how they connected the model with other useful models, and how they took the opportunity to develop their own understanding, ideas, and concepts. So, the exercise worked!

- Concerning the pandemic, we learned that the model fits different phases of companies and institutions—previous normal mode, ongoing crisis, consolidation, and next mode. The sustainable purposes were explicitly emphasized (or questioned), which underlines their importance for people who care about future development—in their team, in their organization, and on the planet. In terms of the travelling organization, we learned that the journey not only is uncertain, but also requires the competence to vary speed very quickly and to understand complex timing issues: slowing down, reaccelerating, and dealing with time loops and hysteresis. And finally, the connectivity of resources, of experts, of politicians, of all people, and of money, material, and communication: These all determine success or catastrophe.
- To come back to the variety of aspects presented in the articles, we have learned about a number of "operating modes" that need to be managed, such as innovation mode, optimization mode, routine mode, crisis mode, and future mode—you need to define the "mode model" that is right for your company. An example of how to integrate them is the product life-cycle curve: All modes have to follow the purpose, are part of the travelling organization, and need competences and resources that have to be linked together, at least to form a fruitful coexistence. The organization must not only be able to cope with them all but also to do so at the right time and in a well-coordinated manner.

2 Alignment of 3-P with Selected New Management Methodology: The Three-Pillar Model as a Starting Point and Complementary Element to Common Methodologies

The beauty of the 3-P-Model is its simplicity. It can be easily communicated, and people typically understand it very fast, which makes it possible to use the model immediately in a discussion about how it can help to solve a problem, regardless of the organization or industry—it uses a universal language so to speak.

Within the framework of the Three-Pillar Model, different methodologies can be utilized such as Lean, Scrum, PMI, or Design Thinking. The complication with some of those methodologies is that people need to invest time to learn them in detail before they can be used effectively. And they are not always straightforward to learn; therefore, you need coaches and training to make sure everybody has the same understanding what the methodology means and how it is applied correctly.

It is interesting to observe that, in essence, each of the different methodologies has a link to the Three-Pillar Model. In the case of Scrum, you start with the "what" defined by the Product Owner, which is basically to give direction to the scrum team. But although the "what" is clear, the team might lack an understanding of the basic purpose as to why the "what" is relevant as a source of motivation. The execution in sprints follows the "travelling organization" principle, where the backlog of tasks is prioritized step by step after each sprint using scrum techniques. Connectivity is then an additional element of the Three-Pillar Model that can enhance a scrum team by thinking through how knowledge and best practices can brought from the outside to the scrum team.

The Three-Pillar Model is thus a great starting point for each transformational activity with the basic goal to frame the purpose, review how to travel toward or within this purpose, and validate how to best connect in terms of resources and knowledge. Based on this foundation, different methodologies or approaches can be applied to work this out in detail or to deliver dedicated outputs—with the Three-Pillar model serving as the bracket to keep everything together and as a tool that helps to continuously discuss and diagnose the status of a transformation in a way everybody understands.

3 Concrete Insights from the Chapters/Articles

Fundamental Thoughts with Which to Start the 3-P-Model Journey

- About Travelling in the Unknown in the Nineteenth Century and Today: Pattern for Leadership and Management in 3-P-Model Context
  Peter Wollmann, Reto Püringer
  Travelling in the unknown has a long tradition. In the article, it is shown that it works very well with a convincing purpose, enthusiasm, curiosity, and openness of the travelling group of people, but preconditions are the right setting and good leadership skills in the whole team.
- Nature Eats Culture for Lunch: About Consonances and Dissonances Shifting or Limiting Harmony
  Frank Kühn, Jan Sølvberg, Mersida Ndrevataj
  The authors further developed the understanding of "connectivity" and proposed "harmony" as a container for the natural, cultural, and structural resources of individuals, groups, and organizations that need to be well balanced. The suggested tools have proven helpful to gain access to additional insights and potentials that are crucial for the individuals and teams in a travelling organization.
- Wicked Problems of Travelling Organizations
  Dieter Haselbach, Frank Kühn
  This article underlines the relevance of the three pillars to deal with the unforeseeable on uncertain journeys. Wicked problems don't correspond to any experiences, prognoses, strategies, or plans, neither in travelling organizations nor on the planet, as the current pandemic shows. Nevertheless, they are a natural part of the VUCA world, and we have to cope with them by connecting our resources in discursive loops.

Leadership in the 3-P-Model: Setting Direction and Motivation

- The Benefits of Improvisational Theatre
  Paul Hombach

Improvisational theatre is a great opportunity to develop one's 3-P skills, especially for travelling in the unknown. The mindset developed by practicing and the consciousness about oneself is perfect for leading oneself and others.

- Leading Organizations Through Intrinsic Motivation
  Ehssan Sakhaee

  A perfect 3-P setting needs much intrinsic motivation in the team and the right leadership skills to foster intrinsic motivation. Furthermore, leadership and motivation theory can be sharpened by interpreting it through the perspective of 3-P—this leads to a new understanding and additional insights.
- The AAUL Framework of Leadership in Times of Crisis
  Ehssan Sakhaee

  3-P is a perfect support for leadership in the crisis, as demonstrated by Ehssan's new AAUL model from. 3-P is especially able to sharpen other more operational tools or tools with a more focused scope.

3-P Application in the Public Sector

- Applying the Three-Pillar Model in UN Agencies
  Peter Wollmann

  In settings like the UN, the overwhelming sustainable purpose and the readiness for journeys in the unknown as well as the ability for connectivity allow ad hoc team building in critical projects, only limited by restrictions through the necessity to best balance the interests of the UN member states in all situations. 3-P is perfectly applicable.
- The Impact of Platform Economies on the Urban Structure
  Mersida Ndrevataj, Peter Wollmann

  Urban planning can be enlightened and sharpened by the 3-P perspective, especially the big sustainable purpose question: How do we want to live in the urban area in the future, and what does this mean in concrete terms for the journey and the connectivity to all stakeholders (citizens, businesses, etc.)
- From the Inside and the Outside: A Learning Journey to Mainstream the Digital Transformation in a Federal Enterprise
  Janina Kempf

  This article sets out the argument that digital solutions in the project delivery of development projects ensure more efficiency, effectiveness, transparency, sustainability, and scalability—five powerful words in international development cooperation. This undertaking aims to establish proof and credibility that digital service delivery is a driver for a meaningful international cooperation. Furthermore, it ensures the continuous improvement of Digital by Default as a project approach corresponding to the 3-P-Model.
- Scientific Guidance on Journeys in Unknown Areas: A Best Practice Example
  Peter Wollmann

  The importance of scientific guidance in crisis situations (such as the COVID-19 pandemic) can be easily made transparent by using the 3-P perspectives. It underlines the need for purpose, journey, and connectivity, and it enriches our understanding of the model application by underlining the relevance of experts' communication, comprehensibility, and credibility to make the three pillars truly effective.

- Cooperation and Development in a Social Organization
  Lisa Schulze, Daniel Kunstleben
  In this article, the 3-P-Model proved its worth to explore and reflect the key challenges in a municipal enterprise: clear purpose, shared and realized in the organization's offers, projects, and processes; dynamic journey in a multi-dynamic educational, social, regulatory and political system; and connectivity of a variety of internal and external stakeholders, requiring a variety of interlinked structures and meetings.

3-P Application in the Private Sector

- Start-Up Development in Traditionally Operating Industries: Regional Subsidiaries of Pharmaceutical Companies
  Stefan Turnwald, Julia Zirn
  The authors shed light on the particularities in the setup and development of regional subsidiaries of globally operating pharmaceutical companies and explore the relevance of the 3-P-Model. A multitude of challenges come with geographical expansion; various internal and external factors limit the flexibility in shaping the subsidiary organization, while the diverse workforce becomes the melting pot for different expectations, motivations, feelings, and experiences. The article offers ideas for developing new perspectives based on the 3-P-Model and suggests practical solutions with a focus on the transition from growth to maturity of the subsidiary organization.
- Applying the Principles of the 3-P-Model to Build an Agile High-Performance Team Within Finance
  Benjamin Rausch, John Gray, Thomas Thirolf, Peter Wollmann
  The authors describe the key success factors needed to build a new agile virtual unit within a classic Finance organization of a global player: to carefully design the "start-up" upfront including having a clear purpose/vision, a perfect setting with strong sponsors willing to accept risks, ensuring to have the people/skills that can travel fast and deliver results early (by giving them a large degree of freedom), as well as investing from the beginning in communication across the organization. The interface to the "classic system of the enterprise" will need some development thoughts as, e.g., the usual planning and budgeting and monitoring tools do not perfectly fit. 3-P gives a perfect perspective in retrospective and for the future.
- Application of the 3-P-Model in a Start-Up-like Environment of a Large Enterprise
  Sebastian Kespohl
  The author describes how a subsidiary of a large global player can be taken on a fast growth journey using mature leadership measures based on the 3-P-Model. The challenges of the start-up environment—he uses the impressive image of "painting the bus while driving"—can be fixed with clear entrepreneurial ownership, focused transparent and honest key stakeholder management, and a prudent

way of coping with the normal systems of the established organization in a hybrid way (being partly inside the systems and partly outside)

- MedTech Companies on Their Growth Journey-Leadership Responses to Growth Challenges in the Light of the 3-P-Model
  Marie Theres Schmidt, Dieter Fellner
  This article highlights that to maintain the purpose/credo to provide innovative solutions for people fighting cardiovascular diseases in a MedTech company, it is crucial to promote this purpose to each employee. To maintain this, it is embedded in management checkpoints and included as a prerequisite when hiring new employees to support the growth. As employees share the purpose, it's easier for them to connect and create new innovations that will then help the company to grow.
- Building a Sustainable Brand in Specialty Chemicals: Carve Out from a Big Corporate
  Jürgen Scherer, Jutta Wenzel, Susanne Marell
  Cognis was a leading global supplier of specialty chemicals in the home and personal care, functional performance, and nutritional ingredients markets. The company was carved out as the former chemical division of Henkel AG & Co. KGaA. In its 12-year lifetime, the management established a corporate culture—"We know how"—to mobilize, bond, and develop all key stakeholder relationships. However, "the magic glue," the differentiating DNA building element, is the combination of the three pillars via awareness, initiation, creation, and continuous learning
- Climate Change and Winemaking: A Significant Transformation in Agriculture
  Christal Lalla, Giancarla Domini
  This article highlights that climate change, a journey necessitated by external forces, is changing the success factors of current wines. Winemakers need to rethink the purpose of their wines and learn how to make wines using new/innovative production methods, but also to link tradition with new insights, in a much warmer climate—if not, the quality of the wines might be reduced, resulting in less demand. To find an answer, winemakers need to connect with each other and oenologists (wine experts) to find solutions as a wider community—all with the purpose of preserving the fascinating world of wine.
- Trapped in the Bermuda Triangle Among Project, Process, and Line Organizations: Accelerating Complex Tech Development Projects
  Markus Beer, Philip Bosselmann
  The article describes an organizational development program deployed to stabilize and accelerate new product development projects in a high-tech industrial company. Initially, functional egotism, conflicts between project and line organizations, and inflexible processes frustrated the ambitions of all concerned. A set of shared guiding principles was formulated, which served as a foundation on which to establish robust and sustainable cooperative work culture. The new solutions significantly helped to deliver the next new product on budget and on time.

Helpful Design Concepts to Best Use the 3-P-Model

- Organizations Meandering in the Product Life Cycle
  Lilian Matischok, Frank Kühn
  Here the 3-P-Model is effectively used to describe a travelling organization from market development, business opportunities, product architecture, and key processes to supportive structures. As the different products are in different phases between genesis and commodity, the resources need to be connected in a hybrid organizational setup and a culture where the coexistence of the new and the routine is appreciated.
- Transformation in the Field of Product Development: A Five-Day Micro-project
  Frank Kühn, Michael Kempf
  The article shows that to rebuild the product development process in the automotive industry, the Three-Pillar model has proven useful. A clear articulation about the purpose helped to create the commitment of the travellers to connect their resources to co-create and manage the future, collaborative process. The rapid development created a new understanding of agile working that became a vivid part of their travelling organization.
- Emergent Change: Embracing Complexity as a Key Challenge in a Travelling Organization
  Nicole Hönig di Locarnini, Frank Kühn
  The authors describe how to navigate companies or institutions through emergent changes adopting the Three-Pillar Model using a complexity mindset. It shows that a common understanding of the nature of a problem (simple, complicated, complex, chaotic) enables the management team to make better decisions on their joint journey and to connect their resources much more effectively in a dynamic map of routes, steps, and methodologies.
- Building and Using a Compass for Travelling Organizations
  Frank Kühn, Georg Wiesinger
  The authors further complemented the 3-P-Model with the idea of creating a compass for the travelling organization that helps navigate the company toward the sustainable purpose and that relates the strategic management to the connectivity of the relevant resources—not only within the company but also in its ecosystem and its wider environment.
- If Not Now: Then When? Learning from the Pandemic for the Application of the Three-Pillar Model
  Frank Kühn, Michael Kempf
  In this article, the authors show that the 3-P-Model is a tool that can also be used in a crisis such as the COVID-19 pandemic. It helps to rethink the sustainable purpose, the corporate journey, and the connectivity of resources during the crisis and how they might look after the crisis, in the "next mode." They argue for initiatives "here and now," e.g., via micro-projects, to learn from experience and virtual practices that seemed nearly impossible before the outbreak of the pandemic.

This brief overview shows again that the 3-P-Model can be applied in a broad range of situations at various levels of abstraction. It also shows how many interesting additional insights can be gained from applying 3-P and how animating and beneficial detailed reading of the chapters or case studies can be.

4 Chapter Linkages and Interfaces

In this context, it also makes sense to explore the most important linkages between the chapters, e.g., between the "start-up" case studies in "Developing Start-Ups (Integrating into Big Corporates)," "Applying the Principles of the 3-P-Model to Build Up an Agile High-Performance Team," "Application of the 3-P-Model in a Start-Up-Like Environment of a Large Enterprise," and "How to Navigate Global MedTech Companies on Their Growth Journey" which gives interesting views from different perspectives on a highly relevant contemporary topic, or to explore aspects of international and national political institutions in "Applying the Three-Pillar Model for UN Agencies" and "From the Inside and the Outside: A Learning Journey to Mainstream the Digital Transformation in a Federal Agency." It is also beneficial to go in sequence through all three articles with "Fundamental Thoughts with Which to Start the 3-P-Model Journey" or through all three articles on "Leadership in the 3-P-Model: Setting Direction and Motivation" or all five articles on "Helpful Design Concepts to Best Use 3-P-Model" as from the different case perspectives a comprehensive understanding is created.

The overall key linkages between the chapters can be taken from the following matrix overview, already shown in chapter "Contributions to the 3-P-Model Application: Overview and Connection of the Detailed Cases Presented in the Book" (Table 1):

5 Outlook: Core Topics for the Next Book and for Further Attention

This outlook will reflect some first core topics for the next book—and for the reader to reflect on. From the overall evaluation of the book and the summarized and focused outcome of the single articles/chapters, we might select the following areas as being of greatest interest and being requirements for further activities:

- In an increasingly complex and hybrid environment, organizations will have to further develop their strategic and operative management systems (from strategy to operations incl. process and project and project portfolio management; to finance incl. accounting, planning, controlling, and budgeting; to HR) to make sure that the systems of the organizations produce optimal results also in the new—and more agile—world. It might become necessary to become acquainted with the thought that systems will have to become increasingly hybrid, combining the classic organization with the start-up, fast, and innovation-oriented worlds.

Table 1 Chapter key linkages and interfaces

Chapter	Chapters	3	4	5	6	7	8	9	10	11	12	13	14	15	16	17	18	19	20	21	22	23	24	25
3	About Travelling in the Unknown in the Nineteenth Century and Today		•		•	•	•	•			•							•					•	
4	Nature Eats Culture for Lunch					•	•					•												
5	Wicked Problems of Travelling Orgs	•																•				•		•
6	The Benefits of Improvisational Theatre	•																						
7	Leading Organizations Through Intrinsic Motivation	•	•				•	•				•												
8	The AAUL Framework of Leadership in Times of Crisis	•	•			•		•			•			•	•	•								•
9	Applying the Three-Pillar Model in UN Agencies	•				•	•			•														

(continued)

Table 1 (continued)

Chapter	Chapters	3	4	5	6	7	8	9	10	11	12	13	14	15	16	17	18	19	20	21	22	23	24	25
10	The Impact of Platform Economies on the Urban Structure										•													
11	From Inside and the Outside: A Learning Journey to Mainstream the Digital Transformation	•					•	••					•	•					•					•
12	Scientific Guidance on Journeys in Unknown Areas: A Best Practice Example	•					•		•									•						•
13	Cooperation and Development in a Social Organization		•																				•	
14	Start-Up Development in Traditionally Operating Industries					•				•				•			•						•	

15	Applying the Principles of 3-P-Model to Build an Agile High-Performance Team in Finance						•								•	•				•				
16	Application of the 3-P-Model in a Start-Up-Like Environment of a Large Enterprise						•							•		•				•				
17	MedTech Companies on Their Growth Journey: Leadership Responses						•							•	•					•			•	
18	Building a Sustainable Brand in Specialty Chemicals: Carve Out from Big Corporate												•			•				•			•	
19	Climate Change and Winemaking: A	•		•							•													

(continued)

Table 1 (continued)

Chapter	Chapters	3	4	5	6	7	8	9	10	11	12	13	14	15	16	17	18	19	20	21	22	23	24	25
	Significant Transformation *in Agriculture*																							
20	Trapped in the Bermuda Triangle Among Project, Process, and Line Organizations						•						•								••			
21	Organizations Meandering in the Product Life Cycle													•	•	•	•				•		•	
22	Transformation in the Field of Product Development: A Five-Day Micro-project																		•	•				
23	Emergent Change: Embracing Complexity as a Key Challenge in a Travelling Organization			•																			•	•
24	Building and Using a Compass for	•											•			•				•		•		

	Travelling Organizations																							
25	If Not Now: Then When? Learning from the Pandemic for Application of the Three-Pillar Model			•			•				•										•			

- To achieve this, it is crucial to become more efficient in learning. The current insights are not always encouraging, and (real) learning from lessons learned turns out to be really difficult and only partly successful.[2] It would be beneficial to explore how to fix learning issues in the future—fast learning will be a significant competitive advantage for organizations as well as for individuals and teams.
- In this context, further reflections on prudent action in or after a crisis—be it a pandemic, a climate change development, a technical or market disruption—are important and necessary. The 3-P-Model is a perfect frame to provide orientation for the development of useful options and scenarios but, in this context, more details and cases should be developed and documented.
- One of the outcomes of the last statement might be to work especially on multi- or even anti-cyclical thinking and acting, especially in or after a crisis situation but also in general. To gain USPs and competitive advantage, one has to do things differently.
- Such forward-looking entrepreneurial thinking requires new, flexible, differentiated, and faster end-to-end control models—that range from weak signals (or ideas) to successful action. The 3-P-Model can provide the central inspiration for this challenge.
- And last but not least, it makes sense to invest in further broadening the collection of 3-P-cases in the public and private sector as each new case leads to new insights and helps to improve the model.

Peter Wollmann has been a responsible manager, initiator, mentor, and facilitator in large, predominantly global transformations and strategic developments for almost 40 years. His specialties are the implementations of the Three-Pillar Model in organizations and focused setting checks to identify strength, weaknesses, opportunities, and threats and facilitate optimization measures. Since 2017, Peter has been working independently in organizational projects and future initiatives. After graduating in mathematics and physics from the University of Bonn, he began his professional career at the Deutsche Herold, then insurance group of Deutsche Bank, took on strategic leadership, and most recently was the program director for global transformations in the Zurich Insurance Company (ZIC). In his professional network, he brought his experience and strategic thinking to the development of various leading companies. He is the author and publisher of a number of books and articles on strategy, leadership, and project and project portfolio management. He also founded a wine business: VinAuthority.

Frank Kühn has been supporting companies and institutions for many years in the areas of organization and leadership, change, and project management. He brings his experience to developments such as the Three-Pillar Model and systemic setting checks. Frank has a doctorate in work science. After leading positions in research and industry, he was a partner at HLP in Frankfurt and the ICG Integrated Consulting Group in Berlin and Graz. Today, he is an independent consultant, business partner of ICG, and associated with other project partners and think tanks. He has published numerous articles in management journals and books.

---

[2]See article "Learning from Lessons Learned" by Peter Wollmann and Frank Kühn (2020); https://www.peterwollmann.com/post/update-learning-from-lessons-learned-or-magicians-rituals

Michael Kempf has been an experienced Management Consultant for over 20 years. The driving force of his professional activities is his strong ambition to design processes and organizations in a sustainable manner. He relishes identifying key challenges, diagnosing complex relationships, and assisting in shaping the future. Gaining experience and learning something new are indispensable parts of his life, which is why he likes to seize new chances. He began his career as a carpenter before studying social work, education, and business administration. His career has spanned various jobs in social work, 10 years as a manager (HR and logistics) in industrial and retail companies and, since 1998, in advising people, leadership teams, as well as working teams and organizations that are all very different. Michael has co-authored numerous publications in the field of leadership and organizational development.

Reto Püringer has worked for more than 20 years in the banking and insurance industry. He has held various senior positions in global companies. His practical experience ranges from Strategy Development, Business Model Design, Product/Proposition Development/Management, Enterprise-Wide Portfolio Management, Program/Project Management, Operations/IT Management, Large-Scale Change Program Delivery to Financial/Actuarial Management over different geographies and time zones, hierarchies and units, and cultures and systems. Reto has managed multinational and multicultural change and transformation efforts across the globe and managed teams of various sizes both on site and remotely. Reto holds a degree in Economical Informatics and Marketing and completed an Executive MBA at the University of Zurich.

Michael Knight has been an experienced Management Consultant for over 20 years. The driving force of his professional activities is his strong ambition to design processes and organizations in a sustainable manner. He enjoys identifying the challenges, dissecting complex relationships, and assisting in designing the future. [illegible]

The Three-Pillar Questionnaire

Peter Wollmann, Frank Kühn, Michael Kempf, and Reto Püringer

Abstract

Based on the articles of their first book on *Three Pillars of Organization and Leadership in Disruptive Times: Navigating Your Company Successfully Through the 21st Century Business World* (Wollmann et al., Three pillars of organization and leadership in disruptive times—Navigating your company successfully through the 21st century business world. Berlin: Springer, 2020) and on the numerous experiences, concepts, and findings described in this second book, the editors have developed a questionnaire to support organizational developers and consultants in applying the 3-P-Model. Working on this latest book, two additional main aspects have emerged: "Navigate the journey" and "Develop a hybrid environment." In addition, the Covid-19 pandemic has brought additional experience. At the beginning of the chapter, a detailed recapitulation of the 3-P-Model is documented, which introduces readers to the core ideas of the three pillars and encourages them to make initial reflections and discoveries about their own organization.

P. Wollmann (✉)
Bonn, Germany
e-mail: pw@peterwollmann.com

F. Kühn
Dortmund, Germany
e-mail: fk@kuehn-cp.com

M. Kempf
Bad Honnef am Rhein, Germany
e-mail: michael@kempf-cp.com

R. Püringer
Ebertswil, Switzerland
e-mail: rpueringer@hotmail.com

P. Wollmann et al. (eds.), *Organization and Leadership in Disruptive Times*, Future of Business and Finance, https://doi.org/10.1007/978-3-030-63034-8_27

1 Developing a Questionnaire Is Also a Journey

In our first book on the three pillars, we evaluated the chapters, conversations, and discussions in our community and collected the results in a questionnaire to support the reviews, diagnoses, and setting checks in organizations. Now, with this second book, we have gathered further insights, experiences, and approaches that will be incorporated into our evaluation and questionnaire. The results have also prompted us to define two new main aspects: "Navigate the journey" and "Develop a hybrid setting." This questionnaire confirms the range and depth of the discussion as well as the 3-P-Model that provided us and our community with the inspiration and framework for evaluating our ideas and experiences. Thus, this extended questionnaire once again gives us important impulses for our transformation work, where we look forward to its further development in continuous reflection, learning, and application loops.

2 First Check Using the Three Pillars Themselves

The three pillars identified as main design principles for future organizations—as described below—can provide initial pointers and inspiration for transformation work. All three pillars are key assets of systemic dynamics and high organizational effectiveness: They provide orientation and inspiration and give fundamental impulses to start the journey and to connect the resources for joint success.

The high-level questions to be answered are about how, and to what extent, these pillars are shared, discussed, understood, engaged with, realized, and monitored in your organization? To what extent do they determine the navigation of your organization through the VUCA world?

- *Sustainable purpose*:
  The employees and teams in the organization, but also its key stakeholders in the entire ecosystem and business environment, must know what the organization stands for and what entrepreneurial value it creates and societal contribution it makes. This includes the reciprocity of enterprises, public and social institutions, science, etc. The purpose must remain sustainable, reliable, and consistent, supported by leaders, employees, and stakeholders and lived by important representatives of the organization. The purpose aligns, convinces, and inspires the people involved in the joint endeavor and makes them confident and proud to be part of it and to contribute to it. Employees and team leaders can then take this overall purpose and translate it into what it means concretely for their teams and for them individually. Even—or especially—in crises, it proves its worth in providing orientation and energy and in keeping the organization together on its journey.
- *Travelling organization*:
  Business consistency, strategic stability, and structural continuity with some episodic change project from time to time: this has long been an illusion in disruptive and crisis-ridden times. Now, we have to understand that organizations

are continuously on a journey, experiencing twists and turns, following their purpose or even striving for survival, and always looking for the best way between poles, alternatives, and options. If the teams don't know what to expect around the next bend, they have to make smaller steps and explore the terrain. Even if they don't know in advance what the best result will be, they will achieve it: They believe in their motivation and ability to manage the journey and to rely on their agile mindset, self-reflection, readiness to embrace change, and willingness to deliver. People in a travelling organization are curious, open, courageous, and keen to experiment, and they deal well with uncertainty, stress, and unforeseen incidents—and they are empowered to take decisions swiftly by themselves and to operate on their own. In the current pandemic, the journey has become part of a global endeavor of entire states, economies, financial systems, social systems, etc., all of them overwhelmed and stressed—they have no chance of not being able to cope with the dynamics.
- *Connecting resources*:
The organization has to be aware that impact, value, and efficiency but also urgent survival need a great deal of connectivity: between humans, organization, and ecosystem; between expertise and influence; between different political and social systems and cultures; between enterprises, scientific research, and public sector; between customer satisfaction and economic needs; between innovation, daily business, and crisis mode; between strategy, processes, and skills; and between risk management and business continuity. This means managing connectivity, preventing unconnected structural silos, boxed competencies, and echo chambers, but also inspiring and supporting multilateral behaviors and initiatives in global and local professional communities, balancing the various, often contradictory, interests between the stakeholders.

Even a first, more generic, high-level reflection on the understanding, application, and evaluation of the three pillars will create some interesting insights since, in our experience, 3-P-Model thinking sharpens, details, and frames views on one's own organization: on its aims, operations, and the methods and tools used and its challenges and initiatives.

But often a more detailed follow-up step is necessary, described in the next paragraph.

3 Second Check Using the 3-P Questionnaire

To design the following detailed questionnaire, or rather collection of helpful questions for reflection, we evaluated the chapters in our book, reassessed and re-sorted the questions from our first book (Wollmann et al. 2020), related the findings to the three pillars, and, on this basis, discussed their relevance.

You can now go through the questions and select those which best meditate on the setting and development of your organization from a very personal perspective. You should—if necessary—sharpen and specify questions so that they best cover the individual demands you make of your organization. You are free to add further questions which better cover your individual initial situation. This means that you will have to select, hone/specify, complete, and finalize a suitable collection of questions to be worked on.

And then, together with your team or a circle of colleagues, you will embark on an "expedition" through the questions. There may be a step-by-step clarification: firstly to gain a common understanding of what a question means for you and your colleagues, secondly to agree on its relevance to the current situation and future development, thirdly to assess the situation and development in your organization, and finally to agree on initiatives to be taken.

We have had the experience that it is worth taking each step with awareness and care, but also with discipline and consistency; and we have also experienced and understood that the way we handle such a questionnaire creates insights into our own culture or, if you like, it can be an explicit expression of an intended, new culture.

It is certainly important to keep in mind that the collection of potentially helpful questions should not be regarded as a tool to be applied mechanically. The process contains different steps under your control and responsibility to tailor the concept in detail before application:

- Start with a generic high-level discussion of the three pillars and their importance for your organization—and evaluate those questions/topics that are worth looking at in detail.
- Select, specify, express in concrete terms, hone, and complete the questions from the catalogue which should be worked on in detail for your organization ("your individually drafted questionnaire for deep diving").
- Design a prudent process to handle your individual questionnaire (in workshops, in parallel teams, in suitable events, etc.)
- Take time to evaluate and document the results and decide how you will proceed further.

Collection of helpful questions to shape the journey of your organization with the support of the 3-P-Model
Awake for the journey
1. How far did you explore the VUCA world with your team and stakeholders?
2. Do you have a common understanding of the volatility, uncertainty, complexity, and ambiguity you will have to cope with? What experience does your team already have?
3. Does the purpose fit into future challenges and opportunities (i.e., digitalization, platform business, new work, global challenges such as pandemics, climate change, more resilience, etc.?)
4. Could you create a common mindset of agility and travelling as a future system mode?
5. Is there a common understanding of the next transition, e.g., from growth to maturity or from classic to hybrid?
6. Is the transition process toward becoming a travelling organization sufficiently prepared?
7. To what degree are your teams and individuals involved and convinced?
8. To what degree are your sponsors aware of and willing to accept the risks of the journey?
Interlink for the journey

(continued)

1. Are all personal and organizational (internal and external) resources needed for the journey connected, agreed, and in place?
2. Is the connectivity mindset strong enough to overcome silos, egotism, and conflicts between project and processes, departments, and management levels?
3. Are mindset factors such as awareness, acceptance, understanding, and leadership agreed and connected throughout the organization?
4. Are the natural, cultural, and structural resources of individuals, groups, and organization related to each other and well balanced?
5. Is the exchange of know-how and experience en route, the journey's iterative character with loops of reflection, learning and development, and its impact agreed and organized?
6. Are differences in opinions and working styles transparent, understood, connected, and used as learning opportunities on the joint endeavor?
7. How is the communication about the three pillars, new policies, and daily work organized?
8. Are facts, figures, and other relevant pieces of information of the journey transparent for the people?
Practice the future mode
1. Is there a real commitment to a sustainable purpose, creating enthusiasm, curiosity, openness, and mobilization in the team and with the stakeholders?
2. To what extent has silo thinking been overcome in favor of collaborative solution working? Which cross-functional and cross-organizational teams, communities, and networks exist?
3. Do you apply rapid and collective development tools, such as micro-projects, to create quick results and promote an agile mindset?
4. What is the outcome of exploring various mindsets, experiences, and expectations?
5. Are discursive loops practiced to cope with crucial, but even insoluble, challenges?
6. Are alternative communication formats (e.g., impro theatre) used to better explore feelings, thoughts, and experiences, as relevant information for our journey?
7. Is the purpose formulated, shared, and realized in the organization's offers, projects, and processes—and are these continuously checked regarding the purpose?
8. Is outside-in logic practiced: from dynamic market development, upcoming business opportunities, innovative product architecture, solid key processes to supporting structures—not vice versa?
Lead on the journey
1. To what extent is leadership as a serving function—based on the intrinsic motivation of people—practiced?
2. How well is the leadership concept aligned, shared, and connected in the entire system (of the organization and beyond) and with key people (e.g., politicians, managers, peers, experts, scientists, citizens, etc.)?
3. To what extent does the leadership concept and culture explicitly support the sustainable purpose, the organizational journey, and connecting resources?
4. Have you applied the three pillars to explore the different expectations, motivations, feelings, and experiences of your team and to offer new perspectives?
5. Is there sufficient care for psychological safety from collective behavior?
6. Is the leadership concept and culture actively supported by qualification, coaching, feedback practices, and reviews or other similar development options?
7. Do people have confidence in the leadership?
Build new practices
1. To what extent are your portfolios, roadmaps, programs, and projects connected and aligned to the purpose?

(continued)

2. To what extent do you apply the three pillars to develop activities and processes: understand their relevance with regard to the purpose, create a travelling mindset in the team, and connect the resources across functions to co-create the solution?
3. Are the purpose, travelling readiness, and openness to connectivity strong enough to build, for example, ad hoc teams to solve urgent issues?
4. Are agile communication platforms, collective practices, and liberating interventions applied in your organization? Are they strong enough to attract special talents?
5. Is the stakeholder system, ecosystem, and wider community—and your connectivity in the systems—appropriate to face future challenges?
6. How fit are the systems of the organization to find fast answers to new situations that need systemic innovation? Is there enough openness to pragmatically further develop, or even question, systems that are not supportive in critical cases or for further development?
7. Do you differentiate and apply different problem-solving practices appropriate to the nature of a problem (simple, complicated, complex, chaotic)?
8. How is success evaluated and how are new practices calibrated?
Enable people and organization
1. Do you evaluate disruptions and crises to learn from them regarding the three pillars and put in place initiatives to transfer experiences and insights into practice?
2. How successful is your learning from lessons learned in terms of sustainable changes?
3. To what extent do you have the teams, people, and skills to connect with each other and with helpful communities and to travel fast and deliver results early?
4. Is your recruiting focus on people with curiosity, openness, and agility?
5. Is there a climate of encouraging people to take on roles and manage processes?
6. To what extent are feedback and learning procedures installed and working?
7. Are projects, etc. understood and used as learning platform to overcome organizational hurdles and practice a sustainable cooperative work culture?
8. Is there a concept in place to evaluate success and calibrate its development?
Navigate the journey
1. Is the sustainable purpose and vision translated in the organization, i.e., "operationalized" in management checkpoints and processes (e.g., recruiting)?
2. Are the dynamics of crises, disruptions, and changes explicitly regarded in reinventing, reconnecting, and making flexible purpose and vision, business and products, technology and methodology, and processes and structures?
3. Are the journeys and developments of all entities and subsidiaries well-connected with each other?
4. How is the journey coordinated with the ecosystem's development, incl. markets, regulatory systems, politics, etc.?
5. Is the connectivity between internal and external systems and players managed by an effective set of interlinked structures, processes, and meetings?
6. Do you share and apply an entrepreneurial map that displays the complexity and connectivity of resources, routes, and methodologies in your VUCA business?
7. Do you use a compass for navigating the organization toward its purpose and connecting the resources in your system and the wider ecosystem, and, if so, what does it look like?
8. Do you countercheck and update your compass regarding current and future market, business, and product development, and, if so, how often?
Develop hybrid setting
1. Is there a common understanding about the hybrid nature of a travelling organization (e.g., between start-up and routine business), its diverse parts, adequate ownership, and different management needs, but also a culture of good coexistence?

(continued)

2. How effective—and flexible—are appropriate practices and systems designed, differentiated, and connected (e.g., the usual planning, budgeting, and monitoring processes and tools)?
3. Has crisis mode become a managed part of the hybrid organization, incl. coordinated resource management? Do you have concepts for special decision-making in crisis situations incl. development of anti-cyclic options?
4. How well are different working modes (e.g., business as usual, change, crisis) managed in a separate, connected, or even integrated way ("paint the bus while driving")?
5. To what extent, and how, are resources coordinated and connected across the hybrid organization?
6. Have you installed a life cycle-oriented hybrid organization whose managed diversity corresponds to the different phases between genesis and commodity?
7. Do your start-ups or spin-offs have a clear purpose, a clear first travelling map, a good blend of resources, and clearly defined difference and connectivity to the surrounding organization?

4 Starting the Journey

After evaluating and documenting the results of your individual questionnaire, your organization can embark on a new journey.

With the help of your individually tailored questionnaire, you can quickly identify the need for action. Collect relevant keywords, rank them in a backlog, and start actions and initiatives. We have experienced this practice in many organizations where managers and teams are under pressure and happy to get tasks done quickly—whatever they are—Or you can discuss the three pillars; create a common big picture of sustainable purpose, the travelling organization, and the connected resources; and then work through the questions and compare their relevance to the big picture—Or you can try a first reading loop to explore the landscape of aspects; discuss impressions, emotions, and experiences; help shape a vision; and then go into a second reading loop to identify relevant factors that need to be developed.

In other words, the process depends on what exactly you want to achieve in your specific context and how open you are or can be to deepen aspects, to accept different opinions and views, and to work toward a common outcome. The faster the business is, the more we need time and space for stopovers and retrospectives: to focus and pursue our shared sustainable purpose, to build and join a travel group we can trust, and to connect and enable the resources we need for our journey. All three pillars serve our resilience for coping with the VUCA world.

Every journey begins in a situation—always in the here and now, and then again and again. Try to preserve or revive this moment of exploration and energy, of high awareness and mindfulness. Research on our "inner time clocks" says that the present time is only two or three seconds long, and then it becomes the past.

To all "travellers in mind"—Thanks for joining our journey.

Reference

Wollmann, P., Kühn, F., & Kempf, M. (Eds.). (2020). *Three pillars of organization and leadership in disruptive times – Navigating your company successfully through the 21st century business world*. Heidelberg: Springer.

Peter Wollmann has been a responsible manager, initiator, mentor, and facilitator in large, predominantly global transformations and strategic developments for almost 40 years. His specialties are the implementations of the three-pillar model in organizations and focused setting checks to identify strength, weaknesses, opportunities, and threats and facilitate optimization measures. Since 2017, Peter has been working independently in organizational projects and future initiatives. After graduating in mathematics and physics from the University of Bonn, he began his professional career at the Deutsche Herold, then insurance group of Deutsche Bank, took on strategic leadership, and most recently was the program director for global transformations in the Zurich Insurance Company (ZIC). In his professional network, he brought his experience and strategic thinking to the development of various leading companies. He is the author and publisher of a number of books and articles on strategy, leadership, and project and project portfolio management. He also founded a wine business: VinAuthority.

Frank Kühn has been supporting companies and institutions for many years in the areas of organization and leadership, change, and project management. He brings his experience to developments such as the three-pillar model and systemic setting checks. Frank has a doctorate in work science. After leading positions in research and industry, he was a partner at HLP in Frankfurt and the ICG Integrated Consulting Group in Berlin and Graz. Today, he is an independent consultant, a business partner of ICG, and is associated with other project partners and think tanks. He has published numerous articles in management journals and books.

Michael Kempf has been an experienced Management Consultant for over 20 years. The driving force of his professional activities is his strong ambition to design processes and organizations in a sustainable manner. He relishes identifying key challenges, diagnosing complex relationships, and assisting in shaping the future. Gaining experience and learning something new are indispensable parts of his life, which is why he likes to seize new chances. He began his career as a carpenter before studying social work, education, and business administration. His career has spanned various jobs in social work, 10 years as a manager (HR and logistics) in industrial and retail companies and, since 1998, in advising people, leadership teams, as well as working teams and organizations that are all very different. Michael has co-authored numerous publications in the field of leadership and organizational development.

Reto Püringer has worked for more than 20 years in the banking and insurance industry. He has held various senior positions in global companies. His practical experience ranges from Strategy Development, Business Model Design, Product/Proposition Development/Management, Enterprise-Wide Portfolio Management, Program/Project Management, Operations/IT Management, Large-Scale Change Program Delivery to Financial/Actuarial Management over different geographies and time zones, hierarchies and units, and cultures and systems. Reto has managed multinational and multicultural change and transformation efforts across the globe and managed teams of various sizes both on site and remotely. Reto holds a degree in Economical Informatics and Marketing and completed an Executive MBA at the University of Zurich.

The manufacturer's authorised representative in the EU is Springer Nature Customer Service Centre GmbH, Europaplatz 3, 69115 Heidelberg, Germany. If you have any concerns regarding our products, please contact ProductSafety@springernature.com

Printed and bound by CPI Group (UK) Ltd, Croydon, CR0 4YY
30/09/2026
02225497-0018